Sketches of Tennessee's Pioneer Baptist Preachers

Being, Incidentally, a History of Baptist Beginnings
in the Several Associations in the State

Containing, Particularly, Character and Life
Sketches of the Standard - Bearers
and Leaders of Our People

Commencing with the oldest communities
of Baptists and covering, substantially, but
not in detail, a period of one hundred years
(1775-1875) of Baptist effort and achievement in Tennessee; with photo illustrations
and an Appendix of Curious Documents
and Bits and Fragments of Church History

IN TWO SERIES
By J. J. BURNETT, D. D.

First Series (Volume I)
Price: $2.50, Postpaid

1919
Press of Marshall & Bruce Company
Nashville, Tenn.

Original Copyright 1919
Reprinted with Index 1985
ISBN 0-932807-11-9
Copyright © 1985 by The Overmountain Press
All Rights Reserved
Printed in the United States of America

The Overmountain Press

JOHNSON CITY, TENNESSEE

Yours to serve,
J. J. Burnett

DEDICATION.

To the memory of the heroic and self-sacrificing preachers who, in the early history of our State, were God's messengers to the people and faithful witnesses to the truth —who, in the name of Zion's King, laid themselves out for a great task, subduing the wilderness and sowing the virgin soil with the good seed of the Kingdom—who, in the enduring Word they preached, laid the solid foundations of Baptist history in Tennessee, pioneering the way for us, their descendants and successors, whose good fortune it has been, in later generations, to enter into their labors and build upon foundations laid by their hands— this volume is dedicated with heartiest affection and appreciation. THE AUTHOR.

◆

"One soweth, and another reapeth. . . . Other men labored, and ye are entered into their labors."—*Our Lord, as reported by John.*

"I have little patience with our aristocrats who are ashamed of the plebeian fathers who made it possible for them to be rich and courted; I have less for those Protestants who affect so much superiority to their Pilgrim sires; and I have none at all for those Baptists who do not highly esteem the character and sacrifices of the men who secured them their high station in the world. Contemptible children are they who do not magnify their parents; but I trust the Baptists of the next hundred years may not be classified with such. They should encourage the preparation of biographies of their ancestors, should place before the world the records of their lives, and should in this way aim to develop in the churches something of their Christian chivalry and heroic devotion to the truth of God."—*George C. Lorimer, D.D.*

"A people who do not honor the deeds of their worthy dead will do nothing worthy of being honored by their descendants."—*Macalay.*

(4)

CONTENTS.

(5)

6   CONTENTS.

PREFACE.

In January of 1896 this writer commenced the preparation and publication of "Illustrated Sketches of Tennessee's Pioneer Baptist Preachers," publishing some of the sketches in the *East Tennessee Baptist,* others in the *Baptist and Reflector.* As field-worker and correspondent for those papers, during a self-imposed Baptist itinerancy of five years, covering nearly every county in East Tennessee, and other historic grounds, in and out of the State, with pencil and notebook in hand, visiting associations and churches, historic places and persons, and making extracts from or abstracts of old church records, family records, tombstone and associational minute records, and records of tradition in the memories of the oldest inhabitants, he had the opportunity to decipher and preserve obscure inscriptions and rare old Baptist ecclesiastical documents, which, but for this or a like good providence, would have been obliterated by time ere now, or been buried with the old and knowing heads which surrendered their treasures of historic lore to the reporter's notebook while the parties were living. Encouraged by the favorable reception given these published sketches and the expressed wish of many to have them in more suitable form for preservation, and, personally, being not unwilling to continue a labor of love, the writer decided it might be a worthwhile task to continue and extend his researches, and really purposed to put in book form, just so soon as he could make the necessary investigations, a history of the self-sacrificing labors and difficult but glorious achievements of the old-time, John the Baptist type of preachers of our State —and thus give them a chance to speak their message of loyalty and devotion to the present generation of Baptists. But the task was greater than he had anticipated. Besides, the prosecution of the work was long hindered by untoward circumstances—perhaps I should say, was *providentially de-*

layed. For the last two or three years, however, in the providence of God, he has been enabled to spend most of his time in selecting and recasting materials already in hand, gathering other materials, typewriting sketches, and investigating by correspondence and otherwise the immediate sources of our history in the Carolinas and in Virginia, with the gratifying result that with some of our oldest churches and preachers he has been able to supply some missing links and connect back with Baptist settlements in the older states, thus supplying a fitting background for sketches of men not less able or worthy but only less noted than the Baptist heroes of Virginia, Maryland and New England, memorialized in the histories of Semple and Taylor, Cathcart and Armitage, and other historians. These sketches, when completed (in a supplementary volume), will constitute a more or less complete history of Baptist beginnings in the territories covered by the several associations in the State, commencing with the oldest settlements or communities of Baptists.

In preparing sketches for the present volume, it was the writer's plan, at first, to run through the State a line of even date, covering a definite period, say fifty years, and to give equal attention to the three sections of the State—East, Middle and West. This plan, however, did not prove to be practicable, owing to the double difficulty of fixing a line and of working to it. As the matter now stands there is a slight disproportion in favor of East Tennessee, which, in a way, has been better worked, and so far as names, great and small, are concerned, is more largely represented in the present volume than the other divisions of the State. This inequality, however, on the eve of going to press, has been remedied in a measure by reserving for the proposed "Second Series" sketches of East Tennessee preachers (mostly middle, connecting links between a remote and a less remote past), which were at first intended for this volume. This change seemed desirable for two reasons. First, a number of the reserved sketches are mere fragments, which might, perchance, be improved by taking more time for research. Second, the reservation of a batch of imperfect sketches would make room for a greater number of prominent pioneers of Middle and West Tennessee— preachers, editors, and teachers, whose names are familiar household words over the entire State.

In the preparation of this work the writer has had to deal with some difficult problems, such as denominational machinery and methods, ministerial education and theological seminaries, Sunday schools and missions, interdenominational fellowship and affiliation, "church succession," etc., questions about which there are differences of opinion among Baptists. In dealing with these questions the writer has tried to be judge and not advocate; has sought to bring to his task the judicial temper, at the same time having a conviction that his findings and decisions ought not and could not be negative and colorless. Throughout the work he has sought *accuracy, justice, impartiality*—endeavoring to give to each of his subjects his true figure and merited place in history. He has not affected elegance of style or cared to conform to conventional rules. Most of his subjects were rugged pioneers of the wilderness, to whom elegant dress would not be natural or becoming. These the writer has not hesitated to clothe with the becoming dress of homespun and home-made garments; he has painted them as he saw them and as they were, "holding up the mirror to nature" and reality. He has chosen to let them speak their mother tongue freely and tell their own story (where there were autobiographies to speak) in their own original way—only using, at times, the editorial liberty of correcting a little of the spelling. The writer esteems it a great privilege to have been permitted to know these men intimately—some of them personally, more of them in the lives they lived; to enter into their inner life and experience was goodly fellowship; to follow them in their "travels and labors," and note their struggles and triumphs, was, and is still, to have a high appreciation of their worth. Should the reader share in a measure the writer's pleasure and profit, that would be cause for thankfulness.

With these words, explanatory and apologetic, and with the hope that these biographies may mean something to the on-going of the Kingdom and serve to stimulate a greater interest in and appreciation of our history, and its makers, this volume, with its fortunes, is committed to the care of the Baptist brotherhood of the State, and other readers personally or sympathetically interested.

Affectionately,

THE AUTHOR.

INTRODUCTION.

The fathers and mothers of our Tennessee Zion are more or less familiar with our denominational history in the State, and, perhaps, need no introduction to the "preachers," whose biographies are here presented. To the younger generation of Baptists in the State I am introducing, in the persons of Tennessee's Pioneer Baptist Preachers, a goodly company of heroic men, fearless champions of Baptist principles and practices, stalwart defenders of the Baptist faith—men, all of them, of high moral worth, many of them men of marked natural ability, and not a few of them of national reputation. They were men of God, who exhibited quenchless, apostolic zeal in preaching the gospel to the destitute; men of dauntless courage, who could fight the Indians, when necessary, and then preach the gospel to them; men, who, though unlearned, and untaught in the schools, were by no means ignorant men, but men self-educated and taught of God, men, for the most part, of one Book; men who had an experience of grace, and knew how to preach the doctrines of grace and experimental religion; rugged and heroic men, who subdued the wilderness, and planted it with churches, thus laying the foundations upon which succeeding generations of Baptists have builded. Let us accord all honor to these early, God-called preachers, who fought the battles of the Lord and of the Baptists, mostly at their own charges, and who, for the cause' sake, suffered privation and braved the perils of the wilderness, finding no "wilderness path too lonely to traverse and no pioneer settlement too crude or remote for them to serve." Some of these men, and many of their sires, fought in the Revolution for civil liberty, and with their compatriots in the older States "led and won the battle for religious liberty in America," and in so doing were a part of the "advance guard of Southern civilization." They were men, for the most part, of Anglo-

American stock, but were spiritual descendants of the Scotch Covenanters, the French Huguenots, and the Ana-Baptists of Switzerland. They were here, many of them, before Tennessee had an existence—when the present State was as yet the "Watauga Association," or a "part of North Carolina," or the "State of Franklin," or the "territory of the United States, South of the Ohio." They had come from the Carolinas and from Virginia. They were not only preachers and tillers of the soil, they were the educated class, the leaders of the people—doctors, school teachers, surveyors, county court clerks, county trustees, and representatives in the legislature. They formed the connecting links between remote communities, and thus were the principal founders of society in the pioneer settlements. Haywood, in his history of Tennessee (1823), speaking of the "eminent men" of his State and their "memorable achievements," asks this natural and pertinent question: "Ought not their names and exploits to be rescued from the obliteration of time and the tomb of silence?" and then adds: "If their splendid achievements cannot be transmitted to after generations in the rich dress they deserve, in a style of elegance suited to the high merits of the actors, still it is better to perpetuate them in the most simple form than to let them wholly be forgotten." The writer of these sketches shares, in a measure, this feeling in regard to the heroic and self-sacrificing old preachers who did so much, not only to civilize the State in which we live, but to Christianize it and make it so largely Baptistic. In clothing and portraying his characters, however, he has purposely chosen the plainest "dress" and the "most simple form"—the dress and form most suitable to their calling and station in life, which also would be most pleasing to them if they were alive and could read what is here said of them.

East Tennessee began to be permanently settled, from North Carolina and Virginia, in the winter of 1768-9; other parts of the State, about ten years later. A company of ex-

plorers, seven in number, in the year 1768, left the county of
Augusta, in Virginia, made a "tour of the wilderness, traveled
to the waters of the Holston, and traversed the country from
Holston to Clinch Mountain." In the month of February,
1769, they crossed the North Fork of Holston and went on
their way as low down as Big Creek, now in Hawkins County,
where they "found themselves in the hunting grounds of a
large party of Indians." Thinking, no doubt, that "discretion was the better part of valor," they turned about and went
back up the river, with the intention of returning home. Re-
crossing the river and proceeding about twenty miles above
the crossing, they found a "cabin on every spot, where the
range was good, and where, six weeks before, nothing was to
be seen but the howling wilderness." When they passed this
way, "on their outward destination," they found no settlers
on the Holston, "save three families on the head springs of
the river." Of these first settlers ten families came from the
neighborhood of the place where Raleigh, N. C., now stands,
and settled on the Watauga, near where Elizabethton, Carter
County, Tenn., now is. This was the first settlement in Tennessee. Soon afterwards it was augmented by settlers from
the hollows in North Carolina and from Virginia. (Haywood.)
Several things contributed to this result. Wonderful things
had been reported of the "great West," the wilderness country,
just beyond the mountains. The love of gain, the lure of the
wilderness, the infectious spirit of adventure that was in the
air, the love of liberty and independence, all these, conjoined
with the dire necessity, on the part of many, to repair their
broken fortunes, made emigration natural and easy. The inhabitants of North Carolina had been greatly oppressed by
exorbitant fees, unreasonable taxes, and other indignities
heaped upon them by the representatives of the mother country. Their rebellion against abuses of power and injustice
had brought on the battle of the Alamance (May 16, 1771),
in which they were defeated by the Royal forces, and two

hundred of them slain, and others captured and hanged. Under existing circumstances the wilderness promised at least exemption from annoyance and oppression, and with this added incentive, "full streams of emigration began to flow in various directions from the misgoverned province of North Carolina." With the stream that poured through Holston Valley came many Baptists, among others Tidence Lane and an Arm of Sandy Creek Church (N. C.), a little later (1779) located and established on Buffalo Ridge, Washington County, Tenn. This church (Buffalo Ridge), it is now generally conceded, was the first church permanently established on what is now Tennessee soil, then a part of North Carolina. Benedict (1848) records an early tradition to the effect that "two churches were gathered" by the Baptists when this part of the State was a "dangerous wilderness, some time before any of those arose whose history we are now about to relate. They were probably (certainly, we might say) collected some time after the year 1765, and broken up in the Indian war (1774). One of these churches was on Clinch River, a few of whose members returned after the war, and the church was re-constituted by the name of Glade Hollow."

The writer has selected (or rather accepted) the date, 1775, as the starting point of the history embodied in these sketches. This seems to be the first definitely known and recorded date of Baptist entry and effort in the State. "Late in the fall of this year" (1775), says Ramsay, "the westernmost settlement" was made "in Carter's Valley" (in what is now Hawkins County), and "Mr. Kincaid, Mr. Long, Mr. Love, and Mr. Mulkey, a Baptist preacher, were the pioneers." The Mr. Mulkey here mentioned was Jonathan Mulkey, of Baptist pioneer fame.

In the application and use of the word "pioneer" in the title to this volume some liberties have been taken. Not all the preachers whose lives are here sketched were pioneers in the sense that a hundred or more years ago they were a voice crying in the wilderness, or heralds of the cross to a primitive and rude frontier people, removing obstructions, building up a highway, etc. Many of them were. Others were pioneers in a relative or accommodative sense; they extended the work of the earlier pioneers into new settlements, into backward communities, into fields and regions "beyond." The work of the two divisions of the army was similar, however, requiring for its accomplishment zeal, courage and enterprise, the true pioneer spirit, which is the spirit of evangelism.

Among the biographies in this volume will be found a number of sketches of "Primitive or Old School" preachers; such they designated themselves in their minutes. These preachers, almost without exception, were men of piety and influence, many of them great men for their day—men of honest convictions and loyal to the Scriptures, as they understood them. They, and their sires, had fought for civil and religious liberty, for the rights of the individual, the rights of the common people, and of the local church. They had thus either contracted or inherited a religious *bias* in the direction of individualism and local church independence, or Baptist democracy. They would naturally, therefore, look with suspicion upon ecclesiastical machinery or organization beyond the local church or district association. Good men actually feared centralization, and the people in general had no taste for an aristocracy of any kind, ministerial or otherwise. Besides, most of these preachers were Hyper-Calvinists, believing that the Lord could and would take care of his own affairs in his own good' time. Neither had they learned by experience or observation the wisdom and necessity of co-operation in order to largest service and greatest results in the Lord's work. Little wonder, therefore, that in the presence of a new order of things among Baptists these men first hesitated, then opposed.

As a people, young and old, Baptists and non-Baptists, we owe no small debt of gratitude to the old-time preachers, who pioneered the way for us and made possible our heritage of good. Let us give them due recognition. Let us acquaint ourselves with the story of their self-sacrificing and heroic lives. They had their shortcomings, to be sure. They made no claims to perfection, and we make none for them. But they were God's noblemen; were the "salt of the earth" in their day and generation. Their example is an inspiration. The memory of their heroic deeds and self-sacrificing labors ought to be a moral tonic to the present and future generations of Baptists—ought to put iron and oxygen in the blood and re-enforce us for more strenuous and sacrificial living.

There will be disappointment on the part of some in not seeing sketches here, which it had been hoped would find a place in this volume. But really it has been impossible to make room for them; they have been reserved for a "second series."

As to illustrations coveted for this volume, it has been a distinct disappointment to the author not to be able to find better pictures of the dear old men whose faces it would be a joy to see in a picture gallery or collection of portraits. But many of them never had a picture of themselves made; really there were no art galleries and few traveling artists in the country places where most of them lived. Of the few old pictures collected, and greatly prized, it has been a problem, in many cases, to get a creditable, or even a recognizable, portrait, with which to grace a sketch. It has been thought best, therefore, to leave out "cuts," made and paid for, that might be prejudicial to a good impression, rather than otherwise.

For helpful suggestions, as well as considerable materials used in the preparation of these sketches, the writer is in-debted to the following works: Benedict's General History of the Baptist Denomination in America, Borum's Sketches of Tennessee Baptist Ministers, Grime's History of Middle Tennessee Baptists, Semple's History of Virginia Baptists, Taylor's Baptist Ministers of Virginia, Cathcart, Armitage, and other Baptist historians; Haywood's History of Tennessee, Ramsay's Annals of Tennessee, etc.; but most of all he is indebted to the kindly, sympathetic co-operation of living witnesses of a generation ago—the real history-makers and interested students of history, the dear fathers and mothers in Israel, most of them now gone to their lasting reward, but who, while living, graciously and gladly helped in furnishing the author a fund of information in the form of "notes," from which the major part of this volume has been produced. To these due credit has been given in the body of the book.

Fraternally and most cordially,

J. J. B.

Jefferson City, Tenn.

2

SKETCHES OF

Tennessee's Pioneer Baptist Preachers.

ANDERSON ACUFF.

The Acuffs have been a prominent and well-known family in Grainger County, Tenn., for many years. Three of the family—Anderson, John D., and Simeon—a cousin and two brothers, were Baptist ministers of good repute, standing well in their community, being men of integrity, honored and useful in their day and generation. They were not pioneers in the strictest sense of the word, but were rather middle connecting links between a remote and a less remote past in the history-making period of Baptists in Grainger and surrounding counties. My sketches of these worthy ministers, like many of the more than two hundred sketches in this volume, are fragmentary and imperfect, on account of a regrettable scarcity of available materials for an adequate history. These sketches, fragmentary as they are, it will also be noted, appear on the first pages of the book, where it might be expected by some the biographies of the oldest preachers, the veritable "pioneers of the wilderness," would be found. This, the author would explain, is not accidental but according to plan: He is writing history biographically, not chronologically, and simply publishing the sketches in alphabetical order, and not otherwise. This, in passing, which might better serve as a *post-script* to the Preface, if the Preface were not already in the hands of the printer.

Anderson Acuff was born in Grainger County, Tenn., October 9, 1809, and died February 13, 1893, at the home of his son, Noah Acuff, in Knoxville, and was buried in the churchyard of the Glenwood Baptist church, near Powell Station, Tenn. He was twice married—first to Miss Lucy Popejoy, a daughter of Nathaniel Popejoy, to which marriage were born five sons and four daughters. His second marriage was to a Mrs. Hubbs, a widow, but of this marriage there were no children. He had a fair education, for his day and time, and taught school some during his early manhood. He was a carpenter and furniture-maker by trade; did honest work and made a living. He was an ordained preacher and was pastor of churches; the record of his ordination, however, we have not been able to find. Revival meeting work had a fascination for him that was irresistible, which led him to travel here and there and hold meetings. He was very much at home when it came to baptizing happy converts, and was considered an admirable and unusually graceful administrator of the ordinance—the comments of those who witnessed his performances in the baptismal waters being, "He was the best hand at the business I ever saw," "He had the greatest sleight in baptizing," "He knew exactly how to put them under," etc.

His ministerial activity was confined mainly to the counties of Grainger, Claiborne, Jefferson, Union and Knox. His associates in the ministry were William Hickle, Joshua Frost, Mark Monroe, and R. M. Wyrick. Elder Acuff was a useful minister, was jovial in disposition, and carried about with him a fund of humor and good nature that was perennial and refreshing. He was also able in prayer and exhortation, enjoyed the confidence of the people, and drew them to him wherever he went. The last few years of his life he was in rather poor health, preaching only occasionally, upon special invitation.

Dr. S. D. Acuff, a successful physician of Knoxville, who kindly furnishes "notes" for this sketch, is a grandson of Elder Anderson Acuff.

JOHN D. ACUFF.

John D. Acuff was born in Grainger County, Tenn., near Washburn, August 8, 1813, and died June 10, 1898. He was ordained somewhere between 1835 and 1840. His ministry was in Grainger and adjoining counties. He was pastor of Puncheon Camp, Big Valley, Alder Springs, Hickory Valley, Elm Springs, Rock Castle, Caney Valley, Cedar Spring, Beech Grove, and other churches. He was a "deep thinker, and in a sense was well educated—educated himself, in fact, by reading and continuous, close study. He was one of the best informed men in Grainger County. He had the care of many churches, and was a good pastor. He had the reputation of being one of the ablest doctrinal preachers in the Northern Association. He was at the same time spiritual and sympathetic, able in prayer and a good mixer." (Dr. J. W. J.) I have also been told that John D. Acuff was a strong advocate of ministerial education and of missions, and that he "stood almost alone" in his community in favoring a revision of the King James Version of the Bible. He endured hardness as a good soldier of Jesus Christ, and was faithful to the cause of his Master and the things for which Baptists stand.

In his young manhood he was maried to Miss Winnie Kitts, and reared a large and respectable family. Two of his sons, W. S. and Joel A., are Baptist preachers of ability and influence, the latter having the reputation of having preached more "funerals," the last quarter of a century, than any man in Grainger County.

Elder Acuff "served his Master faithfully, and the churches of which he was pastor, till by reason of the infirmities of age he was no longer able to serve; and this service, like that of many another Baptist preacher of his day, was a sacrifice on his part, the churches paying him little for his pastoral and other labors." His earthly toils and labors of love are ended. His bright, rich reward in heaven, we doubt not, has begun.

SIMEON ACUFF.

Simeon Acuff, a brother of John D. and a cousin of Anderson Acuff, was born near Puncheon Camp in Clinch Valley, Grainger County, Tenn., February 4, 1818. He was a son of Thomas Acuff, who was a son of John Acuff, and he, or his father, was among the first settlers of this section, and came from a place called Tuckaho, in Maryland. Said Thomas Acuff being a farmer, his son Simeon, with the rest of the family, was brought up to farm life. At the age of eighteen he was married to Susan Strange, and built a log cabin on his father's farm, reared a family of five children, and remained on this farm as long as he lived. He was converted during a series of cottage or community prayer meetings, which he and his wife, who was already a Christian, attended. In one of the meetings, when, as it happened, the service was being held at his father's house, he received the light and made his profession of faith in Christ. Soon after this he was baptized, uniting with the Puncheon Camp Baptist church. Not long after his conversion he began to take an active part in these community prayer meetings and to exercise his gifts in public prayer and exhortation at the church, under the watch-care and encouragement of Elder Asa Routh. In 1847 his church licensed him to preach and a little later authorized his ordination to the full work of the ministry. He continued to farm for a living, preaching as he had opportunity. His education was very limited, being only able to read and write. But by devoting his spare time to reading he became in time a fairly good Bible scholar. His strength and success as a preacher did not by any means come from his educational equipment, but from his reliance upon the Holy Spirit, whose effectual working and gracious help were always in evidence in his preaching and life. His services were greatly in demand, both as pastor and evangelist. He was pastor of most of the prominent churches in his native county of

Grainger, also of different churches in Union, Campbell, Claiborne, Hancock, Jefferson, and perhaps other counties. He was a successful revivalist, and witnessed hundreds of conversions in his meetings. He took great delight in baptizing newly made converts who loved the Lord and wanted to obey him in baptism. He was sent for, far and near, to preach funerals, perform marriages, attend communion occasions, and aid in protracted meeting efforts. He was not a doctrinal preacher so much as he was a preacher of the beautiful and tender and consolatory messages of the gospel. He was sympathetic and had a love for the souls of men. He preached with power the beauties of the Christian life and had the gift of picturing the home of the saved in heaven, the beauties of the New Jerusalem, and the meeting of God's children in their heavenly home with the Father and their Elder Brother, the Saviour, so as deeply to impress his hearers, and make them want to become members, if not already members, of the family of God. He was for some years moderator of the Northern Association, and traveled a good deal as missionary of that body, organizing churches and Sunday schools and fostering "weak interests."

His character was above reproach, and his patience in troubles and adversities was marked; he had faith in God and his goodness. He died May 6, 1893. His nephew, Elder W. S. Acuff, on the occasion of his burial, preached the funeral sermon, which was pronounced by many to be a really "great oration," due in part to the fact that there were "great" things to be said of a great and good man in Israel who had fallen in the harness.

Among the living descendants of Elder Simeon Acuff is his son, Coram Acuff, Esq., of Maynardville, who has kindly furnished most of the items for the above sketch.

LEVI ADKINS.

Elder Levi Adkins was born ———, February 20, 1794. He was married to Elizabeth George, and together they reared a family of eleven children, six sons and five daughters. He and his wife, Elizabeth, were constituent members of Bethel Church, Anderson County, which was organized with sixteen members, March 29, 1833. He was licensed to preach by Bethel Church, in May, 1842. The date of his ordination and the ordaining council I have not been able to ascertain. In 1849 he became pastor of Bethel Church, and continued pastor until 1865. He was also pastor of Bethany, Graveston, and Milan churches. He was moderator of the Clinton Association from 1864 to 1869, successor to Joshua Frost and succeeded by J. C. Hutson. Brother Adkins was a plain old-fashioned preacher of the simple gospel, lived his religion, had the confidence of the people, and was instrumental in leading many souls to the Savior. He lived about five miles from Andersonville.

March 30, 1877, having fought the good fight of faith and having finished his course with joy, he fell on sleep, and was buried in the Bethel Church Cemetery, where sleeps the dust of other faithful "ministers of the Word."

Rev. R. L. M. Wallace, of near Clinton, clerk of Bethel Church and clerk and colporter of the Clinton Association, one of my fellow-helpers, is a great-grandson of Elder Levi Adkins.

JOEL ALDRIDGE.

Joel Aldridge was a well-known minister and noted evangelist in the Northern and Mulberry Gap Associations. He was "licensed" to preach, June 8, 1833, by the Mouth of Richland Church, Grainger County, Tennessee. He was ordained by the same church, August 12, 1837, Elihu Millikan, Samuel Love, James Kennon and William Mynatt acting as a presbytery. The records of this church for August 11, 1838, read: "Chose Joel Aldridge assistant pastor." He was missionary of the Northern Association, and did a great deal of effective evangelistic work north and south of Clinch Mountain. Elder Asa Routh bore this testimony to him as an evangelist: "Joel Aldridge was the best revivalist I ever saw; he swept Clinch Valley by his wonderful power in protracted meeting efforts. From Powder Spring Gap to Puncheon Camp, when there were no churches between these points, he swept the valley clean of sinners, leaving no heads of families in the ranks of the enemy, except a hard knot or two—snarly cases, on which the devil had a first mortgage. He was not a boisterous preacher, as you might suppose; he reasoned and persuaded with tears." I am indebted to Elder Routh for the following incident: "Brother Aldridge lived on the south side of Clinch Mountain. While holding a meeting somewhere up the valley an urgent request came from his wife for him to come home at once; the family were out of provisions, had nothing to eat. Dismissing his meeting he hastened home; but stopping for dinner with 'Uncle Jakie Beeler,' he told him his situation with tears. Dinner over, 'Uncle Jakie' said to him, 'You stay right here and rest a bit till I do an errand and return.' He got together everything that was needed for present emergencies, and said to his guest, 'This will go straight to your home; go back and take up the meeting.' He got on his horse, weeping for joy, and without delay returned to the meeting."

WILLIAM ANDERSON.

A name prominent in the records of the old Bent Creek (Whitesburg) Church, and in the minutes of the Nolachucky Association, is that of William Anderson. He was born in Southwest Virginia, January 4, 1801. He was of Scotch-Irish descent, his father being Scotch, his mother Irish. His parents coming from the old country at an early day, settled in Vir-

ginia. Young Anderson in early manhood came to East Tennessee and settled on Bent Creek, about three miles from
Russellville. February, second Saturday, 1827, he was received
"by experience" for membership in the Bent Creek Church. In
the minutes of the church for the second Saturday, February,
1830, is this item: "The church unanimously calls Brother
William Anderson to exercise his gift in preaching the gospel
in the bounds of Bent Creek, Robertson's Creek, County line,
Bethel South (now the Morristown First), Barton, Concord,
and Warrensburg churches, and gives him written license."
Second Saturday, in February, 1834, the church "calls him to
ordination," and one month later he is ordained. Henry Randolph, Jere Hale, Noah Cate, Andrew Coffman and Pleasant
A. Witt acted as a presbytery. He attended the Nolachucky
Association from 1831 to 1838 as a messenger of Bent Creek
Church. In 1838 he preached the introductory sermon before
that body, from the text: "Say ye to the righteous it shall be
well with him. Woe unto the wicked! it shall be ill with him"
(Isa. 3:10, 11).

The Nolachucky Association had asked the churches composing the body to give an expression of their sentiments on
"the institutions of the day," such as State conventions, missionary societies, etc. Accordingly, Bent Creek Church (June,
second Saturday, 1839) "took up the institutions named in our
minutes, and decided we will not make them a test of fellowship. Vote, 38 to 27. The minority rent off from this church,
and hold their meetings on a different day, claiming to be the
old Bent Creek Church, but call themselves by the name of
Primitive Baptists." At the meeting of the association (Concord Church, fourth Friday, September, 1839) several churches
and parts of others, "numbering about one-third of our association, went off, declaring non-fellowship against us, and left the
house." In this division William Anderson, and other strong
men, went with the minority, claiming to be the "old school,"
or "primitive," or "New Testament" Baptists. He was thor-

oughly conscientious in his convictions, and a most zealous advocate and defender of what he conceived to be New Testament principles and doctrines, and went everywhere preaching them as "the faith delivered once for all to the saints."

William Anderson had few advantages, in early life, for obtaining an education, but he studied his Bible and loved to preach. "He was devout and upright in all the relations of life; loved his people and the doctrines they held; would make any sacrifice to propagate them; and, though lacking the education and culture of the modern preacher, none of his descendants approach him in point of intellectual ability." This is saying a good deal, when it is remembered that Dr. J. M. Anderson, of Tennessee, and Dr. William Anderson, of Georgia, are his grandsons. Dr. Sam Anderson, President at one time of Mossy Creek College, and Lawyer P. M. Anderson, of Newport, and a large connection of Andersons in Jefferson County, Tennessee, are near relatives of William Anderson, of pioneer fame. He was a farmer and chairmaker as well as a preacher, and so numerous were the Andersons of his neighborhood he was often designated, for the sake of distinction, "Chairmaker Billy Anderson." But he made honest chairs. One of them I have seen is made of sugar-tree wood, is a family relic about 100 years old, and I have just heard of another on Holston River.

In 1843 he sold his home on Bent Creek and moved to Jackson County, Kentucky. He preached pretty much "all over eastern and central Kentucky, and was considered the leader of his people in that part of the country. In his last years he made long tours on horseback, being away from home for weeks or months, visiting and ministering to his scattered people. His spirit has greatly influenced my life. I think I preach a fuller gospel, but how I wish I could be as noble a man!" In the year 1868 he fell on sleep and was buried in the old Flat Lick burying ground, in Jackson County, Kentucky, where his "flesh rests in hope."

WILLIAM ATCHLEY.

William, son of Isaac Atchley, was born May 23, 1813, in Sevier County, Tennessee. His grandfather, Thomas Atchley, was a native of Middlesex County, New Jersey, but in early manhood moved to Virginia and served under Washington in the War of the Revolution. He was married to Lydia Richards, of Loudon County, Virginia. He afterwards emigrated to Tennessee, locating in Sevier County.

William Atchley was converted in early life, uniting with Providence Church. He was married to Anna Bowers, a daughter of Elder Augustus Bowers. He was ordained to the work of the ministry in 1860, taking the pastoral care of churches. He was pastor of Providence, Bethel, Red Bank, Henderson's Springs, Ellejoy, Millikan Grove, Jones' Chapel, Alder Branch, Sugar Loaf, and other churches. Brother Atchley was "considered a successful preacher" in his day—a preacher of the old type, "unlearned" in books, but a "missionary"; and "many were converted under his ministry." He was a member of the Alder Branch Church from its organization (1836) to his death, March 3, 1901. He was buried in the Alder Branch cemetery. His preacher-brother, R. S. Atchley, had "outstripped him in the lane of life," and gone on to his eternal reward. The praises of both these servants of the Lord are in the churches of Sevier County. His son, William D. Atchley, now in his 77th year, is one of the substantial Baptists of Sevier County; and his grandson, M. C. Atchley, of Harriman, is one of our best preachers.

The following anecdote of William Atchley is vouched for by good authority: Brother Atchley was holding a revival service at Sugar Loaf Church, in which an old man 72 years of age was interested about his soul, having come forward for prayer a number of times. Brother Atchley was making the round of his inquirers, asking them how they felt and instructing them. Coming to the old man, who, apparently, had been very much concerned about himself, he asked him also "how he felt." Imagine the shock to the preacher's gravity and the amusement of the nearby youngsters, when the venerable mourner answered in perfect seriousness, "I feel like I had swallowed a large green pumpkin, and it is right here in my breast."

Another incident: One dark night, at Alder Branch Church, a "hardshell" preacher was discoursing on the "two-seed" doctrine, and showing how non-elect infants were doomed to dark despair because of the decrees of God. There was only one light in the house, and that was in the pulpit for the use of the preacher. Lucifer matches had not been invented; the putting out of the only light, therefore, might prove to be a serious matter. Unfortunately for the preacher, in bringing his fist down with too great emphasis on the Bible, he put out the only light in the house. Brother Atchley took advantage of the circumstance, and told the preacher he not only put the people in spiritual darkness by his preaching, but plunged them in physical darkness also.

ROBERT S. ATCHLEY.

Robert S., son of Isaac and grandson of Thomas Atchley, was born March 31, 1818, in Sevier County, Tennessee; died July 7, 1880. His birthplace is seven miles above Sevierville, "near the foothills of the Smokies." Brother Atchley never attended a college or a seminary; his library, however, now in possession of one of his grandsons, has in it a number of Greek and Hebrew books, the markings in which by his hand plainly indicate his familiarity with them. His nephew, W. D. Atchley, Esq., tells me his preacher uncle had a working knowledge of Greek, "dug out" at home. He was pastor of Alder Branch, Providence, Bethel, Red Bank, and Banner churches. He had good gifts and was laborious in the ministry, which was mostly in Sevier and Blount counties. Like most preachers of his day he received very little for his preaching. "His heart was always burdened for the lost sheep, and only three hours before he died, with seeming supernatural strength, he sang feelingly that beautiful song, 'The Shepherd of the Hills.'

Brother Atchley was twice married; first, to Louisa Clark. The issue of this marriage, if living, are in the west. His second marriage was to a Miss Watson. To this union were born four children, three daughters and one son. His youngest daughter, Mrs. W. M. Spence, lives at the old home above Sevierville, with a dear, patriotic boy "gone to the war."

Elder Atchley is described as "tall, dark-eyed, always wore a grave expression, talked little, was studious, and seldom laughed; he was of a mild temper, small in his own estimation, faithful in filling his appointments, and a power in the communities where he labored."

For several years, beginning with 1847, R. S. Atchley was a messenger of the Alder Branch Church to the Tennessee Association, his name appearing on the minutes also as pastor of a number of churches representing in that body.

He was also an active and efficient worker both in the East Tennessee and in the Sevier Association, when those bodies were organized.

P. M. ATCHLEY.

Elder P. M. Atchley was born in Sevier County, Tennessee, February 22, 1827. His parents were pious, exemplary Baptists, in moderate circumstances in life, but reverses of fortune reduced them to poverty, so that young Atchley grew up with no advantages of an education. He grew up in a religious communtiy, however, and in early life made a profession of religion and united with the church. Following his conversion he became a lover of good books and attained to a good degree of learning. Brother Atchley was thrice married, and had for wives three excellent Christian women.

He was married to Charlotte Garrett, September 22, 1852, to which union were born two daughters, one of them dying in infancy. April 10, 1856, he was married to Margaret E. Thomas. To this union were born four children, three daughters and one son—three of whom dying in infancy. Losing his companion, he was married a third time, to Martha J. Thomas, who became the mother of two sons, one of them dying when an infant. Recognizing in his many sad losses and sore bereavements the hand of God and a voice calling him into the ministry, and to repent of "vows and promises unkept," to preach the everlasting gospel, he yielded to his "impressions to preach," and was accordingly licensed by the Alder Branch Church, in 1864, to exercise a public gift, and in 1866 was ordained to the full work of the ministry by the sanction of the same church—Elders Robert S. Atchley, N. H. Haggard and Hiram S. Blair acting as a presbytery. Brother Blair says of him: "He has labored with a good degree of success in various places in the surrounding country. He has served as pastor at Boyd's Creek and Zion Hill churches. He is an excellent Sunday school man, is in frequent demand for addresses before Sunday school conventions, and has organized a model Sunday school in his own neighborhood, many of the pupils of which have been brought to Christ and to the church under his labors and influence. His Sunday school has now become a church of ninety-three members. He is one of our best revival preachers, but his health will not permit full-time work. He has held important offices of trust in his county. He is a strong advocate of Baptist principles; is much beloved and highly esteemed by his brethren. He is tender-hearted, ready to sympathize with his fellow-beings in their afflictions or distress, laying himself out to minister to their wants. He is a social and pleasant companion, greatly delighting to converse with his brethren upon the subject of religion and the prospects of future rest and happiness in heaven. He is a good and useful minister in the cause of God, and would be greatly missed.

May the good Lord spare his life to labor in His vineyard." (Condensed from Borum.)

Brother Atchley passed to his reward June 14, 1910, and was buried in the Alder Branch cemetery, Elder S. C. Atchley conducting the funeral services.

All of his ten children preceded him to the better land, seven of them dying in infancy. He survived his last wife some four years, living with his daughter-in-law, Mrs. Dona Atchley, and his grandchildren, preaching occasionally, as he had strength. The last of his family to outstrip him in the lane of life was his son, Elder N. A. Atchley, who died in 1907.

G. A. ATCHLEY.

Elder G. A. Atchley was born in Sevier County, Tennessee, October 8, 1836. He was a son of Elder William Atchley, who was a pioneer before him and a preacher of influence and standing in the county of Sevier. In a meeting held by Elder C. C. Tipton he made a profession of religion and was baptized, in 1853, into the fellowship of Alder Branch Church. September 30, 1860, he was married to Miss Nancy E. Fox, to which union were born eleven children, six sons and five daughters. Losing the wife of his young manhood he was married a second time, to Sarah Lindsey, becoming the father of five daughters and two sons. He was ordained to the ministry in 1876. He was pastor of several country churches at small salaries; he was also a farmer and school-teacher. He taught in the public schools of Sevier County a number of years. His most successful work as a pastor was with Gist's Creek and Providence churches, where he went in and out and served faithfully as an under-shepherd for eight successive years. Brother Atchley was a preacher of ability and a life-long Bible student. This was his one textbook, his chief storehouse of knowledge, his main source of information and inspiration for the business of preaching. He had a good knowledge of the Scriptures, and the Word of God to him was the sword of the Spirit, the one and only effective weapon of his warfare. Brother Atchley obeyed the injunction of the Scripture, "Do the work of an evangelist," and was successful in that work.

He died at his home, in Sevier County, March 10, 1902, and was buried in the cemetery of the Alder Branch Church. His funeral services were conducted by the pastor, Elder D. F. Manly.

He is survived by his wife, five daughters and seven sons. One of his sons, Elder S. C. Atchley, has been in the active ministry for seventeen years and is one of our valuable preachers.

JESSE BAKER.

Jesse, the son of G. W. and Martha Baker, was born near Sneedville, Hancock County, Tennessee, March 20, 1836. On his father's side he is mostly Irish. His mother was of German descent, having been born in Holland. His grandfather, Joseph, was a native of Virginia, but in the early history of the country, moved to Tennessee and settled in Hawkins (now Hancock) County. His great-grandfather, Andrew Baker, was a Baptist preacher in Virginia, a man of great usefulness, but a little eccentric in his habits. For instance, he would conscientiously "walk," and would never ride, to the house of worship on Sundays, in "imitation," as he held, of Christ and His apostles. On any other day of the week he felt at liberty to ride. It happened on a certain occasion, so the story goes, that the venerable old preacher was seen riding on a fine horse and approaching a crowd of worldings. One of the crowd, a smart fellow, who had just the day before been elected Esquire, said to the others: "Now, let's have some fun out of the old man." And so he accosted the preacher: "Well, Mr. Baker, you seem to be prouder than your Master; I believe He never rode on as fine an animal as you are on." "No," was the

3

quick retort, "they have made 'squires of all the asses, leaving me nothing in that line to ride." The tables were turned and the joke was on the other fellow.

Jesse Baker was converted in his seventeenth year, in a meeting held at Sneedville by Asa Routh and Thomas Gilbert, and was baptized by John Gilbert into the fellowship of the Sneedville Church. March 12, 1855, in his nineteenth year, he

JESSE BAKER.

entered Mossy Creek College, graduating June 9, 1859. In the summer before his graduation he was ordained by the authority of the Sneedville Church—Elders A. Routh, T. Gilbert and J. D. Berry acting as a presbytery.

He was married October 3, 1860, to Lucy A. Neil, a daughter of William and Margaret Neil, of Tazewell. I suppose no preacher's wife ever fed and entertained more preachers, and other company, than Sister Baker.

At different times Brother Baker was pastor of the following churches: Tazewell, his first pastorate, ten years; Mossy Creek, sixteen years; Dandridge, seventeen years; Cedar Grove (Alpha), eighteen years; Mouth of Richland, ten years; Dumplin, Island Home, Smithwood, a number of years; also Newport, Rankin, Beaver Creek, Buffalo, Rob Camp, Little Sycamore, and other churches. His greatest work was at Mossy Creek, now Jefferson City, extending over a number of years. First and last, he baptized into the fellowship of the church at this place not fewer than 500 persons, including college students.

He was closely identified with the interests and fortunes of Carson and Newman College from near its founding in 1851. In 1868 he was an associate teacher in the college with Prof. R. R. Bryan. In 1869 he was President of the college, with the Russells (W. T. and T. R.) as associate professors. As agent for the college, in a crisis when its very existence was involved, in ten months he rode horseback 3,500 miles and raised $5,250 to free the struggling and debt-burdened institution from the imminent peril of being sold under the hammer. Closing his agency work, and taking his place in the college as teacher (1870), in less than five months' time he saw a hundred young men matriculate as students in the college. In the fall of the same year a revival wave swept over the college and church (of which he was pastor), and about 100 souls were converted. December 10, 1870, he resigned the presidency of the college to give himself wholly to preaching and pastoral work.

His interest in the college and its work, however, never ceased. He was Secretary of its Board of Trustees for about thirty years, and rarely missed a board meeting in all that time.

In 1882 the college honored him, and itself as well, by conferring upon him the title "D.D."

Dr. Baker passed to his reward May 29, 1902. From an address delivered by Prof. W. T. Russell at a memorial service held by the Trustees and Alumni of Carson and Newman College, I copy the following eloquent words: "The college had just come out of the war a wreck, with a debt of $6,000—her only assets being an unfenced campus and three dilapidated brick buildings, destitute of floors, windows and doors. Dr. Baker had been elected President. I had been elected, a mere boy, to a place in the faculty. We went to look over the grounds and talk over the work, August 7, 1869, the day of the total eclipse of the sun. As we looked over the wrecked buildings and grounds, it seemed fitting to have the light of the sun shut out. Dr. Baker was distressed because the property was in ruins and the people discouraged, the college about to be sold under debt, and its history about to end in dishonor. As we turned to leave the cheerless spot he said, 'Let us undertake it.' That was heroic faith. He rode horseback all over East Tennessee and preached and prayed and plead for money. At the end of the year funds had been secured to pay off the debt, and that was a day of great rejoicing. Dr. Baker then took up his work in the college. He was also pastor of the church, which held its meetings in one of the college buildings. It was during these years that some memorable revivals were held by him in the college. He taught during the day and preached at night. In one of these great meetings 100 souls were saved, and this occasion became an epoch in the history of the church and the college. I remember especially one great sermon at night. He spoke with such pathos and power and eloquence that it seemed the whole audience was moved as I have never seen an audience moved, before or since. His voice was full of fervor and melody. His tongue was eloquent; his hands could speak. His fiery words burned into every soul present. In the midst of his sermon his face shone as it had been the face of an angel, and he said, "My soul's on fire tonight!" He then proceeded to describe a soul about to be doomed to death. He pictured that soul reaching out the hands of faith to take hold on the Christ, and struggling to break loose from the demons of hell, that had come up from their fiery home, clothed with scorpion stings and flames of fire. He painted that soul laying fast hold on Christ. Then the demons loosed their hold and turned in flight. 'Thank God, he's saved!' cried some one in the audience. He rose to such heights of impassioned and entrancing eloquence that many of the audience rose from their seats and stood up. One strong young man fell down and buried his face in his hands, and involuntary shrieks and groans came from all parts of the room. It was after midnight when that meeting closed."

ISAAC BARTON.

On the lookout for Baptist historical data and family relics, at the old Barton residence, near Russellville, we made the valuable "find" of a manuscript history of the Barton family, in Isaac Barton's own handwrite. The document bears date of "October 4, 1825," extracts from which will constitute the major part of the following sketch.

Isaac Barton was born in Maryland, near Fredericktown, August 16, 1746. His father, Joshua Barton, was the son of a widowed mother, from Holland. In 1753, or 1754, his father moved to North Carolina and settled on a branch of the Yadkin River, and, after the death of his mother, moved to Virginia, settling on Pig River, in what is now (1825) Franklin County.

October 9, 1772, Isaac Barton was married to Keziah Murphy, a daughter of William Murphy, a Baptist pioneer preacher of Virginia. This union was blessed with twelve "living children." Soon after his marriage he joined a Baptist church, and in a short while was called from above and encouraged by his church to preach the gospel, "the which I undertook to do," says the record, "with much fear and trembling."

He was ordained to the ministry by Samuel Harris, one of Virginia's most famous preachers, and William Johnson; and took the pastoral care of Blackwater and Pig River churches (Virginia), remaining with them "in love and harmony" until 1780, when he came to East Tennessee, and not long after took the care of a church near Greenville (Warrensburg Church), where "we enjoyed a great degree of love and fellowship, until the prospect of new countries caused the greater part of the church to break up and move. I also moved to the head of Bent Creek, in the bounds of the Rev. Tidence Lane's church (Whitesburg), where I remained thirty-one years, during which time, in general, we lived in mutual love and friendship, until a little before his death (1800), when his mind by some means got dissatisfied with my sentiment on the atonement, though we had preached together for many years." This difference in "sentiment" was doubtless due to the fact that Lane had come to consider Barton too strongly Calvinistic in his views of the atonement and of kindred doctrines.

"About that time" (1800), the record continues, "from the Bent Creek Church there went out a newly constituted church, called Bethel South of Holston (First Church of Morristown), of which I took the pastoral charge, and am yet with them as such" (1825). He was then past 80. "We have lived in general," the record goes on to say, "in harmony and love, and as a church have been able to dismiss members for Head of Richland, Friendship, and Blackwell's Branch churches. Our present number is between seventy and 100 members."

March 25, 1786, Jonathan Mulky and Isaac Barton constituted "the Church of Christ on French Broad River," or "Lower French Broad" Church, three miles northeast of Dandridge, the constituent members being "twelve in number."

At the organization of the Holston Association (1786), Tidence Lane, Isaac Barton and Frances Hamilton were messengers of the Bent Creek Church.

September 14, 1798, William Murphy and Isaac Barton constituted the Church of Christ on Lick Creek (Warrensburg), with a constituency of "twenty members."

He was pastor of what is now the First Baptist Church of Morristown, judging from all the available evidence (the church records having been destroyed), for thirty or thirty-one years. He died November 10, 1831, in his 86th year.

Isaac Barton was father, grandfather and great-grandfather to a number of distinguished men. One of his sons, Judge David Barton, of Missouri, was President of the convention which met in St. Louis, June, 1826, to form a State Constitution, which was afterwards known as the "Barton Constitution." In September of the same year he was elected the first United States Senator from the State of Missouri, with Thos. H. Benton as his colleague. This distinguished son was also the first Circuit Judge that ever held a court west of the Mississippi River. Judge Robert Barton, of Chattanooga, a grandson (recently deceased), and Senator R. M. McKinney Barton, a great-grandson, are both noted men.

Dr. W. A. Montgomery, one of the ablest preachers among Southern Baptists, is also a great-grandson of Isaac Barton, a pioneer of the wilderness nearly a century and a half ago.

The following incident, referred to elsewhere, I believe, may be mentioned in connection with Isaac Barton's preaching in the early part of the last century. Near Whitesburg, on the farm of Brother George Smith, and on the bank of Bent Creek, there stood a historic and noted tree, an elm, something like a hundred feet high, and extending its branches over a circle of at least 300 feet. This tree was old and decaying when the writer saw it. Perhaps it is no longer standing. But tradition says the shade of that elm tree was the preaching place of Tidence Lane and Isaac Barton before the Baptists in

that part of the country were able to build or had not learned
as yet the art of constructing meeting houses for the worship
of God.

N. W. G. BAXTER.

N. W. G. Baxter was born September 11, 1838, near Clover
Bottom, in Sullivan County, Tennessee. He had only a "common school" education, but being a close reader and a sturdy,
independent thinker, he came in time to be a well-posted man.
He was married to Miss Mary A. Devault, a sister of Rev. E. E.
Devault, an associate of the writer in Carson College and a
room-mate in the seminary, and a missionary of the Foreign
Board in China. This union was blessed with a large and well-
to-do family of children. In the early history of the Civil
War he entered the Confederate army, was captured and sent
as a prisoner to Camp Chase. In 1865 he was licensed to
preach by Double Springs Church, and shortly afterwards was
ordained to the ministry by the laying on of the hands of the
presbytery. For several years he served as an evangelist of the
Holston Association. In this capacity he served the Master
and the brethren with marked success, being eminently fitted
by natural gifts and gracious endowment for the work of an
evangelist. In the Holston Association he was pastor of some
of the best churches, as Jonesboro, New Salem, Cherokee, Holston, Bluff City, Blountville, and others; and also several
churches in the Holston Valley Association. As pastor he was
"faithful and efficient, prompt and scrupulous in attending his
appointments, was tender and sympathetic in his ministry,
and loved by all who knew him." As an evangelist he shunned
not to declare the whole counsel of God, and as a consequence
he led most of his converts, which were numbered by the hundreds, down into the baptismal waters. One of his marked
and useful evangelistic gifts was that he was a "good singer."
He was not only laborious and successful in the ministry, he
was an industrious and successful farmer, "raising and edu-

cating a large family of children, supplementing his income by cultivating his own farm, and contributing liberally, according to his means, to all of our denominational enterprises. Few men of his day accomplished a greater work for the people and for the Master than did Brother Baxter."

He died December 23, 1903, and was buried in the "family burying ground" with Masonic honors, being a member of the Fall Branch Masonic Lodge.

REES BAYLESS.

Here in the shadow of the old Cherokee Church, on Cherokee Creek, Washington County, I am standing on historic ground, listening to the silence that broods over the cemetery where I meditate. The church has been in existence since 1783; has outlived two meeting houses, and for years has been worshiping in a third. The old church book (preserved from the beginning) and tombstones show some interesting records. I find in the cemetery a stone erected to the memory of "Rev. Rees Bayless; born August 22, 1787; died October 29, 1864; more than fifty years a Baptist preacher"; and another erected to the memory of his grandfather, "Daniel Bayless, who died in the year 1800." Here also sleeps the dust of Elder John Bayless, father of Rees, and once a minister of the Cherokee Church. In its long list of members the church record shows seven generations of the Baylesses, among them three generations of Baptist preachers.

The subject of our sketch was born on Cherokee Creek, Washington County, Tennessee, four miles south of Jonesboro. On the paternal side he was of sturdy English stock, his grandfather, Daniel, having emigrated from England more than a century and a half ago, settling first in Pennsylvania, afterwards locating in Washington County, Tennessee, with his three sons, Samuel, John and Reuben. In the large family

REES BAYLESS.

connection are a number of interesting land "grants," made
to the older Baylesses before Tennessee became a State.

Elder Bayless was converted in his youth, and, uniting
with the Cherokee Church, was baptized, most likely, by Jonathan Mulkey, a preacher of pioneer fame. He was married
May 17, 1804, to Margaret Young, who became the mother of
his six children, five daughters and one son. In August of
1728 he was married a second time, to the widow Elizabeth
McPherin. In 1810 the Cherokee Church licensed him to
preach, and in 1820 ordained him. He became pastor of this,
his home church, in June, 1827, and continued pastor for more
than a quarter of a century. He was also pastor of Buffalo

Ridge, Sinking Creek, Indian Creek (now Erwin), Limestone, and other churches of the Holston Association. For many years he was a leader in this, the oldest association in the State, and was its Moderator for twenty-two years.

He was a prominent figure among East Tennessee Baptists and influential in the councils of his brethren. His judgment was deferred to and his advice had weight with the churches. At a meeting of "representatives" of the Holston, Tennessee, Nolachucky and East Tennessee associations, held August 25-26, 1843, at Pleasant Grove Church, Cocke County, for the purpose of adjusting doctrinal differences in regard to "election," "free salvation," etc., and to secure, if possible, a basis of union and co-operation in mission work, Elder Rees Bayless was chosen Moderator of the convention, and to his wise counsel and conservative bearing was due, largely, the friendly feeling and harmonious action of the Convention in the substantial adoption of the New Hampshire Confession of Faith and a resolution to co-operate in the work of missions.

Like most of our Baptist preachers of a hundred years ago, young Bayless grew to manhood, having few educational advantages. Being a student, however, of men and books, and a hard worker in the field of knowledge that was open to him, he dug out for himself stores of practical and useful learning, and became in the real sense of the term an educated man I am credibly informed that he was even a "Greek scholar," but whether he got his knowledge of Greek at school or at home, I am not able to say.

I close this sketch of a faithful and honored master-builder in our Baptist Zion with the following characterization of him by one who labored with him in word and doctrine and who appreciated his great worth to the denomination and to the cause of God: "Elder Bayless was not a man of culture or scholarly attainments, in the modern sense of those terms. But he was really educated and a self-made man. He was an old-fashioned gospel preacher, a great preacher for his day. He had great strength of character and was as firm a man as Andrew Jackson. He was a speaker of commanding appearance, standing erect, six feet three inches, rawboned and stalwart, a splendid specimen of physical manhood. He had great compass and strength of voice, and always spoke with ease, never straining his voice, giving the audience the impression of reserved power in the preacher. For a long while before his death ,he was afflicted with rheumatism, and was a great sufferer, much of the time being unable to preach, but he bore his sufferings with Christian fortitude, and endured as seeing Him who is invisible. He was in deed and in truth a man of God and did great good in his day, mightily influencing the people" (W. A. Keen).

To Elkana Bayless, grandson of Elder Rees Bayless, an ordained minister of Cherokee Church, a lover of books and a student of history (deceased, March 31, 1899), I am indebted for considerate kindnesses and practical help in my work.

To Robert Rees Bayless, of Johnson City, a grandson namesake of the elder Rees Bayless, I am indebted for helpful suggestion and service in many ways. He recently (May, 1917) passed to his reward. He was past 73, had been a deacon of Cherokee Church for fifty years, and for forty-eight or forty-nine years had attended, almost unbrokenly, the annual meetings of the Holston Association.

JESSE D. BERRY.

Jesse D. Berry was born near Lee Valley, Tennessee, about the year 1815, possibly a year or two later. He made a profession of religion in young manhood and united with the Baptist Church at Richardson's Creek, Hancock County. He was ordained by this church to the "full work of the ministry," November 21, 1846, Elders Moses McGinnis, John Day and James Greenlee being the ordaining council. He served the Richardson's Creek Church as pastor from 1849 to 1860 "con

tinuously," being at the same time pastor of a number of other
churches. During his pastorate of this, his home church,
he represented his church every year in the Mulberry Gap
Association, being one of the most active ministers in that
body. He was not only active as a pastor; he was also a
popular and effective evangelist. "He had more calls as pastor
and evangelist than he could fill." I note this incident as of
record in the minutes of the Richardson's Creek Church: "Little War Creek Church requests the church at Richardson's
Creek to grant them a part of the time of Jesse D. Berry."
Reply: "If you will help us to pay for a horse for him to
ride, we will grant the request." This is all the information
I have been able to gather in regard to a most useful minister
of Jesus Christ. His family are scattered and the older people who knew him are dead. This mere fragment of a sketch
is the best report I can make, at present, of a man of God who
wrought nobly for his Master and served well his day and
generation by the will of God. Elder Berry passed to his
reward in the year 1864.

WILLIAM BILLUE.

In the old family Bible, which has come down through four
generations and is now in the possession of a great-grandson,
Elder W. A. Catlett, I find the following record of a remarkable preacher, the record made by the preachers' own good
hand: "William Billue was born August 25, 1793, in Mecklenburg County, North Carolina; emigrated to Tennessee in 1812
and located in Blount County; joined the Baptist Church in
Miller's Cove in 1822; was licensed to preach the gospel
March, first Saturday, 1823, and was ordained by the Rev.
James Taylor and William Holloway, November 31, 1823." In
the cemetery of Mount Lebanon Church is a tombstone inscribed, "Rev. William Billue (born, as above); died April 4,
1874," with this tribute to his memory: "By the grace of God

he fought a good fight and kept the faith which was once delivered to the saints."

When William Billue began his ministry (1823), there
were in Blount County only two churches, Miller's Cove and
Sixmile; now (1896) there are twenty-six.

Among the churches served by Brother Billue as pastor,
long and well, are Nail's Creek, Crooked Creek, Stock Creek,
Piney Level, New Hopewell, Ellijoy, Mt. Olive, and Mount Lebanon. The lumber which went into the first meeting house
of the Mt. Lebanon Church was his contribution.

More than any other man he gave impulse and impetus
to the Baptist cause in all this section of country, and was
instrumental in laying the foundation of many of our now
prosperous churches. Spiritually and baptistically, to use the
language of many of the older brethren, "Old Uncle Billy
Billue was the father of his country," that is, of Blount
County.

When corn was ten cents a bushel he rode as "missionary"
for a shilling a day. He and Richard Taliaferro traveled
throughout the bounds of what is now the Clinton Association, and in the surrounding counties, stirring up the churches
on the subject of missions. They were the first missionaries,
I am told, in this part of the country. Brother Billue was
furnished a "missionary horse" by Eleven Hitch, "free of
charge," like the gospel he preached.

Of his early history and conversion old "Uncle Jimmy
Hitch," who knew William Billue longer and more intimately
than anyone else, says: "William Billue, as a young man,
was wild and wicked, dissipated and reckless, lived among the
Indians, apparently a moral as well as a financial wreck,
but when the grace of God took hold of him it transformed
him. At the age of 30, or thereabout, he became a new man,
and soon began to preach. He taught school, farmed and
made money; was sober, industrious and prosperous, being
worth, at his death, from $15,000 to $20,000."

He was a man of affairs, rather than of books. What he knew of the Bible and other books he "dug out" for himself. Though not scholarly, yet with good natural ability, a determined will and a voice incisive and effective, he was a commanding speaker. He was not prepossessing in personal appearance, being spare-made, rather ill-shaped, and club-footed, but his eyes were dark and "keen as a hawk's," and eye and voice and will made him "master of assemblies" in his day. Peter Brakebill, a venerable brother, says of him: "I used to think Uncle Billy could say more in a few words than anybody. When he set up his target and took aim, he didn't shoot all over the board and waste ammunition—he generally knocked the center out."

Brother Billue had no penchant for public debate, but when necessary he knew how and where to find a man to do his debating for him. He was instrumental in bringing about the Pope-Hillsman debate at Eusebia, a Presbyterian church. The Presbyterians in those days, when confronted by an ordinary Baptist opponent, felt pretty safe in intrenching themselves in the "dead languages," especially Greek, when worsted in discussion and dislodged and routed from their English strongholds, so to speak. But Matt Hillsman happened to know Greek, as well as his opponent, and so carried the Baptist flag in triumph to the top of the citadel, unfurled, and easily defended it—with its threefold ancient inscription of "one Lord, one faith, and one baptism."

The subject of our sketch was twice married: first, to the widow Jane James, June 15, 1813; the second time to a Miss Susannah Hitch, August 20, 1846, William Rogers performing the ceremony.

His first wife was a Presbyterian, but became dissatisfied with her so-called "infant baptism." The husband, to satisfy his wife, and make her dissatisfied with her so-called baptism, went to a Presbyterian Doctor of Divinity, President of a college, and laid the case before him. With a twinkle in his eye he said he wanted something to "satisfy" his wife, but was told by the doctor, in whom scholarship and candor united, "I guess, Brother Billue, I can't satisfy your wife with her baptism; I suppose she will have to go to the Baptists."

William Billue was six years Moderator of the Tennessee Association. His labors were abundant in the Master's cause. His influence for good was felt far and wide. I have met many who were baptized by him, and some who by his influence had been led into the ministry. His praise is in the churches. And many, in the last day, will rise up and call him "blessed."

Among his more prominent associates in the ministry we might mention Elijah Rogers, Eli Roberts, Samuel Love, James Lankford, and other dear familiar names that "cannot die," because enshrined in many hearts and destined to find a sure place in the history of Baptists.

JONATHAN BISHOP.

Jonathan, son of Joseph Bishop, was born in Washington County, Virginia, June 8, 1795. In early life he came with his parents to East Tennessee, settling in Hancock County. At the age of 19 he was married to Julia E. Clark, a daughter of Francis Clark, Lee County, Virginia. He was married a second time, to Elizabeth Williams, of Russell County, Virginia. He had ten children by his first marriage and four by the second.

The circumstances of his conviction and conversion are striking. His brother James, who afterwards became a preacher, had married into a Methodist family. When some one urged his wife to become religious, she replied, heart-brokenly, "I'd like to—but Jim is going to hell, it seems like, and I'll just go with him." Pierced by this arrow the husband said, "She shall never go to hell on my account," and at once went to praying for himself, and was converted. Immediately he sent for his brother Jonathan, who lived twenty miles away, to come to see him without delay, although it was the busiest season of the year. Leaving at once their pressing work Jonathan and his wife came in haste to see what was the matter. Riding up to the house he said, "Why did you send for me at so busy a time?" "I want to pray for you," was the reply. Jonathan at once took in the situation, and noting the marked change in his brother was led to pray for himself. He was soon converted, and was baptized, it is supposed, by James Gilbert, uniting with the Mulberry Gap Church, Hancock County. Under Brother Gilbert's influence he developed into a preacher, and at the age of 30 was ordained to the ministry by the authority of the Mulberry Gap Church.

The first five years of his ministry was in Hancock County, the next twenty-five in Lee County, Virginia. Here he was pastor of several churches, witnessed many gracious revivals, and was instrumental in organizing and building up a number of good churches. From 1854 till he fell in the harness, September 8, 1870, his ministry was in Tennessee, at Mulberry Gap, Sneedville, Third Creek, Valley Grove, Salem, and other places.

Jonathan Bishop was an old style preacher, with a limited education, and having some of the "peculiarities" of voice and manner that were common in many places among Baptists of his day. But he had real power over an audience and was a moral force for good wherever he was known. As a speaker he was earnest and sympathetic; he was a rapid talker, and had the gift of exhortation. He had a great zeal for the salvation of souls, and his delight was in holding meetings—protracted meeting work was his forte. An old-time friend and admirer of Brother Bishop gives this testimony: "His courage, his devotion to the cause of Christ, and his untiring labors to elevate the standard of morals in his community, are pleasant memories of that grand old soldier of the cross that I never can forget."

4

Among the many converts of his meetings, Brother Bishop reported one Methodist "class leader," one "household" of *believing* Methodists baptized, and the conversion and baptism of a number of men who afterwards became useful ministers of the gospel.

From J. C. Bishop's "Reminiscenses" of his father I cull the following incidents. A meeting-house was wanted in Lee County, Virginia. Following the leadership of Jonathan Bishop, from forty to fifty men got together on Monday morning and went to work to build a house of worship. By Saturday night the logs "were cut, hewed, put up, the house covered, and the floor laid, all ready for the Sunday service." We give this as a concrete example of "dispatch" in doing the King's business, which "requires haste" more often than we give it. The following also serves to point a moral: Brother Bishop placed great emphasis upon reading the Bible for light and guidance, even upon one's knees. Providence, on one occasion, gave him valuable assistance in enforcing his teaching. It was November 18, 1833, the solemn night when the "stars fell" so wonderfully, and many thought the world was coming to an end. The preacher's house was filled to overflowing with excited people, who had come to pray and be prayed for. There was scarcely a Bible in the neighborhood, on that occasion, that didn't shed its dust in a hurry, and become for once the Book of books. Two men professed religion and turned preacher—but whether they held out faithfully or not the writer is not informed.

The Bishops are a numerous and noted family, of high standing and influential. It is largely a family of preachers. Three brothers, Elisha, Jonathan, and James, were Baptist preachers. J. N. and W. W. Bishop, of the younger generation, and possibly others, are among our most useful ministers.

HIRAM S. BLAIR.

Hiram Blair was born in Blount County, Tennessee, in the first quarter of the last century. His parents were poor but honest. On account of financial misfortunes, the boy Hiram was forced by hard necessity to toil and sweat to help secure for the family the necessaries of life. This necessity of his boyhood life deprived him of educational advantages, and thus handicapped him for life. This disadvantage he could only partially overcome by hard study in after life. But a worse handicap than a lack of education was his moral environment—associations and temptations which made it hard to do right and easy to go wrong. The result was he became the bond-slave of sin, and gave his life and the influence of his example to Satan, until it pleased God, through his abundant mercy, to save him. This He did in a meeting at Bethel Church, Sevier County, under the preaching of Eli Roberts and G. G. Sims. The investigation of the Scriptures changed him from Methodist to Baptist views, and he "went down into the water" to be "buried with Christ in baptism," October, 1847, in his nineteenth year, becoming a member of Bethel Church. Later, at the organization of Jones Chapel, he became a constituent member, beginning, soon after, to exercise the gift of public prayer.

October 7, 1850, he was married to Miss M. J. Patterson, to which union there were born a son and two daughters. In August of '55 he was married to his second wife, a Miss Mary J. Allen, and to this marriage were born eleven children, five sons and six daughters. In 1863 his church (Jones Chapel) licensed him to preach, and December 25, 1864, ordained him —Elders John Russell, R. S. Atchley, and G. G. Sims serving as a presbytery.

As pastor, Brother Blair served Providence, Bethany, Sugar Loaf, Union, Wilsonville, Powder Springs, and other churches. For a number of years he served as missionary of the East

Tennessee Association, holding meetings, collecting funds, strengthening weak churches, witnessing many conversions. His most successful labors were in Cocke and Sevier counties, though preaching considerably, and with good success, in Jefferson and Blount. He was not an idler in the vineyard. He was not afraid of work, and knew how to stick to a job. He gave a great deal of time to the Lord's work, with little or no remuneration.

He was generally in evidence at the associations and other public gatherings of his brethren, and always willing to serve on committees and to do whatever was needed to be done. Brother Blair was a solid man, and a plain, good, old-fashioned preacher. He had the confidence and respect of everybody, and maintained a spotless reputation. He used to visit the churches of Joseph Manning, and preach for him occasionally, when the writer was a boy. Our recollection is that his mind worked slowly in the beginning of his discourse, but he warmed to his subject as he proceeded, and usually gave to his hearers an instructive and edifying sermon. He was faithful to improve his gifts, and wrought faithfully and well for the Lord and the Baptists, who, in his thinking, were the Lord's "chosen people."

Near his home in Sevier County is a grave and a marble slab above it, bearing this his inscription: "In memory of Eld. H. S. Blair: born July 26, 1828; died June 4, 1894—aged 65 years, 10 months, 8 days. A sinner saved by grace.

> " 'Here sweet be my rest,
>   Till He bids me arise,
> And view Him in triumph
>   Descending the skies.' "

SAMUEL J. BLAIR.

Samuel J., son of Thomas and Hannah Blair, was born June 9, 1823, near Madisonville, Monroe County, Tennessee. His father was a farmer in moderate circumstances, and a Baptist deacon. He was ambitious to give his children educational advantages, and young Blair had an ambition to make out of himself a scholar and a worth-while man. So he provided himself with books and "burned the midnight" pine-knot in the pursuit of knowledge. He also organized a neighborhood debating society, for self-culture and practice in speaking.

November 13, 1842, he professed faith in Christ, and on Christmas day, the month following, he was baptized by one of the Taliaferros into the fellowship of the Madisonville Church. On the same day, he said, "standing at the water's edge, in the midst of my associates and surrounded by the fathers in Israel, and looking upon the clear, sparkling stream, as it gushed from its fountain and wended its way so beautifully through the green meadows, I felt the first impressions to preach the gospel to a perishing world."

But he felt he must make preparation for so great a work. His father sent him one term to the Madisonville Academy, which enabled him to teach in the public schools. Alternating between teaching and going to school for four years, by diligent study he prepared himself for an effective ministry of the gospel, to which office he was publicly ordained, September 27, 1847, by a council composed of Daniel Buckner, John Scruggs, a Brother Wilson and a Brother Chapman.

November 11, 1847, he was married to a Miss Nancy Walker, and settled on a farm near Shepherd Hill, James County. Here shortly afterwards he organized a church, which he served as pastor for many years, where also he had many seals to his ministry. He also organized Hopewell Church, serving it as pastor for many years. He was also pastor of Pleasant

Grove, Antioch, Kandis Creek, Phillippi, Salem, Blue Spring, and Georgetown churches. In all these localities he had a successful ministry, and left a fragrant memory. His last pastorate was in East Chattanooga, where he succumbed to what had become a chronic brain trouble—falling "gently to sleep" August 5, 1897, to wake up in the Father's house on high.

Brother Blair was a man of positive convictions, and was ever ready to take a stand for the right; he was at the same time conservative and conciliatory, having a sweet and tender spirit and a disposition to "keep the peace" and to harmonize churches and communities. This made him a safe counselor. On one occasion, it was said, he was moderator of what threatened to be a stormy council. Some delicate matters had been brought before it for adjustment. At one stage of the procedure it seemed that an unpleasant division of the council was certain, when the moderator, by tact, wise counsel, and the exhibition of a tender, sympathetic spirit, saved the day, and united all parties in loving fellowship. "Blessed are the peacemakers."

JOHN BLANCHARD.

John Blanchard, minister and physician, was a native of Cocke County, Tennessee. He was the oldest son of John and Sarah Blanchard, of South Carolina, and was born March 30, 1821. He was of Welsh extraction. His father was a hardy pioneer, with a physical frame built for endurance and a spirit for bold and daring adventure. His ancestors, leaving the old country in an early day and coming by way of South Carolina to what was then the "west" of the new world, were guided by the migratory instinct to seek a home in the mountains of East Tennessee—a genial climate and soil and a place for exploits and adventure. The birthplace of young Blanchard on the French Broad River, in Cocke County, ten

miles from Paint Rock, which marks the boundary line between Tennessee and North Carolina, is one of the most pic-
turesque and rugged spots in the "Switzerland of America."
A young lawyer and writer of descriptive powers, himself a
native of the mountains, and a neighbor and admirer of young
Blanchard, gives the following pen picture of the place and
the scene where the subject of our sketch first saw the light:

JOHN BLANCHARD.

"To the west is Stone Mountain and to the east its twin
brother, rugged old Neddy. Between them, carrying its everlasting toll of grit and sand and gravel, the French Broad
roars and frets and grinds, cutting deeper and broader its
tortuous passage through the last range of the Alleghanies.
The Buncombe Branch of the Southern Railway winds along
its western bank, and from the car window you may see a
wagon trail on the opposite bank, crowded down to the water's
edge by the feet of old Neddy. Just at the foot of this historic mountain to the west, where there begins a narrow fringe
of poor sandy bottom land, John Blanchard was born. Here
his father, in an early day, too poor to do better, settled down
and built his rude log-house." Here in the school of poverty
and hard work young Blanchard learned the lesson of industry,
self-denial, and self-reliance, as well as virtue and honesty.
To help support the family he was compelled to "hire out"; and
as a young man his highest ambition was to be the best wood-
chopper, rail-splitter, and general, all-purpose farm-hand in
the county. His ambition to "stand at the head" was gratified
—for he was tall and straight as a mountain pine, and sturdy
as the oak that wrestles with the tempest, with a frame of
bronze and muscles of steel.

His manly virtues of truthfulness, honesty, and sobriety,
especially his reputation for doing good, honest work, for large
pay or small pay, made him the trusted hired hand and "friend"
of the Stokelys and Huffs, and other men who knew his genuine
worth.

Living in the home of Alfred Lea, justice of the peace,
owner of a mill and a man of letters, young Blanchard learned
his letters, while working for him as a hired hand. Later he
acquired some knowledge of arithmetic and bookkeeping, while
running a grist-mill on French Broad River, making mental
calculations and "keeping the books in his head."

March 24, 1842, he was married by Joseph Manning to Miss
Charlotte Justus, Elder Manning performing the ceremony at

his own house. Alfred Lea, his former employer and tutor, gave him a royal, old-time "wedding dinner."

In 1842 he was converted in a Methodist camp meeting at Parrottsville, in his native county. A little later he attended a Baptist meeting, being held by Joseph Manning in the old French Broad meeting-house. "Jack" Blanchard was profoundly stirred by the preaching, joined the church, and was baptized by Elder Manning.

With his conversion came a new inspiration and an ambition to make the most of himself that it was possible to make, with his limited opportunities. Laboriously; by the light of "blazing pine knots," he learned to read the Bible, and particularly the New Testament Scriptures. His days were given to hard work, his nights largely to study.

In 1843, in the old brick meeting-house at the mouth of Big Creek (now Del Rio) on the French Broad River, Elder Blanchard preached his first sermon. From this time on his constant desire—his prayer and effort by day and his dream by night—was that he might help to improve the temporal and spiritual condition of his neighbors, and to serve the Lord who had saved him and called him to preach the gospel of his grace.

April 18, 1844, he left his native mountains to seek a home in the West. His mode of travel was by wagons. His route lay through Knoxville, where he spent one night, camping at the spring, "out of which the Knoxville Ice Company now gets water to make ice." Leaving Knoxville, he made his way across the Cumberland Mountains, by way of Crab Orchard, Kentucky, to the Ohio River; thence to the Mississippi. Prospecting in Arkansas awhile, he finally located in Illinois. Here he worked hard and saved his earnings; bought and improved lands, built a home for himself and family, educated his six children and set them up in business. Two of his sons became ministers. At 43 he himself took up the study of medicine, and four years later was a practitioner in the art of healing—graduating from the Eclectic College of Medicine.

Cincinnati, in 1869. Two of his sons and one of his grandsons are graduates from the same medical school. Not only
in his native East Tennessee but also in his adopted State of
Illinois he has been a noted pioneer of education, temperance
reform, religion, and good citizenship. He is an illustrious
example of what industry, economy, perseverance, and heroic
endurance, sustained by moral purpose and a determined, unconquerable will, can do, in raising a man from lowly birth
to position and influence in the world.

> "Honor and fame from no condition rise;
> Act well your part—there all the honor lies."

Though an "M.D.," and an active physician, he has been
active also in the ministry, rarely being without a pastorate.
"He still preaches at his home church," though old and nearly
blind. His recollection of passages of Scripture, and their
location, is remarkable, it is said, although he is now scarcely
able to read a word.

As a preacher, his style is quaint and effective. He has no
honeyed words, and to over-refined tastes and "ears polite"
he is not a model of grace—but the common people hear him
gladly. A man of giant frame, of titanic strength and sten-
torian voice, he could scarcely appear before an audience to
speak and not make an impression. The writer has never
heard a preacher with a voice so like the roll and roar and
crash of God's thunder. But, surpassing his equipment of
physical strength and effectiveness, were those qualities of mind
and heart that make the true man and real preacher.

After an absence of many years, Brother Blanchard, full
of years and honors and in good health, has been permitted to
visit the "old home place" and the friends of his youth, under
the shadow of "grand old Neddy" in his native East Tennessee.

CHESLEY H. BOATWRIGHT.

Chesley H. Boatwright was born in Cumberland County, Virginia, November 25, 1797. There are different ways of spelling the name. Heretofore I have spelled it "Bootwright," and sometimes "Bootright," having the impression that some-one of his early ancestors was a maker of "boots." But the people, generaly, have called him Boatwright, and doubtless he is connected, historically, with the Boatwrights of Virginia. So I have changed the spelling. In his twentieth or twenty-first year young Boatwright came to Grainger County, Tennessee, and married Louisa Taylor, a daughter of Elder Hughes Owen Taylor, one of the early settlers of the "new country of Grainger." About the year 1825 he moved to Anderson County. In 1830 he was "licensed" to preach by Mt. Hebron Church, in Knox County. The first Friday in November, 1833, he was ordained by authority of Bethel Church, Anderson County, which had just been constituted (March 29, 1833) of sixteen "constituent members," mostly from the Mt. Hebron Church, and recognized by a "presbytery" consisting of Elders Joshua Frost, Isaac Long, Noah Cate, Samuel Love. Doubtless some or all of these men officiated in the ordination of the subject of this sketch. Elder Boatwright served Bethel Church as pastor from 1840 to 1845, and from 1848 to 1851. In the fall of 1831 he engaged himself to teach a school of several months near Coal Creek. About the same time he began a meeting in the neighborhood, preaching of nights. Elders Joshua Frost and James Hickey joined him in the meeting, ably assisting in the work. "A revival broke out, and Clear Branch Church (now Longfield) was the result. Boatwright became the first pastor, and continued pastor and moderator of the church till he moved to Arkansas in October of 1849, a period of about fifteen years. He died in Arkansas, but the date of his death and the place of his burial are not known to the writer" (W. R. Riggs).

In 1846 Clear Branch Church (C. H. Boatwright, pastor) was the largest church in the Northern Association, reporting a membership of 228. This association "was formed in 1839; it came off from the Powell's Valley community, on account of its opposition to the cause of benevolence. This new and vigorous interest entered at once into the business of domestic missions, and employed Messrs. C. H. Bootright, J. Aldridge, and Wm. Hickle to travel and preach among their feeble churches, and in destitute regions around them. In 1842 their missionaries reported as follows: Traveled upward of 3,000 miles, and baptized 300, save one" (Benedict). This exhausts my "notes." It is a regrettable fact that so little definite information is obtainable in regard to a minister of so great prominence and of such ability and personal force as Chesley H. Boatwright seems to have had. He was active in the ministry for twenty years, before leaving the State, and was widely known in several counties and associations. He was a strong man, and made an impression wherever he went. I have heard many of the old people of the country speak of him with profound respect, and, incidentally, have noted his name in connection with the founding of churches and the ordination of ministers not a few.

ELDER JOHN BOND.

The early history of the Baptists of Middle Tennessee is intimately associated with the name of Bond. Two brothers, James and John Bond, began their ministry in the year 1820 and became and continued dominant factors in the denominational life until their death. John Bond was born in Anson County, North Carolina, February 23, 1787. His parents moved to South Carolina when he was only three years of age. At the age of fifteen he gave his heart to God, and on Wednesday after the third Sunday in July, 1802, having recited his Christian experience to the Padget Creek Baptist church, he was buried by baptism by Elder Thomas Green. The clear waters of old Tiger River witnessed to the joy of the youth.

The Bond family moved from South Carolina to Tennessee and settled near Statesville in 1806. The Smith's Fork Baptist church was organized in this year, and the youth probably became a constituent member and retained his membership with this church until 1815. In this year he was licensed

ELDER JOHN BOND.

to preach; and when Union church, familiarly known as "Old Hurricane," was constituted, as a daughter of the Smith Fork church, he went into the new organization and became the first clerk. In 1820 he was ordained by the Union church, with the presbytery composed of Elders Joseph Lester and David Gordon. He gave to this church 20 acres of land and largely assisted in the erection of its building. The modern church building stands upon the old plot and the visitor may read in the adjoining cemetery the names of the heroes of these long-departed days.

Soon after his ordination Elder Bond was called as pastor of Union church and served through the unbroken period of 39 years. Tradition holds that the compensation for this long pastorate came in the form of a donation, placed one Sunday morning upon the table before the pulpit. It consisted of about $11.00 and a pair of woolen socks. Pushing the spontaneous expression of appreciation toward an aged, but poor brother, the minister said: "Here, Daddy Mack, you need these worse than I do."

As a minister Elder Bond must have combined tact and oratorical ability to justify such a long pastorate. Careful, of informing judgment, tender in his treatment of the brother in error, he was often sought for his counsel to help churches settle their personal and doctrinal difficulties. He was a strong Calvinist who fully recognized that Calvinism did not violate the missionary obligation. When the division in Middle Tennessee occurred over the missionary question, Elder Bond was a strong advocate of the missionary party. His name ranks among the ministers of his day with those of J. R. Graves, R. B. C. Howell, James Whitsitt, J. M. Pendleton, Joseph Marshall, and J. H. Eaton, who were his friends and co-laborers.

His method of speaking was without manuscript. He did not have an ambition for authorship, but in 1859 he compiled the History of Concord Association for the first fifty years, which was published by request of the Association. The sum of $50 was given the author for this service, and by him was presented to Union University at Murfreesboro for a scholarship. Elder Bond frequently served as moderator, and preached on special occasions, for Concord Association. As an expression of the Association's love for him, in 1859, the Association raised a fund for making him life director of the

Southern Baptist Sunday School Union.   Toward the latter
period of his life he was affectionately known as "Father
Bond."

In personal appearance he was of medium height, slender
in build, with an average weight of 140 and of an active disposition.   He was well to do in material things, owning at one
time 1,300 acres of rich land with a number of slaves.   In
1806 he was married to Miss Sallie Cummins, and to them ten
children were born.   The youngest of these, Captain James
Houston Bond, at this writing is a resident of Nashville.   On
March 2, 1861, with his mental and spiritual powers unabated,
and with the record of a long and useful ministry, and just
before the war clouds burst upon the South, this minister of
God laid down his earthly service to take part in the triumph
of those who served well their God and their generation by the
will of God.

The ministerial heritage of John Bond overleaped one generation to fall upon the youngest son of his youngest son.
Dr. Albert R. Bond, the beloved editor of the Baptist and
Reflector, of Nashville, the grandson of John Bond, gratefully
recognizes the pioneer services rendered by his worthy ancestor.
It was the privilege of the editor to take part in the centennial celebration of the organization of old Union church and
stand in the pulpit of his worthy sire.   On the foundation of
our fathers may the larger structure of Kingdom plans be
builded!

DANIEL BOONE.

Col. Daniel Boone, though never identified with the Baptists, was a Baptist in principle, and had a brother, Squire
Boone, who was a noted Baptist preacher in Kentucky.   According to Haywood and Ramsay, Baptists are as much indebted to Daniel Boone for an early and a good start in Tennessee as to any other man.   This is my justification for giving
him a place in this volume.

Daniel Boone was a son of Squire Boone, Sen., and was born in Pennsylvania about the year 1734. When four or five years old he removed with his parents to North Carolina, and settled on the Yadkin, eight miles from Wilkesborough. In 1760, according to Ramsay (see inscription on Boone Tree, in Appendix to this volume), Boone visited the country now known as Boone's Creek, in Washington County, nine years before what is now Tennessee became the Watauga Association and thirty-six years before it became an independent state. In 1764 Boone, with a kinsman, again visited the Watauga to further explore the country. As he approached the spurs of the Cumberland Mountain, in view of the vast herds of buffalo grazing in the valleys, he exclaimed, "I am richer than the man mentioned in scripture, who owned the cattle on a thousand hills. I own the wild beasts of more than a thousand valleys!" Whatever his confusion in his quotation of scripture, it was clear to him that the land, and what was on it, belonged to him who had the faith and courage to go up and possess it. May 1, 1769, Boone, with three others, left his "peaceable habitation on the Yadkin River in quest of the country of Kentucky." In the fall of 1773 Boone made an attempt to take his family to Kentucky. "Before this time no white female, no family, had crossed the Cumberland range. Boone prevailed on four or five other families to join him, and with them advanced towards Cumberland Gap. The little party was joined in Powell's Valley by forty hunters, well armed. The whole formed a caravan of eighty persons. While passing a narrow defile in their march, on the fifth of October, they were startled by the terrific yell of Indians, in ambuscade. Some of the men flew to the protection of the women and children, while the others rushed to encounter the enemy. There was a scene of consternation and confusion for a time, but the Indians, surprised at the fierce and resolute resistance of the men, fled in every direction. The first fire of the Indians, however, killed six men and wounded the seventh. Among the killed was a son of Boone, aged about twenty. The party fell back to the nearest settlement, where the emigrant families remained for a time." (Ramsay.) Boone had no little part in negotiating with the Indians for the purchase of lands connected with the Watauga settlement, purchases being made in 1774 and 1775. (Haywood.)

To Daniel Boone, Cathcart (*Baptist Encyclopedia,* Vol. I. p. 113) pays this high tribute: "He was a man of great integrity, enlarged charity to his race, and profound reverence to God. His bravery was undaunted, and he was almost womanly in the gentleness and amiability of his manners. His love of the beauties of nature, rather than his fondness for adventure, led him to spend most of his life in the great forests of the west. He explored Kentucky in 1769-71, moved to the territory in 1775. About 1795 he went to Missouri, where he died, September 26, 1820, in the eighty-sixth year of his age. His remains and those of his wife were removed to Kentucky and interred in the state cemetery at Frankfort in 1845."

E. D. BOWEN.

E. D. Bowen was born in Scott County, Virginia, January 30, 1856. He was a son of Jason and a grandson of Jesse Bowen, who was of German descent. The family moved to Tennessee when E. D. was a small boy. His mother's maiden name was Ruth Lee, a daughter of Arch Lee, who was a near relative of the famous "Light-horse Harry" and Robert E. Lee, of Virginia. He was converted at the age of 17, and became a preacher of the Primitive or Old-school Baptist faith. He married Miss Mary E. Baker, a daughter of Joseph Baker, of Hancock County, Tennessee, and to this union were born eight children, six sons and two daughters. One of his sons, I. G. Bowen, is a ministerial student in Carson and Newman College.

5

Becoming dissatisfied with the non-progressiveness of his brethren of the Primitive order, E. D. Bowen renounced his allegiance to the church of his first love, becoming a "missionary" Baptist, but still holding the strong Calvinistic doctrines of the Old-school Baptists. Brother Bowen was a strong man intellectually, and a very fine preacher. He was moderator of the Mulberry Gap Association, and was one of the ablest preachers belonging to that body. One of the most delightful sermons the writer ever heard at an association was delivered by E. D. Bowen at the Mulberry Gap Association, some years ago. It was strongly but not unduly Calvinistic, emphasizing the doctrines of grace and good-naturedly touching up the theology of some of his "softer" brethren in the ministry. He was master of his subject, and a charming speaker; the discourse left a good taste in the writer's mouth.

Elder Bowen was pastor of a number of churches, tilled the soil to supplement his salary, and was called upon to fill "offices of public trust in his county." He died February 16, 1915, and was buried in the Testerman graveyard, near Blackwater Church—a church of which he had been pastor for "nearly twenty years." By "resolutions," this church memorialized him as a "brother beloved," a "noble Christian," a "faithful pastor and bold soldier of the cross," a great "power in the church," taking "great delight always in cheering, uplifting and helping" his fellowmen—his life being an "example" for the church and community to follow. Signed by the committee.

J. L. BOWERS.

John Leonard Bowers was born in Carter County, Tennessee, July 30, 1830. He was a son of John T. and Mary L. Bowers. He was a namesake of his grandfather, Elder J. L. Bowers, who came from near Philadelphia, Pa., and at an early day was a pioneer Baptist preacher in North Carolina. His mother was a Lincoln, a kinswoman of Abraham Lincoln, President of the United States.

Brother Bowers made a profession of religion under the preaching of Elder James B. Stone, and was baptized and ordained by him, by the authority of the Watauga Church. More than twenty years ago I stayed all night with Brother Bowers, and learned from him that he had been "pastor of Harmony Church sixteen years; Siam Valley, or Doe River, Church sixteen years; Holly Springs and Butler, fourteen years; Sugar Grove, Pleasant Grove, and Doe churches" for some two or three years.

The house I stayed all night in, on the occasion of my visit to Brother Bowers, was one of note. Brother Bowers had been married three times, and there had been born to him and his three companions twenty-five children in one house—the house in which I was being entertained.

I found Elder Bowers to be a man of good sense and piety, solid and well grounded in Baptist principles and doctrines, of good standing among the churches, and a useful minister. He had been pulling in the Baptist harness for more than thirty years, with a fair promise of a dozen more years of active labors before him. I have not heard from him for several years, but I presume he has gone to his reward.

C. L. BOWLING.

Cornelius Lindsay, son of Caswell C. and Mary (Lindsay) Bowling, was born in Roane County, Tennessee, December 11, 1836. His father was a wood-workman and his grandfather, Larkin H. Bowling, was a worker in iron. He lost his father when but a lad of six summers. He was converted in his fifteenth year, and was baptized by Elder William Lindsay, uniting with the Indian Creek Church.

In 1855 he went to school to J. W. Miller, who was teaching at Clinton. Leaving home with a dollar and a half in his pocket, he started out to get an education. On his arrival at Clinton he found out that his one dollar bill was a "counterfeit" bill—leaving him forty cents for an arithmetic and ten cents for a pencil. He boarded with an uncle, working out his board bill, and hopefully pursued his studies. It was not long till he was able to secure a certificate to teach school.

In 1860, at Wallace's Cross Roads (now Andersonville), he preached his first sermon, from the words, "Ye are the light of the world." He was then teaching. But feeling the need of a better education, in January of this same year (1860) he entered Carson College. But the Civil War coming on, the school was broken up. The next four or five years he taught school and farmed, preaching occasionally. November 29, 1862, he was ordained by Indian Creek Church—William Lindsay, J. C. Hutson, and Levi Adkins constituting the presbytery (Jonathan Lindsay being ordained the same day and by the same presbytery).

From '66 to '68 he was County Superintendent of Public Schools for Campbell County. In the year 1868 he was married to Miss Martha Hall, daughter of Judge M. L. Hall, of Knoxville, who brightened his pathway for three brief years and died. Saddened by this sore trial, he never married again.

In '72 he re-entered Carson College, graduating in '78, and tutoring in the college till '81. While in college he was pastor of Sweetwater, Island Home, Ball Camp, and other churches.

Some years ago he had been pastor of Fincastle seventeen years, Jacksboro sixteen years, Indian Creek and Smithwood quite a number of years; also Caryville, Coal Creek, Powell's River, Salem, Andersonville, in fact almost every church in the Clinton Association. He was missionary for the Clinton the first year after the war, and witnessed 365 professed conversions, baptizing ninety-eight into the fellowship of the churches.

C. L. Bowling made an enviable record as a preacher, but he was confessedly enamored of the school-room. He taught at Jacksboro, Fincastle, Clinton—many places in the counties of Anderson, Campbell, and Knox. "I think I have accomplished a great deal of good by teaching," he was wont to say; "I am proud of many of my scholars." Brother Bowling was a smooth-tempered, quiet, and lovable man, and a good preacher. It was the writer's privilege to know him in college, nearly four years, then to visit him in his home, near Jacksboro, a few years ago, stay over night, and have delightful fellowship with him as of yore, talking over "old times." He started out in life poor, with a widowed mother and three sisters to care for; but he made good, and was comfortable in his old age. He gave a hundred or two dollars to Carson College, and has contributed to many of our mountain schools and churches, liberally, according to his means.

With all his teaching and farming, it is said, I believe, that through all his ministerial life he was never "without the care of a church," and never laid his preaching armor by till he passed from the church militant to the church triumphant, May 16, 1906, while still pastor of the Jacksboro Church. His memory is blessed.

JOEL BOWLING.

Joel Bowling, a son of Larkin H. Bowling, was born in
Anderson County, Tenn., May 2, 1817. His grandfather,
Joseph Bowling, was a native of Virginia. Joel was the son
of a farmer, and was brought up to farm life. He was converted in North Carolina, in his twenty-eighth year, but uniting with Brasstown Church, Georgia, this church licensed him
to preach, soon after his conversion.

August 8, 1838, he was married to Adaline M. Carroll, of
North Carolina, to which union there were born eight children.

About the year 1857 he was ordained by the Longfield
Church, Anderson County—Thomas Sieber, Wm. Lindsay, Paul
Harmon, and J. C. Hutson serving as a presbytery. At the
close of the war he "refugeed" some three years in Kentucky,
preaching to Mt. Hebron, Macedonia, and Pleasant Ridge
churches. Returning to his native State, he was active in the
organization of the Coal Creek Church, becoming its pastor,
and serving as such for about six or seven years. He was also
pastor of Pleasant Hill Church, Anderson County. He also
labored extensively in the destitute sections of Campbell and
Scott counties, and other places.

He was a great admirer of Joshua Frost, and claimed him
as his "spiritual father." His associates in the ministry were
Paul Harmon, the two Sieber brothers, Thomas and John,
Jonathan and William Lindsay, J. C. Hutson, and Joshua
Frost.

He was rather fond of preaching from Old Testament subjects, and was considered by some of his brethren a "law
preacher," and not as strictly evangelical and as fervently
spiritual and evangelistic as they would like.

He considered himself a "landmark Baptist," and when I
last met him he had been a reader of the *Tennessee Baptist*
for forty years. He was getting up in his "eighties," had not

been able to preach "much" for a year or so, and was not quite able to get himself reconciled to some "financial troubles and reverses" that had befallen him.

C. C. BROWN.

Crocket Carter, son of David W. and Permelia A. Brown, was born January 29, 1841, near Warrensburg, in Greene County, Tennessee. He was one of a family of twelve children, four daughters and eight sons. His father was a carpenter, but had a farm, and all the children were taught to work. His grandfather, Isaac Brown, came from the "valley of Virginia," first to Washington, then to Greene County, Tennessee. He was of English stock. His paternal grandmother was a White, from South Germany. His grandfather Wise, from Virginia, was also German. His grandmother Wise, who was a Callahan before her marriage, was of Irish descent, her mother having been born in the "County of Cork, Ireland."

Young Brown was brought up to farm life, and had to work hard to help support the large family. Having a thirst for knowledge, he would often take his book with him to the field that he might study during the "rest" moments. At the age of fifteen he spent one term at the Morristown High School. This was followed by a period of farm-work and home-study. Then came the Civil War, with its demoralizing influences. At the close of the war, returning home, he read and began the practice of law. In a meeting at St. Paul's, a Presbyterian church, near Morristown, in the fall of 1866, he was converted and joined the Presbyterian Church.

In his twenty-seventh year, February 10, 1867, he was married to Miss Mary C. Baker, a daughter of William and Jane Baker, of Greene County, Elder Harvey Smith performing the ceremony.

About this time his impressions that he ought to preach began to deepen, and with the "call" to preach came a call

C. C. BROWN.

to study the New Testament Scriptures to see what he would be called on to preach and teach as "the word of the Lord." He was a Presbyterian, but had not studied the Bible. Then there was Jonas B. Castiller, a Baptist preacher, who kept poking Baptist doctrine at him, saying to him, familiarly, "Crocket, what will you do with this? and this? and where do you get your infant baptism?" and so forth. His doctrinal views undergoing a change, he decided to unite with the Baptists. Approved for baptism by Friendship (later Bethel) Church, and at the water's edge giving his reasons for a change of church relations, he was baptized by Elder Jesse Hale, in May, 1869, his wife, who also was a Presbyterian, joining him in this act of obedience to the Head of the church. In May, 1870, by the authority of his church, he was ordained to the full work of the ministry—Elders Henry Hale, T. J. Lane, and R. B. Godfrey acting as a presbytery. He did evangelistic work and served as pastor of Mansfield Gap Church till 1872, when he made a visit to northwest Missouri, to see his father's family and prospect a little in the new country. Here for two or three years he did monumental work, organizing and establishing churches. Years afterwards the writer visited one of these churches—High Creek Church, Atchison County—now a strong and wealthy church in what is now one of the "garden spots" of the world; and heard the saints speak lovingly and much of "Brother and Sister Brown," expressing their grateful appreciation of their fruitful pioneer labors among them.

In 1876 he entered Carson College, graduating the following year, with Prof. S. E. Jones, D.D., J. M. Susong, and the writer. Later his *alma mater* made him a D.D.

For a few years he served successfully as pastor of the following churches: Concord, Dumplin, Mt. Olive, Mossy Creek, Morristown.

For three years ('84-'87) he was Secretary of State Missions. For some time he had been looking wistfully toward the West, where he had some attractive calls. He mentioned this, confidentially, to a member of the State Board, while entertaining the board's proposition to him to take the secretaryship "Yes," said the member, "that would be pleasant, and would mean more money, but you can do more good in Tennessee. Build your monument here." A few days later the two met again, when Brother B. said, "You are right. I have settled the matter. My life-work shall be in Tennessee and in her bosom my bones shall rest."

As Secretary, he was laborious and efficient, serving the denomination with all his consecrated powers. His work was a great strain on nerve and brain. Few men had stronger sympathies, and his sympathies went out to the poorly paid and struggling missionaries of the board, whose salaries were past due—and many were the times he exhausted his own means to supply their need.

C. C. Brown was popular and magnetic. He had in him a great deal of droll wit. Even before his conversion, on occasions of public gatherings, it was a common thing to "see a crowd gather around him" to listen to his jokes and enjoy his wit. After his conversion by the same magnetic personality he drew men to Christ and the better life. He rarely preached without dewy eyes and tears in his voice. Especially did it seem that he never got done repenting for the grievous sins of his past life—a fact which always added force to his exhortations and appeals. Socially, he was a good mixer. As Secretary, he was a good organizer—and in every way he had power with "the masses" of the people.

For some months before he reached the end of his journey he had been passing through "the valley of dark shadows," not in fear of death, but in unrest and in the vague fear of some unknown evil. Sometimes he would be assailed by doubts. Specters of the night would flit across his brain. His mind would be shadowed by the suggestions of skepticism, as by an evil spirit. A great "if" seemed to loom up before him at times—a result, for the most part, I am sure, of nervous depression and the impaired state of his health. But with a clear premonition of the approaching end the demon of doubt departed. The clouds were rifted, the shadows lifted, and the sun shone. It was "victory" at last. His sun went down without a cloud. When with trembling hand he had signed his will, among his last words were these: "Brethren, Chris-

tianity is true. The best and highest witness for it is what
it does.

> " 'Plunged in a gulf of dark despair
> We wretched sinners lay,'

but God reached down his saving hand and (here making a
gesture) scooped the sinner in, 'saved us by his grace.' Other
systems will fail, but Christianity will go on—it will never
fail." He fell asleep July 2, 1887.

W. A. G. BROWN.

Prof. W. A. G. Brown was born in Blount County, Tennessee, May 23, 1830. He was the son of Deacon Jonathan
Brown and Rebecca (Bowers) Brown. When he was 12 years
old his father moved to Sevier County. No church being convenient, he threw open his own house to church services, which
soon resulted in the organization of what is now Sugar Loaf
Church. Professor Brown was converted at the age of 12 years
and united with Nails' Creek Baptist Church. He graduated
from Mossy Creek College in 1856. Soon after his graduation
he married Margaret Amanda Pattison, who was a direct descendant of the Newman family, who have played such a large
part in the establishment of Carson-Newman College. To
them were born five boys and two girls, one boy and one girl
dying in infancy, the others growing to manhood and womanhood. While Professor Brown was not a preacher, he was the
father of preachers. Three of the four boys who grew to manhood became ministers of the gospel. One of these, H. Dudley
Brown, who was always of delicate health, lived only a few
months after leaving the Southern Baptist Theological Seminary. Another son, Rev. T. L. Brown, a graduate of the
Theological Seminary, is pastor at Lewiston, North Carolina.
The third of the preacher boys is Rev. A. E. Brown, D.D., who
is the founder of the great Baptist Mountain School System

under the Home Mission Board of the Southern Baptist Convention. The oldest son, F. A. Brown, is a teacher of large experience and splendid ability. The only daughter living, Mrs. Sallie A. Walker, is also a teacher,

Professor Brown was of a modest, retiring disposition. Had he not been so timid he would have taken rank among the great mathematicians of his day, for he was noted as a mathematician. He was a man of very broad culture. A thirst for knowledge was born in him. The first money he ever made was spent for a book, and I suspect, if the facts were known, the last money he ever earned went for a book. He had a very large private library, and was so thoroughly familiar with it that on the darkest night he could place his hand upon any book he desired in any of the numerous book shelves.

He had a very large sympathy for struggling boys and girls, and surrendered opportunities of benefitting himself financially in order to give his life to the education of the poor and deserving. Immediately after he graduated he was elected president of Mars Hill College, in North Carolina. A few years later he was called back to Tennessee to become professor of mathematics in the halls of his alma mater, and occupied that position till the Civil War broke out. He served four years in the Confederate Army, and was wounded at the battle of Chickamauga. After the close of the war, with his brother-in-law, Dr. N. B. Goforth, he established Riceville Institute. From this institution went out such men as the lamented Prof. W. T. Russell. When Mary Sharp College was the leading school for girls in the South, Professor Brown was chosen professor of mathematics in that school. Ill health caused him to give up this position and return to upper East Tennessee. He became president of the Masonic Female Institute at Mossy Creek. It was while under his management that this school reached its pinnacle of usefulness, and among the most cultured women of East Tennessee will be found students of this institution, among them the wife of Bishop

James Atkins. In 1879 he returned to North Carolina and became president of Judson College, with which institution he remained until a growing deafness caused him to give up teaching. During his last years, on account of this affliction, he was largely shut off from fellowship with his fellowmen, but through it all he was a regular attendant at church, even though he could rarely hear a word, but by taking the text and outline of his preacher-son, he would be able to work out the sermon for himself. His death occurred on August 25, 1906. He is buried at Fairview, North Carolina, beside his wife and preacher-son.

(As a rule the subjects here sketched are preachers. The notable exceptions are President Z. C. Graves, Prof. R. R. Bryan, and Prof. W. A. G. Brown, pioneers of higher education for women in Tennessee and the South.)

ROBERT REEDY BRYAN.

The present sketch is a tribute, not to a preacher, popularly so-called, but to a distinguished pioneer of higher education among East Tennessee Baptists—a man who, though never officially ordained to the ministry of the Word, was ever preaching, whether in the professor's chair or out of it. He is the first main *pillar* and a large part of the enduring *foundation* of the temple of knowledge at Mossy Creek, which in the last seventy years has grown into Carson and Newman College, Jefferson City.

Professor Bryan was one of a family of fourteen children. He was born in Jefferson County, April 11, 1822. His father was Thomas Bryan, of Irish descent. His grandfather, Peter Bryan, was a member of the Territorial Convention which met at Knoxville, January 11, 1796, to draft the constitution and organize the State of Tennessee. Eleven counties were represented in the convention, each county being represented by five delegates—Peter Bryan being one of five to represent Sevier County.

In his fifteenth year he was converted under the ministry of Elder James Lankford and was baptized into the fellowship of the Dumplin Church.

At the age of 17 he began his career as ·a teacher, though afterwards attending Holston College at New Market, for two years, and later the High School at Straw Plains, one year—teaching and going to school by turns.

In his twenty-third year (about 1844 or 1845) he commenced teaching at Mossy Creek; teaching public schools, private schools, teaching in the old Baptist "brick" meeting-house at Mossy Creek "Zinc Works," teaching for five years in any empty building that could be found—clearing the forest, preparing the soil, and sowing the seed of the future college. In 1849 he was one of a group of six who met in council to consider the vital question of denominational education, and project plans for an institution of learning and a suitable building.   The men who constituted this honored group were Elders C. C. Tipton and Nelson Bowen, Prof. R. R. Bryan, and the three Newmans (William C., Isaac M., and Samuel I.), most of whom largely gave their lives and fortunes to the cause of Baptist education.   Further conference, through C. C. Tipton, was had with Elders "William Billue, Ephraim Moore, Joseph Manning, Woodson Taylor, T. J. Lane, James Lacy, and Grant Taylor, also with Brethren James H. Carson, Coleman Witt, Joseph Hale, Dr. W. M. F. Helm, and others"—the result of the conference being the organization of "The Baptist Educational Society of East Tennessee." The society proceeded at once to elect a board of trustees; also a building committee was appointed and agents were sent out to raise money.   The school having been provided for and "chartered" (1851) as the "Mossy Creek Missionary Baptist Seminary," the first session was opened up in the old Baptist meeting-house hard by the "Zinc Works," with William Rogers, president, and R. R. Bryan, professor. The untimely death of President Rogers threw the whole burden of the college management and work upon Professor Bryan. In September of 1852 the school went into its first new building. In 1853 Samuel Anderson was elected president; in 1857 Matthew Hillsman; in 1859 N. B. Goforth. To these several presidents Professor Bryan was "secretary of state," so to speak, always loyal and in harmony with the administration, always faithful to the interests of the college, and wielding by his magnetic personality a widespread and potent influence for good, not only in the school but in the community at large.

Not unfrequently Professor Bryan had to teach the entire curriculum. This he could do successfully. But when a choice was open to him his greatest delight was in teaching some branch of natural science.

The secret of his success as a teacher, I suppose, was his personality; he was a born teacher. He was friendly, enthusiastic, magnetic. He was not prepossessing or commanding in his appearance by any means—but he was a live wire and shot electric currents through thick skins and drowsy brains, waking up the dormant powers of the mind. One of his most marked characteristics was his *patience*—a cardinal virtue anywhere but absolutely indispensable in a teacher who, like Professor Bryan, had to deal with young men fresh from the farm, unlettered and undisciplined and, for the most part, from uncultured homes in backward communities.

Another marked characteristic of Professor Bryan was his courageous and persistent devotion to the cause of Baptist education. In 1862 the college was broken up by the ravages of war and the building occupied by Federal soldiers. But in 1866 Professor Bryan girded himself and went to work to rebuild the broken fortunes of his beloved institution—being re-enforced in 1868 by Dr. Jesse Baker.

There is a limit to physical endurance. The over-strenuous life of trying to do two or three men's work was too much of a strain on a body that was never strong, and it was only a matter of time when, in spite of a regal will, Professor Bryan's health would utterly break down and he would be forced to give up his school-work, which was the joy of his life. Retiring from active work in the school-room but still battling against disease, he lived to see the college to which he had given his life well on its feet, and passed to his rest June 26, 1878.

Dr. Goforth, one of his colleagues, said of him: "Prof. R. R. Bryan has many and lasting monuments, not of marble or brass, but more enduring—monuments of immortal minds, molded by personal contact of teacher and pupils in the school-room."

Dr. Baker, also a colleague and life-long friend, bore this testimony: "Professor Bryan filled his professorship in the college to the entire satisfaction of the board and of all the patrons of the school. He had a sharp, incisive mind, strong will power, was courteous and affable in his manners, and soon won the hearts of all the young men in the institution. No professor ever connected with Carson College was more universally admired and loved by his students."

Omitting other similar testimonials, I add this note of interest to the family: Professor Bryan was married to Rebecca A. Lankford, a daughter of Elder Jas. Lankford, September 5, 1850, President Rogers officiating at the marriage. The union was crowned with the blessing of eleven children. Some of them, like the father, are born teachers—notably Prof. W. S. Bryan, now of Oklahoma, who is not only a gifted and successful teacher but a useful minister of the gospel.

DANIEL BUCKNER.

Daniel Buckner was born in South Carolina, September 30, 1801. His father, Henry Buckner, was a personal friend and great admirer of Daniel Boone, and named his son for that rugged and distinguished pioneer.

The family moved to Tennessee, settling in Cocke County, when Daniel was quite a lad. Here he was brought up on a farm, and here, in his 15th year, he was converted, "walking twelve miles," we are told, to join the nearest Baptist church— the old Lick Creek (now the Warrensburg) Church, Greene County. He was immersed by Caleb Witt in the Nolachucky River.

In 1817 he was married to Miss Mary Hampton, of Cocke County, a granddaughter of Elder William Dodson, of North Carolina, and a near relative of General Wade Hampton. She was a woman of vigorous mind and strong character. To this union were born five children, three sons and two daughters. The eldest son, Dr. H. F. Buckner, was thirty-five years a missionary to the Creek Indians. He translated into the Creek tongue the gospel of John and made and published a grammar of the Creek language. The second son, B. B. Buckner, was in the Mexican War, went safely through it, but died of sickness the day after peace was proclaimed, and was buried in the City of Mexico. The third child, Miriam Isbel, was the mother of Dr. A. J. Holt, formerly of Texas, later of Tennessee, now of Florida. The fourth is Dr. R. C. Buckner, founder of the "Buckner Orphans' Home" (Texas), the largest orphanage, I believe, in the Southwest; also former editor and proprietor of the Texas Baptist and President of the Baptist General Convention of Texas. The fifth, Ann Hasseltine, is a widowed daughter, living with her brother in Dallas, Texas. We may also add, that Burrow Buckner, a brother of Daniel, was a preacher of no mean ability, and that there are in the Buckner

6

family fifteen Baptist preachers, many of them able and noted men in the denomination.

Elder Buckner was licensed to preach in his twenty-second year. He was ordained (1827) by Chestua Church, Monroe County, Elders George Snider and James D. Sewell acting as a presbytery. This church was greatly blessed by the labors of Elder Buckner, who baptized large numbers into its fellowship. He was the first Baptist to preach in Madisonville, the county seat of Monroe County, preaching at first in the Methodist Church, then in the Academy. Many people of the place turned to the Lord and to the Baptists, and a Baptist church was organized, "March, fourth Saturday, 1828." In a little while a house of worship was erected, and Elders Snider and Buckner were co-pastors for five years. The first fruits of the Madisonville harvest were twenty-five converts, baptized by Elder Buckner in one day, five of whom became ministers of the gospel. One of them was Bradley Kimbrough, D.D., then a young lawyer; another was Dr. Samuel Henderson, a distinguished editor of Alabama; and a third was Dr. H. F. Buckner, missionary to the Indians.

Other fruits of his labor in Monroe County were the organization of Ebenezer Church, which he served as pastor for seven years, and the establishment of the Baptist cause at Tellico Plains.

In 1831 he was called to the pastoral care of Zion Hill Church, McMinn County. His pastorate here was a perpetual revival, resulting in about 100 conversions and baptisms. In appreciation of his services the church made him a present of a home, consisting of a house and small farm, also a fine saddle horse.

He then made a settlement with Big Spring Church on Mouse Creek, moving his membership to that place. While living here and at Maryville, he sent his oldest son, H. F. Buckner, to Maryville College, there being no Baptist college or high school at that time in the State. About this time

DANIEL BUCKNER.

the foundation of the Maryville Baptist Church was laid, chiefly through the instrumentality of Daniel Buckner.

In the early "thirties" he was appointed "missionary" by the State Convention (not our present State Convention, to be sure) to travel in East Tennessee in the interest of missions. At that time there was strong opposition to missions, and church doors, in many places, were closed to the missionary.

For the most part Elder Buckner had to preach in the grove, the schoolhouse, or in private dwellings. Wherever he preached he took a collection for missions. If he couldn't get some one to pass around the hat, he would pass it himself. The gospel of missions was preached by him in well-nigh every county in East Tennessee. He spent a year and a half in Washington County, preaching to some of the oldest churches in the State, indoctrinating them on the subject of missions, and influencing the Jonesboro saints, it is said, to move their interest in from the country and undertake to build up an interest in town.

He then moved to Bradley County and located in Cleveland when the first town lots were being sold. Aided by his brother, Burrow Buckner, he soon established in the new town a Baptist church. Dr. A. J. Holt remembers distinctly hearing his grandfather say that he "established the Madisonville, Tellico Plains, Maryville, and Cleveland churches."

His remuneration as missionary was the customary 50 cents a day; his reward was persecution, the reprobation of his brethren, such epithets as "hireling," "traitor," "booted apostle." The church of which he was a member was not in sympathy with his work, and on his return from his first missionary tour called him to an account for his strange doings. A charge was preferred against him for having been connected with the State Convention, and, refusing to sever his connection with that body, was excluded. The accused was not permitted to say a word in his own defense. The wife asked that she might be excluded with her husband, but was answered: "We have no charge against you." She replied: "If I were a man I would preach missions, just as my husband has done, and as I hope and pray my sons may do." But the church refused to exclude her and she refused to accept a letter of dismission. Elder Buckner demanded a copy of the charges, and with that as his letter of recommendation, joined a missionary church—his wife and oldest son, and a few of the members of the excluding church, joining with him. He was published in the minutes of two anti-mission associations as an "excluded minister"; but "the Word of God was not" and could not be "bound," and mightily grew the missionary spirit.

From 1839 to 1854 he was pastor at Somerset, Kentucky, adding 250 to the membership of the church by baptism; and was afterwards pastor at Lancaster, Rock Castle, Perryville, and Danville, Kentucky.

In the summer of 1861 he moved to Texas, whither his son, Robert C., and his daughter, Miriam, had preceded him. His faithful wife died on the way, and was buried by loving hands in Clarksville, Texas. He was pastor at Boston, DeKalb, and other places, in Texas; and in 1865 he was married a second time.

At the age of 70, his hearing having become impaired and being afflicted with vertigo, he began to retire from the active duties of the ministry and to give himself to reading, meditation and prayer. While he was a "solid and uncompromising Baptist and preached a full gospel for more than sixty-three years, it is pleasing to note the fact, that as he advanced in years and ripened in grace, he became more charitable toward people of other denominations, and often spoke with great love and tenderness of those whom he regarded as in error." In his long and useful ministry he baptized about 5,000 people, not less than twenty-five of whom became ministers of the gospel. His ruling passion was devotion to the cause of Christ.

As to physique and mental characteristics, one who knew him well describes him as a man of "powerful physical frame, standing erect six feet and weighing 250 pounds; voice powerful; mind strong and active; energy unbounded." In a reminiscence of Dr. Sam Henderson is this further description: "My father took me, when quite a lad, to a neighbor's house to hear a strange minister preach. The occasion was a funeral service. There was present a large concourse of people, attracted thither, in great part, by the fame of the preacher, who in due time arrived, and in an impressive way commenced the services. The preacher was medium height, thickly set, with coal black hair, countenance slightly bronzed, and sparkling eyes that would have been brilliant but for a soft. dove-like benignity that at once awakened confidence and affection. The matter of the discourse I did not fully understand, but the appearance and manner of the speaker greatly impressed me."

We may truly say of Elder Daniel Buckner, that he was a "good soldier of Jesus Christ," that he was a fearless veteran who fought many hard but successful battles for his Captain—laying his sword and armor by, at last, in his 84th year, to cross over and join the ranks of the church triumphant.

He had been living for two years with his son in Dallas. The night before his death he sat up till about 10 o'clock, conversing freely with the family and friends and discussing Bible questions with great "interest, clearness and force." After the company had retired, he made disposition of his personal effects, affectionately bestowing presents here and there among his loved ones—then retired for the night. The next morning, going out before breakfast for his "usual walk," he failed to return. Anxious inquiry and search were made, and loved ones found him where he had fallen. "His great heart had ceased to beat. His great soul had gone to meet its Saviour. Reverently we laid his body to rest and erected to his memory a plain marble slab, bearing, by request of the departed, the inscription of verse seven of the 116th Psalm: 'Return unto thy rest, O my soul, for the Lord hath dealt bountifully with thee.'"

J. A. BULLARD.

The writer knows very little of the life and labors of Elder J. A. Bullard. From the records of the First Baptist Church of Knoxville are gleaned the few facts contained in the following brief sketch: Elder Bullard was "sent by the Baptist

Home Mission Society" of New York to do missionary work in East Tennessee. In looking over the destitution in "this section of the country," in 1842, he found some brethren in Knoxville who were anxious to be organized into a Baptist church. In the courthouse, on Sabbath evening, January 15, 1843, a bunch of Baptists adopted articles of faith and an abstract of principles. The next Sabbath (January 22) they were constituted The (First) Baptist Church of Knoxville, of twelve constituent members. The council of recognition was composed of Elders James Kennon, Robert G. Kimbrough, Elihu Millikan, William Billue, John S. Coram, James Ray. The fourth Saturday in February the church voted to "invite Elder Bullard to be pastor" of the new organization for "one year, beginning January 1, 1843." Some time during the year the church sent Pastor Bullard and other messengers to the East Tennessee Baptist Convention, meeting at Jonesboro, reporting a membership of forty-six individuals, "white and colored," and asking aid from the Convention. This same year the Knoxville church was admitted to the Tennessee Association; and January 27, 1844, the church "invited William Billue, James Kennon and J. S. Coram to supply pulpit till a regular pastor could be secured." The one year pastorate had expired, and Elder Bullard, perhaps, had returned to the North. In two months the church had a new pastor, and was going ahead with its work.

W. M. BURNETT.

For forty years there was no better or more favorably known preacher in Knox, Blount and Sevier counties, or a more stalwart defender of the Baptist faith, than W. M. Burnett, son of Jeremiah B. Burnett.

The subject of our sketch was born in Knox County, Tennessee, June 10, 1814. He was not gifted with physical beauty, as his picture shows, but he was gifted with brains and had force of character. His mixed features leave the casual observer in doubt as to whether he was most Roman, Jew, or Indian—or a combination; whereas, in point of fact, he was no blood kin to any of these ancient historic peoples. His physiognomy—high cheek bones, aquiline nose, sunken face and swarthy complexion—as well as the family records, show him to be a scion of an ancient black stock of the Burnetts, which now and then, in all the tribes, puts forth an occasional unexpected shoot.

W. M. BURNETT.

He was converted in his youth; in his twenty-first year was licensed to preach by Hopewell Church, Knox County; and was married, March 21, 1838, to Latitia Sharp, Elder James Lankford officiating. He was ordained by Nail's Creek Church, at the regular May meeting in 1840, James Lankford, William Billue and William Hodges acting as presbytery.

He served as pastor the following churches: Hopewell, Nail's Creek, Ellijoy, Sugar Loaf, Pleasant Grove, Henderson's Chapel, Knob Creek, Maryville, Sevierville, and Boyd's Creek. He was pastor of the last mentioned church twenty-six years.

building a new house of worship to take the place of the old brick house, which was falling into ruins. Besides being pastor, he was Circuit Court Clerk, Deputy County Court Clerk and County Trustee of Sevier County, farmer and school teacher. I have met scores of grown-up girls and gray-bearded boys who went to school to him and received mental training and "physical stimulus" at his hands.

He was not a classical scholar, technically so-called; however, he was a hard student, and knew some Greek. "His learning was varied and extensive, and he was specially familiar with the doctrines and principles of Baptists." He preached in plain, forcible English, easy to be understood by the common people.

As a defender of "the faith delivered once for all to the saints," he was bold and unflinching. Armed with Henry's and Clark's Commentaries, Wesley's Journal, and what he considered a Baptist Bible, he was ready to meet doughty champions of error whenever it seemed necessary. His four days' debate with a champion of Methodism is still fresh in the memory of the Boyd's Creek people. His Moderators were M. Hillsman and C. C. Tipton, and the cause of truth, on that occasion, it is said, "did not suffer in his hands." He was not a "fighting preacher," in the popular sense of that term, but, as his brethren testified, was only and always a 'faithful expounder of the Scriptures, and an able advocate of the principles and practices of the Baptist people," in sermon or debate. That he was not a sectarian or a bigot or bellicose in spirit was evidenced by the fact that, in time of the Civil War, when he was not serving as "chaplain" in the army, he was preaching everywhere at home to men as men, to Baptists and Methodists alike, weeping, like the prophet Jeremiah, over the desolations of Zion and the war-stricken condition of his people.

His last sermon was at Boyd's Creek, from the text: "Keep thy heart with all diligence, for out of it are the issues of life."

A brother preacher, who was in feeble health, had begun the sermon, but began coughing so badly he could not finish. He called upon "Brother Burnett to take up the thread of the discourse and finish." It was an inspiring and uplifting sermon, which the people "never forgot." His greatest sermon was preached from his death-bed, with Paul's triumphant words as a text: "I have fought the good fight." He died April 14, 1881, and was buried in Pleasant Hill cemetery, in the neighborhood of Antioch Church, nearby the old home where the deceased had lived for many years.

By special request the funeral discourse was preached by Elder John Russell, from Paul's words above quoted, "I have fought the good fight." On the minutes of the Boyd's Creek Church is this memorial: "For more than a quarter of a century our brother has served this church with perfect acceptance and without a jar. Under his ministry the church has passed through many precious revivals, and by his solemn appeals and persuasive eloquence many souls were led into the fold of the good Shepherd.

> His toils are past, his work is done,
>   And he is fully blest;
> He fought the fight, the vict'ry won,
>   And entered into rest."

J. M. L. BURNETT.

The subject of this sketch was born in Buncombe County, North Carolina, near Asheville, September 14, 1829. He was a son of Swan P. and Frances Burnett, being the youngest of thirteen children. His grandfather, Thomas Burnett, was a Virginian by birth, of Scotch descent. His mother, a daughter of Thomas and Janny (Montgomery) Bell, of North Carolina, was partly Irish. His father was a well-to-do farmer and ambitious for his children, wanting to give them an education

J. M. L. BURNETT.

and a "start" in life, and, if possible, "settle" them around
him. This, however, he could not do, without more and better
acres of land for a home-basis of operations, and the possi-
bility of additional land purchases in the course of time.
Down the French Broad River, fifty miles west, was an "opening," and in 1835 the family left the old homestead and came
to the newer country, settling down near the Mouth of Big

Creek (now Del Rio), in Cocke County, Tennessee. Here the
lad was brought up to farm life, grew to manhood, lived most
of his life, died and was buried.

At the age of 13 he was converted in a meeting held by
Elders Joseph Manning and Ephraim Moore at Clay Creek
Church, and was baptized by Elder Manning. He preached his
first sermon at Pleasant Grove Church on the banks of Pigeon
River, six miles from Newport.

August 31, 1854, he was married to Evelyn Ann Huff,
daughter of Stephen Huff, a lovable but frail woman, who
brightened his home for three brief years, and died, leaving
an issue of two children, a son and a daughter. December
26, 1861, he was married to Miss H. S. Cody, a daughter of
Elder Edmund Cody, of Alabama, a woman of refined tastes
and consecrated life. To this union were born eight children,
four sons and four daughters.

In 1859 and 1860 he was a fellow-student with Dr. Wm.
H. Whitsitt in Union University, Murfreesboro, Tennessee.
Dr. J. M. Pendleton, then one of the university professors,
made the statement, it is said, that J. M. L. Burnett and
W. H. Whitsitt "were the finest, or among the finest, linguists
he had ever taught." Dr. Whitsitt, in a personal letter, says:
"Dear Brother: I had the honor to be a fellow-student with
J. M. L. Burnett at Union University—studied with him in
several classes. He was a man of marked ability, insight and
independence. Though he was older than myself, we appeared
to fraternize on the spot and were much in each other's company. Perhaps one of the most important ties that bound us
was his taste for Burns, in whom he took more delight than
any other student. He had the ability, too, to read the great
poet in dialect—a thing that I could not accomplish. It was a
revelation to me to hear him recite "Tam O'Shanter." The
inexpressible fun and pathos of it had never got hold of me
before. And I have never since heard anybody who could do
it in his style. I lost my sense of propriety; I rolled on the

floor; I shouted till the landlady sent to inquire if anything had happened. I sometimes seem to hear his tones through these long years as he would say, 'Ah, Tam! Ah, Tam! Thou'll get thy fairin'; in hell they'll roast thee like a herrin'!'" This is an exquisite compliment, coming from one who afterwards became a charming interpreter of the Scotch poet and a delightful lecturer on "Bobby Burns."

In 1861 he was ordained pastor of the Fort Gaines (Georgia) Church, Elders Edmund Cody, Adiel Sherwood and Dr. E. W. Warren constituting the ordaining council. He served this church, and other churches in Georgia and Alabama, some five or six years.

In 1867, with impaired health and a change of life-plans, he returned to his East Tennessee country home, near the Mouth of Big Creek (Del Rio), in Cocke County, where he lived the independent, quiet life of a farmer-preacher the balance of his days. Declining calls to some prominent pulpits and an offer of the chair of mathematics in a leading university, he remained on the farm, serving as pastor of his home church, Big Creek (at Del Rio), Newport, Leadvale, Morristown, and other nearby churches.

From his home at Del Rio, in sight of the mountains and in touch with the mountain people every day, he did a great deal, in an inspirational way, toward fostering missions, Sunday schols, pastoral support, associational and other co-operative work among weak and backward churches in the mountain districts. By his sympathetic touch with mountain preachers he also did real pioneer work, encouraging and helping them, as he did, to equip themselves for effective work among their own people.

Joseph Manning, Ephraim Moore and J. M. L. Burnett were the principal founders of the East Tennessee Association, composed at first of four churches, afterwards covering two counties, Cocke and Sevier. The last of the above mentioned brethren was frequently chosen as Moderator, and was a good par liamentarian. He was at home in deliberative bodies, whether in the presiding officer's chair or on the floor of the body; he would keep the body out of parliamentary tangles, straighten out the tangle, or skillfully "cut the gordian knot," so as to go on with the business.

As to scholarship, he was not a graduate, had no scholastic titles or degrees. He was *educated,* however, in the true sense of the word, and was a trained thinker. He had a good working knowledge of Latin and Greek, and as to his "mother tongue," alike in the pulpit and by the fireside, he drew from 'a well of English undefiled." He was a Fullerite in theology, and Robert Hall was his model of diction and pulpit discourse. He was naturally a good sermonizer, and had the instincts of the orator, but had been denied the orator's voice. He was gifted and able in prayer. As a conversationalist he had the faculty of adapting himself to any sort of company, and was a generous dispenser of sunshine and good cheer. He could be a good listener, or on occasion could play the role of "The Autocrat of the Breakfast Table," in which he was wont to revel with the greatest delight.

When he had preached his last sermon (at Leadvale, one of his charges), the brethren gathered about him to give him the usual invitation to their homes. He declined the invitations with the words: "I must go home; the harvest must be gathered; the Reaper is there awaiting my return," not knowing that the reaper whose name is Death was awaiting him in the dim shadows and that he himself was soon to be harvested. He fell on sleep August 1, 1883, in his 54th year.

The deceased is survived by his widow, Mrs. H. S. Burnett, of Del Rio, Tennessee, and ten living children who are making good in the various callings of life. One of them is a medical doctor in Newport, another a physician in Greenville, South Carolina, another a writer of history on the Carnegie Foundation, Washington, District of Columbia; another a preacher and former President of Carson and Newman College; while one is the wife of a most liberal giver to Carson and Newman; another the wife of a life-long teacher; another the wife of a lawyer, and still another the wife of a successful merchant who is a Baptist, etc.

He received his honorary title, "D.D.", from Carson College, date not remembered.

H. E. BYERLEY.

Henry Edward Byerley was born in Grainger County, Tennessee, August 29, 1849. He was a son of James and Elizabeth (Scaggs) Byerley. His parents moved to Knox County when young Byerley was only about a year and a half old. Here he was brought up to farm life, attending the common district schools in his youth and finishing his education at Walnut Grove Academy and the University of Tennessee. He professed religion at Murphy's Chapel in August, 1865, and was baptized the second Sabbath in November following. June 7, 1879, he was ordained to the work of the ministry by a presbytery composed of H. C. Hamstead, P. A. Morton and J. A. Robinson. He was a successful farmer and a good pastor. By close study of the Scriptures he became a "workman with no reason to be ashamed, knowing how rightly to handle the word of truth."

January 30, 1873, he was married to Martha A. Luttrell, Elder T. W. L. George performing the ceremony. To this union were born ten children, six of them dying in infancy. Four are still living, a son and three daughters. The son, Charles Spurgeon, lives at the old Byerley homestead. One of the daughters lives in Florida, another in Alabama, the third in Knoxville, Tennessee. All have families and all are Baptists.

Brother Byerley passed to his reward April 17, 1890. His companion died June 10, 1915, in Jacksonville, Florida. Both were interred in the burial ground of Union Church, Knox County. A handsome monument marks the last resting place of Elder Byerley, erected to his memory by the following churches, which he faithfully served as pastor: Little Flat Creek, Graveston, Beaver Dam, Sharon, Union, Stock Creek. The monument is also inscribed with these lines:

"Beautiful toiler, thy work is done;
Beautiful soul into glory gone;
Beautiful life with its crown all won—
God giveth thee rest."

HUGH CALDWELL.

Hugh Caldwell was born near Knoxville, Tennessee, January 20, 1827, and died at Bayless, Tennessee, June 5, 1906. He was twice married. His first marriage was to Miss Polly Bayless, who died in 1876. In 1879 he was married to Miss Minerva Hoskins, who preceded him to the better country about the year 1900. He began his ministry soon after the Civil War, and was a preacher of righteousness and of the faith and practices of Baptists about forty years. The churches he served most as pastor were Bethel, Oak Grove, Zion Hill, Texas Valley, Milan, and Bethany. Several years before he died Bethany called him as pastor for life, and here is where he was buried. He was Moderator of the Northern Association for a number of years. At the division of this body and the formation of the Midland Association he became Moderator of the new body. He was a good parliamentarian and a graceful presiding officer, but he preferred the privileges of the floor to the responsibilities of the Moderator's chair. "He was at home in discussions on vital questions of doctrine, church polity, discipline, and order in God's house." In a note of "sundry things" to the *Baptist and Reflector* (October 27, 1898), signed "J. J. B.," is the following: "The Midland Association was an enjoyable meeting. Its fifth annual session was held with the Fairview Church. It is a small body, representing about fifteen churches, but has some good material. Elder H. Caldwell is the venerable Moderator, and Brother J. B. Carden is clerk. The veterans present were Elders Bradford Demarcus, W. L. Smith and H. Caldwell. These brethren have fought and wrought well for the Master for many years." These men of God have all gone to their heavenly home, and are doubtless enjoying their exceeding great reward in the Master's immediate presence.

Elder Caldwell left a number of children and grandchildren to mourn his passing, notably a son, M. F. Caldwell, Esq., formerly of the Knoxville bar, a friend of the writer's and correspondent for one of our Baptist papers, but is now somewhere in the West.

SAMUEL CALISON.

Elder Samuel Calison was born in Grainger County, Tennessee, in the year 1823. He died in October, 1898, and was buried in the Calison and Hammer family graveyard, two miles west of Central Point Church, Grainger County. He was pastor of Central Point, Blue Spring, Indian Ridge, Little Valley, Blackwell's Branch, and other churches. He spent much of his time holding meetings. He believed in and enjoyed "old-time religion," and was a preacher of that type. He was successful in revival meetings. He was an associate, in revival meeting work, of Elder J. S. Greenlee, and it was given to them to witness in their meetings hundreds of conversions and baptisms. His labors were in Grainger and surrounding counties, and he was a "great power in the hands of God in building up the Baptist cause in that part of the country. He was a man of deep piety and great earnestness. Many will bless him in time and eternity for his influence upon their lives."

He was married to Miss Sarah Gilmore, of his native county, and to this union were born three daughters and one son. Two of his daughters, Mrs. Lavena Biddle and Mrs. Roxena McSpadden, survive him.

7

J. H. CARMICHAEL.

John Howell Carmichael was born in Grainger County, Tennessee, February 2, 1833. He was a son of Daniel C and Prudence (Howell) Carmichael, being the third in a family of six children. His parents were natives of Grainger County, and Baptists, who walked in the ways of the Lord "blameless" and taught their children the holy Scriptures from their youth. The boy John was converted at the age of 12. He was brought up to farm life, his father being a farmer, and, having learned the art of farming and being enamored of country life, he stuck to the farm during life, owning at his death nearly 1,000 acres of land. For a youth brought up on a farm he had good educational advantages, and improved them, making the most of the district school and in his later teens attending the Morristown High School. Among the things he treasured as long as he lived was a letter he received from his beloved teacher at the age of 20. In this letter, addressed to his "friend John," a former pupil, the teacher speaks in the highest terms of the pupil's excellent habits of study, his exemplary conduct and his marked proficiency in all of his studies. This letter is greatly prized by the family.

March 28, 1858, he was married to Miss Mary E. Grove, of his native county, to which union were born eight children, two sons and six daughters. In 1865 he was duly ordained to the work of the ministry by the authority of the Head of Richland Church, Elders H. W. Taylor, G. G. Taylor and Lunah W. Lowe acting as an advisory and ordaining council. He became pastor of churches, serving Head of Richland, fourteen years; New Prospect, fifteen years; Kidwell's Ridge, nine years; Liberty Hill (afterwards County Line), six years, and Beech Grove and Cedar Grove, four years each. He was also pastor of Blackwell's Branch, Buffalo, Macedonia, Oakland, Bean Station, Narrow Valley, Central Point, and Puncheon Camp. It was chiefly through his instrumentality and by his labors that the Narrow Valley Church was founded and fostered. For a number of years he was the painstaking and efficient clerk of the Nolachucky Association. The annual sermon preached by him before that body in 1868 is an index to his character as a minister and as a Christian. The theme was Christ's new commandment, That ye love one another (John 13:34).

Elder Carmichael was a "deep thinker and a fine reasoner; he would always take time to study and reason things out before reaching a conclusion. As a preacher he was forceful, but always plain and easy to understand. As a pastor he was faithful as an under-shepherd. As a man and a citizen he was enterprising, public-spirited and liberal with his means. To his family he was all that was noble and good; his memory is sacredly cherished. He was faithful till death, passing to his reward February 9, 1913."

Three daughters survive him—Mrs. M. P. Russell, Grainger County; Mrs. W. P. Sykes, Bradley County, and Mrs. P. L. Brock, Morristown. His nephew namesake, John G. Carmichael, a graduate of Carson and Newman College, and now pastor in Los Angeles, California, is one of our most promising young ministers.

JONAS B. CASTILLER.

Jonas B. Castiller was born in North Carolina in 1814. He was married three times. His first wife was Rhoda Solomon, a daughter of James Solomon, of Cocke County. To this union were born a son and a daughter, William and Isabelle. His second wife was Mrs. Betsy Solomon, widow of John Solomon. This second wife had a daughter, Mollie, by her first husband. His third wife was Mrs. Sarah Solomon, widow of Howard Solomon. Brother Castiller lived near Point Pleasant Church, Cocke County. He was pastor of this church for a number of years, also of Clay Creek, Pleasant Grove, and other churches. He spent a great deal of his time holding meetings about over

the country, frequently associated in his work with Elder
John Russell, of Sevier County. He held a memorable meeting
with Bethel Church, which greatly helped to establish the
church in its feeble beginnings. In looking over the records
of the old Friendship Church I see Jonas B. Castiller was frequently "Moderator *pro tem*." When the beloved C. C. Brown
was a young man, and clerk of the Friendship Church, he was
a great admirer of Brother Castiller. Brown was inclined,
before and after his conversion, to the Presbyterians, and but
for Castiller's influence would likely have been a Presbyterian
preacher. Castiller was constantly prodding him with some
difficult question with regard to the Presbyterian system:
"Crocket, what will you do with this? and this? and this?"
until he got Brown to reading the Bible for himself, and then
led him down into the waters of baptism.

When the East Tennessee Association met with the Big
Creek (Del Rio) Church in 1867, Brother Castiller was a messenger of the Pleasant Grove Church, and at that meeting he
and Elder John Russell were appointed "Associational missionaries for the ensuing year." About 1870 he moved to
Fackler, Alabama, where he became pastor, and continued his
ministerial work, "preaching to from two to four churches till
his death, February 17, 1877. He lived a Christian soldier,
and died as he had lived. He was buried near Fackler, Jackson County, Alabama." His son, William, moved to Arkansas
at the close of the Civil War. His nephew namesake, Jonas
B. Campbell, now 64 years old, lives at Fackler, Alabama. A
host of the Inmans, Holts, Solomons and others, of Cocke,
Jefferson and other counties, are his kith and kin.

The following incident is a sidelight on the character of
Elder Castiller. The occurrence is a boyhood recollection of
Elder P. H. C. Hale. Before the Civil War Brother Castiller
drove hogs (as was the custom in those days) to South Carolina for Esquire James Hale. Brother Castiller was "conscientious about keeping the Sabbath," and with the consent

and endorsement of Esquire Hale, gave his drove of hogs their Sunday "rest" until they reached the market. According to the testimony of both the men, the Sabbath-observing hogs got to market in a shorter time and in better condition than other droves that were taken straight along and not allowed their "Sabbath rest."

WILLIAM CATE.

In the old cemetery at Jonesboro is a slab erected by the Baptist church of that place and inscribed: "In memory of Rev. William Cate, born June 17, 1807; died February 2, 1860. For twenty-five years he was an energetic and efficient minister of the Baptist faith, whose labors in the sacred cause of Christ are an imperishable monument to his memory. 'Mark the perfect man, and behold the upright; for the end of that man is peace.' "

William, the son of John and Mary Cate, was born in Jefferson County, Tennessee, being the sixth son in a family of eleven children, eight sons and three daughters. The Cate family in this country is a multitudinous generation, all akin and most of the stock a Baptist folk, the various tribes being descended, according to tradition, from two brothers who "came over from England" in the early settlement of this country.

Young Cate grew to manhood with few advantages of an education. In his twenty-third year he was married to Mary Thornburg, of his native county. November 10, 1837, he and his companion "went down into the water" together and were baptized, uniting with the Rocky Valley Church. The same church licensed him to preach, and January 1, 1838, he made his "first lecture as a licentiate." He was ordained to the full work of the ministry, January 24, 1840, Elders James Lankford and Robert G. Kimbrough constituting the presbytery.

In 1841, under appointment of the Baptist State Convention, he went to Washington County and commenced his labors as "missionary" in the bounds of the Holston Association. At the close of his first year on this field he reported to the board, "protracted meetings held, 23; sermons preached, 200; addresses delivered, about the same; number of conversions witnessed, 500."

ELDER WILLIAM CATE.

In 1842 he organized the Jonesboro, Elizabethton, and Blountville churches, and later the New Salem, Rogersville and Bristol churches. The same year (1842) he became pastor of the Jonesboro Church, and continued pastor eighteen years (till his death), building for the Baptists of the town two houses of worship. When he commenced his work in Jonesboro there was but one Baptist in the place—the territory having been "pre-empted," so to speak, by people of other faiths. At the close of his pastorate the Baptists were 170 strong. Meanwhile he had baptized thousands of people in the bounds of the Holston, and had canvassed nearly the whole of East Tennessee as collecting agent for church-building, missionary, and educational enterprises. He was the inspiring genius and principal founder of the Holston Baptist Female Institute, Jonesboro, where many of our Baptist young women of other days received their education. Having no children of his own to educate, and believing that the thorough education of Baptist young people, especially our Baptist girls, would be a pillar of strength to the denomination, he took the field, and with much sacrifice of time, energy, and vital force, raised several thousand dollars for the above institution, and erected a number of handsome buildings.

When the Baptists were struggling to get a foothold in Knoxville (1850), and the First Church meeting-house was about to be sold for debt, William Cate was employed as financial agent and saved the building from going under the auctioneer's hammer. When William Cate commenced his work as missionary, the cause of missions in Tennessee was languishing and the workers were discouraged; but his dauntless courage and unprecedented success, and the widespread revivals of 1841 to 1845 inspired hope and put new life in all the associations connected with the State Convention.

Referring to Elder Cate and his labors as missionary for the Holston Association the venerable and now lamented William A. Keen said: "No man ever stirred up so much interest, or aroused such fierce opposition, or made so deep an impres sion upon the people as did William Cate. He was a full Bap tist, and preached the gospel fearlessly, attacking the very stronghold of the enemy. From the very start his preaching was a sensation. He proclaimed the duty of Baptists to go up and possess the land, and led the way. But every step of the way was opposed and every foot of the territory was stoutly contested by Pedobaptist opponents. Every day was a battle, but every battle was a victory; for the hand of the Lord was with him."

William Cate was not robust, nor was he particularly strik ing in his personal appearance. On the contrary, he was leàn and swarthy, and had a weak voice. But his dress was neat, his figure tall and straight, his eyes were dark and piercing, and his voice, though weak, was pathetic and spiritually mag netic. In a scholastic sense he was not educated, but he had a trained mind. His style was not that of a popular preacher, still he was popular. He was not a "revivalist," in the popular sense, and yet he was a wonderfully successful soul-winner. He never failed to command attention and sometimes produced upon his hearers a profound impression. "He was pious, deter mined, persevering. He knew no discouragement, but with faith in God he planned and executed his plans, confidently expecting that if he failed today he would succeed tomorrow."

When the Baptist banner was first uplifted in the old his toric town of Jonesboro, it seemed presumptious to some that such a thing, should be done, and not a little disturbance was thereby occasioned in certain quarters. Wm. G. Brownlow— "Parson" Brownlow, he was called—preacher and politician, and editor of the *Whig*, gave the Baptists some hard knocks in his paper, and wrote a book against them. Among the caricature pictures in the book was one representing William Cate baptizing a female in Cherokee Creek. The pictures in the book were not overly modest, nor its arguments formidable —it is of interest only as a sword or other weapon of war, captured from the enemy, is of interest to the old soldier after the war is over.

One of the marked characteristics of William Cate was his modesty; he always shrank from occupying distinguished or popular pulpits. On his collecting-agency trips he rarely got far from his base of operations, East Tennessee, but on one occasion he got as far as Baltimore, and was urged by the distinguished Dr. Richard Fuller to preach for him on a Sabbath. Brother Cate reluctantly consented and did the best he could. To his surprise and encouragement he overheard one of the old members say, "Well, thank God! we have heard the gospel preached in Dr. Fuller's pupit once more."

As an illustration of the strong prejudice the "agent" or money-getter had to encounter in Brother Cate's day, take the following. On the Dumplin Church records of December 7, 1851, is the copy of a "notice" posted on a tree close by the church-house and addressed to "Mr. William Cate." The notice reads as follows: "It is generally believed you had better not come to this camp-meeting at Dumplin, lest you cause sinners to be lost; for they have no confidence in you. They believe you are not seeking souls, but money. Now for the cause of God and your good, you had better stay away." It is gratifying to note that the Dumplin Church branded the notice as a "base falsehood and a foul slander," and endorsed Elder Cate as a "successful minister of the gospel and an efficient agent in raising funds for benevolent purposes."

Elder Cate, with his usual painstaking accuracy, had kept a detailed account of himself in a diary and had preserved many papers and records with a view to writing a history of the Cate family, which has in it a score or more of preachers; but after his death these documents were turned over to Professor Starkweather, then of Jonesboro, who took them with him to Rochester, N. Y., with the intention of writing a biography of Elder Cate; but the war coming on, the work was abandoned and the records have not been recovered.

In 1860 the beloved Cate left the field where he had sown and reaped so bountiful a harvest, and went to Fayetteville, Ark., to visit relatives, hold meetings, and perhaps make a settlement in the West. Immediately upon his arrival he fell sick of pneumonia fever, which brought to a speedy close a most useful life. The Holston Association, which he had served nineteen years as missionary and eight years as moderator, by committee and vote paid beautiful tribute to his memory. Peaceful was his death and without a struggle.

> "So fades the summer cloud away;
> So sinks the gale when storms are o'er;
> So gently shuts the eye of day;
> So dies a wave along the shore."

NOAH CATE.

Noah Cate was born in Jefferson County, Tennessee, May 17, 1805. He was one of eleven children, eight sons and three daughters. His father, John Cate, was a native of North Caro lina but settled in East Tennessee at an early day.

The Cates in this country, according to family tradition, are descendants of two brothers who came from England in early colonial times, one settling in New England, the other in Virginia. It is a numerous and noted family—a family of preachers.

In his twentieth year (December 4, 1824) he was received "by experience" and approved for baptism by the Dumplin Church, and baptized by Elder Duke Kimbrough, the pastor. June 2, 1827, his church "liberated him to exercise his gift in public"; October 2 of the following year his "ordination" was called for; and on the "fifth Saturday of November, 1828, he was ordained" by the Dumplin Church—Elders Duke Kimbrough, Richard Wood, Thomas Hill, Henry Randolph, Samuel Love, and Elijah Rogers constituting the presbytery.

To equip himself more completely for his ministerial calling he entered the Madisonville High School, where he acquired a fair English education.

August 15, 1833, he was married by Elder James Kennon to Mrs. Margaret M. Lee, widow of Samuel J. Lee, of Hawkins County, Tennessee.

His earliest ministerial labors were in East Tennessee, but about the year 1837 he received a call to the McMinnville Church in Middle Tennessee. Here he organized the feeble Baptist forces, built for them a neat brick house to worship in, and left the church with a considerable working membership. Here and elsewhere in Middle Tennessee, under the patronage of the State Convention, he did successful missionary work until 1842, when he returned to East Tennessee and began work at Blountville, Sullivan County. Here he found a weak church without a house of worship. Through his instrumentality a meeting-house was built for the Blountville saints, and working from this point as a center he was enabled by the blessing of God and the co-operation of his brethren to organize and build up a number of strong, efficient churches.

In 1849 he went to Abingdon, Virginia, as a missionary of the Goshen Association. Here, also, he found a handful of Baptists and no house of worship. Ministering here some three or four years, "strengthening the weak hands and feeble knees" of the brethren, helping them to build a house of worship, and adding to their numbers, he returned to his native East Tennessee, locating in Rogersville. The Baptist cause here was weak, overshadowed somewhat by a strong Presbyterian influence. Brother Cate "strengthened the things that remained" while here, and built a house of worship at Kingsport.

In 1858, he began a tour of the South and West, preaching in West Tennessee, Georgia, Alabama, Kentucky, and Missouri. In the last-mentioned State he spent several years, preaching to a number of churches, and enjoying the confidence and esteem of his brethren.

In 1866, he settled in Arkansas, first in Greene County, afterwards at Jonesboro, where he spent the remainder of his life, through the "dark reconstruction days," in efforts to re-build disorganized society and restore the spirit of education and civilization (banished by the war) by preaching the love and goodwill of the gospel. He had begun the erection of a house of worship in Jonesboro, but was not permitted to witness its completion—death overtaking him October 23, 1871. His widow and two children survived him, one (Wm. H. Cate) a lawyer in Arkansas; the other, a daughter, the wife of a merchant in Texas.

Noah Cate was "six feet two inches tall, of a powerful frame, corpulent in middle life, plain in his dress and manners, kind and conciliatory in his conduct; his eyes were a dark hazel, set deep in his head, his hair was black, his complexion dark, his head somewhat bald." He loved his denomination and the principles for which it stands, and battled fearlessly for what he considered the "faith delivered once for all to the saints."

A contributor to Borum's "Sketches," drawing a characteristic contrast between Noah Cate and his preacher-brother, William, says: "William, the younger, was tall and slender, but a man of fine appearance and an intellectual face. He was always entertaining, and would preach as good a sermon on one occasion as on another. On the contrary, Noah would sometimes be almost dull, while at other times he would preach with wonderful power and pathos and eloquence. William was a man of more cultivation; Noah had greater strength of intellect." They were alike faithful, earnest, and persistent; they were equally consecrated to their Master's cause; neither knew what it was to be discouraged, or to acknowledge defeat.

Noah Cate's first sermon was from I Samuel 17:29: "Is there not a cause?" His last sermon, nearly fifty years later

(June 5, 1871), was from Rom. 6:22: "Being made free from sin, ye have your fruit unto holiness, and the end everlasting life." A fitter text with which to close his ministry could hardly have been chosen, if the preacher had positively known that *that* was to be his "last sermon."

MICHAEL CATE.

Michael, son of John and Mary Cate, was born in Jefferson County, Tennessee, December 20, 1808. He belongs to a family and generation of preachers. Besides his two preacher-brothers, Noah and William, there are in the Cate generation in the South and Southwest more than twenty preachers of influence and standing in the Baptist denomination.

September 5, 1828, the Dumplin Church received Michael Cate "by experience and baptism." April 11, 1835, he was "ordained deacon" by the same church, and served his church faithfully in this capacity for fifteen or sixteen years.

In the division and reconstruction of the Dumplin Church, April, fourth Saturday, 1839, after the "Anti-mission" brethren had entered their protests against 'foreign missions and the societies of the day," and pulled out, Michael Cate, as the records show, stands as one of the twelve firm pillars, supporting, "on constitutional principles," the old organization, declaring themselves the original church and in favor of missions, and resolving to maintain regular worship in the old house, as they had done for years.

May 6, 1848, Michael Cate was "granted the privilege of exercising his gift in the bounds of the church." May 5, 1851, he was "ordained" by the authority of the Dumplin Church. Elders J. S. Coram, William Billue and William Ellis acting as a presbytery.

May 28, 1833, he was married to Mary French, of Jefferson County; and November 25, 1838, he was married a second time, to Nancy Reneau. His home was near Dumplin Church.

In the business meetings of the church he was often Moderator, and did a great deal of baptizing and other official work for this his home church.

He was pastor, at different times, of Rocky Valley, Dandridge, Pawpaw Hollow, Six-Mile, Pleasant Grove. and Ellijoy churches. He was a sympathetic and faithful pastor. Everybody had confidence in him and loved him. The young people reverenced him; the older people were devoted to him. He was a great stay to his home church, and in Dumplin Valley, where he lived eighty years, he was a great lump of rock-salt. He was a benediction to any community where he was known.

"Uncle Mike" Cate, the old people tell me, had very great power in revival meetings, his sermons and exhortations often having an electrical effect upon his hearers. His solemnity of manner was awe-inspiring; his serious, dignified bearing was impressive. There was no levity, or foolishness, about him. He was a fountain of sympathy, and was greatly in earnest. He was alike successful as a pastor and as a revivalist. He was not a traveling missinoary evangelist and collecting agent, like his brothers that were preachers; but holding fast to the center—his home church and community—he maintained a steady and glowing light, which shone far out into the darkness and guided many a wanderer to the Shepherd's fold.

July 2, 1890, Brother Cate closed his earthly career, wept for as a citizen, honored as a "father in Israel," his memory cherished by all who knew him.

ELI CLEVELAND.

In the cemetery of the old Sweetwater Church, in Monroe County, not far from Philadelphia, rests the remains of one of the earliest pioneer settlers of the Sweetwater Valley. From his tombstone I copy this inscription: "In memory of Rev. Eli Cleveland; born October 1, 1781; died November 23, 1859. Born a sinner; saved by grace."

The Clevelands are a numerous and noted family, both in England and in the United States. A book has been written which gives the history of the family as far back as the year 1200, showing the varied spelling of the name to be, "Cliffland, Clyveland, Cliveland, Clieveland, Cleaveland, and Cleveland—the last spelling being the one adopted by the members of the family who came to this State" (Lenoir).

REV. ELI CLEVELAND.

The subject of our sketch was born in Wilkes County, N. C. He was a son of Capt. Robert Cleveland and a nephew of Col. Benjamin Cleveland, both of Revolutionary "fame," making many campaigns together, "fighting the tories." The father of these two American patriots, the grandfather of Eli Cleveland, it is thought, settled in Orange County, Va., about the year 1700.

Eli Cleveland was married to a Miss Mary Ragan, of Ashe County, N. C., December 28, 1803. To this union were born eight children, four sons and four daughters.

He was baptized the third Sabbath in December, 1813. uniting with a Baptist Church in Ashe County, N. C., having obtained a hope in Christ a short time previous. Soon afterward he commenced exhorting and preaching to sinners to "flee the wrath to come." He moved with his family to Knox County, Tenn., in 1817. He was ordained to the ministry in 1818, by request of Beaver Ridge Church. He moved to Sweetwater Valley in 1821. He united with the church at Sweetwater the fourth Saturday in January, 1822. He was chosen moderator of the church soon afterward, and retained the office until his death. This being a newly settled country, he preached much and was instrumental in building up and establishing a number of churches. He also bult up a fine estate and became the owner of several negroes. He had some $30,-000 loaned out, mostly to farmers, at 6 per cent interest. He gave the ground for the meeting house and cemetery of the old Sweetwater Church, and largely built the house, boarding the hands and furnishing teams, and negroes to drive them, as well as to do other work in connection with the building. The house was built of brick, and Elder Robert Snead was a colaborer with him in building the house, Brother Snead being an expert hand at moulding and laying brick and, having charge of the building, put his indellible mark on the house by putting up the front wall with his own hands out of the brick he himself had made.

Eli Cleveland was a good practical surveyor, and did a good deal of surveying in connection with the entry and settlement of the new.and fertile farms in the "Ocoee district," thus help- ing his neghbors to establsh their lines and corners. I have been told the town of Cleveland was named for him; at any rate, it was named for the Cleveland family. As to education, culture, style of preaching, etc., a venerable brother, who knew him well and heard him preach often, characterized him as a "good mathematical man, well versed in the Scriptures, sym- pathetic, powerful in exhortation, a great peacemaker, and a genuine missionary; he was very simple and plain, and never tried to go into the deep doctrines of the Bible before an audience." As to personal characteristics and appearance, he is described as a man of plain manners and plain speech, hav- ing perfectly black hair (in his younger days), a fine physique, weight about 200 pounds, a fine conversationalist, and pos- sessed of a voice of very great power, but a voice that was full of pathos and tears. "His exhortations and appeals had a most wonderful effect upon his hearers. Repentance was the great theme of his preaching, and hundreds of souls were brought to the Savior under the influence of his ministry." His brethren sometimes twitted him, good-naturedly, over his money-making, slightly insinuating that he was too "rich" for a preacher. But he had a talent to make money, and Provi- dence had spread out before him a new, rich country, and all he had to do was to use his good sense and go out and possess the land. He was not grasping, however, but was liberal with his means for a man of his day and environment. He not only contributed liberally toward building a house of worship for his own neighborhood, but helped the First Baptist Church of Knoxville build their first meeting-house, gave liberally to the Baptist Female Institute at Jonesboro, and to other causes of religion, as he had opportunity. He gave his time to the churches, never receiving anything from them in the way of remuneration for his services. It is said, however, that on one occasion a collection was taken for him without his knowledge; but, with the consent of the brethren, he took the money donated and with it purchased an overcoat for a poor preacher in the neighborhood.

In the '30's and '40's, when churches were dividing over the question of "missions" and the "societies of the day," Elder Cleveland, by keeping a cool head and steadying the boat, taking a conservative position, as he did, kept his church a unit and steered it successfully through the straits of those stormy days, landing it at length in tranquil waters, on the "missionary side" of the question.

Elder Eli Cleveland died of heart failure November 23, 1859, aged 78 years, 1 month and 22 days. His last words were addressed to his true yoke-fellow in the ministry, Elder Robert Snead, who was to succeed him in the pastoral care of the old Sweetwater Church: "I shall not long be here; I have given up; I have no desire to stay here at all; this world is nothing to me. I am perfectly resigned to go at any time it is the will of God to take me. I have great reason to be thankful for His goodness toward me. My trust is altogether in Jesus, because I could not trust in anything on earth or in myself. I want you to pray for me that I may go easy, for God answers the prayers of His people. Take care of my little flock." The last words spoken, in thirty minutes he fell asleep in Jesus without a groan or a struggle.

ANDREW COFFMAN.

"Andrew Coffman, born December 22, 1784; died September 1, 1864" (tombstone record, Bent Creek Cemetery). Elder Coffman was born and lived all of his life in a very old house, still standing, between Whitesburg and Russellville, where one of his sons, James Edward, lived for half a century, and where his grandson, John Coffman, now lives. January 16, 1812, Andrew Coffman was married to a Miss Nancy Legg.

This union gave to the country some of its best citizens. I make special mention of his oldest son, William H. Coffman, for a long while Baptist deacon of the Whitesburg Church, and who was a true friend and a father to the writer during his first experience in teaching school.

In the record of Bent Creek Church for August, fourth Sunday, 1816, is this item: "Received Andrew Coffman by experience." The presumption is, he was baptized by Caleb Witt, who was pastor of the church at the time. July, second Saturday, 1819, he was made one of a committee appointed by his church to settle a difficulty between two prominent brethren. April, second Saturday, 1820, he was licensed, with two other brethren, to exercise his gift of preaching in the bounds of Bent Creek, Lick Creek and County Line churches. Later the bounds of his license were extended so as to take in "Bethel South (the Morristown First) and Robertson's Creek churches." He was ordained deacon the second Saturday in May, 1825, and was ordained to the work of the ministry the second Sunday in September, 1827, by a council composed of Caleb Witt, Daniel Howery, Wm. Senter, Hughes O. Taylor, Jacob Coffman and Pleasant A. Witt.

He and Pleasant A. Witt were three times chosen co-pastors of the Bent Creek Church, the first and second time for a period of twelve months, the last time an indefinite call was made, to continue "till dissatisfaction should arise." He was a constituent member of the Nolachucky Association in its organization at Bent Creek Church (1828), and year after year, as long as he lived, attended that body as a messenger from Bent Creek (now Whitesburg) Church. He served on various committees, as the minutes show, preached two introductory sermons, and represented the body, almost every year, as a messenger to one or more "corresponding" associations.

Andrew Coffman was a solid, old-fashioned preacher, as he was a solid man, having the confidence of everybody who knew him. He was not pastor of many churches but was a mainstay to his home church. His most intimate associate in the ministry was Pleasant A. Witt till they parted company in the division of the association (1839), Witt going with the minority, or so-called "Primitive" party, Coffman remaining with the "missionaries." Another of his associates was Brother T. J. Lane, younger in the ministry, but a true yoke-fellow.

Elder Coffman farmed for a living and preached as he had opportunity. He was frequently called upon to go north of Clinch Mountain into the Mulberry Gap and other associations, to preach "funeral" sermons. The "biggest thing" he ever got for preaching, I have been told, was a colt some brother north of the mountain gave him for being missionary enough to "come over and preach where the people need the gospel and love to hear it." The colt "lived," it is said, and "made a fine horse."

JAMES B. COGDILL.

"A very interesting and remarkable man is the faithful Shepherd of Mount Zion, James B. Cogdill. The church was constituted in 1853. Brother Cogdill has been its pastor for twenty-two years. During that time he has baptized into its fellowship 200 persons. The church is located in the Grassy Fork District of Cocke County, and is 300 strong, with an ever-green Sunday school. When Brother Cogdill commenced his work with this mountain people he had to make his way afoot, through underbrush and laurel thickets, creeping along Indian trails and hog paths, to reach his appointments. Many a time has he waded Pigeon River, braved snow and ice, wind and storm, in order to preach the gospel to the poor of the mountains, a people "after his own heart," and over whom he had a wonderful influence. He has been a father to them, and in his twenty odd years of ministry among them has wrought a great change, witnessed many marked improvements. In the mountains of Cocke and Sevier he has powerfully preached the

plain "old story," and baptied 1,200 people into the fellowship
of Baptist churches. Great changes have taken place. The
roads are better, the population has increased 200 per cent, the
morals and manners of the people have greatly improved, much
of which is due to the efforts, the influence and the spirit of
Brother Cogdill." (Contributed to the E. T. B. by J. J. B.).

"Grassy Fork is as notably Baptist as it is unanimously
Republican. The Baptist Church, Mount Zion, is 300 strong.
Elder James B. Cogdill has received from the church twenty-
six annual calls to be pastor, and has accepted them all. He
has baptized for the church some 300 candidates for membership. He is a tower of strength to the Baptists of this mountain country and to the cause of God. He is pastor of six
churches. With two of them, Bethany and Gess's Creek, Sevier
County, he has recently held successful meetings, resulting in
some fifty conversions and forty accessions to these two bodies."
(Author's note in *Baptist and Reflector*.) Brother Cogdill is
a spiritual son of Elder Joseph Manning and the Big Creek
(Del Rio) Church, and was set apart to the ministry by that
body, with the laying on of the hands of the presbytery.

J. W. H. COKER.

J. W. H., son of J. H. and Elizabeth Coker, was born, June
4, 1847, in Yancy County, N. C. He was converted early in
life, and commenced preaching before he was 19. He was licensed and ordained by the Protestant Methodists, and
preached two years for that denomination. Reading the New
Testament and contact with "Uncle Dicky" Evans, of Sevier
County, made him a Baptist. I have heard this version of his
change from Methodist to Baptist views, and the cause there-
of, and am now confirmed in the belief that it is a true version,
since the story has been circulated and been published in the
papers for twenty years, and I have not heard of any denial.
Anyway, Brother Coker, being rather belligerent in his younger

days, and perhaps feeling himself under the necessity of "whistling" some "to keep up courage," was anxious—so the story goes—to have a debate with Brother Evans over the mooted questions of "baptism, close communion and falling from grace." Time, place and subjects for discussion were agreed upon. But Evans was a seasoned veteran, and Coker but a tender youth. What would be the result of the debate?

J. W. H. COKER.

Before the crowd had fully gathered, imagine the surprise and amusement of everybody—Brother Evans had already converted his opponent and was leading him down into the water to baptize him. He was received and ordained by the White Oak Flats Church, Sevier County, November 12, 1871.

He was pastor of White Oak Flats, Evans' Chapel, Friendship, New Salem, Allen's Grove, Pleasant Grove, Jones' Chapel, Red Bank, Powder Spring, Henderson's Springs, White Church, Sugar Loaf, Ellejoy, Shady Grove, Beech Spring, Bethel, and other churches, in the counties of Sevier, Jefferson, Knox and Cocke. He was pastor of Bethel for thirty years.

Brother Coker was almost uniformly successful in holding protracted meetings. In 1878 he made a six weeks' evangelistic campaign in Western North Carolina, in which great numbers were converted and added to the churches. In a ministry of forty-five years he witnessed 5,000 conversions and baptized some 3,000 into the fellowship of Baptist churches. He preached a full gospel and used no "clap-trap" methods. He was a "strong and fearless preacher, always standing for the right. His life was devoted to the ministry; he was always working for the Lord. He contended earnestly for New Testament and Baptist principles, and was opposed to pulpit or other affiliations that would compromise the truth or weaken the Baptist conscience."

March 15, 1865, he was married to Miss Matilda Ogle, of Sevier County. This union was blessed with a family of eleven children. Some of them are dead, but the father lived to see nearly all of them converted and become members of a Baptist church. One of them is a preacher, now in Oklahoma.

Brother Coker had often expressed the wish that he might fall in the harness and not outlive his usefulness or be laid on the shelf. Accordingly, May 18, 1911, "he was taken ill at night and the next morning departed to be with Christ."

His mortal remains were buried in the cemetery of Red Bank Church, tender memorial services being conducted by Elders D. R. Mullendore and S. C. Atchley.

ANDREW CONNATSER.

Andrew Connatser was a preacher in Sevier County in the early half of the last century, noted in several ways, and particularly gifted in exhortation and prayer. He was of German descent, and could speak the German language, but was born in this country. He was ordained deacon of Bethel Church, Sevier County, "August, fourth Saturday, 1829," and later was ordained to the ministry by authority of the same church. For a number of years he was a messenger of Bethel Church to the Tennessee Association. He was pastor of Alder Branch and other churches. In physical build he was raw-boned, muscular and sinewy, a man of rare physical strength and endurance. Before his conversion, according to the custom of his day and neighborhood, he drank some, and would "treat" his associates and receive "treats" in return, on special occasions. After his conversion, even after he had become a preacher and "had preached his third sermon," I was told, seven of his companions undertook to get him to drink with them and to "treat" in the old-time way. To prove his hospitality and to show that he was not "stingy," he yielded to their solicitations and furnished the "treats." But they were not satisfied; they wanted him to drink *nolens volens,* and undertook to force him. Thinking he had gone far enough on the "two-mile" road with his persecutors, or had taken enough of their abuse to satisfy the law of "non-resistance to evil," instead of turning the other cheek to the smiters, with his good fist he landed blows on the cheeks of about seven of his assailants, knocking them down as fast as they approached him. After that they "let him alone," the argument of hard knocks proving effective where the gentle means of moral suasion had proved a failure.

For many years before his death Andrew Connatser lived in pioneer style in an old house in Sevier County which had been used as a fort in fighting the Indians. It had holes in the sides, corresponding to the port-holes of a ship, through which the whites could poke their guns and fire in case it was necessary to defend themselves from the Indians.

In 1851 he was pastor of Tuckaleechee Church (Min. Tenn. Association). He was also pastor of Bethel and Bethany churches. He married a Miss Mary Blevins. He and his wife both lived in Kentucky before coming to Tennessee. He has a number of living descendants in Sevier County.

CHAMP C. CONNER.

Elder Champ Carter Conner, son of John Conner, was born March 13, 1811, in Culpepper County, Va. Upon a profession of his faith in Christ he was baptized, September 14, 1828, by Elder Cumberland George into the fellowship of Broad Run Baptist Church, Fauquier County, Va., and in a short time thereafter entered the ministry. December 23, 1833, he was married to Ann Eliza Slaughter. In November, 1835, he moved to West Tennessee. He was a sturdy pioneer in this part of the state, where he had to "meet and combat anti-nomianism in all its varied forms, but he lived to see it almost extinct." He was a landmarker both in faith and practice; "was utterly opposed to pulpit affiliations with teachers of error." He was a great friend of missions and Sabbath schools, and all co-operative work along Baptist lines. He was a skilled debater and able defender and advocate of Baptist doctrines and principles. He was pastor of Brownsville and other churches in West Tennessee, was president of the Baptise Female College, Hernando, Miss., also pastor of the Baptist church at that place, for a number of years. He was called to be pastor of St, Francis Street Baptist Church, Mobile, Ala., but for some reason did not accept the call. He was a minister of brilliant parts and rare oratorical gifts, but better suited to evangelistic work than the commonplace visiting and teaching work of the pastorate, although he possessed good social qualities, had a sprightly intellect, and was jovial and friendly. As a minister of the gospel he possessed "rare talent, and almost unequalled eloquence, being able to hold his audience spellbound for hours. He had a soft, mellow voice and a melting eye, nearly always preaching with tears." He was not only gifted as a preacher; he was a man of acquirements, knew medicine and law, and was posted on matters pertaining to state and national governments. He was a skilled parliamentarian and an able presiding officer, often presiding with dignity over the Big Hatchie Association and the West Tennessee Baptist Convention. He died at his post, of Pneumonia, February 14, 1875, and was buried at Indian Mound, the place of his residence, in Lauderdale County. At the time of his death he was pastor of four churches: Woodlawn, Grace, Society Hill and Zion.

"Servant of God, well done; praise be thy new employ!"

There were some subjects, it is said, which Elder Conner could hardly bring himself in his later years to preach upon. One was "The awful condemnation of the finally impenitent." While preaching from the text: "If the righteous scarcely be saved, where shall the ungodly and the sinner appear?" his mind would be seized with such inconceivable horror in contemplating the doom of a lost soul in perdition that he could not go on with his discourse. But to the end of life he ceased not to declare the whole counsel of God and to plead with sinners to flee from the wrath to come.

HEZEKIAH C. COOKE.

Hezekiah Cantrell Cooke was born in Greenville District (county), S. C., November 4, 1806. He was the second son of William Henry and Mary (Cantrell) Cooke, being one of a family of twelve children. He was a direct descendant of Robert Cooke, a Scotchman, a "saddler and shoemaker by trade," whose wife was Sarah Fielding, from Devonshire County, England. This couple came across the waters and settled in Maryland, "St. Mary's County," in the year 1720. Another Robert Cooke, grandfather of Hezekiah, was married to Susannah Watson, Culpepper County, Va., January 6, 1778, and died at his home in White County, Tenn., November 12, 1841, in the 90th year of his age. Young Cooke came with his parents to Tennessee in 1819, and settled in McMinn County. At the age of eighteen he made a profession of religion and was baptized by Elder William Wood into the fellowship of Connessauga Church. In 1830 he was married to Miss Mary Wood, a daughter of Elder William Wood, which union was blessed with a large family of children. In November, 1847, he was "licensed" to preach, and later was "ordained." For a long time he "fought his impressions" to preach, but the Lord "chastised" him into duty by the rod of affliction; both his health and his business projects failed. He promised the Lord if he would give him back his health, and not kill him, he would preach. His health was restored, and he kept his vow. Laying himself as a minister of Christ on the altar of service, he not only regained his health, but prospered financially and spiritually, the Lord's work also prospering in his hands. In giving an account of Elder Cooke's call to the ministry, and his resistance, justice requires, I think, this additional statement: It was not simply his original, natural, Adamic stubbornness that made him rebel, but his high ideal of the qualifications of a minister made him hesitate and shrink from the responsibilities of preaching the everlasting gospel to dying men.

In his earlier ministry Elder Cooke was somewhat inclined, it is said, to Arminian views, in regard to God and man and the plan of salvation; but as he went deeper into the questions of theology he adopted the Andrew Fuller theory of the atonement, and became what is known as a "moderate Calvinist," one who is a thorough believer in the "doctrines of grace" but who also believes in the just accountability of man as a moral agent. "As a preacher he was not what the world would call eloquent, but he presented the truth with a power, force and perspicuity seldom excelled and rarely equaled." He was a pastor of some three or four churches in the bounds of the Sweetwater Association, and was gaining considerable reputation as a theological debater when death cut short his career of promising and increasing usefulness. He died of pneumonia January 24, 1859, leaving a widow and several children, a great number of relatives and a host of friends to mourn his departure. The temporary resting place of his mortal remains is the homestead burying ground on Connessauga Creek. "Dust thou art, to dust returnest, was not spoken of the soul."

LINDSAY COOPER.

Lindsay Cooper was born in Campbell County, Tenn., November 1, 1833. He was a son of John Cooper, who was born at Ellicott's Mills, in the state of Maryland, and served in the War of 1812. In May, 1850, young Cooper professed faith in Christ and was baptized into the fellowship of Indian Creek Church, in his native county. December 21, 1856, he was married to Miss Mary Gaylor. To this union were born nine children, seven sons and two daughters. In December of 1860 he moved to Morgan County. At the outbreak of the Civil War he "refugeed" for a time in Kentucky. August 8, 1861, with Capt. Joseph A. Cooper, who afterwards became General Cooper, and three other brothers, he was mustered into the service of the Union army, as a member of "Company A, First Tennessee Infantry." He served in the war three years and seven months. Returning from the war he changed his church membership from Longfield Church, near Coal Creek, to Liberty Church, in Morgan County. By this church he was "licensed to exercise a public gift," and in 1866 Pleasant Grove Church "ordained" him to the full work of the ministry. He was pastor of Union, Liberty, Pleasant Grove, Indian Creek, Coal Hill, Pine Orchard, Crab Orchard, Emory, Black Creek, New River, Cooper's View, Pisgah, Glen Mary, and other churches. He was chiefly instrumental in the constitution of five new churches and in the erection of two new meeting houses. He did a great deal of missionary and evangelistic work, and baptized hundreds of people. His ministry was mostly in Campbell, Scott, Morgan and Roane counties, extending over a period of forty-nine years, and, for the most part, was pioneer work, laying Baptist foundations and fostering weak Baptist interests in a comparatively new and undeveloped country. His mission was to preach the gospel to the poor, to supply "destitute" places with the Word of God. He had good evangelistic gifts and was an uncompromising Baptist, contending always and under all circumstances, conscientiously and earnestly, for the "faith delivered once for all to the saints," never shunning to "declare all the counsel of God."

From the home of one of his daughters, near Wartburg, Morgan County, February 17, 1916, Elder Cooper departed this life, being in his 83rd year. At the time of his death he was a member of Cooper's View Church. Funeral services were conducted by Elder John Wilson, who drew lessons for the living from the respective and divinely contrasted character and destiny of the rich man and Lazarus (Luke 16:19-31). The remains of the deceased were the first to be deposited in the new church yard of Cooper's Chapel, a meeting house just built and named in honor of the chief builder, Brother Cooper.

Elder Cooper is survived by his widow and six children, twenty-eight grandchildren, two great-grandchildren, an only brother, Sylvester Cooper, who is upwards of 90, and two nephews, deserving of special mention on account of their marked service to the denomination: Dr. D. H. Cooper, formerly of the East, at one time a schoolmate of the writer, now of Oklahoma, and W. R. Cooper, since 1874 a deacon of the Broadway (or McGee Street) Church, Knoxville, for nineteen years clerk of the Tennessee Association, and for other "nineteen years" the efficient and stalwart moderator of that body.

J. S. CORAM.

The substance of the following sketch was published for the occasion of the celebration of the one hundredth anniversary of the Dumplin Church and the meeting with that church of the Tennessee Association in its 95th session, September 30, 1897. The subject of our sketch had been twenty-six years pastor of the church, during his lifetime, and seventeen years moderator of the Association.

J. S. Coram was born in Virginia, November 5, 1811. He was the son of William and Elizabeth (Allen) Coram. He was converted in a Presbyterian meeting at Washington Church, Knox County, but the date and place of his baptism I have not been able to find. The Mouth of Richland records, of July 14, 1833, read: "We give Brother John Coram privilege to exercise his gift in prayer and exhortation in the bounds of this church." May 10, 1834, the church voted to "extend the bounds" of Brother Coram's privilege, and, January 10, 1835, "lettered him out" to join elsewhere.

He was ordained by Little Flat Creek Church the third Saturday in February, 1835, the "council being composed of delegates from the Mouth of Richland and Beaver Dam churches, Samuel Love, Moderator; Martin L. Mynatt, Clerk."

He was pastor of Little Flat Creek, Mouth of Richland, Ball Camp, Prospect, Union, Dumplin, Gallahar's View, and other churches. Little Flat Creek and Dumplin were his long-

J. S. CORAM.

est pastorates, each being about twenty-six years. He was an acknowledged leader in his Association, the Tennessee, for more than a quarter of a century, serving as moderator seventeen years, and preaching the introductory sermon eleven times. He was a prominent figure not only in his own association but in the history of East Tennessee Baptists, being called upon, far and near, to aid in meetings, to take part in the ordination of preachers and deacons, the organization and recognition of churches, and to sit in council with his brethren, in many ways and on various and sundry occasions.

In his young manhood he was married to a Miss Rachel S. Forgey, who became the mother of an interesting family of children, two of his sons becoming preachers.

J. S. Coram was not a man of letters or of wide culture, but he was brainy, and was possessed of extraordinary will-power. Added to these were a splendid physique, a powerful voice, the orator's temperament, and a taste for handling great pulpit themes. These elements of natural strength made him a commanding speaker and a master of assemblies. But it is the special temptation of strong minds to want to wrestle with mighty problems, to pry into the mysterious and the inscrutable, to try to solve the unsolvable. And so it happened with the strong and gifted Coram, that the subtle "pride of reason" became a temptation and a snare to him in his later years. I refer to his peculiar views of the millennium and the large place he gave to that subject in his preaching. In grappling with the mystery of "Babylon" and the "beast," the "false prophet" and the "man of sin," and the overthrow of these mighty enemies at the "second coming" of Christ at a near and fixed (?) date, he drew crowds to hear him and made them sit up and take notice; but a majority of his brethren were not in accord with all of his views on this difficult subject; and also an occasional outsider might be heard to say that "the Reverend Coram missed it a little today." This is only another instance of the rule of history, that a man's greatest endowment and most splendid gifts, unless safeguarded by eternal vigilance, may become a source of weakness and an occasion of stumbling. But J. S. Coram did a great work in his day. He was a commanding figure among East Tennessee Baptists of a bygone generation, and his name will not be forgotten.

The last Association Brother Coram ever attended was at Ball Camp, in October, 1881. Being an invalid at the time, he was brought on the grounds in a farm wagon, remaining in the wagon pretty much through the day, while the "brethren fellowshipped him and expressed regrets that he could not be with them in the meeting." (W. R. Cooper.)

His death occurred January 26, 1882, and he was buried in the "family" burying ground on the Coram homestead near Ball Camp. At the time of his death he was a member of the Mouth of Richland Church, Grainger County. By committee and resolutions the church memorialized him as a "brother beloved, a sterling citizen, a kind father, a bright and shining light, an earnest and faithful minister of Christ, a great man in Israel, and a fallen chieftain."

SIDELIGHTS.

The following incidents, vouched for by good authority, give additional light on the subject of this sketch:

1. "Uncle Jack Coram," as he was familiarly called, had a hard time to make a living. His churches were paying him very little for his preaching, and he was in debt for his home. So when the government offered him the chaplaincy of the "Sixth Tennessee Infantry," at a salary of $1,200 a year, the offer looked pretty good. The commission papers signed and his home affairs adjusted, he was ready to go to the army. He went out to the gate where his gray horse, Jim, the only horse he had, was standing, ready for his master's departure. About to mount his horse, he stood for a minute in deep meditation, and soliloquized as follows: "Well, I am going to give up all my churches to make money, bad as I need it. Old Jim," he said to his horse, "I can't do it. You may go back to the stable. I'll preach if I starve!"

2. In a meeting with Prospect Church, Loudon County, a number of sinners were under deep conviction, it seemed, but were too stubborn to come forward for prayer. Among the number was a Mr. Green. The preacher, noting the deep concern of Mr. Green, started to go to him, but Mr. Green, hat

9

in hand, struck for the door, the preacher following. When out of the house the sinner ran, and so did the preacher, exhorting as he ran. Seeing the convict about to escape, as a prisoner fleeing from the officer, the preacher shouted, "Watch him, Jesus; arrest him and bring him back!" When about one hundred yards from the church house the escaped convict fell prostrate on the ground, so the story goes, and had to be carried back to the house, where he was prayed for and labored with, and where, in about forty-eight hours, he rejoiced in a Savour's pardoning love. (W. Whitlock.)

3. The following story has been told me by different parties, and has not been contradicted. On one occasion, it is said, after Brother Coram had several times preached on his favorite theme, the "millennium," and had figured the "end of the world" down to a pretty fine point, he left home to hold a meeting, giving the usual instructions, before leaving, as to what he wanted done, and charging his boys particularly about sowing the oats and planting the corn. He was gone from home, on this occasion, considerably longer than he had expected to be. Returning home at length, he found, to his surprise, that the boys hadn't struck a lick toward putting in the crop. He remonstrated with them sharply for their slothfulness and disobedience. The boys innocently (?) replied that they thought the world was coming to an "end" in a very short time and, under the circumstances, they didn't see the use of spending time and wasting seed in putting in a crop. This story is an exaggeration, doubtless, and an unwarranted and unforeseen application of Brother Coram's preaching, but it serves to point a moral: The prophets didn't know the full significance of all that was given them to foretell; Jesus himself didn't know the exact time of his second coming, nor the angels; man should not be wise above that which is written.

NOAH CORAM.

Following is a brief account of one of God's noblemen, once a useful minister of the gospel and a brother greatly beloved among Baptists, whose praise is in the churches and who was greatly respected by all who knew him.

Noah, son of William and Elizabeth Coram, was born December 16, 1822. He united with the Mouth of Richland Church by experience and baptism November 14, 1840. In 1843 he was married to Miss Caroline Zachary. He was licensed to preach by the Mouth of Richland Church, and September 10, 1853, his license was "extended."

February, second Saturday, 1855, he was ordained to the full work of the ministry, Robert G. Kimbrough, J. S. Coram, James Kennon, and Elihu Millikan constituting the presbytery. Mouth of Richland was his first pastorate. He was also pastor of Dumplin, Alder Branch, Smithwood, Pawpaw Hollow, Union, Mill Springs, Dandridge, and other churches. Dumplin was his "home church." Having served this church faithfully as pastor for a long time, on the third Saturday in February, 1876, the church gave him a final call, which he declined, on account of failing health and increasing weakness. He had long been afflicated with a weakness of the spine, and for years had done his preaching from his "gospel chair."

"Noah Coram, though physically weak, had a strong and penetrating voice, a clear head, and a big heart. He was clear and strong on the plan of salvation, and was a sound gospel preacher. He had a great soul in a weak body. He was a tender and persuasive preacher, a sweet-spirited brother, universally beloved." (Dr. Jesse Baker.)

Perhaps his greatest effort as a preacher was the introductory sermon before the East Tennessee Association at Henderson's Chapel, Sevier County. His text was, "God forbid that I should glory save in the cross of our Lord Jesus Christ,"

and, notwithstanding he had to preach from his chair, so
gracious were the words of the preacher and so great was the
effect of the sermon, that the hearers wanted the speaker to
"go on," one brother being sorry that the preacher did not have
strength to preach "three hours" for his special benefit.

At another Association a certain well-known and able
brother preached a sermon on the so-called "Lord's Prayer,"
and called on Brother Coram to "conclude," which he did
with an exhortation that set things "on fire," so much so that
his older and more distinguished brother (J. S.), who didn't
at all believe in shouting, was walking the floor, "happy" and
shaking hands with everybody, carrying a "full cup" with exceeding care, lest it run over.

Noah Coram could not only move an audience mightily;
his influence was for good and "only good." He had salt in
him, and his life was savory.

He fell asleep April 26, 1882, and loving hands laid the
mortal part to rest in the cemetery at Dumplin.

"As a pastor he was much beloved by the churches he
served, and by all who knew him. In all of his long and sore
afflictions he bore up with calm and patient resignation."
(Record of Dumplin Church, July, first Saturday, 1882.)

W. L. COTTRELL.

William Lindsay Cottrell was born in Knox County, Tenn.,
July 8, 1833. He was a son of Samuel Cottrell. His mother,
before her marriage, was Miss Louise Summers. Young Cottrell enjoyed the benefits of the public schools of his county
from his youth and when grown entered the East Tennessee
University (now the U. T.), graduating from that institution
in 1853. He was converted in 1854 and joined the Mt. Olive
Church, under the pastoral care of J. S. Stansberry, and was
baptized by Isaac Hines. December 22, 1857, he was married
to Miss Mary E. Currier. To this union were born seven chil-

dren, two sons and five daughters. Six of the family the father saw grow up and become members of Baptist churches. This same year (1857) he was ordained to the ministry at Mt. Olive Church, Knox County, Elders Hines and Stansberry acting as the advisory and ordaining council. During his ministry he served as pastor the following churches: Mt. Olive, Cedar Ridge (now Island Home), Pleasant Ridge, Valley Grove, Hickory Creek, Loudon, Clear Springs, Sinking Creek and Laurel Bank. He was the principal founder (1892) of Rocky Hill Church, and was its pastor for a number of years. He also helped to organize the Baptist church at Loudon. Moving to Knoxville, he became assistant pastor of the Centennial (now the Deaderick Avenue) Church, under the pastoral oversight of J. H. Snow. In his earlier life and ministry Brother Cottrell taught school a good deal, and at one time had as a distinguished pupil, Pleasant B. McCarroll, who afterwards became a great power for good in Knox and Blount counties.

Losing his first wife, Brother Cottrell was married a second time, to Mrs. Addie Winkle, of Knoxville. He died March 29, 1908, at the home of his son, Henry Cottrell. At the time of his decease he was a useful and honored member of Grove City Church in Knoxville. He was buried at Rocky Hill Church (near Lions View), beside his first wife. His funeral discourse was preached by Pastor F. E. White, who paid a beautiful and touching tribute to the life, labors and ministerial character of the deceased. Brother Cottrell witnessed many conversions during his ministry, and baptized more than 500 converts. Brother Cottrell was a strong man in the ministry. He was greatly loved and greatly missed.

THOMAS HITER CROUCH.

The subject of this sketch was born February 10, 1833, on the Watauga River, near the mouth of Boone's Creek, Washington County, Tenn. He was a son of John and Sarah (Epperson) Crouch. Young Crouch was converted in his early teens in a meeting held with Buffalo Ridge Church by Elders W. A. Keen and Asa Routh. He was ordained at the same time with John Davidson and George P. Faw by the authority of the above church, of which all three were members, Elders Keen, Routh and Eli Ratliff acting as a presbytery. March 20, 1861, he was married to Sophia Bowers, a daughter of Lawrence A. Bowers, of Boone's Creek, who lived to be 95 years old, and was a member of the County Court of Washington County for thirty or forty years, and many years its chairman. To this union were born ten children, seven sons and three daughters, a family of born teachers, it would seem; at least seven of them are, or have been, teachers of the youths of the country. There are twenty-one grandchildren, and four out of the number are teachers, while others perhaps are candidates for the office.

He was pastor of the following churches: Limestone, Philadelphia, Harmony, Antioch, Whitesburg, Johnson City, Sinking Creek, Fordtown, New Salem, Muddy Creek, Clear Fork, Double Springs, Boone's Creek, and perhaps others.

Elder Crouch had the true missionary spirit. He helped build church houses for the Baptists, and freely and liberally gave time and money to the Lord's work. He was a "modest and unassuming man, preached the gospel in a quiet but earnest manner, and was a sweet singer in Israel." His death occurred June 11, 1894. He died as he had lived, victorious through faith, and was buried in the Boone's Creek Cemetery, where the "mortal" waits to put on the "immortality" of the resurrection state.

JOHN DAY.

John Day was born in Jefferson County, Tenn., January 15, 1795. He was a son of John, who was also a son of John Day, of Virginia. John, being a favorite name in the family, has been handed down from sire to son, or grandson, there being only one missing link in the chain of namesakes for seven generations. The latest John is a live and promising youngster who is a grandson of a certain John who is an efficient deacon of the First Baptist Church of Knoxville.

John Day was married to a Miss Fannie Holdway, of Jefferson County. To this union were born thirteen children, two of them dying young, eleven living to raise families of their own. The fifth child, Mrs. Elizabeth Haynes—"Aunt Betsy," we call her—now in her 94th year, well preserved, and having been a Baptist for seventy years, has been a great help to the writer in his work.

Most of his life Brother Day lived in Hawkins County. Making a profession of religion, he joined War Creek Church, and was ordained by the same, by the "laying on of the hands of the presbytery," Hughes O. Taylor and Woodson Taylor.

He was pastor of War Creek, Richardson's Creek, Bean's Creek, Blackwater and other churches. His "rule was, four churches at a time to serve as pastor, and fifth Sundays for funerals." One of his associates in the ministry and his helper in protracted, or "revival," meetings was Daniel P. Morris. He was also a fellow-helper and co-worker with James Lacy, James Greenlee and the Taylors.

His labors were in the bounds of the Nolachucky and Mulberry Gap Associations. He stood for righteousness, New Testament teaching and example, and when the denominational "split" over missions and methods came he remained with the "missionaries."

In March, 1853, Brother Day closed his earthly career. Having fought the good fight of faith and finished his course with joy he wears the victor's crown.

A. C. DAYTON.

Dr. A. C. Dayton (not a D.D. but an M.D.) was born at Plainfield, New Jersey, September 4, 1813. He was a son of Jonathan and Phoebe Dayton, and a "descendant of the Dayton who was the first speaker of the national House of Representatives." At the age of twelve he became a recognized member of a Presbyterian church. From his boyhood he had a taste for books and a thirst for knowledge. He worked on the farm and attended the village school till he was sixteen years old, when, on account of serious trouble with his eyes, he was compelled to quit school and give up his studies for a time. A little later he taught school and increased his stock of knowledge by further study. Choosing the profession of medicine he bent his efforts in that direction, his eyes still giving him trouble. Employing a boy to do most of his reading for him he pursued his professional studies with energy and success. This method of study made it necessary for him to cultivate the habit of giving attention and relying on his memory, instead of his eyes, a habit which resulted naturally in giving him a remarkable memory, which served him in good stead throughout his life. In 1834, in the twenty-second year of his age, he graduated in medicine, receiving his diploma from the medical college of New York City. With enfeebled health and finding the duties of his profession too great a tax on his strength, he relinquished the practice of medicine and, turning his face southward, started out on a lecture tour, lecturing on phrenology and temperance. At Shelbyville, Tenn., he became acquainted with Miss Lucie Harrison, third daughter of Capt. Robert P. Harrison, a woman after his own heart, whom he courted and married. Seeking health and healing from the balmy air of a more southern climate he took his bride and, going to Florida, sojourned in the land of flowers for two or three years, then going to Columbus and then to Vicksburg, Miss. It was about this time he became dissatisfied with his church relations.   After a careful study of the Scriptures and prayerful self-examination, with a thorough investigation of the whole subject of denominational differences, in the year 1852 he became a Baptist.   In a serious illness, when near death's door, he had promised the Lord if he would raise him up he would renounce every worldly ambition and preach the gospel.   This promise he kept, and on the next Sabbath after his baptism he preached his first sermon, on the "love of God" (John 3:16), the theme of his first and last sermon and the keynote of his ministry.

Accepting the agency of the Bible Board of the Southern Baptist Convention, then located at Nashville, he moved to Nashville, in July, 1855, where, in connection with his duties as secretary of the Bible Board, he became associate editor of the Tennessee Baptist and the author of several books.   His first book, "Theodosia," was a phenomenal success, running through several editions and being sought for eagerly on both sides of the Atlantic.   This was followed by the "Infidel's Daughter," a work of ability and merit, and very popular. These two works established the author's reputation as a writer of religious fiction and signaled him as a pioneer in this sort of Baptist propaganda in the South, particularly in Tennessee. Other publications, especially in connection with our Sunday school literature, met with a like favorable reception everywhere.   "The war coming on, Dr. Dayton removed with his family to Perry, Ga., where he temporarily assumed the presidency of Houston Female College, and employed his pen as an editorial contributor to the Baptist Banner, then published at Atlanta, and in preparing a religious encyclopedia, which he designed to be the crowning work of his life.   But he was disappointed, for he fell a victim of tuberculosis (an enemy he had held at bay for twenty years), dying calmly and peacefully at his home in Perry, Ga., June 11, 1865.   In the quiet cemetery of this southern city rests his body, awaiting the summons of the arch-angel's trumpet."   (J. M. P.)

Dr. Dayton, though dead, still lives and speaks to the world through his writings. His mantle fell upon at least two of his daughters. His oldest daughter, Mrs. Laura Dayton Eakin, of Chattanooga, recently deceased, was the popular editor and beautiful story writer of the "Young South" department of the Baptist and Reflector. His second daughter, Mrs. Lucie Dayton Phillips, wife of Dr. J. M. Phillips, inherited a large portion of her father's genius. She was the popular author of "Thread of Gold," for twenty-five years was a writer of serial stories for the Baptist Sunday School Board, and was also a contributor to the publications of the American Baptist Publication Society. Mrs. Lucile (Phillips) Burnett, wife of Dr. J. M. Burnett, is a granddaughter of Dr. Dayton. Her stories in Kind Words exhibit quite a bit of the ancestral genius, and she hopes to give more time to writing when her large family are older grown and make fewer demands upon her time and attention. Only three members out of Dr. Dayton's large family are now living: Hugh L. Dayton, a lawyer, of Shelbyville; Mrs. W. W. Kannon, of Nashville, and Mrs. Elizabeth W. Stocks, of Chattanooga.

BRADFORD DEMARCUS.

Bradford Demarcus was a son of Solomon and Mary Demarcus. He was born near Andersonville, Anderson County, Tenn., May 5, 1820. He was one of eight children, and was brought up to farm life, his father being a farmer. His grandfather, William Demarcus, was a native of France, but at an early day came to this country and settled in North Carolina. His mother was a daughter of Wm. James, from England. She was a "pious woman and a strong Baptist. She knew Bunyan and the Bible pretty much by heart, and would have been a preacher if she had only been a man." Young Demarcus owed much to the piety and godly counsel of his mother. He was converted in his twenty-second year, in a meeting held by

Elders Chesley Boatwright and Woodson Taylor in a school-house where the New County Line Church (Grainger County) now is, and was later baptized into the fellowship of that church by Elder Taylor. Soon after his conversion he began to exercise his "gift" in the way of prayer and exhortation. In 1842 he was "licensed" to preach by Bethel Church, and in August of 1847 was ordained by Beaver Dam Church, Elders J. S. Coram, Homer Sears and Gordan Mynatt constituting the ordaining council.

Elder Demarcus made a remarkable record as pastor. In November, 1847, in connection with the venerable Joshua Frost, he organized the Mount Harmony Church (Knox County), and was called to the pastorate of the church the following April. To this church he received fifty-two annual calls, the last one being extended him just one hour before his death. He was pastor of Beaver Dam Church twenty-nine years, of Zion Hill twenty-five years, of Third Creek Church twenty odd years. He was also pastor of Fair View, Valley Grove, Pleasant Hill, Sharon, Union, and other churches. He was mainly instrumental in the organization of four of the above churches. During his pastorate of Beaver Dam, Zion Hill, Mt. Harmony, and Third Creek churches there went out from these churches fifteen new churches to keep house for themselves.

Elder Demarcus was eminently successful in revival meetings. In a ministry of more than fifty years he witnessed over 2,000 conversions, baptizing nearly that number with his own hands.

Brother Demarcus was an East Tennessean by birth, and never was off his native heath. He traveled considerably in his preaching tours, went "around the borders" pretty well, but was "never out of East Tennessee" till he went to heaven. He "believed in foreign missions," he said, "but never could get very far from Jerusalem." He never preached for a "set salary," but received whatever the churches would "give." If a church was "hot," the pay was good; if the church was "lukewarm," he didn't get much; if the church was "cold," he got nothing at all.

Next to his mother his greatest helper, in his younger days, was Chesley H. Boatwright, who taught him his letters in a log cabin, in Hickory Valley, Anderson County, who also for some years was a father to him in the ministry. His true and most constant yoke-fellow in the gospel was William Hickle, a man after his own heart.

Elder Demarcus was, we might say, a self-made man, and for the most part a man of one book—the Bible—although in his twenty-fourth year he spent some time in the University at Knoxville, where he received training and equipment enough to teach school.

Brother Demarcus was married three times: First, to a Miss Emily Weaver; second, to Mary Smith; third, to Mary Ellis. By his first wife he had seven children; by his second. twelve. One of his sons, J. W. Demarcus, is an alumnus of Carson and Newman College and a Baptist preacher.

Like Barnabas, Elder Demarcus was a good man. He lived his religion, and had the confidence of the people. He preached more funerals and married more people, it is thought, than any country preacher in all East Tennessee.

Just a week before his passing he preached at Salem Church on the subject of forgiveness. He stood to the last firm and unshaken on the solid rock, and sung with his expiring breath, 'How Firm a Foundation." He died at his home in Knox County, near Beaver Dam Church, April 22, 1899, near the close of his 79th year.

JOHN B. DENTON.

John B. Denton was born in Jefferson County, Tenn., near Dandridge, August 16, 1826. He was converted at the age of 16, at the old Antioch Church, south of the French Broad River, in his native county. He was ordained to the ministry at the age of 20. He was pastor of Antioch and Leadvale churches in Jefferson County, and Alder Branch Church in Sevier County. He was pastor of Antioch a number of years, and was chiefly instrumental in building up the spiritual body at that place, also in rebuilding their house of worship, after the old meeting-house had burned down, giving of his means, his time and his labor. Most of his ministerial life was spent in Jefferson County. He was a great stay and pillar to his home church, rarely failing to attend the regular meetings. He was a thoroughly dependable man, a good preacher, and a wise counsellor. He loved to meet and associate with his brethren, and nearly always attended the meetings of his own and of sister associations. One of the writer's earliest recollections is of meeting Elder J. B. Denton at the East Tennessee Association, and of seeing him in his father's home and hearing them discuss Bible doctrines and questions of theology.

Elder Denton was married four times: First, to Martha Baker, in 1858, to which union were born seven children, five sons and two daughters. His second marriage was to Mrs. Jemima Butler. To this union was born an only son, who died in infancy. His third wife, before marriage, was Margaret Swann; his fourth Dorcas Click.

In the minutes of the Nolachucky Association for 1911 the committee on obituaries reports. "Brother John B. Denton, aged 85 years, and probably the oldest minister of our Association, has passed from our midst to the great eternal city of God, greatly beloved by all who knew him, and a devoted member of the Dandridge Church. He died January 8, 1911." The following notice is taken from *The Journal and Tribune:* "Dandridge, Tenn., January 8, 1911. Rev. John B. Denton died at his home about two miles from this city at nine o'clock this morning. He was in his eighty-fifth year, had been a Baptist minister more than sixty years. His death was caused by pneumonia, from which he had been suffering for two weeks. He was one of the best known and most highly respected men in the county, and has always been considered one of the best men that ever lived in the county. Although beyond his 'four score years' he had not given up his ministerial work. He preached in Dandridge quite recently; he has not been preach-ing regularly, however, for some time. Mr. Denton is sur-vived by his widow, who was his fourth wife, his son, Hugh W. Denton, who lives near Dandridge, also two brothers, Berry, aged 92, living in Cocke County, and David, aged 80, whose home is in Jefferson County." Elder Denton was buried in the family graveyard at his late home, near Dandridge. Peace be to his sleeping dust, and blessed be his memory.

JESSE DODSON.

"In memory of Rev. Jesse Dodson; born November 22, 1752; died November 22, 1843. A minister of the gospel sixty years." (Tombstone record, Eastanallee Church.)

The deceased was born in Halifax County, Va. His first settlement in Tennessee was in Claiborne County. From there he went to Middle Tennessee. In 1819 he came to the Hiwassee Purchase, making a settlement in McMinn County, a few months before the county was "erected." On the Eastanallee is a house still standing, I believe, built ninety-eight years ago by Jesse Dodson.

Soon after his settlement in the Hiwassee district he be-gan pioneer work. He and seven others constituted themselves into the Eastanallee Church. He and Silas Witt organized New Hopewell. He and James Courtney founded the Hiwassee Church. Salem Church was organized by him and Richard Wilson, while he and John Short were co-founders of the Friendship Church. He was preacher to and pastor of these and other churches for many years.

He was of Welsh extraction and had the Welsh fire. He was not trained to methodical sermonizing or systematic ex-position of Scripture, but was earnest and fervent in exhorta-tion, and was successful in revivals.

Elder Dodson owned 300 acres of land in the heart of Eastanallee valley, and ten negroes, whom he "freed," it is said, after the death of his wife (by whom he came into possession of them), giving as his reason that he had "concluded that a bill of sale of negroes in his pocket would be a bad passport at the gate of Heaven."

His wife was a Miss Ruth Johnson, of South Carolina, of a well-to-do family, but the date of his marriage and other family and ministerial records have perished, were washed away or destroyed, it is thought, by the high waters of the Eastanallee in the year 1875.

He lived to preach and exhort sinners to repentance about sixty-one years, and on his 91st birthday died in the triumph of a living faith.

ROBERT DONALDSON.

Robert Donaldson was born in Manchester, England, August 12, 1835. He was a son of Thomas Donaldson, a native of Scotland. His mother, before her marriage, was a Miss Tudor, born in Liverpool, England. Young Donaldson was educated in the old country, but when old enough to take care of himself left his native England and his father's home and, in company with three older brothers, took passage for New York City (about the middle of the last century), seeking a home in this country of larger opportunity. About the year 1856 the brothers left New York and came to the coal fields of the South. December 24, 1858, Robert Donaldson and Miss Hulda Marlow, of Kentucky, were united in marriage. To this union were born eleven children, four sons and seven daughters. He was converted about the year 1861, in the state of Kentucky, and in the same state was ordained to the ministry, somewhere in the seventies, probably in 1872. In 1873 he came to Caryville, Tenn., interested in coal mines and "miners." Here he found a few Baptists but no house of worship, no church, no Sunday school. With the help of the good people of the place a house of worship was soon erected, Brother Donaldson becoming pastor. He continued pastor of the church for three years, building up, by the blessing of the Lord, a good Baptist interest in this new mining town. He was called to the Jacksboró Church, a cultured people, and in a town long famous for good schools. He served this church as pastor for a number of years. He was also called to Coal Creek and Heiskell's Station, and served these churches jointly some seven or eight years. He then went to Birmingham, Ala., where his brother, Edward, was in the coal business, with the intention of casting his lot in that city. But he only stayed a short time, and returned to Coal Creek for a second pastorate of that church. He now witnessed new additions to the membership of the church, and was enabled to build, by the help of the brethren, a "nice new house of worship" for the Baptists, the house in which they now worship.

He was pastor of the church at Robertsville, preached the first sermon (April 19, 1891) in the new Baptist meeting-house at that place, and visited and preached for the church often. He was also pastor of Poplar Creek, New Salem and Fairview churches. The last church of which he was pastor was the Moran Memorial Church, at Dossett. Here he "fell on sleep," September 27, 1898, and here rests his body in the quiet church yard,·awaiting the resurrection of the last day.

Elder Donaldson is survived by two sons and four daughters and many relatives and friends, who revere his memory.

A. J. DUNCAN.

"The venerable brother, A. J. Duncan, is an ordained preacher of intelligence and gifts. He has been a Baptist fifty-four years. He has not been physically able to preach for some years, but he has been greatly useful in Sunday school and 'fifth Sunday meeting' work, in fireside conversation, in his talk and walk on the streets and in the stores. He believes

in 'contending earnestly for the faith delivered once for all
to the saints,' and he defines 'saints' as Baptists and 'the
faith,' as the New Testament system of doctrines. He believes
strongly and persistently in church 'discipline,' which he says
is his 'forte.' My visit in his home, in Calhoun, has been most
pleasant. The infirmities of age are creeping over him. May
he be spared other years to do good. He has given his estate,
210 acres of land, to the new Cleveland Church, reserving
only $1,000 out of it for his living, the rest of the proceeds to
go toward building a house of worship. (Notebook entry.)
Brother Duncan has long since gone to his reward.

JOSEPH H. EATON.

Dr. Joseph H. Eaton was born September 10, 1812, in Ber-
lin, Delaware County, Ohio. According to the genealogy given
by his distinguished son, Dr. T. T. Eaton, "Joseph H. Eaton
was the son of Joseph Eaton, who was the son of David Eaton,
who was the son of John Eaton, who was the son of Joseph
Eaton, who was the son of John Eaton, who emigrated from
Wales, A.D., 1686." He was the youngest of twelve children
and lived with his widowed mother after all his brothers and
sisters had begun life for themselves, his father having died
when young Eaton was but a lad of twelve. He attended the
neighborhood school till about fifteen or sixteen years of age,
at which time he went to Worthington Academy, near Columbus, Ohio, to prepare for college. Once during his childhood
he was supposed to be dead; the physician pronounced him
dead, and dead he was to all human appearances. But his
mother insisted that he was a child of prayer and was not
dead, but would live to fulfill his God-given mission in the
world. So his mother, though needing his presence, by faith
sent him away for his life equipment, saying to him, "My son,
it is hard to part with you, but you need advantages our
neighborhood cannot give, and I bid you go." Spending a year

or two in academic work, in 1832 he entered Georgetown College, Kentucky, where his brother, Dr. George W. Eaton, afterwards president of Madison University, New York, was then a professor. He pursued his studies at Georgetown, and tutored till 1835, when he followed his brother to Madison University, graduating in 1837. He taught school near Nashville, Tenn., till the spring of 1838, when he went to Fayetteville, to

DR. J. H. EATON.

take charge of the academy there. In the summer of 1840 he was married to Miss Esther M. Treadwell, of Plattsburg, N. Y., a granddaughter of Thomas Treadwell, a member of the Continental Congress. In 1841 he went to Murfreesboro, where in connection with others he began an educational institution, which, in 1848, became Union University, Dr. Eaton becoming its first president—a position which he held as long as he lived. He preached his first sermon in Dr. Howell's pulpit—that of the First Baptist Church of Nashville. Professor Eaton had had "impressions" to preach, but was timid and shrinking. So. Dr. Howell, being a little " crafty, "caught him with guile"; he took Prof. Eaton into the pulpit with him, to help in the service, and then said to him: "Now, sir, you have got either to preach, or apologize to the congregation." It was as easy to preach as to apologize, so he preached. He was ordained in Murfreesboro, September 10, 1843—Dr. R. B. C. Howell, T. B. Ripley and others taking part in the ceremonies.

In 1853 Madison University conferred upon him the degree of LL.D.

Union University, under his administration as President, had almost phenomenal success. The student body was easily 300, being representative young men from Georgia, Alabama, Florida, Mississippi, Texas, Louisiana, Arkansas, Kentucky, Missouri, Illinois, North Carolina and Virginia, and from all parts of Tennessee. Dr. Eaton was not only a fine administrator with executive ability, he was *scholarly,* and at home in the classroom. In the absence of any of the professors of the University, Dr. Eaton would take their classes, and the young men, it is said, "never failed to understand that he was *master* of the *situation."* His special "fondness was for metaphysics and the more occult sciences. He taught logic and Butler's Analogy without a text-book. He held up to his students a high standard and was exacting in his demands for study, but was patient and long-suffering with dull pupils. An idle student, however, found no favor in his eyes. He had high hopes for young men, he believed in them, laid himself out for them without stint or grudging, had great enthusiasm for his work, and therefore was greatly beloved by all his students, though the discipline was rigid and the tasks heavy. There are hundreds of men now scattered over the Southwest who can testify to his purity of heart and his unfailing fidelity in all the relations of teacher and friend. Few men have left their impress upon the minds and habits of the young men of the South more indelibly than he. His students regarded him as a perfect model and copied his style. In their eyes he was faultless. He was remarkable for his affability, his geniality, his wonderful versatility of character. Long will his memory be cherished by those whose good fortune it was to know him intimately, or come under his influence." (Dr. G. W. Jarman).

Dr. Eaton had a remarkably vigorous constitution, but with looking after the class work, the discipline and the finances of the University, and preaching every Sunday, and sometimes oftener, the strain was more than his constitution could bear. After a lingering illness, brought about by over-work, "he died January 12. 1859, aged forty-six years, four months and two days, leaving a wife, a daughter and two sons."

Dr. J. M. Pendleton, who taught theology under Dr. Eaton, and who followed him as acting President of the University, or chairman of the faculty, in his "Reminiscences of a Long Life," bears this testimony to a fellow-worker, one of God's noblemen: "Dr. Joseph H. Eaton, the President, was a man of intellectual power and broad scholarship, not inferior, as I think, to his brother, George W., who died President of Madison, now Colgate University. Dr. Joseph H. was a very laborious teacher, enthusiastic in his work; when I first knew him he was a fine specimen of manly beauty, and his sermons and addresses were replete with vigor and eloquence. But his noble physical frame succumbed to disease and he died in the prime of his life, leaving a bereaved University, a bereaved church, and a more bereaved family. It devolved on me to preach the funeral sermon. The general feeling was, a great man has fallen in Israel. Mrs. Eaton, left to feel the desolateness of widowhood, was a remarkable woman, equal in intellectual and spiritual qualities to her husband. She spent many years of her life in teaching, and left her impress on the minds of many young ladies. She lived a widow more than twenty-five years, and died in Louisville, in 1886. I preached her funeral sermon also, from the words: 'Blessed are the dead who die in the Lord,' etc. Two children survive, Rev. T. T. Eaton, D.D. and Mrs. J. E. Peck, who are worthy representatives of their parents, and who are occupying positions of usefulness."

As a *preacher,* Dr. Eaton is thus described by Cathcart (Baptist Encyclopaedia) : "As a preacher, Dr. Eaton was earnest and impressive, of impassioned utterance and rapid delivery. His power to fix attention and impress his thoughts upon his hearers has seldom been equaled. He won the enthusiastic devotion of those who knew him, of all classes and grades of society. His fellow-ministers, professors, the churches to which he preached, his many students, and his servants, all loved him as few men are loved. Handsome in person, gracious in presence, genial in manners, and winning in conversation, he was eminent in the qualities which make men charming in the home circle, as he was in those which make a great teacher and preacher. There was about him a sense of reserved power. The strength of the man was always felt beneath his genial graciousness. His children and his students would face any danger rather than have him know that they had been guilty of a dishonorable action, so much did they dread the glance of his eye, so much did they value his approving smile. His virtues live in the memories of all who knew him."

Of the descendants of Dr. Joseph H. Eaton, there are now living his daughter, Mrs. "Jo Eaton" Peck, of Murfreesboro. Tenn., seventy-six years of age, a grandson namesake, J. H.

Eaton, a lawyer of Denver, Col., and a granddaughter, Mrs. Maria Eaton Farmer, of Louisville, Ky., the last two mentioned being a son and a daughter of the lamented Dr. T. T. Eaton.

JOSHUA EDWARDS.

Joshua Edwards was born in Henry County, Va., August 11, 1781. He came with his parents to upper East Tennessee when he was four years old. In the year 1800 he was converted, and was baptized by Jonathan Mulky, uniting with the Cherokee Church, one of the oldest churches in the state. He was a member of this body twenty-seven years.

September 30, 1802, he was married to Nancy Erwin, and on December 9, 1838, was married to Drusilla Delaney.

In the constitution of the Holston Church, June 16, 1827, he was a constituent member, and on the same day was chosen clerk of the church. December 20, 1834, he was ordained deacon, Benjamin White and James Poindexter acting as a presbytery. March 20, 1836, he was licensed to preach, and soon after was ordained by the same presbytery, as above mentioned. He at once became pastor of the church and continued as such for some sixteen years, till the infirmities of age made it necessary for him to resign. He was chiefly instrumental in building a house of worship for this newly constituted church, holding church services in his own house till the meeting-house was ready for use.

In 1845 this church was the fifth largest in the Holston Association, numbering 135, with "J. Edwards the spiritual guide." J. Edwards, we might say, was the founder and builder of this church, under God, almost all the converts who came into the church being his spiritual children.

Joshua Edwards was a good preacher, a good clerk, and a good writer. In 1845 he was Benedict's correspondent for the Holston and other associations. In the capacity of correspondent or reporter for our great historian he rendered a great service to the denomination, preserving and giving publicity to valuable matters of history which otherwise might have perished. In the "extensive revivals of religion in the Holston community," reported by him, and by which the "numbers of the Association were augmented," he himself had no mean part.

He was greatly loved by his people, and upon his death, March 18, 1859, his church memorialized him in her minutes, and the same year sent an obituary notice to the Association, speaking of him in the very highest terms.

ISAAC ELLEGE.

News has just reached me of the death of the venerable brother and minister, Isaac Ellege. If he had lived to the 16th of this month (April, '97) he would have been 86 years old, having been born in Knox County, Tenn., April 16, 1811.

Brother Elledge had been a minister of the gospel sixty-four years, continuing to preach right on almost to the very time of his death. He was licensed to preach by Pawpaw Hollow Church, Sevier County, and was ordained in Alabama, at the age of 27. His ministry was in East and Middle Tennessee, North Carolina, Alabama and Mississippi. He was the faithful pastor of Nails Creek, Crooked Creek, Sulphur Springs and Laurel Bank churches.

He is a valuable witness to the stirring events of the "anti-mission war" from its beginning, in his section of the country, about the year 1834. He knew personally the leaders on either side of the question. He knew Joshua Frost as a tower of strength to the cause of "the missionaries," and Dr. Thomas Hill, with his "iron-jacket" views of predestination, proclaiming the "decrees" and making war on missions. He knew "Sam Love," and heard him preach with such unction and melting tenderness and Holy Ghost power that a good deal of ice had melted from about the hearts of Baptists and their "hard doctrine" had largely disappeared.

April 20, 1897, I overtook Brother Ellege on the roadside near his home, one mile from Ball Camp. I took him up in the buggy with me, told him who I was and what I wanted, asked him some leading questions, and "took notes." I knew his mind had failed some of late, but his recollection was good. His view of the atonement was that Christ "died for all alike," that the gospel was for "all the world," and that "whosoever will" might come to 'the feast and be filled." He challenged "discussion" on those points. He told me he had just preached the day before on his favorite theme—the doctrine of election; its two sides—at New Salem Church, near Clinch River, in Anderson County, where, more than sixty years before, the Tennessee Association had split on the rock of missions. With remarkable memory he recalled the controversies, divisions, methods, misconceptions, and reconstructions of those early times, and of the wonderful revivals that attended the labors of the missionaries everywhere.

Brother Ellege realized he could not remain in the harness long, and was anxious to do what he could. One part of his mission was, as he told me, to "get his anti-mission brother back into the fold." He had just recently preached at Cave Creek, and called on a hardshell brother to pray, and he "prayed all right."

RICHARD EVANS.

With this sketch I present the face of the venerable brother, Elder Richard Evans, "Uncle Dickey," as he is familiarly called by his mountaineer neighbors and friends. He is now in his 73rd year, but well preserved and full of rugged strength. He was born in Sevier County, Tenn., January 4, 1824. He was the only son of Jacob Evans, but had three sisters. His mother, before marriage, was Martha Ogle, Ogle being a historic name among Sevier County Baptists. His grandfather, William Evans, was of Welsh descent. The subject of our sketch is of Welsh-English extraction, inheriting the English sturdiness and the Welsh fire, and looks, both as to physical features and mental characteristics, as though he were a direct descendant of the historic Christmas Evans, a preacher of Baptist fame.

At the age of 16, in a meeting held by Eli Roberts and William Ogle, he was converted, and joined the White Oak Flats Church. In the same year, January 30, 1840, he was

RICHARD EVANS.

married to a Miss Ollief Ownby, to which union there were born twelve children. In his twentieth year he was licensed to preach by the White Oak Flats Church, and in his twenty-second year was ordained by the same church, Elders Eli Roberts and Isaac Kimbrough constituting the ordaining council. Of this, his mother church, Brother Evans has been a member for fifty-six years, and pastor for forty-six years, and bids fair to continue pastor for many years to come.

He has also been pastor of the following churches: Ware's Cove, Red Bank, Bethany, Friendship, Hill's Creek, New Salem, Lebanon, Evans' Chapel No. 1, Evans' Chapel No. 2 (most of these in Sevier County); Tuckaleechee, in Blount County, and Lufty, Shoal Creek and Bird Town (an Indian church), in Swain County, North Carolina. Of Bird Town, a church of 100 Indians, he was pastor for two years, receiving a larger salary than from many of his white churches. His salary was always small, never more than $25 from a single church, and more often from ten to fifteen dollars a year.

Brother Evans has been wonderfully successful as a revivalist. In meetings with his preacher brethren, and in those held by himself he has witnessed not less than 10,000 conversions, and has with his own hands baptized 1,805 converts into the fellowship of Baptist churches.

Brother Evans has preached to the Cherokee Indians, through an interpreter, has held protracted meetings among them, in the same way and with the same results as among his own people, and has baptized sixty converts from among them.

He has been a marvel in his day. He has been a mountain preacher, for the most part, and has revolutionized large districts in Sevier County and in Western North Carolina. There are no more moral communities anywhere than the "coves" where "Uncle Dickey" Evans' voice has sounded out the glad tidings and the note of reform of the gospel message. So great was his influence in the community, in politics as well as religion, that it was commonly said that "a candidate for office didn't need to canvass the eleventh district, if Preacher Evans was for him, the voters would be for him; if the *preacher* was against him, he could save time and trouble—the voters would be against him."

Brother Evans was a soul-winner, and rarely ever preached, even at an Association, without calling for penitents. When comparatively a young man he attended the Tuckasege Association (N. C.), where the Baptists had borrowed the Methodist "camp ground" to hold their associational meetings. He was appointed to preach Sunday afternoon at 4 o'clock. At the close of the sermon he called for "mourners." The meeting wouldn't close but continued through the night, resulting in fifty professions of faith. This was the beginning of his missionary and protracted meeting labors in the mountains of North Carolina, which he kept up for several years with marked success.

His prominent associates in the ministry were Eli Roberts, Asa Layman, Robert Atchley, John Russell, and W. M. Burnett. His favorite text was, "By grace are ye saved"; his favorite hymn, "How Firm a Foundation," etc.

In his boyhood days Brother Evans had few educational advantages and few books. Later in life, however, he read Bunyan, Buck's Theological Dictionary, Smith's Dictionary of the Bible, Hedge's Logic, and Smith's Grammar.

Not being a trained polemic, or a skilled debater, Brother Evans thought discretion was the better part of valor, and generally left "controversies" and controverted subjects to his more "gifted" brethren. He avoided, if possible, a "regular engagement" with anti-mission and Pedo-Baptist opponents. He preferred a sort of "running fire." When forced to fight, however, he would give the enemy the "best fight there was in him." In one little bout with a Methodist preacher he not only won the day but converted his opponent to the Baptist position, as the preacher confessed to him afterwards.

Brother Evans was fond of relating the following rather sensational incident: He was preaching on one occasion in an old and somewhat dilapidated building, from the text, "And as Moses lifted up the serpent in the wilderness, even so must the Son of Man be lifted up," when the sudden scream of a woman interrupted the devotions of the assembly. A black snake had lost its grip on some overhead timber and had fallen into the woman's lap. The congregation adjourned without the benediction, to chase the fleeing reptile, but reassembled, to finish their devotions.

Brother Evans is still pastor of his home church, White Oak Flats, and Evans' Chapel No. 1. He has lived nearly three-quarters of a century, and, so far as we can calculate human "probabilities," barring the accidents to which old age is peculiarly liable, he has a fair prospect of living over into the century ahead of us and making in due time his 100th milestone on the road of life before he goes hence to receive his crown.

(The above was written and published February 28, 1896, twenty years ago.)

The following incident comes to light from an out-of-the-way page in a "notebook." The note is anonymous, and I have forgotten my authority, though I think it was not Brother Evans himself. The incident nevertheless is trustworthy and characteristic of the man and, though sensational and rather a risky experiment, some of us may be disposed to think, it will serve as a sidelight on a preacher who believed in being always on his job. When a young preacher Brother Evans happened to stay all night at a house where they had planned to have a dance. The young people gathered in due time and began their operations. Brother Evans was off in a remote room. At a late hour of the night one of the young ladies invited the preacher to join her in the dance. The invitation was accepted, and the fiddlers were ready to proceed with their part of the performance when the preacher interrupted, "Hold on, one minute, if you please. I never go into anything that I can't talk to the Lord about. Let us have a word of prayer." By the time the preacher was through with his prayer the young lady had collapsed, a change having come over the spirit of her dream, embarrassment and confusion were written in the faces of the youngsters, nobody was in the notion of going ahead with the dance. "And this was the beginning of a meeting in which there were 200 converts."

JAMES AND JESSE FEARS.

These two men seem to have been brothers in the flesh; anyway, they were brothers in the Lord and labored together in the gospel ministry. Their names stand together and are conspicuous on the pages of some of our oldest church records. The Bent Creek (Whitesburg) records of May, second Friday, 1790, give this: "Jesse Fears upon offering his impressions of mind to preach is tolerated to preach upon trial." Some differences unfortunately occurring between him and some of his brethren, the church felt constrained, November, second Friday, 1790, to take the following action: "Under consideration of some difficulties subsisting between Brother Jesse Fears and some members in this church we suspend the public improvement of his gift till further labors." These difficulties were satisfactorily straightened out, we presume, since a few months later the church granted Brother Fears a "letter of dismission." November 10, 1792, the Mouth of Richland Church "chose James Fears to act as their minister for the present." February 10, 1798, the above church "approbates" Brother Robert Fristoe's gift "in the preaching line," and "do request Brother Barton, Brother James Fears and Brother Jesse Fears to act as a presbytery." May, first Saturday, 1796, James Fears "takes the pastoral care" of Lower French Broad (now the Dandridge) Church. This church (August, 1897) called for the ordination of Brother Duke Kimbrough, and petitioned

Brother Richard Wood and Brother James Fears to attend on the occasion, the fourth Friday in October following. This exhausts my notes on these men of God. But little of their history has been preserved. Their record is on high.

ASA FITZGERALD.

One of the pioneer preachers of lower East Tennessee was Asa Fitzgerald. He was born on Duck River, in West Tennessee, October 11, 1809. His father, Archibald Fitzgerald, who was also a minister of the gospel, came from South Carolina. Brother Fitzgerald belonged to a family of thirteen children, three of whom, Asa, Archibald and Aaron, were influential country preachers in Southeastern Tennessee and North Georgia.

The family moved to Indiana when Asa was four years of age, but returned to Tennessee in 1823, locating in Monroe County. Young Fitzgerald went back to Indiana, and was married to Miss Judith Warren in the year 1829. To this union were born twelve children. He was converted about the time of his marriage, but was not ordained to the full work of the ministry until the year 1851, the White Plains Church calling for his ordination. He was pastor first at Shiloh. He was afterwards pastor of various country churches, including Corinth, Gum Springs, Blue Springs, Providence and Salem, in North Georgia.

In 1874, his first wife having died several years before, he was married to Miss Margaret Whittle, a native of Sevier County, Tenn., but at the time of her marriage living in North Georgia. To this union were born a son and a daughter, the daughter dying in infancy. The son, Dr. William H. Fitzgerald, formerly pastor of the First Baptist Church of Jefferson City, now pastor of the Mount Olive Church, near Knoxville, is a sweet-spirited, scholarly, lovable preacher, one of our very best pastors.

In 1898 the subject of this sketch fell on sleep, his companion having preceded him to the better country by the space of two years. His tired body rests in the Antioch Cemetery, near Apison, Tenn., where he had lived and held his membership many years. His praise is in the churches to which he preached and in the community in which he lived. His name still lives in the memory and on the lips of the older residents of lower East Tennessee.

The characteristic and outstanding features of Brother Fitzgerald as a man were his genuine piety, his love for the Word of God, and his faithfulness to duty under all circumstances. He always kept to his farm as a means of support but made it secondary and subservient to the interests of spiritual religion and the advancement of Christ's Kingdom.

JOHN FREEMAN.

John Freeman, son of John and Mary Freeman, was born in Greene County, Tenn., July 25, 1813. His father was a soldier in the War of 1812. He was converted in his twentieth year, and was baptized by Elder Enoch Simmons, uniting with Davis' Creek Church, Claiborne County, Tenn. He was licensed to preach by Town Creek Church, and in 1852 was ordained by Gap Creek Church. For thirty-five years he lived among the "anti-missionaries," affiliating with them and preaching for them to the best of his ability, but he was too liberal to suit some of his "very hard" brethren. In 1869 he and Gap Creek Church, of which he was pastor, came over to the missionaries. He was pastor of Town Creek, Gap Creek, Providence, Cave Spring, Pleasant Point, Cedar Spring, Mossy Spring, Carr's Branch, Nave Hill, and Blair's Creek churches, some of which he was instrumental in founding. He baptized into the fellowship of some of the above churches a hundred or more members. He helped ordain, or otherwise encouraged and "put forward," some twenty-five young preachers, most of whom are doing effective work among the churches.

January 9, 1834, he was married to Miss Anna Sharp, a daughter of Wm. Sharp, Sen., of Claiborne County. This union was crowned with a family of eleven children, eight sons and three daughters. Brother Freeman is still living (1898), nearly 86 years old, well preserved in mind and body, and enjoying life. His home is near New Tazewell, Claiborne County, Tenn.

ROBERT FRISTOE.

July, second Saturday, 1791, Bent Creek (now the Whitesburg) Church appointed Robert Fristoe, along with Elders Tidence Lane, Isaac Barton and Caleb Witt, messengers to the Holston Association. The Association minutes for 1794 show that Phillip Hale and Robert Fristoe were messengers of Lick Creek (now the Warrensburg) Church. In 1795 Robert Fristoe was a messenger of the Lick Creek Church, and was chosen moderator of the Association. He seems to have been a layman, and not a preacher, at this time. In May, of '96, Cove Creek Church called for the ordination of Robert Fristoe, and a letter of dismission for him, both of which were granted. In 1797 he appears on the Holston Association minutes as a messenger of the Richland (Mouth of Richland) Church, and is again elected moderator. The following year (February 10, 1798) the Mouth of Richland Church "approbate Brother Robert Fristoe's gift in the preaching line and consider him ripe for ordination. In consequence of which we appoint next church meeting, three days in course: Friday as a church meeting, Saturday for fasting, and Sunday for preaching; and do request Brother Barton, Brother James Fears and Brother Jesse Fears to act as a presbytery in the ordination of Brother Fristoe at that time." At the April meeting the call for a presbytery was "repeated," and the odination effected, we presume, since the church at its next meeting (May 12th) extended a call to Brother Fristoe to be pastor, which call was accepted. June 14th, the church "receives Brother Fristoe by letter, giving him the right hand of fellowship." In June of the following year the church "grants Beaver Dam a part of Brother Fristoe's time." After a continuous pastorate of twenty-one years the church (September, 1819) "grants letters of dismission to Robert Fristoe and wife"; but in December, 1822, he is "reinstated to the pastoral care of the church and serves as pastor three more years. He was pastor of Little Flat Creek Church twenty-nine years (1798-1827), being followed by Samuel Love in a pastorate of thirteen years, and he by J. S. Coram, who served the church as pastor for twenty-six successive years.

Elder Fristoe was a peacemaker, and was wise and tactful in adjusting differences between churches and brethren who happened to be at variance. December 12, 1801, he was chosen by the Bent Creek Church to act with five other ministers as a presbytery in settling a "distress" existing between two of her members who were preachers.

In a council of nineteen churches, met with Beaver Creek Church, December 25, 1802, to organize the Tennessee Association, Robert Fristoe and two other brethren were "representatives" of the Mouth of Richland Church.

In 1805 he was moderator of the Tennessee Association; in 1809 he preached the introductory sermon, from I Peter 2:19, his theme being, "Suffering Wrong for Conscience' Sake."

JOSHUA FROST.

Joshua, son of Thomas Frost, was born in Lee County, Va., December 22, 1782. His father moved to East Tennessee in 1796, and "entering" a section of land, five miles south of Clinton, built on it "the first house" that was built in Anderson County. Here young Frost was brought up to farm life, with few advantages of an education.

11

He was married July 19, 1803, to Miss Annie Chiles. To this union were born six children, five sons, one daughter.

The date of his conversion and baptism was lost with the old records of the Beaver Ridge (or Ball Camp) Church, Knox County, with which he united. The record of March, 1818, places Joshua Frost at the head of a list of the "nineteen constituent members" of the Raccoon Valley Arm (now Zion

JOSHUA FROST.

Church), which the mother church agreed might be established. His church licensed him to preach September 12, 1820, and by request of the above-mentioned Arm he was ordained, March, 1822, Thomas Hudiburg and Obed Patty constituting the presbytery.

The ministerial career of Brother Frost begins, therefore, with the history of the Raccoon Valley Arm, in the beginning of 1818, this new interest growing up around him. In 1819 an acre of land was given by a Brother Norman, on which to build a house of worship. In 1823 the Arm assumed the name of "Zion meeting-house," and the year following became an independent body. The old meeting-house, many of whose logs Brother Frost cut and hewed, is still standing (1897), and close by is the old dwelling house built by his father and inherited by the son, who lived in it till upwards of 80 years old, when he went on a visit to his children in Illinois.

Elder Frost was pastor of Zion Church about forty years. Of the old mother church, Beaver Ridge, otherwise known as the "brick chapel," he was pastor for a great number of years, baptizing into the fellowship of the church, first and last, so the old brethren say, at least "200 members." He was also pastor of Salem, Clinton, Mt. Horeb, Bethel, Fairview, Union and other churches, in Roane, Anderson and Knox counties, many of which he was chiefly instrumental in founding.

"He was the prime factor in the organization of Mount Harmony, Zion Hill, Blowing Spring, Pine Grove, and Third Creek churches." (Azariah Harrell.)

He did a great deal of work in out-of-the-way and destitute places, and while he had the misfortune to lose his record of converts, baptisms, churches organized, etc., he was heard to say that he had organized and built up, pretty much by his own efforts and the Lord's help, "twenty-two churches."

From 1818 to 1863 Elder Frost, almost every year, was either a delegate or a corresponding delegate to the Tennessee Association. The minutes show that he preached five intro-

ductory sermons before that body. He was for some years
Moderator of the Northern Association, and from 1853 to
1864 he was Moderator of the Clinton.

Joshua Frost had an "impressive voice and manner that
made him a power in the pulpit. A wave of his hand made an
impression." (B. Demarcus.) His voice was not only powerful, but clear and penetrating; he could be heard distinctly
a great distance. It is said that his wife at home, a full half
mile from the church, could hear him read or quote his text
and line out his hymns, and tell him all about his performances
at church when he would get home.

As a minister and as a man he was firm, fearless and outspoken. He never allowed an oath or sin of any kind, in his
presence, to go unrebuked. There was an air of gravity and
sanctity about him that caused all classes of people to reverence him. Was there a bunch of youngsters, or of older people, engaged in frivolous conversation in or about the church?
the approach of Elder Frost was a signal for silence or rever-
ential behavior.

He is said to have had wonderful tact in introducing on
all occasions the subject of religion. He lived on the public
highway and kept a sort of public tavern or stopping place for
stock-drivers, lawyers, judges and other travelers, but he
would rarely have a person in his home an hour, it is said, or
ride a mile with a stranger on the highway, without finding
out whether he was a Christian or not.

In his preaching he quoted freely from the Scriptures, proving all things by the Word of God, giving chapter and verse.
He was also a good singer, and was gifted in exhortation.

He was a thorough believer in free salvation and missions,
and had little sympathy with the doctrine of predestination
as held by many Baptists of his day. Perhaps the greatest
sermon of his life was at the Powell's Valley Association,
when that body was settling down into "fixed fate" and anti-
mission sentiments. The question was up as to who would

preach and some of the brethren were excusing themselves as not being "prepared." Elder Frost said, "If ever I was prepared to preach it is now"; and he commenced his sermon by saying, "They have slandered my God, and I am here to vindicate him. They say he is a respecter of *persons*. My Bible teaches most plainly that he is a respecter of *character,* and willeth not the death of any."

One of the notable characteristics of Elder Frost's ministry was the conscientiousness with which he filled his preaching appointments. It is said that in a ministry of nearly fifty years he never disappointed more than one or two congregations.

He was also a great believer in prayer, and had a firm and abiding faith that if God had called him to preach his everlasting gospel he would take care of his family while he was doing it. At one time he had an engagement to begin work in the destitute regions of Kentucky. When the time came for him to leave home to go to his appointment, his youngest child was very sick. His companion hung on his neck and wept sorely, beseeching him not to go. It was a sore trial for him to leave home under the circumstances, but, kissing the child and taking leave of his wife, he rode away with great heaviness of heart. He had gone only a little way, however, when his burden of anxiety had left him and he felt assured that his child would get well. The child was better from that same hour, and soon recovered.

With all his seriousness and prevalent sobriety of manner, Elder Frost had in him a vein of droll humor which sometimes cropped out unexpectedly. Seeing a Baptist preacher, in time of the Civil War, carrying a gun on his shoulder, he gave his preacher brother a mild and good-natured rebuke by telling him, he "didn't like to see a minister of the gospel carrying a gun, going about to kill people."

As already mentioned, Elder Frost had gone to see his children in Illinois. He had finished his visit and had a desire to

meet with the Clinton Association once more, especially since
the meeting was to be with his home church, Zion. He was arranging for his return home, and it was only a week to the
set time for his home-coming, when he was stricken with
paralysis, which resulted in his death, July 30, 1865. He died
at the home of his youngest son, Paul C. Frost, tenderly cared
for. He wanted to return to his Tennessee home, but by the
Father's appointment he went to his better home on high.

PETER S. GAYLE.

Peter Smith Gayle was born in Charlotte County, Va., May
20, 1802; was married to Mary M. Pettus, March 27, 1823; and
was baptized in his native county of Charlotte some time before his marriage, perhaps by Elder Abner Clopton. He moved
to Tennessee in 1826, settling in Giles County, and was shortly
afterwards ordained to the ministry. In the early thirties
(about '31 to '33) he was a pioneer minister and pastor in Nashville, predecessor of Dr. R. B. C. Howell, in the pastorate of the
First Baptist Church. The church had suffered from the in-
roads of Campbellism, having lost the larger part of its membership and its house of worship. Elder Gayle rallied and banded
together the faithful and elect few (some seven or eight) and
built up the church to a membership of something like forty,
and turned the work over to other hands. In 1836 he moved
to Haywood County, in West Tennessee, taking charge of Russell Spring (now the Brownsville) Church. He was pastor
of this and the Woodlawn Church, in the same county, for six
or eight years, both of the churches prospering under his administration. In 1845 he moved to Denmark, Madison County,
taking charge of the Jackson and Big Black (now Denmark)
churches. In 1846 he became pastor of the First Church, Memphis, serving the church as pastor two years. The next three
years he was pastor of Beale Street Church, a new interest
just organized. He now moved to Madison County, Miss., and

took charge of Mound Bluff and Clinton churches, serving them efficiently till his death, which occurred June 8, 1853, at the age of 51. At the time of his death he was holding a meeting with the Clinton Church with great success, the church having already received for baptism some seventy-five persons and he himself having baptized fourteen of the candidates the day before his death. He had been heard to say many times: "If it is the Lord's will for it to be so, I should like to die in the midst of a protracted meeting of great interest." So it was that his wish and prayer were answered. The Clinton and Madison Masonic Lodges published very complimentary resolutions in regard to Elder Gayle, making mention of him as a "useful member of society, as a distinguished and devoted minister, and as having spent a handsome fortune in the service of his divine Master, in building churches, paying ministers," etc.

Elder Gayle was one of the originators of the first State Convention, organized at Mill Creek Church, Davidson County, 1833, and was the first president of the West Tennessee Convention. He was in the organization of the first Baptist education society in West Tennessee, formed at Brownsville, July 26, 1835, and became the agent of the same. In the agitations and divisions of churches and associations in the thirties and forties, over mission and anti-mission, effort and anti-effort, questions, Elder Gayle was known as an "effort man," being a zealous advocate of missions and education, "performing more arduous labor and doing more for the Baptist cause in the convention and throughout the state" than almost any other man. "He was above medium size, somewhat stooped in his shoulders, of pleasing address, usually wearing a smile, especially while preaching. His whole soul seemed to be absorbed in his Master's business, but his smile and manner seemed to say, 'It is always pleasant to obey Jesus Christ." (J. H. B.)

In 1838 Elder Gayle was requested by the Big Hatchie Association to prepare a circular letter to be read before the body at the next annual meeting. The letter called forth a good deal of discussion and opposition, and was finally rejected. At that time there was considerable confusion, uncertainty and suspicion in the public mind. Campbellism was rife in many places, and Hyper-Calvanism (Hardshellism) everywhere. These were like Scylla and Charybdis, in avoid ing one you were liable to make wreck on the other. So Elder Gayle, I take it, in seeking to refute the errors of his antimission brethren, was suspected by some of falling into the opposite error of Campbellism. The four propositions of his letter are interesting, whether we consider them entirely defensible or not: "First, that Jehovah intends to save sinners; second, that he works by means; third, that all the knowledge of man is received through the senses; fourth, that all the means used by God are exerted on man through the senses." He defended his position from the charge of being Campbellistic by saying that "Campbellism denies the doctrine of all Divine agency, other than that contained in the means alone, while his position declares God's truth and God's agency to be two things, the divine agency using and operating through the means (the Word of truth) to the accomplishment of the end, and without the Divine influence the means employed would never produce a single conversion." Living in an atmosphere of controversy, at a time when there was considerable excitement among Baptists over Boards, Conventions and Associations, Elder Gayle developed a penchant for polemical warfare, but his contention was always for Scriptural and New Testament practices. In an article in *The Baptist* (August, 1838), on the subject of a proposed "General Association" for the State, he stoutly opposed such an organization as a substitute for the State Convention till they had thoroughly tried out the convention idea. He urged his "brethren to be firm and zealous in their efforts to build up the Tennessee Baptist Convention, just as it was, without addition or diminution, as to its construction; also to foster three other societies, as nearly on the same plan as the Convention as possible: A Tennessee Baptist Bible Society, a Tennessee Baptist Foreign Missionary Society Auxiliary to the Baptist Triennial Convention for Foreign Missions, and a Tennessee Baptist Education Society." But he advises to "move cautiously and to walk in the truth, and nothing but the truth"; and as to certain heretics who had given trouble to the Baptists he says, "it would be anything else to me, to say as little as possible on the subject, than a cheering hope and pleasing anticipation to be identified with them."

Benedict, in the revision of his great history (1845), had Elder Gayle as his correspondent for the Big Hatchie Association. The Baptists seem to be getting more solidly together and moving more unitedly along Scriptural lines. Among other things in his communications it is gratifying to see this note of harmony and progress: "In 1844, at an extra meeting of the delegates from the churches of this and some of the neighboring Associations, the following questions were freely and fully discussed, and unanimously answered in the affirmative: '1. Ought each church to have her own bishop and deacons? 2. Ought the bishop to devote himself wholly to the duties of his office, and should the church sustain him in so doing? 3. Ought each church to assemble every Lord's day for public worship?' In ten years from 1835 there were added by baptism to this body upwards of twenty-four hundred members."

Elder Gayle had a fine family of eight children, two sons and six daughters. One of the daughters, Mrs. Fannie Gayle Job, was a mother to the writer when as a boy-preacher he was supply pastor of the Central Church, Memphis, during the summer of 1880. Perhaps all the family ere now are united on the "evergreen shore," where the voices of the glorified are tuned to "sing the song of Moses and the Lamb."

JAMES GILBERT.

James Gilbert, son of Hiram Gilbert, was born on Walker's Creek, in Giles County, Virginia, in the year of our Lord 1787. The family moved to Lee County, Virginia, when James was quite a lad. In 1813 he was converted and united with the Thompson Settlement Church. He was baptized by Elder Andrew Baker, the great-grandfather of Dr. Jesse Baker, and was the "last person, save one, baptized by that devoted servant of God." They went down into the water, like Philip and the eunuch, and when they had come up out of the water, the spirit of prophecy came upon the venerable man of God, and he exclaimed, "I have baptized a preacher." And so "the mantle of Elijah fell upon Elisha."

In early manhood he was married to a Miss Sarah Marshall. To them were born ten children, two of whom, John and Thomas, became able and useful ministers of the gospel.

James Gilbert enjoyed few advantages of a school-education, and never was a man of many books. But as a preacher of the old-school type he was mighty in the Scriptures, one of the ablest preachers of his day.

His ministry was largely in Virginia, where he was pastor of the Thompson Settlement Church, and did successful work as missionary and evangelist. In Tennessee, the larger part of his labors was in Hancock, Claiborne, Sullivan, and one or two other counties. Dr. I. B. Kimbrough, who as "secretary" and "agent" went almost everywhere, used to say that when he struck Powell's Valley and Lee County, Virginia, "where old Jimmy Gilbert preached," he found "nobody but Baptists." He was the founder and builder of the Mulberry Gap Church, and was pastor of Sneedville, Beech Grove, Little Sycamore, and other churches.

Of the Mulberry Gap Association he was moderator for sixteen years in succession. He presided over the conference or convention at the organization of the association (1835), and was for years the leading spirit, the "big preacher," of the association. He fought long and hard against the "anti-mission" heresy in the association. Frequently he would call some brother to occupy the moderator's chair while he went down into the arena, to "hew to pieces" the bold and defiant spirit of anti-Christ, which thus dared to lift its head among Baptists.

At other times he would turn the association into a protracted meeting. When the association met at Little Sycamore, he preached and called for penitents. The vast throng, as if moved by one impulse, came forward. Only two sinners in all the crowd were unmoved. On another occasion the association met at a private house. After the regular sermon, Brother Gilbert was called on to "conclude" the service, according to the custom of those days. The preacher arose and said, "I have a headache, brethren, and, what is worse, I have a cold heart"—but before he had talked ten minutes the fire had kindled and he was launching out on an exhortation. The audience was stirred. One woman, a "hard-shell," shouted. She had broken her iron jacket, and was shouting herself hoarse, as she came out from among the "antis" to join the "missionaries."

As a visitor to the Holston Association, when that body met with the Muddy Creek Church, Elder Gilbert was appointed to preach out of doors. His text was, "I have a message from God unto thee." In the midst of the sermon it began to rain. The preacher told his hearers they had better find shelter, but they said, "Go on!" The few umbrellas at hand were lifted. The preacher preached and the rain poured. Most of the audience were drenched, but still they listened. More than one offered to hold an umbrella over the preacher, but he said, "No; if you can listen in the rain, I can preach without a shelter."

Brother Gilbert's special gift was that of an evangelist. His greatest work was in revival meetings. He was instrumental in the conversion of more than 2,000 souls, who were added to the Lord through his ministry.

East Tennessee and the mountains have had few men, if any, who had greater power over an audience than James Gilbert. Under the lightning strokes of his fiery denunciations of sin hard-hearted sinners would quake and tremble—would sometimes fall to the floor, crying out, "Pray for me! I am a lost sinner!" A noted preacher and competent critic said of James Gilbert, that "when the spirit of exhortation was upon him he was simply irresistible."

In personal appearance, Elder Gilbert has been described by those who knew him as a man of "portly mien, tall and commanding, eyes dark and flashing, voice powerful and trumpet-like, as if given to awaken sinners and call them to judgment. His manner was grave and impressive. He had a fine delivery, and was a persuasive, melting preacher." He was also a great singer, and had a voice not only of great power but of wonderful melody and sweetness, both in preaching and singing the gospel.

January 21, 1858, this noble servant of God passed to his reward, at the age of 71. His brethren memorialized him in their Associational Minute as "an able minister of the gospel," and his death as removing "one of the few remaining ancient pillars of the sanctuary among the Baptists of East Tennessee."

This "venerable father" was laid to rest in the old graveyard under the shadow of the church at Mulberry Gap. When the writer was on the ground no stone marked his resting place. His monument is in the life he lived, the good he was enabled to do—but, some day, Baptists and others will bethink themselves and place a stone at his grave.

JOHN GILBERT.

John Gilbert, second son of Elder James Gilbert, was born in Lee County, Virginia, November 26, 1812; died in Tennessee, March 20, 1891. Converted at the age of 17, he united with the Mulberry Gap Church, Hancock County.

He was ordained to the ministry at the age of 24, and was 54 years a preacher of the gospel. He was pastor of Mulberry Gap, Thompson Settlement, Beech Grove, Sneedville; in fact, most of the churches in Hancock County and within the bounds of the Mulberry Gap Association. He was missionary and moderator of that body for a number of years.

In his twenty-third year he was married to Miss Orpha Baker, a kinswoman of Dr. Jesse Baker; and in 1852 he was married to another of the Baker family—Lydia, a daughter of Jackson Baker. The issue of the first marriage was eight children, while to the second marriage were born nine children. The responsibility of providing for two large families made it necessary for him to work hard and live hard—if he gave much time to preaching. A good deal of the time he was away from home in meetings. When at home he worked on the farm and in the tanyard, five days in the week, giving his Saturdays and Sundays to the churches.

Elder Gilbert had only an "old-field school education, but he was a great power among the churches. He possessed all the attributes of a good man. His heart was always overflowing with the love of God, and his zeal for the cause of religion never tired. He baptized 2,800 people." As to his temperamental make-up and disposition, I have been told, he "was a Woodson Taylor sort of man, smooth and conciliatory—exactly the opposite of his brother Thomas." Both were powerful preachers, in their way. In his last sickness he selected as a text for his funeral Paul's triumphant words, "I have fought the good fight," etc., with the request that "Brother Tom preach his funeral." His end was peace. His body was laid to rest in the graveyard of the Mulberry Gap Church, where it awaits the resurrection morning. His praise and the savory influence of his life are in all the churches.

THOMAS GILBERT.

Thomas, the son of Elder James Gilbert, is one of a family of ten children. He was born October 27, 1825, in Lee County, Virginia. His grandfather, Hiram Gilbert, came over from England, at an early date, and settled in Giles County, Virginia. He was a soldier in the Revolutionary War. His grandmother Gilbert was of German descent—a small, dark-skinned woman, with a heavy suit of long, wavy black hair reaching nearly to the ground.

Growing up in the mountains of Virginia and East Tennessee, where schools were poor and far between, young Gilbert had few advantages of an education. Speaking of his early life, he said he "grew in years and in sin, till converted in his twenty-second year." He dates his "conviction" for sin from a meeting held at Greasy Rock (Sneedville) by his father, James Gilbert, and his older brother, John Gilbert, who was a preacher of great power, as well as his father. For weeks he was as "the stricken deer." Like the "unclean spirit," he wandered in desert places, seeking rest and finding none." He even went over into Kentucky, to attend a meeting, but returned, still in darkness and unrest. Of this sad period of his life and experience he said:

> "How I did wander up and down,
>   And no one pitied me;
> I seemed a stranger quite unknown,
>   A child of misery."

This prolonged despair and agony he attributed to the then prevalent "blue doctrine" in regard to predestination and reprobation. He was at last found by the seeking Savior, and was converted, or "born again," November 7, 1847. But immediately he fell to doubting on this wise:

"I thought it was Satan deluding me here;
 I thought that my case was as bad as before;
 I had lost my conviction, and could not grieve more.
 But Jesus returned with a kind, loving smile,
 'To seek for your sins it is not worth your while;
 For, lo! I have nailed them all to the tree;
 You cannot retain them—but look unto me.'
 All glory to Jesus! my soul then replied;
 All glory to Jesus! for me He hath died.
 I'll show forth his praises as long as I live,
 Because He is glorious and mighty to save."

November 24, 1847, he was married to Malinda McNeal, a daughter of Neil S. McNeal. In 1849 he was licensed to preach, and in 1850 was ordained by the authority of the Sneedville Church. He was soon sent out as a "missionary" of the Mulberry Gap Association.

In 1859 and 1860 he served as missionary of the General Association of Virginia, in Lee County—baptizing hundreds of people. The next five years, during the terrible civil strife, he remained at home, preaching to the women and children, and the old men, who were not in the army, managing to live the best he could, and baptizing about 400 converts. At the close of the war the Virginia board again employed him to labor as missionary in Tazewell and Buchanan counties, at a salary of $600 a year. While in Virginia, besides his general missionary and protracted meeting work, he was pastor, first and last, of some fifteen churches.

THOMAS GILBERT.

In 1871 he resigned his work for the Richmond (Va.) Board and came to Tennessee to labor under the auspices of the Mission Board of the East Tennessee General Association. In this position he had his usual marked success.

As a pastor-evangelist, Elder Gilbert held successful meetings with nearly all the leading Baptist country and village churches over several counties in East Tennessee, frequently adding from fifty to seventy-five or eighty converts to the membership of a church from a single meeting, and often doubling the church's financial strength. Notably was this true in the counties of Claiborne, Hancock, Hawkins, Hamblen, Greene, Grainger, Jefferson, and Cocke. Nearly all the churches of the last-named county received wonderful ingatherings from Brother Gilbert's meetings. It was through his instrumentality and as a result of his great meeting (February, 1876) that the Newport Church was organized, and the money, for the most part, raised, to build their first house of worship.

He was pastor of the following churches: Union Grove, Big Spring, Concord, Warrensburg, Persia, Antioch, Bethel, Clay Creek, and Pleasant Grove. As pastor he indoctrinated his churches faithfully, teaching and urging them to give to all good causes—pastoral and ministerial support not excepted.

Elder Gilbert witnessed in his meetings about 4,000 conversions and baptisms; and, being always and on all occasions a "doctrinal" preacher and making revival meetings a special occasion for preaching on baptism, "close communion," the doctrine of a New Testament church, and the duty of the churches to support the gospel, he never failed to baptize about all the converts in his meetings, or to get an adequate remuneration for his services.

Elder Gilbert was combative in disposition, and frequently aroused opposition—sometimes made enemies; but he baptized many a sinner, and many a pedo-Baptist as well, whom he first made mad. His preaching generally bordered on the controversial; and if at any time it seemed to him necessary to defend the truth by public debate, he rather gloried in it. During his ministry he had some five or six public debates with the local champions of the Methodist or Presbyterian faith, and never failed to acquit himself creditably or fully sustain the Baptist position.

In his palmy days few men were more powerful in exhortation than Brother Gilbert; not many were better acquainted with the human mind, or better understood the plan of salva-

12

tion. In dealing with inquirers he was like a skillful physician who understands the disease and knows the remedy and how to apply it.

For half a century Thomas Gilbert was a true yoke-fellow in the gospel with Asa Routh. The last time the writer saw him he was a battle-scarred veteran, retired from the field of conflict but with the trophies of victory about him—a good deal of the old-time fire in him still. "Monday morning I drop in on Brother T. Gilbert at Whitesburg, and find him still suffering with rheumatism but joyously conversing with his brethren about the Lord's work and the condition of our Baptist Zion." (J. J. B., February 9, 1899.)

Brother Gilbert answered the summons to "depart and be with Christ," February 11, 1904; and was followed to the better land by his son, Henry Gilbert, who was a useful minister, March 27, 1909.

By report of committee and unanimous vote the Nolachucky Association memorialized Elder Thomas Gilbert as an "able and effective minister, performing more hard labor, baptizing more people, and organizing more churches than any other single preacher, perhaps, in all the surrounding country—being sound in the faith, bold in defense of the truth; he at last stacked arms at the feet of his great Commander, received an honorable discharge, and went Home to join in a re-union with his worthy comrades, Routh, Baker, and Brown." (J. B. Bundren, for committee.)

JEPTHA B. GINN.

Jeptha B. Ginn, son of Sherwood Ginn, was born in Georgia, November 15, 1815. He came to Tennessee when 16 years of age. He was of Irish descent, belonged to a poor family, and got a late start in life. At the age of 19 he was married to Sarah Davis, a daughter of Michael and Nancy Davis, to whom were born eight children.   November 6, 1862, he was married a second time, to a daughter of Edmund and Sallie Davis. By his last wife he had a family of seven children.

He never went to school enough to "go through the blue-back speller," it is said; and never learned to read till he was married.   His first wife was a "good reader and taught her husband to read."   He was converted at the age of 40, and commenced to preach at once.   He owned a poor farm, but had a large family to support, which means that he had very little time to study.   His equipment for preaching was Bible and hymn-book, and Barnes' Notes on The New Testament.   He was a member of Mount Olive Church, Blount County.

He was pastor of New Hopewell, Miller's Cove, Tuckalee-chee Cove, Nail's Creek, Sinking Creek, Ware's Valley, Six-Mile, and other churches.   I am told he was "earnest and consecrated, a good exhorter, and did a great deal of good in the mountains and coves.   He was a fiery speaker, and depended too much on the thunder and not enough on the light-ning of his power—and killed himself by over-exertion in preaching."

As missionary evangelist in Knox and Blount counties Brother Ginn did a good work in strengthening many of the weak churches.

As pastor, few men of his day, even in the mountains, were more poorly paid.   He was not the first nor the only preacher that has had to wear "seedy clothes."   His farm gave him a scanty support, large as was his family; his churches were poor, as a rule, and not trained to give, and the pastor had not been trained to train them.   As a result the preacher's clothing was generally "the worse for wear," and his family had to skimp.   I was informed by a reliable party that he preached for a certain church a whole year and didn't collect salary enough to "keep his horse shod."

He passed from labor to reward April 27, 1879.

N. B. GOFORTH.

(The substance of the following sketch was published in the *Baptist and Reflector*, July 28, 1898.)

With this sketch appears the striking and familiar face of one of East Tennessee's pioneer preacher-educators, Dr. N. B. Goforth, erstwhile president of what was to be Carson and Newman College. The subject of our sketch is the son of Hugh and Mary Goforth, and was born in Sevier County, Tennessee, May 20, 1828. On the paternal side he is of English descent, his grandfather, William Goforth, having descended from one of three brothers, who (according to a family coat-of-arms) came from England early in the seventeenth century, one settling in Pennsylvania, one in North Carolina, and one in Virginia. Dr. Goforth belongs to the Virginia branch of the family, and was named for the famous French emperor and noted man of destiny, Napoleon Bonaparte.

Young Goforth spent his boyhood days on the farm, in his native county, with few advantages of an education. In his nineteenth year, at Central Campground, under the soul-stirring preaching of William Billue and Joseph Manning, he was converted, and, uniting with Boyd's Creek Church, was baptized by Elder Manning in Pigeon River. In his twenty-second year he attended school at Sevierville. At the age of 23 he entered Maryville College, where he took a four years' course, graduating in 1854. His "A.M." degree he received later, from the Mossy Creek Baptist College, as also the honorary title, Doctor of Divinity. In college he was a hard student, having a special fondness for the classics and being most proficient in Latin. In May, 1855, he was called to the chair of languages in Mossy Creek College. In 1859 he became president of the college and continued as such till the school was broken up by the ruthless hand of war in 1862.

December 24, 1856, he was married to Miss R. A. Pattison, daughter of Nathan and Rebecca Pattison, of Jefferson County. This union was blessed with a large family of children.

In 1859 he was ordained by Boyd's Creek Church, Elders William Billue, W. M. Burnett, William Ellis, and C. C. Tipton constituting the presbytery. His first pastorate was that of the Mossy Creek Church, and his first official work was the

REV. N. B. GOFORTH, D.D.

baptism of nineteen college students. He has since been pastor of the Riceville, Mouse Creek, Eastanallee, Hiwassee, Mount Harmony, Double Springs, New Hopewell, and other churches in East Tennessee, and of three churches in Texas, during his short sojourn in that State.

But his greatest work has been that of teacher, rather than pastor. At the close of the war, in connection with Prof. W. A. G. Brown, a true yoke-fellow, he established the Riceville Literary and Classical Institute, and taught in the same till December of 1870, when he was re-called to the presidency of Mossy Creek College, which position he held for twelve more years, resigning in 1882. He then returned to Riceville, where he has been teaching and preaching, with a short vacation or two, for the last sixteen years. Eighteen years of successful teaching at Mossy Creek and twenty at Riceville, working ten hours a day and preaching on Saturdays and Sundays, is an enviable record.

Hundreds of young men, from all parts of East Tennessee and elsewhere, received mental and moral quickening from Dr. Goforth at Mossy Creek, and had their lives shaped by his molding touch. Under his influence the mind of many a dull boy waked up and felt the thrill of a new life. He was not only a successful teacher but a great moral force in the school. As a disciplinarian he had few equals. The observance of a few reasonable rules and a moral purpose to study and to get an education was emphasized as the law of the school and the "whole duty" of the student. If the moral purpose was found wanting, the student was not wanted in the school, and was sent home, or elsewhere, till he came to a better mind.

Dr. Goforth was characterized by mental energy and rugged strength rather than polish; he was a diamond in the rough. He believed in *education,* in the truest sense of the word— training, discipline—rather than polish or cramming; and, teaching by example, his life bore fruit in that direction. He was naturally a good metaphysician and logician, and taught metaphysics and logic, as well as theology, but he was most at home in the dead languages.

His work at Mossy Creek was measurably pioneer work in the educational line, paving the way for those that were to come after him. With rude implements, so to speak, that is, with meager equipment in the way of buildings, apparatus and endowment, and with a maximum salary, perhaps, of $500, he and his colleagues did a work for the Baptists of East Tennessee that deserves their most cordial recognition and sincerest thanks. In that group of familiar names—Prof. R. R. Bryan, William Rogers, Dr. M. Hillsman, Dr. Jesse Baker, and the Russells (W. T. and T. R.)—let us give Dr. N. B. Goforth an honored place as a worthy pioneer of higher Christian education for our East Tennessee Baptist Zion and the youth who look to us for light and guidance.

Dr. Goforth believes in the religious training of the young people as well as their intellectual development, and is therefore a great advocate of Sunday schools, or Bible schools, as he prefers to call them—believing that the churches of the future will assuredly be just what we make out of the boys and girls in our homes and Bible study schools today.

Since writing the above we had an occasion to visit Dr. Goforth in his Riceville home. He had had the misfortune to fall and seriously injure one of his hips. He is perhaps permanently injured. Without suffering much pain, he sits in his easy chair and cheerfully talks about "the first rest" he has ever had, and letting others "do the work." He has a "supply" preacher for his church (Riceville), and his daughter and another young lady have charge of his school. The doctor hopes sometime to get out and "talk Sunday Schools and Missions."

NOTE: He has entered the "city that hath foundations, whose builder and maker is God."

J. R. GRAVES.

Distinguished *editor, author, publisher,* fearless *advocate* and faithful *defender* of the *New Testament system* of *doctrines, champion* of the God-given *prerogatives* of a *New Testament church, pulpit orator.*

Dr. Graves was born in Chester, Vermont, April 10, 1820. He was the son of Z. C. Graves, a well-to-do merchant, and a grandson of a French Huguenot who "fled to America," after most of his ancestors "had perished" in the persecution which followed the revocation of the edict of Nantes. His mother was the granddaughter of a distinguished German physician and scholar by the name of Schnell. Dr. Graves was the youngest of three children. President Z. C. Graves, of the Mary Sharpe College, was an older brother, and Mrs. L. M. Marks was his sister. The loss of his father by sudden death, when young Graves was only three weeks old, and the subsequent loss, to the widow and children, of an estate involved in a partnership business, were seemingly unfortunate events, but proved in the end to be "blessings in disguise"; the youngsters, of necessity, were brought up to work and save, and formed habits of self-reliance. At the age of fifteen James was converted and baptized, uniting with a Baptist church in Vermont. In his nineteenth year he was elected principal of the Kingsville Academy, in Ohio, where he remained and taught for two years. He then went to Kentucky and took charge of Clear Creek Academy, near Nicholasville. Uniting with Mount Freedom Church, Kentucky, he was "licensed" to preach, but without his knowledge or consent. For so great a work he felt himself wholly unqualified. But he believed in preparedness for any calling and in hard work as an essential to suc cess. He was notably a self-educated, self-made man. For four years he gave six hours a day to teaching and eight hours to private study, covering a college course without a teacher, and mastering a modern language each year. Meanwhile he was

digging into his Bible, with great admiration for Paul as a
model preacher, and purposing in his heart to be himself a
preacher when he should be "qualified" for a calling so high
and holy. At the age of 24 he was called to ordination and
set apart to the work of the ministry, Dr. Dillard, of Kentucky,
being chairman of the "council" and preacher of the ordination sermon.

DR. J. R. GRAVES.

July 3, 1845, at the age of 25, he came to Nashville and opened, in a rented building, the "Vine Street Classical and Mathematical Academy," joining "by letter" the First Baptist Church. In the fall of the same year he took charge of the Second (now the Central) Baptist Church, served the church one year as pastor, but declined further service, in order to become associated with Dr. R. B. C. Howell as one of the editors of *The Baptist.* His connection with the paper was editorially announced November 21, 1846, as follows: "We have the pleasure of announcing to our readers that the committee of publication have, at length, succeeded in procuring the services of an assistant editor for this paper, whom we here introduce in the person of our beloved Brother J. R. Graves, the indefatigable and successful pastor of the Second Baptist Church in this city. Brother Graves is already favorably known to many of you as an eloquent speaker and a very handsome writer." This was the beginning of an editorial career which lasted nearly half a century.

As *editor,* Dr. Graves wielded a facile and a pungent pen, and, week after week, did a prodigious amount of editorial and other work. When he took charge of *The Baptist* he was only locally known, and his paper had about 1,000 subscribers; at the beginning of the Civil War it had attained the largest circulation, it was claimed, of any Baptist paper in the world; and no man in the South was more widely known than its editor, or had a greater influence upon the denomination. In addition to editing and publishing his great paper he edited a monthly, a quarterly and an annual, besides editing hymn-books for our churches and the great numbers of standard works issued from the presses of the Southwestern Publishing House, such as Robinson's History of Baptism, Wall's History of Infant Baptism, Orchard's History of Foreign and English Baptists, Moses Stuart on Baptism, and other similar works— a character and volume of literature that necessarily influenced in a marked degree the thinking, the pulpit teaching and the denominational life of the Baptist people.

As *author,* he wrote and published, among other works, the following: The Desire of All Nations, The Watchman's Reply, The Trilemma, The First Baptist Church in America, The Little Iron Wheel, The Great Iron Wheel, The Bible Doctrine of the Middle Life, The Exposition of Modern Spiritism, Old Landmarkism—What Is It? and The Work of Christ in Seven Dispensations. Most of these works, as nearly all of his writings, were of a controversial nature and exerted a distinct influence wherever read.

As an *organizer* and *promoter* of Baptist interests he originated the first ministers' institute in the State, and perhaps in the South, to train and equip pastors and help young ministers who were unable to attend theological schools. Without salary, or other compensation, he raised funds for the endowment of a theological chair in Union University, and without "fee or reward" he solicited and collected funds and other equipment with which to start the Mary Sharpe College—and drafted its "admirable curriculum." In 1848 he planned and set on foot the Southwestern Publishing House, Nashville, for the publication and dissemination of a sound Baptist literature, and later was instrumental in establishing the Southern Baptist Sunday School Union. Both these institutions did great good, and promised large success, but were destined to be destroyed by the Civil War. In 1870 he submitted to the Big Hatchie Association the plan and constitution of a Southern Baptist Publication Society, and, in 1874, turned over to the society $130,000 in cash and bonds; but the financial crisis which followed, and other adverse conditions, wrecked the society's plans and caused its suspension.

As a *logician* and *thinker,* he was masterful and lucid, possessing in a high degree the gift which enabled him to so state his propositions that they came from his lips or pen with the force of axiomatic principles or self-evident truths. A

judge in the city of Memphis, lecturing the bar on the importance of a clear statement of propositions, said: "The gift
is as rare as genius, but may be cultivated. Of living ministers I know of no one who possesses it in a higher degree
than Dr. Graves of the First Baptist Church in this city. He
lays down his propositions so clearly that they come with the
force of axioms, that need no demonstration—you can see all
through and all around them." (Borum.)

As a *polemic, controversialist, debater,* Dr. Graves was a
master. He was quite certain that he, and every other divinely
called Baptist preacher was set for the *defense* as well as
the propagation of the truth, that he was directly commis-
sioned by the great Head of the Church to contend earnestly
for the faith delivered "once for all" to the saints; and this
he did amidst shot and shell from every quarter throughout
a stormy life. His conviction in regard to truth and duty
forced him to unsheath the sword—"the sword of the Lord
and of Gideon," against the Lord's enemies, against *error*—
and the sword was never sheathed; he fell fighting. Dr. Graves
had something like a dozen public oral discussions with representatives of other denominations, the last one, "The Graves-
Ditzler Debate," being a two weeks' discussion with Dr. Jacob
Ditzler, a professional debater of the Methodist persuasion.
The debate was published, making a volume of several hundred pages, and was widely read. This contest has been called
the "battle of the giants;" in it Dr. Graves fully sustained his
reputation for fairness and scholarship, for ability and skill
as a debater, and again proved himself to be a fearless, peer-
less and successful champion of Baptist and New Testament
orthodoxy. He did not lend himself and his great powers to
sarcasm and invective, vices all too common in polemical discussion. His one serious purpose was the refutation of error
by correct interpretation of the Scriptures and sound reasoning. He would be courteous toward his opponent, but not at
the expense of loyalty to Christ. He esteemed loyalty to Christ

and his truth, above everything else, a cardinal virtue in a Christian minister. He found no Scripture which commanded him to love error, or tolerate false doctrine; and if in his zeal for the truth and in the heat of debate he failed to exemplify perfectly the apostolic injunction to speak the truth "in love" (which is ideal), and if in his effort to cut off the head of error with the sword of truth he decapitated the errorist at the same time—that only proves that he was "human." The truth is, that while Dr. Graves could not make much allowance for the *teachers* of error he very greatly sympathized with the *common people* who, blindfolded, were led into the ditch by their "blind guides." The spirit and bearing of Dr. Graves, among his brethren and elsewhere, also his appearance and márked personality, are justly represented in the following newspaper reports: "On the rostrum sits Dr. Graves, upon whose forehead is stamped strength, activity and vim, whose power from the press and pulpit is felt and acknowledged all over the Southwest; a man on whose every lineament is strongly marked immobility and stern inflexibility, driving with ungloved hand his Damascus blade into the vitals of error—a bold and fearless defender of the faith; yet gentle and meek as a child."

"One of the most quiet and unassuming men in the convention is the great landmark champion and upholder of the most strictly Baptist principles, Dr. J. R. Graves, formerly of this city but now of Memphis, editor and proprietor of *The Baptist.*" (*Nashville American.*)

"In personal appearance Dr. Graves is about five feet ten inches high, will weigh about 160 pounds, and has a fine face with a well-balanced head. His dark and almost black eyes show the true ring of metal, his fine brow and broad forehead give evidence (from the phrenologist's point of view) of a more than ordinary brain, his finely chiseled nose marks him as a man possessed of penetrating thought, indomitable zeal and energy, his mouth is expressive of sublime sentiments,

and upon the whole his physiognomy indicates great reasoning ability. His discourse, full of unction, full of logic, was
eloquent and convincing." "As an orator, he is very powerful,
and as a writer he unites strength, pointedness and clearness.
He is fearless and boldly avows his sentiments and opinions,
though they may differ much from those of others."

"He has a wonderful command over his audiences, holding
them spellbound for hours at a time. He uses no clap-trap,
no trick of oratory, no prettiness of speech, but he is deeply
in earnest, utters the strong convictions of his own mind and
carries his hearers with him as by the force of a tornado.
Teachers, doctors, lawyers, judges, statesmen, as well as the
illiterate, all go to hear him, and bow before his power. Men
bitterly prejudiced and hating him, hear him and are fascinated, go away resolved never to hear him again, but break
their vows and hear him as often as they have opportunity.
His sermons are mostly doctrinal and as a rule strongly controversial. He is a great preacher, in the best sense of the
word."

Controversial as he was and with all his fierce antagonism
to error, he was nevertheless a gospel preacher in the fullest
sense of the term. He never failed to emphasize the vital doctrines of grace and the necessity of the new birth. As in
ancient times, "all roads led to Rome," so in Dr. Graves'
preaching, "all roads" led to Christ and the plan of salvation.
Great crowds went great distances to hear him, not altogether
or mainly through curiosity, not because he was personally
magnetic, which he was, but because they wanted to hear a
man who was master of great subjects as well as of assemblies
discuss the great doctrines of the Word of God. The writer,
when a boy, went thirty miles to see and hear J. R. Graves,
of the *Tennessee Baptist* and the *Great Iron Wheel,* and listened closely to a two hours' sermon, a part of the time
standing.

It is not generally known, I believe, that Dr. Graves was a specially gifted revivalist; it is of record, however, that in his earlier ministry and before he was thirty years old he had witnessed, in special meetings and under his immediate ministry, more than thirteen hundred conversions.

We have spoken of Dr. Graves as the author and recognized champion of a system of teaching known as "old landmarkism." The system, the author claims, is contained, expressly or by necessary inference, in the New Testament Scriptures, and consists of ten distinct points of doctrine, constituting, like the ten commandments, an organic whole, so that, in the author's view, to "break one" is to "break all."

The title of the little book was suggested by two Old Testament Scriptures, "Remove not the ancient landmarks which thy fathers have set" (Solomon), and "Some remove the old landmarks" (Job). I let Dr. Graves state the points himself, since his book is before me. At the close of chapter XI he asks the question, What is the mission of landmark Baptists? and his tenfold answer constitutes the substance of old landmarkism: 1. As Baptists we are to stand for the supreme authority of the New Testament as our only and sufficient rule of faith and practice. This is *the* distinguishing doctrine of our denomination. 2. As Baptists we are to stand for the ordinances of Christ as he enjoined them upon his followers, unchanged and unchangeable till he come. 3. As Baptists we are to stand for a spiritual and regenerated church, the motto on our banner being, *Christ before the church, blood before water*. 4. To protest, and to use all our influence, against the recognition on the part of Baptists of human societies as scriptural churches, by affiliation, ministerial or ecclesiastical, or by any alliance, etc., that could be interpreted as putting such societies on an equality with Baptist churches. 5. To preserve and perpetuate the doctrine of the divine origin and sanctity of the churches of Christ, their unbroken continuity, etc. 6. To preserve and perpetuate the *divine, inalienable* and *sole* prerogatives of a Christian church, (1) to preach the gospel, (2) to select and ordain her own officers, (3) to control absolutely her own ordinances. 7. To preserve and perpetuate the scriptural design of baptism, and its validity and recognition only when scripturally administered by a gospel church. 8. To preserve and perpetuate the true design and symbolism of the Lord's Supper, as a *local church* ordinance, and for but *one* purpose—the commemoration of the sacrificial death of Christ, and not as a *denominational* ordinance, etc. 9. To preserve and perpetuate the doctrine of a divinely called and scripturally qualified and ordained ministry, holding office and acting for and under the direction of local churches alone. 10. To preserve the primitive fealty and faithfulness to the truth, that shunned not to declare the whole counsel of God, and to teach men to observe all things whatsoever Christ commanded to be believed and obeyed. This is the author's own synopsis of his system, to which he adds these words: "Not the belief and advocacy of one or two of these principles constitutes a full old landmark Baptist, but the cordial reception and advocacy of all of them." Of course these are not intended to be the landmarks bounding the whole Biblical system of truth or of Christianity, but only the landmarks of a New Testament church. He contended most earnestly for the preservation of all the great landmarks of the world's spiritual heritage in the truth of God; not only for the local church and church ordinances, but for (1) the inerrancy, the all-sufficiency and supreme authority of the Scriptures; (2) the proper deity and atoning work of Christ; (3) justification by faith; and (4) the personality, power and work of the Holy Spirit—landmarks, and more than landmarks, the very *essence* of Christianity, to be preserved at any cost by the churches of the nineteenth and twentieth centuries.

As to the acceptance by the denomination of Dr. Graves' view of a New Testament church and its ordinances, it may be said: 1. Many brethren (pastors and churches) gave him their endorsement and adherence, avowing their full belief in the landmark system, going the full figure and refusing to "commune" except in the local church where they held their membership, and only with fellow-members of the same church. 2. Other churches and pastors, making a difference between membership rights and nonmembership privileges and recognizing the doctrinal unity and solidarity of the Baptist family, continued the practice, as aforetime, of so-called "inter-communion," the members of one Baptist church communing, upon invitation, with members of another Baptist church. 3. Still other churches (but very few in the South or Southwest), holding that the ordinances belong to the "kingdom" and not to the local churches and considering that the validity of baptism depends upon only two necessary things, no more and no less, that is, the right faith and the right act (immersion in water), continued the practice of recognizing so-called "alien immersion," or the immersion of a professed believer by a denomination other than Baptist, or by no denomination, and at the same time practiced, accordingly, a communion more or less unrestricted. As to the question of "church succession" the denomination has ever been divided. Everyone who believes the Bible believes, of course, in some sort of succession, perpetuity or continuity for the church builded by the Christ; and certainly every true Baptist is interested in discovering and verifying the succession promised by the great Head of the Church, and would be glad to see any visible foot-prints, to catch any possible glimpse, of a genuine Baptist or New Testament church along the track of history through the "dark age" of Catholic apostasy and Romish persecution, when the true church was evidently "in the wilderness," whither she had been driven by Satanic power and where she was "nourished" and preserved by her divine Lord. But whatever may be the truth of history and whatever our individual beliefs may be in regard to the question of succession, all must admit, I think, that "visible" succession, however well or however

13

poorly established, is not the most vital thing about a church; the *vital* thing is that it succeeds directly from Christ and the New Testament. The subject has its difficulties, involving three questions of importance: (1) a question of correct interpretation of a passage of Scripture; (2) a question of history; (3) a question of emphasis. Dr. J. B. Gambrell's illustration of the "lost horse" gives the gist and relative merit of Baptist contention and Baptist differences on this point. "I do not place much stress," he says, "on historical succession—but the New Testament reads as though things were started to go on. Let me illustrate my idea of succession: A man lost a gray horse. He finds some horse tracks step by step for a hundred miles. Then he comes upon the horse—but it is a black horse. That is historical succession. Tracks are not worth a cent. If, on the other hand, you find the gray horse, it does not make any difference if you do not find any tracks. The whole business lies in the identity; we have the horse hunted for. So, the man who takes the New Testament and finds a church in his neighborhood or elsewhere like the one in the Book, has succession." This puts the main emphasis in the right place, while it may be thought to depreciate in a measure, at least inferentially, the value of a history of an ancient and "peculiar people" with whose fortunes have been bound up in an age-long conflict the fortunes of the kingdom of God. In this connection I may be permitted to say that while Dr. Graves was a successionist there is no evidence, I think, that he put undue emphasis on the fact of succession or on any sort of "mother-church" notion; he did emphasize church *authority* and with apostolic zeal contended for the recognition of the same.

As to the "validity" of ordinances the Baptists of the South and Southwest stand almost solidly for four *necessary* things: A proper subject (a believer), a proper act in baptism (immersion), a proper design (to show forth), and the proper authority (a New Testament church)—all these being held as Scriptural requirements conditioning the valid administration

of baptism and the Lord's supper alike. The Baptists of the
North and East, we think, are coming, and will come, more
and more to this position—a position that would seem necessary, if Baptists are to justify their continued existence as a
separate denomination and assure for themselves a denominational future.

And these results, it must be admitted, have come about,
in large measure, through Dr. Graves' strenuous contention
for a "thus saith the Lord" in all matters of religion. His
slogan was "back to the New Testament," and whatever may
be our theory or practice in regard to some of the questions
involved, or supposed to be involved, in landmarkism, there
can be no doubt that Dr. Graves' manifold contention and protest, by voice and pen, has been a great service not only to
the Baptists but to the whole religious world. For well nigh
half a century he stood as a bulwark against error, as a mighty
breakwater against the incoming flood of a false liberalism
which is the constant menace of a pure Christianity in a
"Laodicean age." Corroborating this view is the statement
of Dr. E. T. Winkler, editor of the *Alabama Baptist:* "Extreme as the views of Dr. Graves have by many been regarded
as being, there is no question that they have powerfully contributed to the correction of a false liberalism that was current in many quarters thirty years ago." Dr. S. H. Ford, in
his *Christian Repository,* endorsed this statement, adding these
words: "We differ with Dr. Graves in some things, but honor
his heroic life-work in meeting and exposing error wherever
uttered." Dr. Cathcart, in the *Baptist Enclycopedia,* speaking
for Northern Baptists, says: "Dr. Graves in his peculiarities
represents a section of the Baptist denomination, a conscientious and devoted portion of our great apostolic community,
but in his earnest and generous zeal for our heaven-inspired
principles he represents all thorough Baptists throughout the
ages and the nations."

Dr. Graves, as already indicated, took a great interest in young preachers. He was jealous of any influence that might affect their moral or doctrinal stamina, or turn them aside from apostolic ways. He was ever anxious that our theological seminaries turn out New Testament prophets after the order of Paul and John the Baptist. The writer has a vivid recollection of his first personal acquaintance with Dr. Graves. It was during a seminary vacation and while acting as a supply-pastor for a church in Memphis. In going his rounds he dropped into the office of *The Baptist* to have a talk with the editor. Though busy furnishing "copy" to the printer, he arose from his desk to greet his visitor, but most of the greeting, as we remember, was a sudden and dramatic reference to a "Jacob staff," a "Gunter's chain" and a "compass." For five or ten minutes he warmed to his subject, giving the young preacher "points" on theological surveying, running boundary and divisional lines, giving metes and bounds, establishing corners, setting up landmarks, etc., that in future generations no "true Israelite might ever lose his inheritance"; in it all laying special emphasis on the fact that there is and can be no true "orientation" of doctrines, creeds and systems, except as they are brought to and examined in the light of the New Testament Scriptures.

Dr. Graves was a thorough believer in the *equality* and spiritual democracy of all believers, and was opposed to a minister accepting any title of distinction that would put him above or apart from his brethren. For this reason he refused more than once to be made a D.D. Whether or not he accepted the LL.D. conferred upon him by Union University and appearing after his name on the title page of some of his works, I cannot speak advisedly. Perhaps the publisher, following a time-honored custom, used his own discretion in the matter.

Dr. Graves was a popular presiding officer and a skilled parliamentarian, presiding with dignity and consideration for his brethren. He knew how to preserve order and dispatch business, and was ever watchful in keeping from before a Baptist deliberative and advisory body matters over which it could have no jurisdiction. He was frequently president of the West Tennessee Baptist Convention and for a number of years was moderator of the Big Hatchie Association.

Dr. Graves was married three times—all "fortunate" marriages, his companions being women of "taste and refinement." His first marriage (1845) was without issue. His second and third wives were sisters, Miss Lou and Miss Georgie Snider, daughters of Dr. George Snider. The living children of the second marriage are Mrs. O. L. Hailey and James R. Graves, of Dallas, Texas, and Mrs. R. H. Wood, San Antonio, Texas. The living children of the third marriage are W. C. Graves and Z. Calvin Graves, of Memphis, Tenn. Mrs. Dr. Graves still lives at the old Graves' home, once "Arcadia," in a delightful suburb of Memphis, now part and parcel of the city. About to leave the city, I stopped in to see her, and found her on the "sunny side" of life, bright and cheerful, and delightfully reminiscent, at the age of 75. Dr. and Mrs. Hailey have four sons who are officers in the United States Army, and another one "wanting in." Mrs. Wood has a son in the army and a daughter training for Red Cross work. W. C. Graves has one son, "Captain Will," in the infantry. So Dr. Graves, in his grandsons in the world war, is helping his ancestral country, France.

Dr. Graves died at Memphis, Tenn., closing his earthly career, June 26, 1893.

In this sketch the writer has purposely refrained from eulogy, believing that facts are more eloquent than eulogistic words. As to Dr. Graves' gifts as an orator many competent judges will agree in the opinion and endorse the unqualified statement of one of our ablest speakers and writers when he says: "I regard J. R. Graves as the greatest orator America ever produced in any calling."

The following article, entitled "The Greatest Sermon I
Ever Heard," was written some years ago for the press by
Dr. J. B. Gambrell, and was copied by several religious papers.
The writer clipped the article, intending to give it a place in
the appendix to this volume. The clipping was unfortunately
lost. But the author, at our request, has kindly reproduced
the scene from memory, and I append the article here, letting
it serve as a climax for my sketch.

THE GREATEST SERMON I EVER HEARD.

By J. B. Gambrell, D.D.

The place was in a village church in Mississippi. ·The time
was Saturday. The community had been for years a battle-
ground for the Baptists and the Methodists. The Baptists
were weak and the Methodists strong. Dr. Graves had been
invited to come and preach on Sunday, and not being well
he came on Saturday. My pastorate was near by and I went
on Saturday to meet him, expecting that he would preach,
since it was the regular Saturday conference day. It was
generally understood that he would be there and a hundred
or so people turned out—among them a number of prominent
Pedo-Baptists, notably an elegant and elegantly-dressed Pedo-
Baptist lady. Under strong pressure Dr. Graves agreed to
talk—said he was not well enough to preach. His subject was
"The Rending of the Veil of the Temple." His reading of
the incident was magnetic and marvelous. Then he began
to talk, very quietly. He reproduced the scene in Pilate's hall,
the journey to Golgotha, the tragic nailing of the Savior to
the cross, the jeering crowd, the weeping disciples—all of it.
The congregation, subdued and moved, saw it all. We were
there, beholding. The description went on until the dying
Savior's cry was uttered, and then the scene shifted back to
the temple where the thickly twined veil, impenetrable to
human eyes, by an invisible force was rent in twain and rolled

back, exposing the Holy of Holies. An awe, inexpressible, was on every soul. Then the preacher began the expository part of the sermon—what it all meant. He, of course, followed the Scripture teaching. The days of the human priest were over, and direct access to a throne of mercy was guaranteed to every human soul. One passage in the sermon was the most striking piece of description I ever heard. It cannot be reproduced, because a good deal of it was by gestures. He described the long line of mitred priests passing into the history of the past and out of the lives of the people, to give Christ not only the pre-eminence in the priestly office but to leave him alone forever in that office. Then there was another line of discussion. It was a merciless *exposé* of the folly and assumption of all priestly functions affected by men of today. With withering sarcasm the preacher ridiculed people who go back beyond the cross and beyond Christ to get their religion out of the old Jewish economy. Here infant baptism came in for a merciless excoriation. While this was going on, the finely dressed lady, above referred to, rose in her place at the back of the house and came down the aisle, with her nose in the air, entering her protest against the preaching at this point by quitting the place. She had to pass out right by the pulpit. Dr. Graves was looking somewhat in the other direction, but when she came near he turned and with a compelling gesture said, "Sit down, lady, sit down! This may be the only chance that will ever be given you for your soul. Stay and hear me through." The lady dropped into her seat almost as if she had been struck by a pile-driver. Then the discussion turned again. All irony was out of his voice and with a pathos and power unexcelled he preached salvation through Christ, the one great High Priest, offering his own blood a sacrifice for sinners. The lady's face began to relax—the tears came. She felt among the flounces of her elegant dress for her handkerchief; she might have had one, but she never found it. The tears rained off her face. The sermon was over,

the benediction pronounced. Without waiting for an introduction the lady, springing to her feet, rushed to Dr. Graves,
saying: "I will thank God to the longest day I live that you
did not let me go. I see it now. I always thought I had to
work to save myself, but Christ saves me." The conference
had been omitted, and the people silently went their ways.

This is an imperfect sketch of the greatest sermon I ever
heard.

Z. C. GRAVES.

Veteran teacher, lover of learning, pioneer of higher education for women, for more than a third of a century president of Mary Sharpe College.

The subject of this sketch was the oldest of a family of
three children, and the namesake of his father, Z. C. Graves.
a well-to-do merchant in the State of Vermont. President
Graves was born in Chester, Vermont, in 1816. He was of
French extraction and a lineal descendant of the French Huguenots. In early life he was lacking in robustness and on
the advice of a physician was sent to the country to build up
a stronger body on pure air and plain living in God's out-of-
doors. Here he remained till he was sixteen, working on a
farm through the crop season and through the winter months
going to school. In his seventeenth year he made a profession
of faith in Christ, uniting with the Baptist church in North
Springfield. He now returned home to enter Chester Academy,
where he prosecuted his classical and mathematical studies for
five or six terms. Leaving his home school for better educational advantages, he entered the Baptist Normal High School,
at Ludlow, where he further pursued his studies, supporting
himself by teaching district schools through the winter months.
The success of these winter schools and his genius for school
management marked him out as a "coming teacher" long before his education was completed. At the age of 21 he went

DR. Z. C. GRAVES,
PRESIDENT MARY SHARP COLLEGE.

West and opened a private school at Ashtabula, Ohio, and a little later succeeded his brother, J. R. Graves, as principal of Kingsville Academy, a historic school in a neat little village on the shore of Lake Erie. In this institution men who have become "eminent as jurists and statesmen, missionaries, professors and college presidents, received their academic training" under the instructions and vitalizing touch of Z. C. Graves. Here he married Miss Adelia C. Spencer, an intellectual and accomplished woman, who, in later years, was to be known as the author of "Jephtha's Daughter," a poem of merit and promise, and more widely known, in literary circles, as the author of "Seclusaval, or the Arts of Romanism." She was also to leave her impress on hundreds of young women of the South as "matron" of the Mary Sharpe College.

It is as a *pioneer of higher education for women* in Tennessee and the Southland and as president of Mary Sharpe College that Z. C. Graves did monumental work. Through the efforts of his brother, J. R. Graves, who had preceded him, five years or more, in pioneer work in Tennessee, the Mary Sharpe had been founded at Winchester, Tenn., in the year 1850; and when the school was ready to be opened Z. C. Graves was elected its first president, which position he held with distinguished ability and success for more than a third of a century. The aim of the president was to give girls a "classical education; an education as thorough as their brothers had been acquiring at their colleges and universities." It was his ambition and plea for women that they should have the "same knowledge, literary, scientific and classical, that had been for so many generations the peculiar and cherished heritage of the other sex; that the sister should be placed on an equality with the brother, for the development and unfolding of all the qualities of her mind, thus making her what she was designed to be by her Creator, a thinking, reflecting, reasoning being, capable of comparing and judging for herself, and dependent upon none other for her free, unbiased opinion." The Mary Sharpe curriculum, it is rightly claimed, was practically equal to that of Brown University, and it was intended that her graduates should be able to pass an examination with the seniors of that university, or of the University of Virginia. If space permitted it would be interesting to note the varied and extended courses of study prescribed in her catalogues for four years of proper college work rigidly required in order to graduation; and the claim of Mary Sharpe to being the first college in the United States to make a thorough study of both Latin and Greek necessary to graduation has not been seriously challenged. The Mary Sharpe has been called "the Vassar of the South." And in that delightful little book, "Before Vassar Opened," a valuable "contribution to the history of the higher education of women in America," by Dr. James Monroe Taylor, the author, with piles of documentary evidence from all quarters before him, frankly admits that the Mary Sharpe "was veritably a pioneer, ten years before Vassar," and while claiming a more "developed curriculum" for Vassar, when that institution was fully established, does not hesitate to concede to the Mary Sharpe that hers "was certainly the most developed curriculum of which we find clear evidence, ten years before Vassar opened, among the colleges for women in the South, and at that date there were no separate institutions for women in the North that claimed collegiate rank."

The school commenced its operations in the basement of the Baptist church with two or three teachers and a few earnest girls who hungered for an education; when the Civil War came on it had "patronage from twelve States, but more from Mississippi than from any other State. Often the girls came overland, long distances, in carriages, accompanied by some male relative, with a colored man for driver. But the war came on, and the news of the Northern invasion of Tennessee spread panic, and Southern planters made haste to call their daughters home. It tried our very souls to see something over three hundred girls, representing the flower of Southern womanhood, fleeing before the advance of an invading foe, our buildings used for stable and hospital, our fine old pianos dumped on the rubbish pile, or split into kindling wood, and our library and other equipment scattered over the highways for miles around." (Dr. Graves to an old student, Mrs. J. F. Miller, and reported in *Souvenir Bulletin,* Tennessee College, 1910.) In this wreck Dr. Graves suffered heavy financial losses, for he had invested his hard-earned savings in college equipment. But the college survived the desolations of war and resumed its work. And more than twenty years afterwards it could be truthfully said, that "by her thorough work and high standard of culture she has become famous in every State as the 'Woman's University of the South.' She has won her prestige, not by endowments and magnificent edifices, but by honest, patient effort to educate the women of the land, to unbind the shackles of error and free them from the despotism of ignorance. Those who hunger for knowledge she welcomes to her gates; those who thirst for the waters of truth she invites to the fountain. Her mission is that of every true school of learning, to increase the power and range of the human mind, and to furnish it with the knowledge which shall most signally promote the well-being and true progress of humanity." (Catalogue.) The building of this institution was to be Dr. Graves' supreme life-work; in it he put his life-blood. During his thirty-nine or forty years' presidency, aided by his associate fellow-teachers, he educated in part and graduated more than four thousand young ladies at the Mary Sharpe, who are "occupying the first positions in social life, and not a few of them are among the noted teachers of the South."

It is not generally known that President Graves was an ordained preacher. He was pastor for three years while teaching, but the "call" to him became more and more emphatic, "Go, teach; go, teach," rather than, "Go, preach"; and he gave himself to the high vocation of a teacher. He was an LL.D., but preferred the title of teacher to that of doctor; as a teacher he "magnified his office." He was a born teacher —had a passion to learn new truth and to teach it to others. He sometimes forgot to eat, in his zeal to impart truth to an inquiring mind. He had a penetrating mind and was highly cultured. His books were his companions and friends, his teachers; he was devoted to them. He was a philosopher rather than a theologian—in his abstemious habits reminding one of the old Stoics, in his manner of teaching reminding you of Socrates. As a Christian he was devout, reverent. As a teacher of religion he was not dogmatic; he was somewhat of a mystic, more like John than Paul. He found Christ, the pre-incarnate Word, the Logos, in conscience, the light of all minds, the light of the heathen world. With him all true education was Christian, the highest knowledge was the knowledge of the Highest. With Augustine he found Christ and Christianity "enfolded" in the Old Testament, especially in the Book of Proverbs, which he was fond of studying with the whole school at the chapel hours and which every girl well-nigh knew by heart, with its personified "wisdom" and her call to virtue and honor and uprightness, to true happiness and success—its "knowledge" and "fear of God," the beginning and the crown of all true knowledge and the most important thing in an education.

Dr. Graves was a man of marked politeness and very great modesty. He was always approachable; in a word, he was a most lovable brother, and was greatly loved by his pupils and by all who intimately knew him. It was the writer's privilege to be his pastor in the palmy days of the Mary Sharpe. It was the first pastorate of a poorly equipped and inexperienced youth. But the young pastor always found Dr. Graves sympathetic and helpful, in his study, in the pew, on the street. He was always in his place at the hour of worship, and was always loyal to his church, as were his faculty and the student body. The pastor was a welcome visitor at "chapel" and in the President's home, and received great quickening from his sympathetic touch.

The prophecy concerning old age for the righteous is that "at evening time it shall be light"; but there is a tinge of melancholy, a note of sadness, in old age—there are shadows with the light. So it was with Dr. Graves, after he had passed his "four score years." In a letter written by him to Dr. Folk, and published in the *Baptist and Reflector,* August 4, 1898, on the occasion of Dr. J. R. Graves' retirement from the paper, we have this: "I am so grateful to our Heavenly Father that he has placed the mantle of my beloved brother upon one so worthy as I consider you to be. I am truly proud of our denominational paper. I am now in my eighty-third year. I have lost my hearing to that extent that I cannot understand anything said in public or at my own table. My health is not good. I have lost my physical strength so much that I cannot work in my garden." Three years later he said: "Old as I now am, in my eighty-sixth year, my desire to teach still lives, and if I could hear well, I could find no greater pleasure than that of teaching my dear little granddaughters (children of his son Hubert, whom death had removed from the home). Ada is now eight years old; I have taken her to the fourth grade, and started her in Latin. (Annie was younger.) Seeing to the education of these children is my only incentive to live." One week later, early Sunday morning, May 18, 1902, it was announced, "Dr. Graves is dead; died last night, two hours after midnight." And then this note: "Grandfather was 86 years old in April, and his death came on a beautiful Sunday in the middle of May. He fell into his last, long sleep as peacefully as a child, worn out with play, falls into a sweet, refreshing nap. The Doctor said the machinery was old and the wheels run down. Grandmother and my aunt and uncle were buried down in the yard, and he wished to be placed beside them. But his pupils begged so that his body might be laid in the City Cemetery, that their request was granted. These loyal pupils, from all over the land, have erected a handsome monument to his memory. May their lives be as long, as happy and as useful as he would wish them to be, is the sincere wish of his granddaughter, Ada Graves, Tennessee College, May 14, 1910."

Dr. Graves has passed to his reward, and the Mary Sharpe is no more, but many are the daughters, now mothers and grandmothers, who bless the memory of their alma mater and revere the name of the long-time president of their beloved institution. One of the first two graduates (1853) from this historic school, Mrs. Wiley S. Embry (nee Miss Nannie Meredith), of Winchester, is still living, well preserved in body and mind. She was neighbor to Dr. Graves, and it is gratifying to know that she was able to minister to him in his extreme old age.

Tennessee College, Murfreesboro, might be considered the daughter of Mary Sharpe. It was founded to take the place and do the work of that institution. It has only come to pass that the fountain of learning "lost in one place" has broken out "in freshness in another place," while Murfreesboro has the same Middle Tennessee "Grecian skies," the same religious "traditions," educational "ideals" and "inspirational" surroundings that Winchester had in the olden time. So that, if we may not say that the mantle of a great college president has fallen upon his duly elected successor in office, we may at least be sure that the spirit of Dr. Graves and of the Mary Sharpe College "goes marching on" in the spirit and work of the Burnett brothers and Tennessee College. Cherish and nourish it—give it ample endowment, and it will live; with a generous endowment the Mary Sharpe, most probably, would not have died.

JAMES GREENLEE.

James Greenlee was born in Grainger County, Tennessee, November 1, 1800; his death occurred April 24, 1857. He was ordained to the ministry, the "first Saturday" in April, 1845, after having given satisfactory proof of his gifts and his purpose to preach. He was a member of Blackwell's Branch Church, and was a messenger of his church to the Nolachucky Association about every year from 1830 to 1852; and from that date to the close of his life his name appears on the minutes as a member and messenger of the Head of Richland Church. For several years he was a missionary of the Nolachucky Association, Elders James Lacy, W. J. Reed, George Grant Taylor, Hughes Woodson Taylor and others being often associated with him in the missionary work of that body. His report to the association for the year 1851 is as follows: "Labored sixty-five days," eighteen of which are "donated"; ' baptized twenty-nine persons, witnessed eighty-nine professions, spent nine days in destitute places." He received "fifty cents a day" for work not "donated." When the association met with the Antioch Church, August, fourth Thursday, 1850, Elder Greenlee preached the introductory sermon—doubtless a practical and helpful discourse, from John 4:29: "Is not this the Christ?" Brother Greenlee began his ministry as an "ordained" preacher late in life, having only twelve years of life before him, but these years were given to active missionary and evangelistic work, a work that appealed to him and enlisted his every energy. He had the confidence of his brethren and of everybody who knew him, and was a useful and beloved minister of Jesus Christ in his day and generation.

J. S. GREENLEE.

J. S. Greenlee was a son of John and Polly (Mays) Greenlee, and a nephew of Elder James Greenlee. He was born in Grainger County, Tennessee, August 17, 1824. He made a profession of his faith in Christ in his seventeenth year. In his twenty-seventh year he was "licensed" to preach by Beech Grove Church, Grainger County, and later in the same year was "ordained" to the work of the ministry by a council composed of Elders James Greenlee, Samuel Jones and Elias Wester. His ministerial labors, for the most part, were in Grainger, Hawkins, Hancock and Claiborne counties.

He was pastor of New Bethel, Cedar Springs, Central Point, New Prospect, Kidwell's Ridge, Cedar Grove, Pleasant Grove, Rock Bridge, Big Hill, and other churches.

J. S. Greenlee was a messenger of Central Point Church to the Nolachucky Association for a number of years, and for several years was a successful missionary of that body. His report to the association, for 1865, shows, "seventy-two days' labor, sixty sermons preached, 190 professed conversions, forty-two baptisms, salary received $69.65."

"For nearly fifty years, with untiring zeal, he went forth proclaiming life to lost men and women. His labors were attended with great success, hundreds of souls being converted under his ministry. He was a great defender of the Baptist faith, and a great missionary and church-builder. Few preachers helped organize more churches than did Brother Greenlee. In his last years he was a great landmark in the Mulberry Gap Association. He died June 12, 1898, at his home near Mooresburg, Tenn." (G. H. Cope.)

I am credibly informed that Elder J. S. Greenlee baptized and was instrumental in bringing into the ministry eight Baptist preachers: J. B. Bundren, Elihu Tittsworth, James Kitts, William Wise, Chrisly Shelton, Eli Jones, B. Riggins, and a Brother Collins.

JEREMIAH HALE.

In the old cemetery, near Bethel Church, Hamblen County, Tenn., is a tombstone bearing the inscription: "Sacred to the memory of Reverend Jeremiah Hale, pastor of the united Baptist Church at Friendship; born February 7, 1803; ordained November 27, 1830; died in the full triumph of faith, July 3, 1849."

Jeremiah Hale was a son of Richard and a grandson of John Hale, who at an early day came from Maryland to Tennessee, and settled on Horse Creek, in Sullivan County. Richard Hale lived to be 107 years old. The large and widely scattered family of Hales in the country belong to one stock, it is believed, and are of English descent.

Jeremiah Hale was married to Mary Ann Crouch (date not obtainable), daughter of John and Sarah Crouch, of Washington County, to which union were born seven children, four sons and three daughters.

The date and place of his conversion and baptism I have not been able to ascertain. He was ordained, as above stated, in the year 1830. The first Saturday in August, 1834, he was called by Friendship Church as an assistant pastor and served the church as pastor and assistant pastor till the first Saturday in July, 1839, when the party in the church, calling themselves "regular Baptists," excluded him, with eleven others. Friendship, constituted with thirty-six members, March 13, 1819, and recognized by a presbytery composed of Elders Duke Kimbrough, Richard Wood, Caleb Witt, Isaac Barton, Charles Kelley, and William Wood, became, in time, the mother of churches—the daughters being Mansfield Gap, Cedar Grove, Leadvale, Bethel, Witt's Foundry, and White Pine. The church represented in the Tennessee Association from 1819 to 1833. From 1834 to 1839 she represented in the Nolachucky, but in this year, in the division of the association (at Concord Church), when a third of the constituency of that body withdrew and repaired to the grove to constitute themselves an association of "old school" or "Primitive Baptists," a majority of the Friendship Church went with the seceding body. Jeremiah Hale remained with the missionaries, having the watchcare of Friendship Church as long as he lived. He was a messenger of his church to the association for a number of years, rarely missing a meeting.

The year the association split (1839) he was preacher of the introductory sermon. His text was: "The Lord is good, a stronghold in the day of trouble; and he knoweth them that trust in him" (Nahum 1:7). Elder Hale was an earnest advocate of missions, believing that it was God's purpose of love and grace that all nations should have a chance to hear the Gospel. A favorite text with him was the famous text used by William Carey, May 30, 1792, at Knottingham, England: "Enlarge the place of thy tent, and let them stretch forth the curtains of thine habitations; spare not, lengthen thy cords, and strenghen thy stakes; for thou shalt break forth on the right hand and on the left; and thy seed shall inherit the Gentiles, and make the desolate cities to be inhabited" (Isaiah 54:2, 3).

For years he was a useful and influential minister of the gospel in the Nolachucky Association, passing to his reward in the year 1849, the same year in which his co-worker and associate, Elder John Kidwell, departed to be with Christ. In the association minutes of that year the clerk, Elder T. J. Lane, makes note of the death of these two beloved servants of God, calling attention to "their distinguished piety and eminent usefulness in the ministry."

Jeremiah Hale had two sons, Henry and Jesse, who were able ministers of the Word; two nephews, Elder P. H. C. Hale (recently deceased), who was one of our best men and a great country pastor, and Elder J. F. Hale, of New Market, a successful pastor and evangelist. We also note the fact that W. C. Hale of Morristown, a useful pastor and many years the moderator of the Nolachucky Association, and Drs. Fred D. and P. T. Hale of Kentucky, sons of Dr. Philip Hale, formerly of Warrensburg, Greene County, Tennessee, are of the same stock and close of kin to the elder Hale, and are all able ministers of the New Testament. Jeremiah H. Hale of Eldorado Springs, Missouri, is the youngest son of Elder Jeremiah Hale, and the only member of the immediate family now living. W. H. Mullens, a money-making, public-spirited and liberal Baptist and citizen of Morristown, son of the only daughter (Martha) who lived to grow to womanhood, is a grandson of Elder Jeremiah Hale.

HENRY HALE.

Henry Hale, son of Jeremiah Hale, one of our older pioneer preachers, was born November 30, ·1828. He was reared in Jefferson (now Hamblen) County, Tennessee, some four or five miles southeast of Morristown. He was converted in his youth, uniting with Friendship Church. By authority of this church he was ordained to the ministry, November 3, 1867, Elder T. J. Lane officiating as a presbytery. His ministry was mostly in Hamblen, Green, and Hawkins counties, doing missionary and revival meeting work, and preaching to Friendship, Warrensburg, Liberty Hill, Bull's Gap, Rocky Point, Bethel, Witt's Foundry and other churches.

July 16, 1868, he was married to Mary Louisa Cunningham, to which union were born eight children.

In 1873 he moved to Vernon County, Missouri, where he was pastor of Virgil City and other churches. In March, of 1896, he moved to Texas, and was pastor of Oklahoma Church till failing health compelled him to give up all ministerial work. He died "triumphant in the faith" January 16, 1904, and was gathered to the fathers and elders and saints in Israel in the better country.

Henry Hale was a valuable man in his denomination, was a good preacher and well connected, belonging to a family of preachers. He spent the larger part of his ministerial life in the West, but did solid and serviceable pioneer work in his native State. The house in which he grew up as a lad he had the misfortune to lose by fire, with valuable records and relics—a loss to history, very much to be regretted.

JESSE HALE.

Jesse Hale was born in what is now Hamblen County, Tennessee, August 8, 1831. He was a son of Elder Jeremiah Hale. His mother's maiden name was Mary Ann Crouch, a daughter of John and Sarah Crouch, of Washington County, Tennessee. He was converted at old Friendship Church when a very small boy, only "seven years old," I have been told. His father, who was pastor of the church, "stood him up on a table" in front of the pulpit, saying to the church as he did so: 'Brethren, this little lad is my son. He says he loves the Savior and wants

to live with his people.' " It is not certain that he was received for baptism; if so, his baptism was deferred, presumably
on account of his extreme youthfulness. He was baptized,
according to the church-book record, on the "Sabbath after the
second Saturday in March, 1842," in his eleventh year. He
was "dismissed from the church in full fellowship, August,
second Saturday, 1850." He commenced preaching when nineteen years of age, but when and where he was licensed and
ordained to preach I have not been able to ascertain. As a
preacher he had varied gifts and more than ordinary ability.
He had unusual influence over an audience; at one time he
would have his audience "mad" and the next moment or two
everybody would be "in tears." His force and personality were
always "felt."

In his young manhood he was married to Diana Moore, a
daughter of John Moore, of Hawkins County. To this union
were born five children, three sons and two daughters. His
home was St. Clair. Besides doing active evangelistic work
he was pastor of Robertson Creek, Concord, Choptack, White
Horn, and perhaps other churches. The testimony of his
brethren and friends was that he was a "gospel preacher, full
of love and the Holy Ghost."

During the Civil Har he was chaplain in the Federal army,
ministering to the soldiers in Ohio and instructing all who
came to him in the "things of the kingdom of God." After
the war he came home for his family, and returned to Ohio,
where he preached for three years, "every Sunday but one"—
that being a fifth Sunday. On that particular occasion his
wife, with apparent seriousness, called for an ax. "Wife, what
in the world do you want with an ax on Sunday?" She replied,
"Why, I thought I would cut out a joist, to mark this day as
one to be remembered; for once you are at home on Sunday."
He was very much loved by his churches in Ohio. They proposed to "deed" him a good house and lot in town if he would
remain with them as pastor. But his wife wanted to come

back home. So he returned, locating near St. Clair, in Hawkins County, Tennessee, where he lived the balance of his life. He fell in the harness before he had reached the full maturity of his powers, passing to his reward, December 22, 1869. He was buried by the side of his father in the old burying ground of the Bethel Church, near the place of his birth, some four miles from Morristown. While still living but anticipating his death he "outlined his own funeral sermon," his daughter tells me, from the text: "I have fought the good fight, I have finished my course, I have kept the faith" (2 Tim. 4:7). He doubtless heard with joy the Master's "Well done, good and faithful servant."

Elder Hale is survived by an only daughter, Mrs. Jane Hazlewood, who lost her father when only twelve years old, but not until he had baptized her, and a son, W. A. Hale, who lives in Iowa. The daughter was very much devoted to her father, and "his memory is still fresh in her heart."

P. H. C. HALE.

Elder P. H. C. Hale, son of Esq. James Hale, belongs to a numerous and noted family of preachers. He is a grandson of Elder Ephraim Moore and a near relative of Elder T. J. Lane, both of pioneer fame. He is a nephew of Jeremiah Hale, brother to J. F. Hale, uncle to Tom and Arthur, a distant relative of W. C. Hale, and a near kinsman of Drs. Fred D. and P. T. Hale, of Kentucky. The writer was Brother Hale's pastor at the time of his decease and was appointed by the Nolachucky Association chairman of a committee to draft suitable resolutions to present to that body at its annual meeting, 1917. The association memorialized him in her minutes by publishing the following sketch, graced with a picture of his kindly face: "Brother Hale was born in Jefferson (now Hamblen) County, Tennessee, October 23, 1842. He was converted when

P. H. C. HALE.

a boy, in his fifteenth year, uniting with the Bent Creek (now the Whitesburg) Church in 1857. He entered the ministry in 1868, and was ordained by the Bethel Baptist Church in 1870. He fell in the harness and passed to his heavenly reward May 28, 1917, aged 74 years, 7 months and 5 days, having been a preacher and a leader in the Nolachucky Association for nearly fifty years. He prayed and labored for the peace of Zion and was always a unifying and constructive force in his association. Under his ministry and supervision the new meeting houses of Central, Witt's Foundry, Point Pleasant, Baileyton and Russellville churches were erected. Brother Hale was in-terested in all the enterprises fostered by his denomination, and not only contributed of his own means to their support but was ever willing and ready to raise collections to carry on the Lord's work. The lad who drove me to the funeral said to me: 'Uncle Pat has held his hat under more nickels than any man in this country, and never failed to put in something himself.' He was particularly interested in Christian education, more especially in our Baptist schools; and when he had educated his own children (a large family) in Carson and New man, he commenced to hunt up worthy poor girls in the country, to make them the beneficiaries of his own gifts and the gifts of others, as students in a Baptist school. Brother Hale was a great stay to his home church, Bethel, was always in evidence at Sunday school and the regular church meetings, and took nearly all the extra collections. He was a great help to his pastor, and will be greatly missed not only by the pastor, but by the church and the entire community in which he lived, and by this association, whose annual gatherings he rarely failed to attend.

He was married September 10, 1867, to Miss Esther Brandon, to which union were born eleven children, six of whom survive him. September 10 of last year, when the children were all at home, Brother and Sister Hale were craftily lured to Bethel Church, where a surprise program had been arranged for the celebration of their 'Golden Wedding,' anticipating by a year the fiftieth anniversary of their marriage.

On May 30, 1917, at Bethel Church, a funeral and memorial service was held on behalf of Brother Hale in the presence of the largest crowd of people the writer has ever seen gathered together at a country church, numbering from 2,000 to 3,000 people. The crowd represented six counties, twenty Baptist churches, and people of all denominations, all having it in their hearts to honor a noble man of God and a beloved father in Israel. Appropriate songs of Zion were rendered by the choir and a touching solo was sung by a young woman. The pastor preached a ten minutes' discourse from the words of the Psalmist (Ps. 37:37) : 'Mark the perfect man, and behold the upright; for the end of that man is peace.' Then followed beautiful and touching tributes to the memory of the deceased by Drs. Spencer Tunnell and J. M. Anderson, Elders J. M. Walters and W. C. Hale, and the local Presbyterian pastor, a Brother Smith. The speakers struck a responsive chord in the hearts of all present as they spoke of the unenvious, the brotherly, sympathetic and peace-loving spirit of the deceased; his perfect freedom from ministerial jealousy, his shepherd-heart, his forward-looking, progressive spirit, his spirit of helpfulness, his faith in God and the brethren, and his optimistic outlook upon life and the future of God's kingdom. His body was laid to rest in the cemetery at Bethel. Blessed be his memory. His life was a benediction. His praise is in the churches. His memory will not perish.

" 'Servant of God, well done; rest from thy loved employ;
  The battle fought, the victory won, enter thy Master's joy.' "

H. C. HAMSTEAD.

Henry C., second son of Charles P. and Rachael Hamstead, was a native of Ohio, born September 16, 1829. His father was a native of New England, of English descent. His mother, whose maiden name was Rachael Crawford Craig, was of Scotch-Irish descent, but a native of Augusta County, Virginia, and a granddaughter of Alexander and Mary Crawford who were murdered by the Indians in Virginia, in 1764.

Young Hamstead was educated at Central Presbyterian College, in Franklin County, Ohio. He was married twice. His first wife was Miss Ida Perkins. To this union were born three children. Losing his first wife he was married to Miss Eliza J. Olmstead, to which union were born two children. He came to Tennessee in 1866, locating at Clinton, where he

practiced law and edited a newspaper. In 1872 he was elected
principal of Big Valley Academy, at Andersonville, Tenn.,
where, the following year, in a meeting hed by Elder Frazier
Demarcus, he professed faith in Christ, becoming a Baptist.
January 25, 1874, by order of Mt. Harmony Church, near
Heiskell Station, he was ordained to the ministry—Elders
J. S. Coram, Bradford Demarcus, and F. M. Long constituting
the ordaining council.

H. C. HAMPSTED.

He was pastor of the following churches: In Knox Coun-
ty, Beaver Dam, Ball Camp, Sharon, Smithwood, Third Creek,
New Hopewell, Little Flat Creek, Union, Meridian, Valley
Grove, Lovel, River View, Mt. Harmony, near Heiskell, and
Mt. Harmony, east of Knoxville; in Blount County, Mary-
ville, Nails Creek, and Lebanon; in Jefferson, Dumplin, Shady
Grove, and Deep Spring; in Sevier, Beech Spring, Boyd's
Creek, French Broad Valley, and Sevierville; in Grainger,
Mouth of Richland; in Anderson, some five or six churches—
names not known to the writer. Into these thirty or more
churches, and other churches in the same counties, it is thought
Brother Hamstead baptized not fewer than 2,500, and perhaps

as many as 3,000 professed converts—and "converts," in his counting, were those only who went into the water and into the church. Nearly a score of those converted under his ministry and receiving baptism at his hands became useful ministers of the gospel. He died November 14, 1914, aged 85 years, 1 month, 28 days. He was buried at Beech Spring, Sevier County, Elder S. C. Atchley officiating at the burial.

H. C. Hamstead had a trained and logical mind, was a fine reasoner, and a good debater. He did not seek popularity, but stood like a rock in defense of what he conceived to be the truth. He was what is popularly called a "doctrinal" preacher, and was strongly Calvinistic in his views.

He was thoroughly missionary, however, though "hard a-plenty in doctrine." At Hall's X-Roads he had a friendly tilt with an "anti"-missionary preacher, who made the usual claim: "We are the Primitive Baptists; you are not." Hamstead replied: "It is a well-known fact that we all belonged to the same denomination till the body split, in the 'thirties' on the question of missions. Split a hog in two, can you tell me which half is primitive hog and which not?" The argument may not have been entirely convincing, but it was unanswerable and effective, ending the dispute.

AZARIAH HARRELL.

Azariah Harrell was born June 26, 1823, in Knox County, Tennessee. He was a son of John Harrell and a grandson of John I. Harrell, who was a soldier of the Revolutionary War and an officer under Washington. He was a member of a large family, being the oldest of twelve children, nine sons and three daughters. At the age of seventeen he made a profession of religion and joined Zion Baptist Church. He was ordained to the ministry in 1861, Elders Joshua Frost and Jonathan Bishop acting as a presbytery. July 21, 1842, he was married to Rebecca Keisling. To this union were born two sons. July 8, 1877, he was married a second time, to Mary West, to which union was born an only daughter.

Brother Harrell was active in the ministry for more than fifty years. His field of labor was Morgan, Roane, Anderson, Campbell and Knox counties. He was a member of Zion Church seventy-four years, preached 545 funeral sermons, married 256 couples, baptized 722 persons, and witnessed 1,200 conversions. Brother Harrell was a useful minister of Jesus Christ. He died March 16, 1915, near Powell's Station, within three miles of where he was born and where he had lived all his life, aged 91 years, 8 months and 20 days. His widow, one daughter, one son, and four brothers and sisters survive him. He was buried by the Masonic Order, of which he had been a member nearly half a century, under the shadow of Zion Baptist Church, of which he had been a member three-quarters of a century, lacking only a few months.

J. L. HARRIS.

A devoted and useful servant of the Lord was the Rev. J. L. Harris, a pioneer worker and general missionary in the backward districts of Cocke County and other territory contiguous to North Carolina. He was the son of James Harris, and was born in Lincoln County, N. C., July 23, 1827. In 1853 he was married to Miss Sarah Jane Spangler, of his native state of North Carolina. He was sixty years a minister of the gospel of the Baptist denomination, for three years in Cleaveland County, N. C., for ten years in York and Union counties, S. C., afterwards one year in Rutherford County, where he held successful meetings and baptized at one time 100 converts into the fellowship of a single church. During the early periods of his ministry he was generally pastor of four churches. Nearly fifty years ago he moved to Cocke County, Tenn., and preached his first sermon in the old brick meeting-house at the mouth of Big Creek, now Del Rio.

He was "regular in the work" most of the time, almost to the time of his death, retaining his memory and "right mind" to the very hour of his departure. He ever stood for righteousness, was happy in the Lord, and kept young. September, 1918, he died, triumphant in the faith, at the age of 90, leaving a large connection and many friends to mourn his departure. During his ministerial life he baptized 1,000 persons and married about 800 couples. "The memory of the just smells sweet and blossoms in the dust."

WILLIAM HICKLE.

William Hickle was the son of John and Katherine Hickle. He was born in Virginia, March 9, 1807, and died June 23, 1891, aged 84 years, 3 months, 14 days.

He professed faith in Christ at Little Flat Creek, was approved by the church for baptism August 19, 1726, and was baptized September 11th of the same year. His church granted him license to preach October 21, 1826. In June, 1827, he was ordained by the imposition of hands, Samuel Love, William Billue, and William Williams constituting the presbytery.

He preached his first sermon at Little Flat Creek Church in his twentieth year. June 7, 1827, according to the record, "William Hickle and Nancy Rutherford were married by Wm. Sawyers, Esq."

At some time during the sixty odd years of his ministerial life William Hickle was pastor of the following churches, and not infrequently five or six of them at a time: Cedar Ford, Powder Spring Gap, Locust Grove, Puncheon Camp, Hickory Valley, Elm Spring, Head of Barren, Carr's Branch, Cedar Grove, Little Barren, Adair's Creek (now Smithwood), Mount Pisgah, Little Flat Creek, Central Point, Buffalo, Mill Springs, Sulphur Springs, New Market, New Prospect, Alder Spring,

WILLIAM HICKLE.

Milan, Maynardville, Graveston, Lyon's Creek, Blackwell's Branch, Lick Branch, and Warwick's Chapel, in all twenty-seven churches, and these scattered over several counties.

Added to the pastoral care of all these churches was the vast amount of protracted meeting and missionary work which he did. He was a missionary of the Northern Association for a number of years, and organized several new churches within its bounds. He also served the Association as Moderator for twelve years, and was for ten years its clerk. He was largely instrumental in organizing the Northern Association, the origin of which is as follows: In 1838 the Powell's Valley Association declared against "missions and the societies of the day." Whereupon the following churches, belonging to that body, namely, Puncheon Camp, Powder Springs, Mount Pleasant, and Clear Branch, by their appointed messengers, "met in convention" at Glade Spring Church, Campbell County, for the purpose of effecting a new organization. Elders James Kennon and William Hickle were appointed a "presbytery" to examine the articles of faith of the churches proposing to go into the new compact, and report on same. The presbytery made a satisfactory report and, accordingly, the "Northern Association of United Baptists" was organized, November 30, 1838.

Elder Hickle was a leader and an active preacher in this Association up to within a year of his death. He was pastor of Cedar Ford and Prospect churches till only a few months before his confinement to his room in his fatal illness.

Brother Hickle held a great many successful meetings and was instrumental in "turning many to righteousness," but I find no evidence that he ever kept a record of the number of professed conversions made under the influence of his ministry. He was untiring in his labors, had a robust frame, a large store of health and good nature, and was always lively and full of innocent pleasantries. He preached so well when in the pulpit and was of such a jovial and joking disposition when out of the pulpit that not a few of his friends and admirers said: "When he was in the pulpit, you would think he never ought to be out, and when he was out, you would think he never ought to be in." For the most part he was serious in the pulpit and, on account of his good nature, was popular out of it, and, upon the whole, his humor was an element of power.

He had a powerful pair of lungs and a good voice for singing. He could preach and sing for weeks in a meeting without
getting hoarse in the least. He loved to sing, and only a week
before his death, after seven weeks of confinement to his bed,
he sang with delight, "Jesus, Lover of My Soul," and "Nearer,
My God, to Thee."

The following incident is vouched for by good authority.
In his younger days Brother Hickle was holding a meeting
with Lyon's Creek Church. One of the attendants was a good
Methodist brother, a Brother Trent, who was accustomed to
"shout" in Methodist meetings when the "spirit moved" him.
As the preacher, one day, was preaching away on some glorious
theme Brother Trent, getting too "full" to contain himself and
observe the proprieties of a Baptist meeting, cried out, "Hold
on, Brother Hickle, hold on! I don't want to interrupt you!
But I can't stand any more!"

Among Elder Hickle's associates in the ministry I mention
James Kennon, Joshua Frost, Chesley Boatwright, Bradford
Demarcus, Joel Aldridge, Samuel Love, J. S. Coram, Asa
Routh, and the Acuffs, Simeon, John D. and Anderson. All of
these have long since gone to their reward.

Three miles north of Luttrell, in Union County, stands the
old house where William Hickle lived, labored and suffered in
the ministry for sixty years. He had a family of eleven children to support. His farm was poor. His churches paid him
but little. He had devoted himself to the ministry and given
his time to preaching. The result was poverty and suffering.
Many a time has the writer heard the remark: "Uncle Billy
Hickle did more work as a preacher and received less pay than
any man in Tennessee."

M. C. HIGDON.

Michael Columbus, a son of Deacon Thomas and Rebecca (Cate) Higdon, was born January 30, 1823, in Jefferson County, Tenn. He was one of a family of fifteen children, ten sons and five daughters. He was the oldest of five brothers who became ordained Baptist preachers. His father moved to McMinn County when young Higdon was a small boy. Remaining here two or three years, he moved to Monroe, locating about four miles from Tellico Plains. Here the lad grew to manhood, receiving a limited education from the public schools of the county.

June 5, 1843, he was married to Mary Ann Crawford. In his twenty-first year he went on a visit to Illinois, where he was converted. Returning to his native state, he united with the Baptists, being baptized by Elder Carroll Lee, in the fall of '44. The second Saturday in July, 1845, he was licensed to preach by Shoal Creek Church. In '47 he was ordained by Friendship Church (Polk County), Elders Z. Rose, I. Simmons and Wm. Sims acting as a presbytery.

He was pastor of the ordaining church, as above, also of another church of the same name, in Bradley County, of Ocoee, Ocoee Union, Greasy Creek, Hiwassee, Union, Smyrna, and other churches. He held a great meeting with the Ocoee Church in the time of the Civil War, in which there were 100 conversions. As a result of the meeting he baptized eighty into the fellowship of the Ocoee Church, and twenty to twenty-five into the Smyrna fellowship. In the "fifties" he spent seven years in Georgia, organizing a church of fourteen members, "swiping in the whole of a Methodist congregation, except one or two members," and building up the membership to 175. At the close of the war he served two years as missionary of the Sweetwater Association. He was Moderator of the Association twelve or thirteen years, was also Moderator of the Eastanallee several years.

15

He has baptized from 1,500 to 2,000 people, including three Methodist churches. He doesn't work well in "union meetings"; can pull better in "Baptist harness," and thinks that Baptists have to give account to their own Master, and, therefore, ought to do their own work in their own way. He doesn't call on excluded members "to pray"; let them be "as a heathen and a publican" till restored to confidence and fellowship.

In the days of lawlessness and misrule, following the Civil War, Brother Higdon and Brother Z. Rose wanted to hold a meeting at Roger's Creek. On their way to begin the meeting they were met by a number of parties who warned them that a gang of outlaws had threatened to "ride them on a rail" if they undertook to hold the meeting. They had already given a Methodist preacher a "lesson" of that kind. A number of the members said, "If they ride you on a rail they will have to do the same for us." The preachers went on to the church. Brother Rose preached and Brother Higdon followed. The meeting continued. Quite a lot of ruffians were present, with guns, pistols and swords. A great many came to the "mourners' bench" for instruction and prayer, among the number two rough fellows with sword and pistol hanging to their belts. Rose unbuckled the belt of one of the fellows and Higdon the other; handing the arms back to the crowd to take care of they went on with the meeting. There were a number of conversions, and at the close of the meeting a good collection of "greenback" money was taken, showing that the soldiers had a part in paying the preachers.

NOTE.—"Father Higdon, who has been a preacher for fifty-six years, was present (at the Eastanallee Association), giving inspiration and encouragement to the brethren." (J. J. B., in report to *Baptist and Reflector,* September 27, 1900.)

Elder Higdon has since departed to be with Christ.

THOMAS HILL.

Dr. Thomas Hill, physician and preacher, was one of the most brilliant, able and influential men among the Baptists of East Tennessee during the first quarter of the last century. He was born in Sevier County, Tennessee, about the year 1770 or a little later. He was first a member of the Forks of Little Pigeon (now the Sevierville) Church, baptized, most likely, by Elder Richard Wood, the first pastor of that church. July, 1801, the Dandridge Church "appointed their pastor, Elder Duke Kimbrough, to attend a presbytery at the Fork of Little Pigeon, for the purpose of ordaining Thomas Hill to the ministry" (Church records). The following year (December 25, 1802) he represented his church (Forks of Little Pigeon) at the organization of the Tennessee Association. August, fourth Saturday, 1803, he was appointed by the Tennessee Association as a fraternal messenger to the mother Association, the Holston, meeting with the old Cherokee Church (1804). At this time, 1803, he appears on the minutes as a member of the Fork of French Broad and Holston Church. In 1807 he preached the introductory sermon, from Eph. 2:10: "For we are his workmanship," etc. He was elected Moderator of the body the same year. He also preached the introductory sermon in the year 1813, his text being I John 1:3. At the formation of the Hiwassee Association (1823), Thomas Hill was moderator and Micah Sellers clerk. The two or three preceding years he had been a messenger of Big Pigeon Church, Cocke County, to the Holston Association. The minutes of that body for 1825 say, Item 9th: "The churches composing this Association declare against Big Pigeon Church for restoring Thomas Hill over the heads of distressed brethren, and appoint a committee of six brethren to 'wait on Big Pigeon Church the first Saturday in September.'" The church protests against the action of the Association, and the following year gets from the Association this message: "We only act as

an advisory council, and as such request the churches to receive or remonstrate against our proceedings, and record it
on their church books." There is no intimation as to what
the offense or "distress" was.

At the organization of the Nolachucky Association, at the
Bent Creek meeting-house, "the first Friday in November.
1828," Dr. Thomas Hill was elected Moderator, and was re-
elected Moderator the two succeeding years. In 1839, when
the Nolachucky divided over the question of missions and
methods, societies and what not, Thomas Hill went out with
the seceding minority, declaring a "non-fellowship" for all
extra-Biblical movements and all the societies and "institutions
of the day."

Thomas Hill is said to have been a strong doctrinal and
historical preacher. He preached a great deal from the Old
Testament prophecies. His nose and mouth were drawn considerably to one side, disfiguring his face in a measure. But
he had a brilliant mind, was resourceful, ambitious, strong,
had unusual gifts of leadership, and was prominent in denominational affairs throughout his ministerial life. He was a doctor, and a "good" one, I am told; but he rarely made out a
"bill" against a patient, especially against a poor man. In
explanation of his practice he would say: "I have a clear
conscience, if I do have an empty pocket. I can live without
the fee." Many in his day were like him. They thought "doctors' medicine" and *religion* ought to be free.

A. O. P. Hill, one of the oldest members of Buffalo Grove
Church, near Jefferson City, a thorough Baptist and a good
citizen, is a grandson of Dr. Thomas Hill.

JOAB HILL.

Joab Hill was the fifth son of William and Hannaniah
Hill. He was born in North Carolina, but the date of his
birth is not known. His father was a Virginian by birth and,

after his conversion, became a Baptist and a Baptist preacher. His grandfather, William Hill, Sr., was a devout religionist after the Church of England, or Episcopal, order, and was greatly angered, it is believed, that his son should unite with the Baptists, a people everywhere spoken against. The unfriendly attitude of the father doubtless had much to do with his son's leaving his native state of Virginia for North Carolina, where he lived and died. The elder William Hill was a patriot in Virginia, as was his son, Elder William Hill, in North Carolina. William Hill, Jr., father of Joab, was a member of the Provincial Congress at Hillsborough, N. C. (1775), was a "member of a committee of safety," after the battle of Lexington, when "congresses were formed in all the colonies and committees of safety were appointed to call out the troops and provide for any emergency," was lieutenant of a regiment of North Carolina Continental Troops, and, later, was chaplain in the American army at the battle of Guilford Courthouse (March 15, 1781), a battle "between the armies of Cornwallis and Greene, in which the former was repulsed with loss." Of the illustrious father of Joab Hill, Wheeler (Reminiscenses, N. C. Hist.) says: "He was a Baptist minister, a sterling patriot, and an honest man; during the Revolution his stirring appeals stimulated the whigs in his section" of the state.

In 1802 Joab Hill married Elizabeth Lane, a daughter of Lieut. Isaac Lane and a granddaughter of Elder Tidence Lane, of pioneer fame. To this union were born nine children, seven sons and two daughters.

In the War of 1812 Joab Hill was Lieutenant Colonel in Colonel Booth's Regiment of Tennessee Militia, being in active service in 1814-15. According to records at Tazewell, as quoted by Mr. P. G. Fulkerson, Joab Hill represented Claiborne County in the Tennessee Legislature more than one term, it would seem, between the years 1803 and 1815. At Powell's Valley Association, held at Cedar Fork meeting-house, Claiborne County, the third Saturday in October, 1818, Joab Hill was one of three representatives of the Big Spring Church, and was appointed by the Association "assistant clerk." In 1832 we find him in the Sweetwater Association, and a messenger from Mt. Pleasant Church. He is appointed by the Association "to write a letter of correspondence to the Tennessee Association," and Daniel Buckner and George Long are appointed "bearers of the letter." The minutes for 1834 show him to be a "licentiate" of Mt. Pleasant Church. It is likely he was ordained the following year, but the minutes, by oversight, I take it, still carry his name as a "licensed" preacher. In 1836 his name stands on the minutes at the head of a committee of eight prominent and influential preachers appointed by the Association to frame and submit to the body a report on the vexed question of a "State Convention." The Convention was a new thing, and was bitterly opposed by some of the brethren. As a conciliatory measure it is "unanimously agreed," by the committee and the Association, "to abandon the Convention, if the churches and the Association will agree to unite in spreading the gospel."

I close this fragmentary sketch with quotations from two letters at hand. The first is from a note of Dr. I. C. Simmons, clerk of New Friendship Church, near Cleveland, who says: "I find on the old church book that Elder Joab Hill was at our church in April, 1836. Alfred Cooper was ordained to preach on that day, and Brother Hill preached the ordination sermon. He preached at our church several times, but that is the only time I find it on record. He was never pastor of the church. I am now 72 years old, and he preached here nine years before I was born. I have heard my mother and Uncle Jackson Cate and Leroy Bates talk so much about Joab Hill that it seems I almost knew him. Brother Bates, who died last fall at the age of 96, knew him well. From what I have heard him and my mother, and other old people, say about Joab Hill, I know he was a prominent preacher." The other quotation is from a kinsman of Brother Hill, who, writing at the age of

82, says: "My grandfather, Thomas Hill, had a younger brother named Joab Hill, who lived in McMinn County, East Tennessee. He was a prominent divine in that part of the state.
He moved to Missouri about the year 1841." He died in Clark
County, Mo., in 1847.

MATTHEW HILLSMAN.

Matthew Hillsman was born near Knoxville, Tenn., August
7, 1814. He was one of a family of eleven children. His parents, John and Rebecca Hillsman, were natives of Virginia,
born in Amelia County. John Hillsman was born November
17, 1764; died December 8, 1850, in his 87th year. His oldest
son, "Uncle Billy Hillsman, a Knox County pioneer, passed
away," according to newspaper announcement (January 15,
1896), "at the age of 90." John Hillsman, though but a youth,
was a "gallant soldier in the war of the Revolution, saw Cornwallis surrender at Yorktown, Va. (1781), heard Washington
deliver his farewell address, taking leave of the army at the
conclusion of the war." At the close of the war, following
the instinct of adventure, with a company of young friends,
he went as far "west" as the Sewanee (now the Cumberland)
River, in Middle Tennessee. For a time he was an inmate
of Colonel Bledsoe's fort, a few miles east of where Nashville now stands. He taught school in the village of Cumberland (now the city of Nashville), and numbered among his
pupils boys who afterwards became men of influence and
standing in the community. Returning to East Tennessee,
about the year 1793, he located and entered into the mercantile business where Knoxville now stands, retiring to his farm,
near Third Creek, Knox County, in 1809 or 1810. (Inman.)
"I am now (1896) in the house in which Dr. Matt Hillsman
was born, taking "notes" for my sketch from Sister Nancy
Johnson, a sister of Dr. Hillsman and the only surviving member of a family of eleven, well along in her eighties, well pre-

served in mind and memory, and a thorough Baptist." (Note-book No. 1.) There is a creditable and uncontradicted family tradition that John Hillsman built the "first" dwelling house (a log cabin) on the ground where the present city of Knox-ville stands, the only other building at the time being the sol-diers' "barracks." The country was still a wilderness. The Cherokees and Creeks were a terror. Killing and horse-steal-

MATTHEW HILLSMAN.

ing were an everyday business. The state of Tennessee was not yet in existence. Knox County was not on the map, had not been "erected" into a county, and Knoxville had not as yet been "laid off." There was not a "shanty" in sight, and the "seat of the territorial government" was only a coming event, when John Hillsman left his native Virginia for the "west."

The "first" baptism ever witnessed in the city of Knoxville was that of John Hillsman by Elijah Rogers, who, in the presence of 3,000 witnesses, led his candidate down into the waters of the Tennessee River and baptized him, August, 1825. Richard Wood and Elijah Rogers, pioneer preachers of the Baptist faith, had been holding a meeting in the Presbyterian church, and this was the first fruits of their labors. This fact I glean from a trustworthy old manuscript.

As to young Hillsman's education I have this note from Sister Johnson: "Brother Matt. was pretty nigh a self-made man. His father paid his way one session in Knoxville (at the East Tennessee College, which later became the University of Tennessee) ; he got the rest by himself." To which we may add, that he was a life-long, painstaking student, lived a good deal in the atmosphere of schools as well as of books, and became a classical scholar.

In the summer of 1832, in a meeting held at Third Creek by that devoted and greatly beloved servant of the Lord, Elder Sam. Love, Matthew Hillsman made a profession of religion, being in his nineteenth year, and was baptized by Elder Love, uniting, most likely, with Beaver Ridge Church, the nearest and only Baptist church in reach of him at that time. February 8, 1833, the Third Creek Church was constituted, with Samuel Love "pastor" and Matthew Hillsman "clerk." At the April meeting, of the same year, it was "moved" by the pastor and "approved" by the church, that Brother M. Hillsman "exercise a public gift in preaching, prayer and exhortation in any of the sister churches." In December of the following year he was granted a "letter of dismission." In 1835 (June

7th) he was "ordained" by Bethel Church, Anderson County, Samuel Love, Chesley H. Boatwright and James Kennon acting as a presbytery.

January 28, 1834, he was married to Ann Eliza Mynatt, of Knox County. To this union were born eight children. He now spent one year working on the farm, preaching as he had opportunity. But in the fall of 1835 he went to Talladega, Ala., where he remained eighteen months, preaching and looking after the struggling interests of Baptists in that part of the country.

In 1837 he returned to Tennessee, locating at a ferry and Indian trading place known as "Ross's Landing," now Chattanooga. Here he went into the mercantile business, had a partner, and was going to "get rich." The Indians and white men around, who had more "credit" than cash or honesty, got the "goods," while the merchant got the "experience." Young Hillsman soon learned in the school of experience that the Lord "had not called him to be a merchant." I remember reading an interesting editorial in *The Chattanooga Times*, some years ago, on "Dr. M. Hillsman, a Pioneer of Ross's Landing and Founder of the First Baptist Church of Chattanooga. 1839." There appeared also in the *Baptist and Reflector*, in 1880, a series of articles by Dr. Hillsman, giving many interesting reminiscences of his early ministerial life. On Baptist begininngs in Chattanooga I quote him as follows: "But few persons now living know anything of the origin of the First Baptist Church organization in Chattanooga, which was the germ from which the present First Church has grown. In 1838, while the Cherokee Indians were still residing in the country, I became a resident of Chattanooga, then known as Ross's Landing. The Indians, having sold their land to the government, it was being rapidly settled upon by immigrants who were expecting to be allowed preemption of their settlements at government prices. Chattanooga was settled in the same way and had a population of several hundred, living in log cabins and board shanties. It had, however, an extensive trade with the Indians and with the back country in North Georgia and with the older settlements north of the Tennessee River. Among the settlers were many excellent people, a fair proportion of them being professors of religion, the larger number being Presbyterians. But there was no church organization or minister of any sort in the place or near it. The citizens had built a good-sized log schoolhouse, and occasionally visiting ministers would occupy it as a preaching place. Although I had been preaching for three or four years I had never received a cent for preaching and had not come to Chattanooga to engage in ministerial work, but, like others, to engage in a secular business. No Baptist preacher in East Tennessee at that time, so far as I know, received anything for preaching, or ever expected to. With the Baptist preacher of that day the first thing to do was to make a living, and then preach all he could. After the people found out that I was a young Baptist preacher they requested that I should preach for them on Sundays, when no one else had an appointment, which I did for two or three years, with a good deal of regularity. In the meantime the Indians were removed, the land was sold, and the town was laid off and rapidly increased in population, when the different denominations began to prepare for organization. The Presbyterians, being the strongest, took the lead, and, by the assistance of others, built a pretty good frame house on their lot, with the understanding that the Baptists and Methodists might have the use of the house by courtesy till they were able to build. Several Baptists had moved into the place and others lived in the neighborhood near by, who attended my preaching, but I had not intended an immediate organization. In the summer of 1840 I was called to Nashville on business, had a talk with Dr. Howell, pastor of the First Baptist Church, who urged that an organization be at once gone into and a regular pastor be secured. A young Brother Lindsley, educated and gifted, was conferred with.

agreed upon, ordained by the Nashville First Church, put in charge of the Chattanooga interest, and in a few weeks Dr. Howell came over the mountains in the stage, and a small church was organized. Following the organization Dr. Howell preached some strong sermons on the subjects and the act of baptism, which excited an interest and drew the crowds, also the fire of the other denominations. Brother Lindsley stayed with the church three or four months and sought another field, leaving me to keep up the meetings of the church. I had occasional visits from other ministers, especially from the well-known evangelist, Richard H. Taliaferro, under whose labors converts and accessions to the church were made. In the summer of 1841, to escape the prevailing malarial fever, I moved my family to Knoxville, stayed a year, and returned to Chattanooga, to preach for the Presbyterians and the Baptists alike in the Presbyterian house of worship. This I did for several months, leaving Chattanooga and the struggling Baptist interest, in the spring of 1843, to go to Middle Tennessee. Elder Sidney Dyer followed me as supply, Elder William Wood followed him, and about 1853 Elder Eugene Strode came to the city, gathered together the scattered elements of the church, reorganized the church, perhaps, and built a house of worship. I was never pastor of the church but gave it such volunteer labor as I was enabled from time to time to bestow, which amounted to little more than holding it together." These essential facts are followed by incidents bordering on the sensational and the romantic, but our space limits forbid their being recited here.

In April, 1843, Dr. Hillsman had calls to churches in Middle Tennessee, with a guaranteed support for all of his time. For the next six years he was pastor, at one time or another, of Fairfield, New Hope, McMinnville, Winchester, Mulberry, and Shelbyville churches. In January, 1849, he took charge of the Murfreesboro Church. During his successful pastorate here for three years and a half the church sent three missionaries to the foreign field. From '52 to '58 he was pastor of the First Baptist Church of Knoxville. During a part of this time he was editor of the *Baptist Watchman,* a paper published in Knoxville in the interests of East Tennessee Baptists. I see the paper and its editor strongly endorsed and enthusiastically recommended in the minutes, both of the Tennessee and the Nolachucky Associations.

May 21, 1858, he was elected President of Mossy Creek College, and Professor of Logic, Rhetoric and Moral Science. He served as president one year, preaching meanwhile to the Knoxville, Morristown and New Market churches. One of his associate professors said of him: "Dr. Hillsman was the finest reader of the Scriptures I ever heard. His chapel lessons were Scripture readings, generally from Proverbs, with a word of comment, and every reading was equal to a sermon."

In '59 and '60 he was Corresponding Secretary of the Bible Board of the Southern Baptist Convention, with headquarters at Murfreesboro. The following year he was pastor at Jackson, till the church was broken up by the ruthless hand of war. In February of '62 he began his twenty-one years' pastorate in Trenton and vicinity, West Tennessee, giving two Sundays a month to Trenton, one to Poplar Grove, one to Hickory Grove. Of the last mentioned church he was pastor twenty-six years, during which time, under his wise and efficient leadership, the church took on new life and built an elegant new house of worship. His Trenton pastorate was one of the longest and most successful pastorates of his life. He enjoyed the esteem of everybody, and his appointment as postmaster of Trenton, under the first administration of Mr. Cleveland, was an expression of public confidence in his integrity and ability.

For twenty-seven years he was Vice-President of the Foreign Mission Board for Tennessee, was several years Moderator of the Central and Tennessee Associations, was President of the West Tennessee Baptist Convention a number of years, and the President of its Board of Missions; he was a trustee of the Southern Baptist Theological Seminary, and one of a committee to locate the seminary in Louisville. He was also on the committee which presented a plan for the organization of the Southwestern Baptist University. In addition to these responsibilities and duties he was editor, associate editor, or corresponding editor for more than one of our denominational papers, and was recognized as a practical and pungent writer.

As a preacher he was "sound in doctrine, clear in exposition, and entirely free from sensationalism. His style was plain, practical and direct, his best efforts being those of his regular services. A judge of the Tennessee Supreme Court said of him: 'I know no preacher whom I would prefer to hear, Sunday after Sunday, year after year.' He was not demonstrative, but felt deeply. He was somewhat lacking in imagination, but had a mind of quick discernment, was discriminating and logical, and had the ability to make you see things as he saw them."

Dr. Hillsman "had a peculiar dignity and bearing that always impressed a congregation before he commenced preaching. He was a good parliamentarian, a good debater, and did a great deal toward getting the churches out of their hard doctrine." (W. A. Keen.)

For years Dr. Hillsman supported himself, preaching without salary or pay. The first pay he ever got for preaching was a "bag of flour and a dressed hog," the donation of a Presbyterian brother. He always had a friendly feeling and great respect for his Presbyterian friends, although he had several tilts with them over controverted points of doctrine, both in private and public debate.

In 1870, in recognition of his scholarship and ability, Union University conferred upon him the merited title, Doctor of Divinity.

From his home near Trenton, October 2, 1892, having served well his day and generation by the will of God, as a preacher of righteousness for nearly sixty years, he laid his armor by and departed to be with Christ. His body rests beside the "remains of his beloved wife and children" in the cemetery åt Trenton, awaiting the resurrection of the just.

ISAAC HINES.

This venerable brother was born in Knox County, Tenn., July 20, 1816. His father, Robert Hines, was a soldier in the Creek War. He was converted in his twentieth year and was baptized by Samuel Love, uniting with Boyd's Creek Church, Sevier County. In his twenty-first year he was married to Cynthia Ann Householder, who was his helper and companion for fifty years, and the mother of his twelve children. He was ordained by the New Hopewell Church, where he is still a member (1897).

Brother Hines served as pastor the following churches: Ellijoy, Knob Creek, Sugar Loaf, Cedar Grove, Mt. Olive, Stock Creek, and New Hopewell. The "greatest meeting" ever held at New Hopewell Church was held by Brother Hines. In this meeting, it is said, almost everybody in the surrounding country, young and old, was converted.

Brother Hines is an uneducated man, but has great sympathy, and has done a great deal of good. He has the gift of tears and the confidence of the people; and these are great assets for a preacher to possess. He never claimed to be a "big preacher," he tells me; but "by the grace of God he could do something." He has witnessed many conversions, and has "baptized hundreds." The Lord didn't call him to "sit down and wait, but sent him out to hunt up sinners and bring them in." "I can't preach much," he says, but "a good many churches want me to help in meetings; and the pastors want me to come and cry for them."

Brother Hines is the oldest preacher in the Chilhowee Association. He was 81 last month. In his last years he has been afflicted and not able to preach much. He has also been troubled over the loss of property and having to pay "security" debts." But when he was strong he took care of the Lord's cause, and now the Lord will take care of him. Many will bless his memory on earth, and many will rise up in the last day and call him blessed.

(The above was written September 1, 1897.)

R. C. HORNER.

Rufus Calvin Horner, son of Thomas and Catherine Horner, was born in Jefferson (now Hawkins) County, Tenn., April 4, 1822. His grandfather, William Horner, was one of the constituent members (1785) of the old Bent Creek (now the Whitesburg) Church. He came from North Carolina to Eastern Tennessee, during the early settlement of the new country. In youth and young manhood Calvin Horner had few opportunities to secure an education. In his twenty-first year he went to school four months. From that time on he kept up his studies, and taught some. At the age of 26, in a meeting held by Woodson Taylor and Samuel Jones, at Robertson's Creek Church, he was converted, and in 1854 he was baptized by Elias Wester into the fellowship of Mount Zion Church, Hawkins County, where he kept his membership the rest of his life. January (first Saturday), 1856, he was licensed to preach, and that night preached his "first" sermon. In September, 1857, he was ordained, Elders Andrew Coffman and Thos. J. Lane acting as a presbytery.

Elder Horner was pastor of his home church (Zion, or Mt. Zion) for thirty-five years. He was pastor of Robertson's Creek, at different times, some fifteen years, and of Poplar Spring and Cedar Creek, ten or eleven years. He was also pastor, at different times, of Cloud's Creek, Whitesburg, Catherine Nenny, Pleasant Hill, Speedwell, Hickory Cove, Liberty, Persia, Grigsby's Chapel, County Line, and other churches. Brother Horner felt that he was "not called to be an evangelist, but to be pastor and indoctrinate the churches"; his "gifts" were in this line. He also thought the evangelist, as a rule, "ought not to take charge of churches, but aid the pastors in special meetings."

Brother Horner was twice married, and raised a splendid lot of children. December 4, 1847, he was married to Sarah Ann Cockraham, a daughter of Daniel H. C., Esq., of Hawkins County. His second marriage (December 16, 1868) was to Nancy Robertson, of the same county.

"Uncle Calvin Horner," as he was familiarly called for many years, stood for righteousness, and had the confidence of the people. Everybody believed in him. His style and manner of preaching was thoughtful and methodical; he was a doctrinal preacher, and a close reasoner. His idea of preaching was that it should be sound, plain and practical. He read the old standards in theology—Baptist, Methodist, and Presbyterian, but the reading of the Bible moulded his doctrinal beliefs and shaped his ministerial life. He counted himself a "land-mark Baptist."

In the Minutes of the Nolachucky Association for 1904 is the following: "Elder R. C. Horner, of Mt. Zion, one of her oldest and most useful members, has been called home the past year. He was one of the strongest and most effective ministers and pastors in the Association. He died with the armor on and went home to God." (Com. on Obituaries.)

16

R. T. HOWARD.

R. T., son of Allison and Margaret Howard, was one of a family of four children. He was born in Rhea County, Tenn., May 9, 1826. He is of English descent, his parents coming from Virginia to Tennessee in the year 1796, settling in Rhea County. In 1842 he was converted in a meeting held at Macedonia Church, and was baptized by Elder Richard Taliaferro. In 1844 he was married to Penelope Majors; and to this union were born seven children, six sons and one daughter. In 1852 he was ordained by the Macedonia Church, Elder Absalom Vernon acting as a pesbytery. In September of the same year he was elected Clerk of the Hiwassee Association, and was re-elected to the same office for thirty consecutive years. He served the Association as Missionary for twenty-seven years and attended the Association thirty years without missing a single session.

He was pastor of the following churches: Macedonia (now Bethel), Yellow Creek, Privet Spring, Rhea Springs, Smyrna, Salem, Washington, Gum Spring, Friendship, Union Hill, Lone Mountain (in Rhea County), Mt. Vernon, Union Fork, Mountain Creek (in Hamilton), New Union, Georgetown, Birchwood, Friendship, Snow Hill, Salem, Ooltewah (James County), Concord, Decatur, Goodhope, Walnut Grove, Shiloh, Bethsaida, Shoal Creek, Short Creek (in Meigs), Old Sequatchie, Dunlap, Little Hopewell, Bethsaida (in Bledsoe). To the prodigious task of taking care of the above thirty-three churches he added the extra labors of missionary and evangelist.

Brother Tate Howard was a "born evangelist," and was especially gifted for that kind of work. For three years and a half he was Chaplain of the "19th Tennnessee Regiment" (Confederate Army), but he was never off the job of evangelizing, of preaching the gospel to the needy and the destitute.

"Endowed with extraordinary physical strength and endurance, and with a heart burning with zeal for the cause of

Christianity, he accomplished an amount of work that seems almost incredible. He encountered rain and storm, snow and ice, sometimes imperiling his life, to deliver his message of peace and goodwill." Like Paul, he was not only "in perils of waters, in perils in the wilderness and in perils by the heathen, but in perils among false brethren"—the "shafts of vilest calumny often leveled at his heart." In weariness and painfulness, in watchings often, in hunger and thirst, in fastings often, in cold and privation, his faith was tried and purified as by fire. Out of it all the Lord delivered him, and enabled him to finish his course with joy and his ministry to the mountain people, to whom he had been sent, with "phenomenal success."

He passed to his reward February 8, 1891, breathing his last, as he had often prayed he might, "in the bosom of his family," from which he had been almost an exile during his strenuous ministerial life. As death rolled its dark waters at his feet he exclaimed, "All is well! All is well!"

The venerable William Whitlock, an old time friend and co-laborer, says of his fellow-worker and companion in the ministry: "Brother R. T. Howard was a strong preacher, a noted revivalist, and a successful pastor. He was a devoted husband and a kind father. He was greatly admired and loved as a minister, and wore his life away in the service of God and his fellow-men."

Brother J. L. Henry, a near neighbor and intimate acquaintance of Brother Howard bore this testimony: "Brother Howard was a man of stalwart Christian character. He had a rare knowledge of human nature and knew how to deal with and influence men. He was consecrated and spiritual; was pleasing in manners and captivating in his address. His education was limited, but it always seemed to me that God gave him special preparation and had set him apart to the special work of evangelizing the people of the mountain country, among whom his success was phenomenal. He had a fine personal appearance and his moral courage was unflinching. He gave his whole time and energy to the ministry, and his labors were abundantly blessed. Under his ministry there were more converts, perhaps, and more additions to the churches, than under any minister who has ever labored in this part of the country. His convictions of right and duty were strong, and he was outspoken on all subjects pertaining to religion, morals and temperance, never shunning to declare all the counsel of God."

R. T. Howard had a preacher-brother, Elder John Howard, who was a strong man; also a son, W. A. Howard, of near Dayton, Tenn., who is one of our very best preachers and pastors.

JOHN HOWARD.

John Howard was born in Rhea County, Tenn., in the year 1820. He was a son of Allison and Margaret Howard, who came from Virginia to Tennessee about the close of the eighteenth century, settling in Rhea County. I have no record of his conversion, baptism, or ordination. I knew him as a man of rugged strength, physically, mentally, morally. He was a good man, with a "character unblemished." He did missionary and evangelistic work in Rhea and Meigs, and adjoining counties. He was pastor of Washington, Clear Creek, Smyrna, Wolf Creek, Privet Spring, Cotton Port, and other churches. His labors, for the most part, were with weak and struggling churches, and largely in destitute places. He "loved to preach and would go to his appointments in all kinds of weather; if he had no conveyance, he walked. He got little for his preaching, but he labored on, with a bright reward in view in the future. I am sure he is enjoying it now, on the other side of the river."

Brother Howard was an uncompromising Baptist, and "hewed to the line," always and everywhere, on doctrinal questions. He couldn't tolerate error or heresy or the least trim-ming, among Baptists, or elsewhere. He expressed himself pub-licly and without reserve on these questions, sometimes giving offense, or provoking criticism from his brethren. But he had a conviction that the preacher ought to contend earnestly for the faith delivered once for all to the saints, and that when he stood up as a witness he ought to speak the truth, the whole truth and nothing but the truth, without fear or favor of man. He loved the truth, and really loved men whom he considered in error and teaching error, but possibly he might have won them more effectively and better served the cause of truth which he loved, if he could have toned down his speech, which somtimes seemed "harsh, rasping and exasperating." Brother Howard was what would be considered a doctrinal or contro-versial preacher. He believed in the doctrine of missions, and thought the "poor heathen" ought to have the gospel, as well as the "poor" at home.

God uses different gifts, and chooses instruments wholly unlike, to accomplish his purposes. John Howard and Tate Howard were wholly unlike in temperament and disposition, were "opposite as the poles" in their make-up, yet they were preacher-brothers, and loved each other. They did not work together much in meetings. There would have been a lack of harmony and fitness. So each rightly served God in his own way, according to his special gifts and calling. Both "live, and will continue to live in the hearts of the Baptists of this country as long as any men that ever preached here; and seeing the crowds that attended their funerals, one could but feel that their lives were being lived over again in the people to whom they had preached."

In 1893, at the age of 73, Elder John Howard died, and was buried two miles north of Dayton, Tenn., and within half a mile of his birth-place.

Elder Howard was married, in young manhood, to a Miss Sophira Vanpelt, to which union there were born one son and three daughters. The daughters are dead. The son, J. T. Howard, an excellent citizen and a Baptist, now lives in Merkel, Texas.

R. B. C. HOWELL.

Dr. Howell (Robert Boyte Crawford Howell), a pioneer preacher in Nashville in 1834, and, later, one of the most widely known preachers of the Southland, was a son of Ralph and Jane (Crawford) Howell. His father was a native of North Carolina; his mother was a Virginian by birth. Dr. Howell was born March 10, 1801, in Wayne County, N. C. He was educated in Columbian College, Washington, D. C. He commenced preaching in 1825, and in 1827 he was ordained in Cumberland Street Church, Norfolk, Va., where he was pastor till 1834, when he went to Nashville to pioneer the way for the Baptists in that city. Here he built up the congregation of the First Baptist Church to a membership of about 500, whites and blacks, and led the way in the erection of a house of worship. In April, of 1850, he resigned his charge to go to the Second Baptist Church of Richmond, Va., where he labored successfully for seven years. In 1857 he was recalled to Nashville. Resigning the charge of his flock in Richmond he returned to "the scenes of his early triumph, where he had built up his great fame as one of the most learned and eloquent divines of the age." The success of his second pastorate with the flock he had gathered in former years, was not less signal or enduring than that which had crowned the first. His ministry in Nashville for more than twenty-five years was in every sense monumental work.

As a pioneer of Baptist religious journalism in Tennessee Dr. Howell stands at the head. From an old copy of *The Baptist,* an eight-page, semi-monthly paper published at Nashville (price, $1.00 a year), dated December 13, 1837, being Vol. 3, No. 24, with an editorial announcing the "Rev. Mr.

DR. R. B. C. HOWELL.

Howell's resumption of the editorship" of the paper with the next issue, it is reasonably certain that Dr. Howell was the founder and first editor (January, 1835) of the first Baptist newspaper published in the state. November 21, 1846, *The Baptist* had become a 16-page paper, with "R. B. C. Howell, D.D., and Rev. J. R. Graves" editors. In the first editorial of this number is this statement: "We have the pleasure of an-

nouncing to our readers that the Committee of Publication
have, at length, succeeded in procuring the services of an assistant editor for this paper, whom we here introduce in the
person of our beloved Brother J. R. Graves, the indefatigable
and successful pastor of the Second Baptist Church (now the
Central) in this city. Brother Graves is already favorably
known to many of you as an eloquent speaker, and a very
handsome writer."

Following is a pen-picture of Dr. Howell in "Sketches of
Some of the Ministers Attending the Southern Baptist Con-
vention, in Richmond, Va., June, 1846," by Dr. S. H. Ford, in
"Ford's Christian Repository," of May, 1876: "Reverend R. B.
C. Howell, D.D., is bishop of the First Baptist Church, of
Nashville, Tenn., and editor of the *Tennessee Organ*. The same
rotund face, beaming with good feeling, marks the man that
distinguished him while a youth at college, twenty years ago.
Whenever I come in contact with such a man as Dr. Howell,
I feel a love of my species strengthened within my bosom. Dr.
Howell is a native of the Old North State; was educated at the
Columbia College, and settled first as bishop of Norfolk, Va.,
where his memory is still embalmed in the hearts of his brethren. Subsequently he assumed the care of the church at Nashville, Tenn., where his labors have been herculean. With a
handful in a rented room to begin with, he continued to labor
until the few have become a powerful band, and the rented
room has been changed for one of the most beautiful edifices
devoted to the worship of God to be found in the valley of the
Mississippi. Dr. Howell is about 45 years of age, but bears his
years well. His eye is still lively and swimming in emotion
when the heart is touched—it needs not the aid of glasses in
reading; complexion is florid and healthful, forehead ample,
hair abundant and brilliant in hue as at eighteen."

As preacher and editor Dr. Howell would naturally and
necessarily be drawn into debates with his religious opponents.
In the '30's and '40's he had to contend with the anti-mis-

sionaries of his own denomination, had to cross swords with the followers of Alexander Campbell, and sometimes to take up or throw down the gauntlet with the Episcopalians and the Methodists. In these polemical bouts with tongue and pen he acquitted himself loyally to Christ and his denomination and honorably to himself.

As an author Dr. Howell was laborious and fruitful. He put forth volume after volume of permanent value. His work on "The Deaconship" ran rapidly through six editions. His next work, "The Way of Salvation," was eagerly read, running through several editions. "The Evils of Infant Baptism" had a wide reading, exciting popular interest in the subject and calling forth a good deal of comment from Pedo-baptist denominations. At the request of the Tennessee Baptist Convention (1854) he wrote "Terms of Christian Communion," which run through several editions in this country and three or four in England. About the same time two other popular works, from his fertile pen, came from the press, "The Cross" and "The Covenants." "The Early Baptists of Virginia," written in 1857, and published after his death, was a valuable contribution to the historical literature of the Baptists. "The Christology of the Pentateuch," a "Memorial of the First Baptist Church of Nashville " (1820-1863), "The Family," Eighty Bound Volumes of Sermons in manuscript, are literary remains showing Dr. Howell to have been a prodigious worker in his lifetime. Some of these manuscripts may yet be published, and their publication will add to the literary fame of the author. Dr. Howell's published works, as well as his pulpit ministrations, evince both genius and scholarship. He knew Hebrew, Greek and Latin, and was universally admired for his scholarly attainments. The degree of Doctor of Divinity was conferred upon him by Georgetown College, Ky., about the year 1844.

Dr. Howell was for many years president of the Southern Baptist Convention and one of its vice-presidents at the time of his death. He was vice-president of the American Baptist

Historical Society, was a member of the Historical Society of Tennessee, and was president of the board of trustees of the Asylum for the Blind, an institution endowed and sustained by the State of Tennessee. As Moderator of the Concord Association and other religious and deliberative bodies he was a gracious and efficient presiding officer.

"As a minister Doctor Howell was regarded as one of the ablest and most learned in the South. His Christian career was ennobled by the highest virtues. His life was unspotted. His genial courtesy and kindness of heart made him a universal favorite, notwithstanding the fierce theological debates in which he was often engaged. He was a thorough Baptist, always jealous of the fair fame and name of his denomination. Under his ministry many souls were added to the Lord and received the ordinance of baptism at his hands. His death occurred on Sunday, about noon (April 5, 1868), at the very hour in which, for more than forty years, he had stood up for Jesus in the pulpit. For a week he had been stricken with paralysis, speechless but not unconscious. When his pastor, Doctor Skinner, spoke of the infinite pity and compassion of the Saviour for his suffering servant, he burst into tears. When asked if he saw Jesus, he answered by pointing first to his heart and then to heaven." (A. N.) "Of Doctor Howell's labors as a voluminous author and a vigilant pastor it is not necessary to speak, as he attained a more than national reputation. He has been long considered a standard bearer in the communion in which he was so great an ornament. He was, moreover, held in high esteem in the community at large, without respect to church relations." (Nashville paper.) At a meeting of the pastors of the leading churches of Nashville a committee was appointed to draft suitable resolutions on behalf of Doctor Howell, with Dr. T. O. Summers as chairman. At a memorial service at the First Baptist Church, on the following day, with fitting ceremonies in the presence of a vast throng of people, gathered to do honor to a great man and a prince in Israel who had fallen, the committee reported in part as follows: "Whereas, Doctor Howell was possessed of great intellectual and moral endowments, qualifying him for the ministry, in which he was most laboriously and successfully engaged for a long period, being highly esteemed, not only in his own church but also in the community at large, and particularly by us, his brethren in the ministry; therefore, *Resolved*, 1, That we bow with submission to this dispensation of Providence, knowing that it was ordered in infinite wisdom, power and love, and that while God buries his workmen he carries on his work. 2, That while God is glorified in the useful life and peaceful death of his servant, we will endeavor to imitate his fidelity, that in due time we may, like him, enter into the joy of our Lord." Brethren of the different denominations bore their testimony to the character and talents of Dr. Howell. Dr. J. B. McFerrin, the veteran Presbyterian minister and editor, said: "Dear brethren, I feel sad this morning. There are only two of the old preachers left now who were co-laborers in the ministry with Dr. Howell when he first came to Nashville, nearly forty years ago, Doctor Green and myself. I lived on most intimate terms of Christian friendship with Doctor Howell. At one time we were both editors of church journals, and our expression of opinion on doctrinal differences sometimes, as did those of the apostles of old, became sharp, but our warm and fraternal regard for each other was never broken to the last. Doctor Howell was a scholar, a gentleman and a Christian. He enjoyed the abiding affection of his congregation, the high esteem of the community and, what was better than all, the signal favor of God, as the abundant success of his pastoral labors testifies. I could not, were I disposed, pronounce a suitable eulogy upon him. May the same rich blessings of God be upon his successor, Dr. Skinner."

He was buried in the beautiful cemetery of Mount Olivet, Nashville, where his sleeping dust awaits the resurrection of the just.

Thursday morning, April 23, 1829, Doctor Howell, was married to Miss Mary Ann Morton Toy. Of this marriage ten children were born, two of them dying in infancy. Of the remainder, three are still living: Robert Henry Howell, Mrs. A. J. Grigsby and Joseph Toy Howell, all of Nashville.

WILLIAM HUFF.

Following is a life sketch of a lamented veteran standard bearer, who fell at his post, October 20, 1898.

William, the fourth son of Samuel and Nancy Huff, was born in Botetourt County, Va., near James River, December 21, 1825. Young Huff was brought up to farm life with the usual advantages of a Virginia farmer's boy of his day—plenty of work in summer and in winter the country school. In early life he professed faith in Christ and by baptism was received into the fellowship of Zion's Hill Church. With what he conceived to be a divine call to the ministry there came to him another call, the clear and abiding impression of duty to prepare himself as thoroughly as possible for his high vocation. Accordingly he entered Valley Union Seminary, Virginia, where he began that lifelong course of study, self-culture and discipline, which made him the self-educated, self-reliant man that he was, and enabled him to realize in ever-increasing measure his life purpose and ambition to be an "efficient minister of Jesus Christ." Other years of teaching and home study were a further preparation and training for his life work.

He was ordained September 19, 1851, and began his ministerial life as a pioneer missionary in the mountains of Virginia, first under the auspices of the Western Virginia Association, afterwards of the General Association of Virginia, his field of labor being, for the most part, Russell and Tazewell counties. Lebanon, the county seat of Russell County, and a stronghold of the Methodists, was the center of his operations. There was no Baptist congregation or house of worship in the

place, and only one Baptist. Here he built a house of worship
and left the church 100 strong, with a commanding influence
in the community. At Marion, the county seat of Smith County, also with South Fork and Rich Valley churches, he labored
with like signal success, building houses of worship, organizing and extending the mission work and indoctrinating the
churches in the principles of the Baptists.

WILLIAM HUFF.

The war of the sixties coming on, Brother Huff secured an appointment as army colporter, to distribute Bibles and religious literature among the soldiers in Confederate camps, in this way rendering real service to suffering humanity and to the cause of God.

Coming to Tennessee in October, 1866, he located near Fairfield, in Bedford County, becoming pastor of New Hope Church. Here, more than in Virginia, he found churches and communities rent asunder as a result of the war; but with his conciliatory spirit and the disinterestedness on his part as of an outsider or stranger, Brother Huff proved to be the Lord's appointed instrumentality for healing the breach of fellowship that threatened disaster to the cause of Christ.

At Shelbyville Brother Huff was pastor for two years, preaching first in a hall, then in the Cumberland Presbyterian church, laying the foundation of a Baptist church in this important center. At Big Springs also he built up the Baptist cause and was instrumental in erecting a house of worship.

In a ten years' pastorate at Wartrace he laid the solid foundations of an efficient church, developing his people in mission and Sunday school work, inaugurating a church-building enterprise, and obtaining the testimony of the brethren, that they were "greatly edified by his sound Scriptural preaching and teaching, and that the love and faithfulness of their shepherd and leader had greatly endeared him to his flock."

In January, 1871, Elder Huff moved to Bell Buckle, with the purpose of planting a Baptist church there. At that time there was not a church of any denomination in the place. The dominant influence in the town was Methodism. A little way in the country, however, was a handful of Baptists, and hard by was a schoolhouse. From a successful meeting here was formed the nucleus of a church. Brother Huff became pastor and remained with the church for more than ten years, building a house of worship, organizing the work, building up and training the membership for constantly increasing usefulness from year to year.

The churches at Fayetteville and Tracy City owe, in large measure, their establishment and present efficiency to the self-denying labors of Brother Huff. Enjoying the confidence of his brethren and willing to undertake a hard job, Brother Huff, at different times and much of the time, was missionary or secretary of one or another of our several boards, and as such did real effective pioneer work on his many fields of labor.

For many years he was the efficient Moderator of the Duck River Association. Judge M. B. Tillman bore testimony to the "signal ability with which he always presided over that body," as well as the "uniform pleasure" it gave the body to be presided over by so "able and so distinguished a brother." Brother D. S. McCullough, the clerk of the Association, justly characterized Elder Wm. Huff as a "sound theologian, a deep thinker, an able expounder of the Scriptures, and a good preacher. He was conservative, amiable, broad-minded, progressive, having faith in God and his brethren, and ever ready to press the claims of Christ and of the Baptists, even at the risk of imperiling his personal popularity." Dr. J. M. Robertson said of him: "No man in Tennessee, in the reconstruction period of denominational affairs in the State, did more to make possible the present unity and success of Tennessee Baptists than did Brother Huff."

The writer can testify personally to his unusual sound common sense, his level-headed thinking, practical judgment, firm grasp of doctrinal and practical truth, and, above all, to the tender and sweet-spirited brotherliness of his character. He was a good preacher indeed, but his greatest sermon was his life.

His contributions to the religious press were clear expositions of the truth, always forcible and practically helpful. There were few better writers among us. Few of our preachers have made a better record.

He witnessed something more than 2,000 professed conversions, baptizing with his own hands not less than that number into the fellowship of Baptist churches.

May 7, 1856, he was married to Mattie E. Johnson, daugh-ter of Thomas Churchill Johnson, of Carter County, Tenn., a woman of culture and consecration, the Lord's hand-maid, and a help-meet indeed for the Lord's servant. They two walked and toiled together in their earthly lot till October 20, 1898, when the Master called him to his heavenly home. He was ready to lay his armor by and go home, for his testimony was, as he wrote to his son in Texas, while waiting his summons: "I have fought the good fight, I have finished my course, I have kept the faith."

URIAH HUNT.

Uriah Hunt was one of a family of eleven children. He was born March 3, 1775, died October 7, 1824, and was buried in the old family graveyard, near Limestone Church, Washing-ton County, Tenn. He had a son, a namesake, Uriah Hunt, who was a preacher, three grandsons, all bearing the name John, who were preachers, and a great-grandson, D. J. Hunt, who is both teacher and preacher.

"I am now in the house, a log house of the primitive type, which Uriah Hunt built, and in which he lived till his death." (Note.)

Uriah Hunt was an honest, honorable, reliable, everyday sort of man, a man who could be trusted to handle church collections, associational funds, business transactions of any kind, for his brethren. He was "first treasurer of a joint board of the Holston and Tennessee Associations," appointed for co-operative work.

He came from North Carolina to upper East Tennessee at an early day, and was said to be of English descent, as his sober disposition and sturdy character would indicate.

He was a contemporary of Jonathan Mulky, Tidence Lane, William Murphy, Caleb Witt, Isaac Barton, and Thomas and Richard Murrell, with other veterans of the Holston Associa tion. "He was a solid old man, and an acceptable preacher." (W. A. Keen.)

J. C. HUTSON.

James Coal Hutson, son of William and Elizabeth Hutson, was born in Montgomery County, Va., November 21, 1821. His father moved to Tennessee when James was six years old, settling in Campbell County. From six to beyond seventy years he has lived within "calling distance" of his first Tennessee home.

He was converted in his eighteenth year, and was baptized by Elder C. H. Bootright, the fourth Sunday in October, 1838, uniting with Indian Creek Church. He dates his "conviction" to a sermon preached by Elder J. S. Coram, some time before his conversion. Indian Creek Church, in 1844, licensed him to exercise his gift, and in 1846 ordained him, C. H. Bootright, William Lindsay and Alfred Agee acting as a presbytery. When I saw him he had been pastor of Big Valley Church, Union County, for nearly twenty-five years. He has also been pastor of New Salem, Clinton, Andersonville, Oak Grove, Murrayville, Indian Creek, Big Creek, Jacksboro, Sugar Hollow, Powell's River, Chestnut Grove, Grantsboro, Liberty and Big Spring churches, most of them for long terms of service.

Brother Hutson has been a tower of strength in the Clinton Association; was its Moderator for fifteen years, and two years its missionary, his work being mostly in Scott County, where he organized the first Misisonary Baptist church in the county. For his first year's work as missionary he got a "shilling a day," for the second, "20 cents a day." He has baptized over 600 people.

Brother Hutson has been married twice. June 18, 1840, he was married to Isabella Gray, and was married to Mary Cox, July 19, 1888. At the last report he had ten children, forty-nine grandchildren, and forty-one great-grandchildren. making his posterity an even 100.

"J. C. Hutson was unlettered, had few opportunities for study and self-improvement, living in a backward community

17

and having a large family to support, but he was able in prayer and exhortation and, considering his disadvantages, did as much good and made as great a success of his life as any man I know of. He baptized a great many people." (J. S. Lindsay.)

Brother Hutson was a good singer, and in this respect was the "successor of Chesley H. Bootright." He had a "smooth, strong voice, was able in prayer, and powerful in exhortation; he was a good expounder of the Scriptures for a man of his limited education; he was consecrated and spiritual, had a good reputation, and was a successful evangelist." (Lindsay Cooper.)

Brother Hutson was a devoted servant of the Lord, was as wholly consecrated to the ministry as was possible under existing circumstances, his influence was wholly for good, his life being his greatest sermon. One of his associates in the ministry, and a near neighbor, was C. L. Bowling, a school-mate of the writer's, who bore testimony to the sterling worth of Brother Hutson as a man and to the savory influence of his exemplary life.

He passed to his reward, December 30, 1898, in his 78th year.

J. H. HYDER.

Jonathan Hampton Hyder was a son of Jonathan Hyder. He was born on Powder Branch, Carter County, Tenn., October 20, 1812. His grandfather, Michael T. Hyder, was of German descent, but a native of Virginia, and one of the earliest settlers of Carter County, Tenn. His mother was an Edens, also of German descent.

Elder Hyder was fairly educated for a preacher of his day. He attended the Jonesboro Academy, was also a student in Emory and Henry College, Va., and in Maryville College, Tennessee, but was not a graduate. He received the greater part of his education in the school of life and experience. In 1843 he was married to Elizabeth Fletcher, a daughter of John Fletcher, of Carter County, a woman of sterling worth. This union was blessed with a family of fourteen children, one of them, A. J. F. Hyder, one of our best preachers; another, L. F. Hyder, a successful physician and farmer, and the entire family, I believe, Baptists.

ELDER J. H. HYDER.

"Hamp Hyder was converted through the instrumentality of a tear." So said William A. Keen, in relating to me the circumstances of his conversion. He was attending a meeting at old Sinking Creek Baptist Church, where two missionaries were preaching. He was then in his twenty-fourth year, and a Methodist, but without religion, hard-hearted, and full of prejudice. The preaching of the missionaries had little effect upon him. He could easily resist their most powerful appeals. But when a "homely old preacher" went to him in the congregation where he was sitting, and in the earnestness of his affectionate pleading happened to let a hot tear fall on Hyder's hand, a change came over his spirit, his heart softened, and he gave himself in penitence and faith to the Lord. Uniting with Sinking Creek Church he was baptized by the pastor, Elder Rees Bayless. He was ordained by this church, May 18, 1849, Rees Bayless, James Edens and Peter Kuhn acting as a presbytery.

Among the churches served by him as pastor we mention the following: Watauga, Stoney Creek, Poplar Grove, Zion, Sinking Creek, Indian Creek (now Erwin), Cherokee, Chinquepin Grove, Elizabethton, which he helped to organize, and Taylorsville, which is now Mountain City.

With all his manifold duties and labors as preacher, farmer, missionary, and evangelist, he was for thirty years county surveyor for Carter County.

He was Moderator of the Watauga Association from its organization (1869) to his death (March 5, 1886), with the exception of only a few sessions. As a presiding officer he was popular, but not less so as a preacher. Though a firm, outspoken man and a pronounced Baptist, he was greatly beloved by his brethren and respected by people of all denominations. His labors in the ministry were greatly blessed of the Lord. It is thought that he was instrumental in the conversion of some 10,000 souls. Through his labors and sacrifices many waste places in Zion were built up and multitudes added to the churches.

Elder Hyder was a man of marked peculiarities and distinct originality. He never failed to attract attention or make a distinct impression. In the mountains of Johnson and Carter, where he was most familiarly known, "Hamp Hyder" is the synonym for original genius, good humor, and droll wit. He was distinctly, but in a good sense, a sensational preacher. His quaintness, though bordering on eccentricity, was accompanied by an original freshness that secured the unfailing attention of his hearers, who felt that while the preacher was "odd" he was nevertheless interesting, and they wanted to hear more of him. As a speaker he was also highly emotional, possessing that pathos of voice and tears that gave to many of the early preachers their wonderful power over an audience.

As an example of Elder Hyder's wit and outspoken candor take the following incident, as told me by old Brother Routh and other witnesses. On one occasion he went to hear a Campbellite preach. In the sermon the preacher took occasion to ridicule what he called the "popular notions" of religion, grace and the so-called "Holy Spirit," saying that he "would not know religion if he were to meet it in the road." Brother Hyder believed in "answering a fool according to his folly." So, at the close of the service, he went forward with a grim smile on his face and in the hearing of all the congregation thus addressed the preacher: "Sir, I want to endorse a part of your discourse. You said you would not know religion if you met it in the road. We have no right to doubt that statement. It seems that you and religion are not acquainted. Of course we couldn't expect strangers to know each other."

For the following remarkable incident I am indebted to Brother A. Carter, the truthfulness of which is confirmed by many eye-witnesses. At one time Brother Hyder was very low with typhoid fever. His sweat had been cold and clammy for a week. At last his breathing stopped and his pulse ceased to beat. For several minutes he was thought to be dead; in fact, was pronounced "dead" by the attending physicians, one of whom, his own son, had closed his eyes. Everybody thought the end had come and the family were all crying, when suddenly, and to the utter astonishment of all present, he who was supposed to be dead opened his eyes, and with a firm, clear voice, spoke to his wife, telling her he was not dead, that he had been sent back on an errand, and was new-commissioned to preach the gospel. The doctors, ordinarily, would call this an instance of "suspended animation." But Brother Hyder thought it was a real "coming to life," and that the hand of the Lord was in it. The circumstance also deeply impressed the neighbors. The preacher lived sixteen other years, with the abiding impression that he had received from the Lord a new lease of life to preach the gospel more earnestly and to give himself wholly to the ministry. And this he did, the Lord working with him and greatly blessing his labors. He was away from home on the King's business, preaching the gospel, when he reached the end of his earthly journey, and was called to his home above. The summons came March 5, 1886.

From the marble slab above his grave I have copied these words:

"For more than forty years he fought,
    As few beside can boast;
Then died as he had longed to die,
    While standing at his post."

A. J. F. HYDER.

A. J. F. Hyder was born September 3, 1846, on Doe River, Carter County, Tenn., about two miles from Elizabethton. His father, Elder J. H. Hyder, was a preacher before him of ability and distinction. His mother's name was Elizabeth. Young Hyder, in his early "teens," enlisted in the Federal Army, taking an active part in the Civil War. He belonged to Company B, Fourth Regiment of Tennessee Infantry, and was honorably discharged on the second day of August, 1865. He was converted and united with Zion Baptist Church on a relation of his Christian experience and submission to the ordinance of baptism. October 25, 1868, his church, recognizing his gifts and his call to the ministry, ordained him to that work by the advice of a council and the "laying on of the hands of the presbytery." He was pastor of the following churches: Elizabethton, Doe, Mountain View, Butler, Sinking Creek, Cherokee, and other churches. He was one of the best pastors in the Watauga Association. He was a strong advocate of the temperance cause, was the first man, perhaps, to introduce clear cut, uncompromising resolutions on the liquor traffic before his Association. Brother Hyder was a farmer and school teacher, as well as a preacher. He taught several public schools, and for six years was Superintendent of Public Instruction for Carter County. He had the confidence of the people and was an efficient public servant.

June 19, 1872, he was married to Margaret A. Hyder. They had a good home but no children, so they felt it their duty and pleasure to rear two adopted daughters as their contribution to society. The writer had the pleasure, more than once, of meeting Brother Hyder at the gatherings of his Association, but remembers with peculiar pleasure enjoying at one time the hospitality of his home.

Brother Hyder, in his last illness, was taken for treatment to the hospital at the National Soldiers' Home, Johnson City, where he finished his earthly course, passing to his reward March 3, 1912. He was taken to Elizabethton for burial.

Elder Hyder is survived by his widow, who lives at Butler, in Johnson County.

JOSEPH JANEWAY.

Joseph Janeway was born in Claiborne County, Tenn., June 28, 1831. He was the son of a minister and farmer, and was brought up to farm life in his native county, enjoying such educational advantages as his part of the country afforded in his day. Later he took a literary course in Mossy Creek College, now Carson and Newman, Jefferson City, Tenn. February 12, 1852, he was married to Jane Helms, of Claiborne County, a cousin of Editor John Helms, of Morristown, Tenn. To this union were born nine children, six sons and three daughters. Soon after his marriage he moved to Loudon County. In 1855 he located in McMinn County. The second Saturday of July, 1859, he was ordained to the ministry by the Mt. Harmony Church. He was the beloved pastor of many of our strongest and most influential churches, among others the following: Cedar Fork, Post Oak, Stockton's Valley, Providence (Roane County), Prospect, Philadelphia, Loudon, Blair's Cross Roads and Mars Hill, in Knox County, Union, in McMinn, Goodfield, Decatur, Sewell, Mt. Harmony, County Line, Eastanallee, Hiwassee, and New Friendship.

Elder Janeway was a benediction wherever he went, was greatly admired for his even temper and smooth disposition, and enjoyed the confidence of all who knew him. He retired from the active ministry at the age of 70, not wanting to stand in the way of the progress of the churches.

He passed to his reward June 16, 1913, having read his Bible through more than fifty times, and having served the Lord and the Baptists, by the will of God, as a faithful minister of the Word for more than fifty years. He leaves a large connection of kindred and a host of friends to mourn his loss. Blessed be his memory.

WILLIAM JOHNSON.

William Johnson was the first Moderator of the Tennessee Association, as appears from the following: "Minutes of a conference of nineteen Baptist churches, being assembled at Beaver Creek meeting-house on the twenty-fifth day of December, in the year of our Lord 1802. 1st. Brother William Johnson was chosen Moderator and Francis Hamilton Clerk." He was a messenger of Boyd's Creek Church. The next year he was also chosen Moderator. He continued a member of the Boyd's Creek Church as long as he lived, representing his church almost every year at the annual meetings of the Association. In October, 1814, the Association met with the French Broad (afterwards the Dandridge) Church, when a request came to the body from the East Fork of Poplar Creek "to perpetuate the memory of Elder William Johnson, deceased," and it was voted to publish "a piece" sent up by that church, as follows: "We have to mourn the loss of our elder brother, William Johnson, who, in the cause of his Great Master, on the 26th day of February, 1814, after an illness of more than twelve months, encountered his last enemy with all the courage and fortitude of a Christian, and carried with him all the evidences and tokens of a conqueror, triumphing forever in that great prize obtained for him through the blood of the Lamb, having been in the ministry nearly fifty years and leaving behind him for an example an unspotted character. "His bow abode in strength; a conqueror he left the globe." (Genesis 49:24.)

LAYMAN JONES.

Layman Jones was born October 1, 1803, in Sevier County, Tenn. He was a son of John Jones. His mother was a Layman, sister of "old Daniel Layman," for whom the nephew was named. From the family Bible we get this additional information: He was married to Rebecca Henry, November 25,

1824. After preaching four years he was "ordained a minister of the gospel, November 14, 1830; died August 8, 1845."

In young manhood he was a school teacher, the "second" teacher to help Uncle John Russell "to get a start" in life. Later he helped Elijah Rogers "to fight the battle of missions" in Sevier County. When missionary zeal was burning low in the Holston Association it was Layman Jones and C. C. Tipton who "kindled a fire that burned like stubble."

Elder John Russell attributes his conviction to a mild rebuke of Layman Jones, administered at old Providence Church in Sevier County. The occasion was a "communion service." Young Russell had come to church through mere curiosity to see what was "doing." The preacher, taking in the situation, said: "See how the line of separation is drawn; only those who love the Lord and are washed and separated from their sins can come to the Lord's table. In the judgment day the line will be drawn again, and the separation will be forever, the sheep on one hand, the goats on the other." The arrow struck deep, and he never got rid of it till, "washed in the blood," he walked out of the "dark, rough wilderness into the light of day," and took his stand on the Lord's side.

"Layman Jones had system about his sermons; I could always tell when he was going to quit." (J. R.)

GEORGE JONES.

Elder George Jones was born, October 3, 1830, in Roane County, Tenn., where he has lived and labored almost his entire life. He made a profession of religion in 1858, united with the Baptists, and entered at once upon an active Christian life. He was ordained to the work of the ministry in 1870, and has been pastor of a number of churches.

He is in many respects an exceptional man. For accuracy of judgment, industry and executive ability he outclasses most of his ministerial brethren. Prosperity seems to follow his steps and fortune smiles upon whatever he turns his attention to or touches. He is broad-minded and progressive in his ideas and plans. He has no children, but is interested in the education of the youth. He has contributed many hundreds of dollars out of his limited and hard-earned means to the founding and support of Roane College (near Wheat), an institution which may be justly considered his own legitimate offspring.

Another monument to the Christian spirit and self-sacrificing devotion of this man of God to the Baptist cause is "The George Jones Memorial Missionary Baptist Church," a magnificent church edifice, toward the building of which he contributed $3,000, and much labor besides. The church and college, in which he has invested himself as well as his means, located as it is in a good community, are destined to bear fruit to the honor of Baptists and the glory of their Lord when the founder and builder lies beneath the sod.

Elder Jones' generous contributions to various public enterprises, religious and educational, have so nearly exhausted his humble fortune it is very doubtful whether he has enough left to guarantee him a comfortable maintenance during his declining years. Yet he withholds not his hands from giving.

Brother George Jones, living in the country, a tiller of the soil, pious, zealous, liberal with his means—may his tribe increase!—is one of God's noblemen, satisfied only to "live in the country," where he ever recognizes the voice of God mingling with the melody of nature.

SAMUEL JONES.

Samuel Jones was one of the notable preachers of the Nolachucky Association, a fine singer and wonderfully gifted in exhortation. He was born in Grainger County, Tenn., April 14, 1813. He was married to Frances J. Willis in the year 1835, the issue of which marriage was a family of thirteen children. From 1845 to 1867 he was a messenger of Black-well's Branch Church to the Nolachucky Association, rarely missing a meeting. In 1845 he appears on the minutes as a "licensed preacher," and the following year his name appears in the list of "ordained" ministers. He was "missionary" of the Association for a number of years. His report for the year 1848-49 is as follows: 'Labored 109 days, attended ten pro-tracted meetings, witnessed about 200 professions of faith, preached sixty-nine sermons, baptized eighty-six persons, as-sisted in the ordination of four deacons, passed forty-five days of my time in destitute places.—S. Jones." In 1859 the As-sociation met with Mt. Zion Church, Hawkins County, Samuel Jones preaching the introductory sermon, from John 15:22, a statement of the fact that the sinner has "no cloak for his sin," since Christ has come and spoken to the world. Brother Jones was not a methodical sermonizer, I am told, but he never failed to strip the sinner of every cover for his sin (ex-cept the robe of Christ's righteousness) and lay bare the guilty secrets of his heart of unbelief. He was fiery, earnest, sym-pathetic, powerful in exhortation. He was energetic, and pushed out into the byways and the out-of-the-way places, seek-ing the wandering and the lost. He helped Elder Asa Routh in a meeting with the Buffalo Church, Grainger County, in which there was an ingathering of more than 100 souls, ninety-one coming into the church by baptism. The meeting was re-membered for years and years, and spoken of as "the wonder-ful revival held by Brother Routh and Brother Sam Jones."

Brother Jones loved to attend the Associations, and was appointed by the Nolachucky, almost every year, to attend sis-ter or corresponding Associations. The writer is indebted to Elder A. Routh for the following incident: At an Association in North Carolina, Joseph Manning, from the East Tennessee Association, and Sam Jones, from the Nolachucky, were ap-pointed to preach at the same hour but at different places. Crowds of people from every direction were hurrying to get to the grounds by the preaching hour. As they moved hurriedly along one would say to another. "Which preacher are you going to hear?" An admirer of Manning would ask, "Are you going to hear Manning?" and one of Brother Jones' admirers would answer, "No, I'm going to hear a preacher that can *preach*—I'm going to hear Sam Jones." Brother Jones' friends and admirers almost idolized him, and Elder Routh appreciated him very much as a co-laborer, and spoke of his character and gifts in high terms (nobody could "excite and stir up people like Sam Jones"), but he thought "Manning could say more than Jones when it came to preaching the gospel."

Elder Jones accomplished great good in Grainger County, extending his evangelistic labors at times into Virginia. He was a self-sacrificing minister, receiving very little for his labors. To the manuscript minutes of the Nolachucky Association, for 1867, the clerk, according to the time-honored custom of the body, appended this brief note: "Another minister has fallen. Elder S. Jones departed this life July 25, 1867." He was buried in Grainger County.

WILLIAM A. KEEN.

Twenty years ago (August 5, 1896) the author published in *The East Tennessee Baptist* a sketch of William Arthur Armstrong Keen, dedicating it to the Holston Association. A lapse of twenty years, and six years of added life to our subject, make necessary some changes and additions. So I recast my sketch, making it practically new.

William A., son of Elijah and Rosanna Keen, was born in Washington County, Tennessee, April 20, 1820. His mother was a daughter of Isaac White, who was of English descent. His father was also English, a man with an "ambitious, driving disposition," full of energy and will-power. His grandfather, Joseph, was an "honest" stonemason, born in Maryland.

His great-grandfather, Matthias Keen, lived near Harper's Ferry, in Virginia, and married a Harper. His grandmother, on the maternal side, was a Vaughn, of German extraction, while the paternal grandmother, a Waller, was Welsh. It is to these elements—Welsh, German, English—our subject was indebted for his oratorical temperament and fire, his unconquerable will and splendid physique, a massive frame, six feet

ELDER W. A. KEEN.

one inch, 240 pounds avoirdupois, lungs of brass, a voice deep, sonorous and commanding, brain and head made to fill a 7¾ hat.

Brother Keen's spiritual birthplace was Fall Branch, and the date, November 16, 1841. Many a time he had been "torn up," as he described his experience, by the powerful preaching of James Gilbert, but his conviction did not ripen into conversion until the time of that marvelous "five days' meeting" at the Fall Branch Church, a meeting held by Pastor Jesse Riggs and Missionary William Cate, in which seventy-five souls were made willing captives of Christ, W. A. Keen one of them. As soon as converted he offered himself to the church for membership, was baptized by "Father Riggs," and, putting on the armor, began forthwith to lead in public prayer and hold prayer meetings.

He was licensed to preach by Fall Branch Church in August of 1842, and preached his first sermon in September of the same year. In 1845 he was ordained to the full work of the ministry, Elders Jesse Riggs, Emmanuel Rutledge and John P. Baxter constituting the presbytery.

In his early years young Keen was providentially denied the privilege of attending school, having lost his father when he was only eighteen months old. This providence made it necessary for his widowed mother, "with needle and loom," to support and educate as best she could her four "helpless" children till they were able to support themselves and help her in return. As the boy, William, grew to manhood, however, he "cradled, mowed, grubbed and plowed at $8 a month, and bought home-made jeans at $1.12½ a yard, to wear to school, now and then, a little at a time," as he had opportunity. He attended a "grammar school" some, but gleaned most of his grammar from critical reading of books in after life. In the schoolroom he learned to read, largely, from the New Testament, which gave him his Baptist bias, in spite of his Methodistic environment. In his academic course he had fairly begun the study of Latin and was arranging to go to college, when an attack of fever disarranged his plans, and ended his school days. He has been a great student, however, in the school of everyday life. His text-book in Logic was Carson on "Baptism," which he carefully read through once a year for several years in succession. "Carson taught me how to conduct an argument," was his tribute to that Baptist scholar and polemic. Locke's "Essays on the Human Understanding" was his text-book in Metaphysics. "Paul to the Romans" was his favorite exercise in mental gymnastics. Parts of this epistle he would read over as much as "fifty times," to get the clew to the apostle's great argument. It was discipline like this, persisted in for more than half a century, added to the natural endowment of a great mind, that made him what he was at 75, a truly educated, self-made, masterful man, an intellectual giant.

William A. Keen was *par excellence* the historian of our denomination in upper East Tennessee, if not in the entire state. None of us know Baptist history as Brother Keen knew it. He was familiar with the whole field of Baptist history and polemic warfare, knew every foot of disputed territory between Baptists and all other denominations. Booth's "Pedo-baptism Examined," with its citations of authorities, was the nest-egg, or seed corn, of what became a standard historical library. He devoured Pengilly and the "Baptist Library," and mastered Wall's "History of Infant Baptism" and Gale's "Reflections" on the same. Jones, Backus, Cramp, Orchard, Mosheim and Benedict were to him old familiar acquaintances. He knew Neander, Robinson, Moses Stuart, Cathcart and Armitage, and numbers of smaller works on both sides of controverted questions, besides keeping up with *The Tennessee Baptist* from its beginning. He was master of "Dutch Martyrology," Ramsey's "Annals of Tennessee," and the Minutes of the Holston Association. He knew our pioneer history to perfection. I count it my special good fortune to have been providentially permitted, during the lifetime of Brother Keen, to spend days with him in his library and take "notes" as, with remarkable memory and evident delight, he recounted the self-sacrificing deeds and portrayed in character sketches the lives of our veteran preach- ers of the cross.

He was not only a historian but a theologian as well. He could have been a master in theology, if he had chosen to study the text-books on the subject. He chose, however, to formu- late his own system of theology (a modified Calvinism) directly from the Bible, and solely for preaching purposes. His ser- mons were small bodies of systematic theology and practical divinity.

As pastor, he served the following churches faithfully: Fall Branch, twenty-one years; Buffalo Ridge, twenty-five years; Limestone, about the same; and, for a shorter term, Muddy Creek, Holston, Indian Creek (now Irwin), Harmony, Clear Fork, New Lebanon, Roaring Spring, Beech Creek, Long's Bend, New Hope, Hickory Cove, McPheeters' Bend, Walker's Fork, Kingsport, Double Springs, Blountville, Cherokee, New Salem, Lovelace, and Bethany. Through a period of more than fifty years of pastoral life he fed the churches of his charge with the "pure milk" and the sound "meat" of the Word, emphasizing the "doctrines of grace" and holding up the New Testament pattern of church polity and practice, never receiving a salary of more than $250 a year—on an average about half that amount. As associate missionary of the Holston Association, with Elders William Cate and W. C. Newell, he received a compensation of thirty cents a day. Associated with "Asa Routh and others," under the direction of the General Association, he had "glorious times" in revival meetings, receiving "souls," but little else "for his hire." Those were days of "small things" in the way of missionary enter- prise, and there was little in the treasury to reward the mis- sionary.

18

Elder Keen was not only looked up to as a "father in Israel," but for years was an acknowledged leader in his association--the Holston. For fourteen years he was its moderator, and eight times preached the annual sermon. As a presiding officer he was dignified and capable, was well posted in parliamentary law and Baptist usage, and eminently just and impartial in his rulings. He not only presided with dignity and ability over the deliberations of his own association; as a representative he was often in the councils of the denomination, a credit to himself and an honor to his association. In conference he was distinguished and able, always having weight, and, sometimes, by his influence and wise counsel, saving churches from schism and the cause from disaster. The open secret of his leadership was his sound sense, his knowledge of Baptist affairs, his conservatism, his preaching and executive ability, his personality, and, last but not least, his life.

On account of a "lame" right hand, which made writing awkward and laborious, Brother Keen never wrote a great deal for the religious press—a regrettable fact, I feel, and a distinct loss to the denomination. For the same reason he has left few notes of sermons or other literary remains. We have, however, a partial compensation in the fact that Brother Keen, during a long and active life, made every effort to represent himself in person and to meet face to face with his brethren in all their denominational gatherings. This he did, conscientiously and always, to "the building up of his brethren in love."

Another regrettable fact is that one of our Baptist colleges did not fall heir to Brother Keen's splendid library. I coveted a wagonload of his rare old books, documents, files of papers, minutes, etc., for one of our college libraries; and I am sure it was his intention at one time to make Carson and Newman the beneficiary of his gift or will. But time passed and circumstances altered the situation, and the library is now scattered. May be the books will still preach and do good.

Brother Keen was first married in his twenty-eighth year, and was married five times. His first wives were delicate women and brightened his pathway but a little while. His last companion, a most excellent Christian woman, shared his joys and sorrows for nearly thirty years, and now survives him. Twenty years ago he had eight living children, and several that were dead.

Elder Keen, mourned and lamented here, passed to his reward yonder, January 27, 1902. He rests from his labors and his works follow.

SIDELIGHTS.

1. About the middle of his ministerial life Elder Keen became keenly conscious of having lost, to some extent, his effectiveness in revival meetings, and wondered why it was. In a meeting with his Limestone Church he poured out his heart on this subject to a young brother of the church, who afterwards became a preacher. "I know more," he said, "than I used to know about God and the Bible, and want to tell it. Why is it I can't have the success in revivals that I had when I was younger and knew less?" The reply was: "Maybe you are diving too deep into theology and the deep doctrines—putting the hay too high in the rack. Try something simple; for instance, John 3:16." Studying a little bit, the preacher said, "Well, I'll try that, with the Lord's help." That night the text was, "For God so loved the world," etc., and the sermon had only fairly begun, when the "spirit of revival" came, and the preacher "praised God" for His great mercy. At the close of the sermon about eighty persons came forward for prayer, and 100 joined the church during the meeting. (W. K. Cox.)

2. Brother Cox also relates how, at Harmony Church, on one occasion, Brother Keen took for a text God's question to

Abraham: "Is anything too hard for the Lord?" (Gen. 18:14) ; and, beginning with creation, with its manifold manifestations of the Divine creative power, then taking up the dim promise of a Savior (the seed of the woman shall bruise the serpent's head) made to man in the twilight of history, and pointing out the renewal of the promise to Abraham, God confirming the promise by a miracle (the birth of Isaac), and then, as a further staging of the great drama yet to be enacted, there was the portrayal of the immaculate and miraculous conception and birth of the Christ, and then, in fulfillment of prophecy, the tragedy of the cross, with its attendant horrors, the preacher reaching his climax in the description of the glories of redemption, in this world and the next, when suddenly, like the bursting of an electrical storm, "everybody shouted at once."

J. P. KEFAUVER.

J. P. Kefauver was born December 19, 1819, near Roanoke, Virginia. He was an only son of Jacob and Nancy (Vinyard) Kefauver. His father was from Maryland, and was of German extraction. His mother was from Washington City, and her ancestors were French. Brother Kefauver was a classical scholar, having had good educational advantages from his youth, first in the nearby district schools, and later a five years' course in what is now Hollins Institute, then a first class high school for boys as well as girls. In early manhood he was married to Miss Sarah Sively, of Virginia, who brightened his life for one brief year and died.

At the age of 20 he was converted and received what he felt to be a divine call to the ministry. He was ordained to the work of the ministry, December 11, 1857, by the authority of Blue Ridge Church, of which he was a member—the credentials given him by the ordaining council bearing the signatures of "Thomas C. Goggin, David Staley, Geo. W. Leftwich, Pleasant Brown." He came to East Tennessee in the fall of 1861. On December 12, 1861, he was married to Miss Nannie R. Cooke, daughter of Dr. Robert F. Cooke, of Madisonville, Monroe County. To this union were born two sons and two daughters.

For seven years Elder Kefauver had the pastoral oversight of the First Church of Chattanooga, during and following the Civil War, protecting the sheep as best he could from the dogs of war, and rehabilitating the church, by the kindly aid of the brethren of the North, after the desolating winds of war had passed over it, leaving wreck and ruin in their wake. At the close of the war, in company with Dr. J. R. Graves, he attended the General Convention of Baptists, meeting in Chicago, and was invited to make a statement before that body of the condition of Baptist affairs in Tennessee, and particularly in Chattanooga. When he had made his talk, the convention with one accord voted to furnish money with which to re-seat and repair the house of worship for the Chattanooga brethren. The house was repaired and Brother Kefauver still served as pastor till the death of his father-in-law, Dr. Cooke, made it necessary for him to turn over the work of rebuilding Baptist interests in Chattanooga to other hands, in order to take charge of a large farm and business which had been willed to his wife. But notwithstanding this extra burden thrust upon him, he continued to do a great deal of preaching and pastoral work, in Monroe, McMinn and adjoining counties. He was pastor, at different times, of Sweetwater, Old Sweetwater, Prospect, Madisonville and other churches. He was a great constructive force in the Sweetwater Association. He was a man of convictions and used great plainness of speech in teaching the churches their duty to support the ministry and to give to missions. In emphasizing the apostolic injunction that "they that preach the gospel should live of the gospel," he did real and effective pioneer work. He believed that a church ought to have a Scripture warrant, a "thus saith the

Lord," for every item of its faith and practice, and that the preacher ought to "declare the whole counsel of God" on all questions of truth and duty, the question of "giving" included. When he took charge of the Madisonville Church the church was considerably in debt. Instead of preaching to the church for nothing till it could pay off the debt, he instructed the church to pay on the debt what they "owed" him as pastor. For a number of years he served, under the direction of the Home Mission Board of New York, as a missionary to "destitute fields," on a salary of $1,000 a year, and did effective work in that capacity—his labors being greatly blessed of the Lord in leading souls to Christ. His sermons, on all occasions, were "argumentative, backed up by Scripture quotations, and were convincing and effective. He was composed and dignified in the pulpit, and his manner more conversational than otherwise." Such men as W. A. Nelson and I. B. Kimbrough and others paid him this compliment: "To attend his preaching and hear his lectures is like being in a theological school; he knows how to expound the Scriptures and teach the people." From a Baptist layman, who heard him often, we have this testimony: "Elder Kefauver was clear-headed, scholarly and sound. He was systematic in the discussion of any subject, setting his Scripture proofs in order with great clearness and force. In receiving members into the church, I have noted that he was always careful to stress the Scriptural evidences of conversion, thus safe-guarding the purity of the church and at the same time keeping many a soul from Satan's snare of self-deception."

After a long illness, this faithful servant of the Lord was called from his earthly labors to the heavenly rest, June 6, 1893, trusting in God and rejoicing in Christ as his Savior, making the request that nothing be placed on his tombstone but the words, "Saved by Grace." His association (Sweet water) memorialized him by a committee report, which bore testimony to the "integrity" of his character, his "devotion" to the cause of Christ, his great "interest in the fifth Sunday meetings, and the faithfulness of a ministry that was blessed of the Lord in winning many souls to Christ."

Elder Kefauver is survived by his widow, a woman of Christian culture and consecration, and the four children, two sons and two daughters.

NOTE: As a sidelight on the character of Elder Kefauver I append the following incident: On a certain occasion, at the close of a protracted meeting, Elder Kefauver was to preach by request on "The Subjects and Mode of Baptism." The house was filled with an expectant audience. Entering the stand to begin the services, he found a note on the pulpit, addressed to the preacher, which read as follows: "Will the reverend gentleman please tell us how Paul was baptized? The Bible says he was on a street called Straight, in the house of Judas. We suppose he will construct a pool in that house for the purpose of dipping." Reading the note aloud he said to the audience, without a moment's hesitation: "I will let Paul answer this question for himself." So he turned to the sixth chapter of Romans and the second chapter of Colossians and read to the audience where Paul speaks of his baptism as a "burial," as a "baptism into death," and as a "resurrection" to a new life. Having read the passages, letting Paul answer for himself, he laid the note aside and proceeded with the services.

J. J. KENNEDY.

Jackson J. Kennedy was born in Wilkes County, North Carolina, November 18, 1812, and at a very early age moved with his parents to Anderson County, Tennessee. He learned the trade of cabinet-maker and carpenter, and had "no superiors in his trade."

In his earlier years he had but limited educational advantages, but he was a student and in course of time acquired stores of knowledge. In 1840, upon a profession of his faith in Christ and submission to the ordinance of baptism, he became identified with the Baptists. The same year (July 6) he was married to Miss Eliza H. Yarnell, a young woman of excellent Christian character and worth. The issue of this union was a family of six children, three sons and three daughters. All the children "felt the influence" not only of the mother but were drawn in the right way by the piety and exemplary conduct and teaching of the father, and "maintained a respectable position in their respective communities."

In 1857 he was duly ordained to the ministry, Elder Joshua Frost officiating at his ordination. He spent some six years in ministry to churches not far from Clinton, "particularly Salem, Zion, Bethel and Blowing Springs." In 1863 he removed with his family to Cleveland, Tennessee, where he was especially active in Sunday school work as long as he lived. He was the first minister, I am told, to organize a Sunday school in the town of Cleveland after the Civil War. He was always an active worker in the church but he seemed most pleased to lay himself out in Sunday school work.

Brother Kennedy was a man of "pure mind and clean life, chaste in thought and conduct, an example to old and young— his influence being felt for good in all circles where he mingled. He never was heard to use a profane word, and would not use tobacco or whiskey in any form or way."

He died shortly after a stroke of paralysis, his earthly career ending October 10, 1898. He was buried in the cemetery at Cleveland, his tombstone bearing the inscription: "A sincere and practical Christian—He kept the Faith." In his last illness he said, "My house is in order, but I regret that I have not utilized my time more effectually." He was a great reader of the Scriptures. A little less than a year before his death he bought him a new Bible, and after making the family record in his "bold, clear hand" he added, "This November 18 (his birthday), 1897, I bought this book to read through this year and began reading." Whether he finished the book I do not know, but he finished his earthly pilgrimage before another birthday rolled around.

Elder Kennedy is survived by an only son, John L. Kennedy, an attorney in Nashville, now in his seventies, and an only daughter, who lives in Los Angeles, California.

JAMES KENNON.

James Kennon was a son of Thomas and Rachel (Walker) Kennon, who came from Virginia in the last quarter of the eighteenth century, settling in Jefferson County, Tennessee. He was a double brother-in-law to Hughes O. Taylor—he marrying Taylor's sister Rebecca, and Taylor marrying his sister Elizabeth.

There is no record of James Kennon's conversion and baptism. He was most likely baptized by Isaac Barton into the fellowship of Bethel South (Morristown First) Church. He was a messenger of this church to the Holston Association, along with Hughes O. Taylor, Elihu Millikan and others, from 1815 to 1825. In the last-mentioned year he was likely lettered off with other Bethel South members, to form Blackwell's Branch Church. In 1827 he represented Blackwell's Branch in the Powell's Valley Association. He was a messenger of Blackwell's Branch to the Nolachucky Association, and moderator of that body in 1831 and the three following years. He preached the introductory sermon in the years 1833, 1840 and 1845. In March of 1826 he "was received to the pastoral care of" the Mouth of Richland Church, and remained with the church as pastor twenty-nine years and a half. Church "agrees to let Brother Kennon or any other brother have house to preach on temperance, except church-meeting days" (August Minute, 1835). "April, 1837, received by letter Jas. Kennon and wife, Rebecca." "August 11, 1838, choose Joel Aldredge assistant pastor." "August, second Saturday, 1853, J. Kennon offers his resignation as pastor, having served the church twenty-seven years." Old pastor is re-elected "indefinitely" and serves till September, 1855.

In 1828 Elder Kennon was a corresponding messenger from Powell's Valley Association to the Tennessee Association, meeting with the Forks of Little Pigeon (now the Sevierville) Church. "Brother Kennon and Brother S. Love, by appointment, preached on the Sabbath, after which, having been invited by the church, the association joined in commemorating the death and sufferings of the Lord Jesus Christ, and the sympathetic tears which flowed in abundance on the occasion was satisfactory evidence of the propriety" of the observance. In 1840 Brother Kennon was elected moderator of the Tennessee Association, and in 1846 was preacher of the introductory sermon. At this time he was pastor of New Market, Adair's Creek and perhaps other churches, as well as his home church, the Mouth of Richland. He was elected pastor of the Mossy Creek Church (now the Jefferson City First), "November, second Saturday, 1848," and continued in that connection for six years. He was pastor of the Sevierville and Boyd's Creek Churches I know not how many years.

James Kennon was one of the ablest men of his day. As a preacher he was a man of dignified and courtly mien and a commanding speaker. He was at home in preaching, on occasions, to lawyers and judges and the best scholars of his day. Tall and imposing in appearance, with a massive physique and a massive voice, he was a commanding figure anywhere, in the pulpit, in the presiding officer's chair, in the social circle. He was ambitious, strong and uncompromising in his views of truth or duty, and when he took a stand it was hard to change him.

The following incident related to me some years ago by one of the old members of the Boyd's Creek Church, of which Elder Kennon was pastor, will be of interest as illustrating the value to a preacher, at times, of a powerful voice, as also showing how Providence sometimes co-operates with the preacher in securing results. It was August of 1848. The pastor was in a meeting with his church. Saturday was an election day, and the people were late getting to church at night. Then a great storm came up; the thunder and lightning were terrific. But the preacher had a powerful voice; the louder the thunder the louder he preached. The storm subsided for a minute or two, then reinforced itself with fury. The rain poured, the wind blew like a hurricane, the thunder roared. "God is speaking," said the preacher, "we must speak too, and the sinner must listen." Every sinner in the house was forward for prayer but one. The meeting continued till past midnight. The church door was opened to receive members some two or three times, and twenty-odd members were received on the one night. The text of the occasion was, "Come, for all things are now ready." The preacher went home with the one unsaved sinner, a Methodist by prejudice, and by way of improving the occasion and the opportunity said to his host: "Well, Brother W., you see the Lord knew what I had to do, and helped out with the sermon, and sent plenty of water; let the Lord have his way with you, and cast in your lot with his people."

Another incident: Elder Kennon was holding a meeting in Union County. One of the neighbors, an old man and a sinner had to go for the doctor, riding horseback for some miles. A sudden and very heavy rain raised the waters till fording was exceedingly dangerous. Everybody was anxious for the man's safety, some telling him he had better be religious before he got into worse trouble. The man was afterwards heard to say: "The prayers of Uncle Jimmy Kennon saved my body from a watery grave, and will not let my soul go to hell." Whether the man was finally saved or lost my informant could not say.

"Sabbath day, June 28, 1846, Elder James Kennon delivered a very able sermon on the subject of baptism, after which and a short intermission, the Rev. William Minnis, a Presbyterian minister, delivered a sermon on the same subject, advocating sprinkling to be the true mode of baptism. The meeting was then dismissed." (Records of the Dandridge Church.)

James Kennon was assistant, associate and acting pastor, with Elder Duke Kimbrough, of the French Broad (later the Dandridge) Church, from 1843 to 1847, preaching to lawyers, judges and other educated men, and greatly admired by James Harvy Carson and others of his hearers.

JOHN KIDWELL.

John Kidwell was born in Grainger County, in the latter part of the eighteenth century. He was contemporary with Isaac Barton, Robert Fristoe, James Lacy, Hughes O. Taylor, and the Witts. At some unknown date he became a member of Bethel South (now the First Church of Morristown), and was most likely baptized by the pastor, Isaac Barton. In the first list of ministers of the Holston Association, given in the minutes of 1817, are the names of Isaac Barton and John Kidwell, "messengers of Bethel South." Afterwards he transferred his membership to the Head of Richland Church, and in 1827 he represented that church in the Powell's Valley Association. In the preceding year he was a corresponding messenger of the Powell's Valley to the Tennessee Association. He was an active minister and preached to a great many churches. John Kidwell is a familiar name, one of frequent occurrence in the records of our country churches. This, for example: "Church appoints the third Sunday in May as a sacramental occasion, and invites John Kidwell, James Kennon and Hughes O. Taylor to attend. July 4, 1831: Brother

John Kidwell resigns his pastoral charge of the church at Buffalo," etc.

He was influential in the founding of Kidwell's Ridge Church, admitted to membership in the Nolachucky Association, as "a newly constituted church," in 1848. The church, I take it, was named in his honor. The church appointed him a messenger to the association in 1849, but before the association had met in August of the same year, God called him home; and this is the clerk's record: "We take this method of announcing to all inquiring friends, that Elders J. Kidwell and Jeremiah Hale have departed this life; and, from their distinguished piety and eminent usefulness in the ministry, there is not a remaining doubt but they are now receiving their reward in heaven."

DUKE KIMBROUGH.

(For fifty years pastor of the Dandridge Baptist Church, Jefferson County, Tennessee).

On a tombstone in the old family graveyard, near Jefferson City, Tennessee, is this inscription: "Sacred to the memory of Rev. Duke Kimbrough: Born November 19, 1762; died September 21, 1849; aged 86 years, 10 months, 2 days."

The Kimbroughs are a numerous and noted family. According to history, believed to be authentic and reliable, the first Kimbrough to come to this country was John, who came over from England in early colonial times. The original stock is said to be Irish, as the name Kimbrough would seem to indicate. The patriarch of the family in this country, the distinguished head of a noted line of preachers and a man of marked ability, was Elder Duke Kimbrough, the subject of this sketch. He was the third son of Bradley Kimbrough, Sr., and was born in Rowan County, North Carolina, date of birth as above given. His mother, before marriage, was Miss Sarah Thomp-

son, a daughter of a wealthy planter in South Carolina. At the
age of 21 young Kimbrough left his native state and came to
what is now Jefferson County, Tennessee. Here he met a Miss
Mary Gentry, daughter of Robert Gentry, who lived near Dandridge, and owned a fine farm on the French Broad River.

ELDER DUKE KIMBROUGH.

Falling in love with Miss Gentry he sought and obtained her
hand in marriage. His father-in-law not only gave him his
daughter but also a handsome farm near Dandridge, where
he lived for some years, and then bought a farm near Mossy
Creek (now Jefferson City), where he lived the rest of his
life. To this union was born one only child, a daughter, Mary,
who married William Chilton. His second wife was Susan
Hunter, daughter of Isaac Hunter of Washington County, Ten-

nessee, who became the mother of four sons, William, Isaac, John and Elisha. William became the father of the widely known Dr. I. B. Kimbrough, formerly of Tennessee, later of Texas. His third wife was Eunice Carlock, daughter of Christopher Carlock, of near Dandridge. To this union were born nine children, six sons and three daughters. Of the issue of this marriage two of the sons, Bradley and Robert G., became distinguished Baptist preachers. Isaac Kimbrough, a son of the second marriage, also became a useful preacher. I also note, in passing, that Rev. I. N. Kimbrough, of Indiana, a great-grandnephew of Duke Kimbrough, is one of the strong men East Tennessee and Carson and Newman College have given to the world.

Of Elder Kimbrough's conversion we have no particular account, except that when the Lord made him a Christian the New Testament made him a Baptist, in spite of his inherited prejudices, which were strongly Episcopalian. Also the record of his baptism has perished. It is reasonably certain, however, that he joined what is now the Dandridge Baptist Church, by experience and baptism, soon after the organization of that church, the record of which is as follows: "The Church of Christ on French Broad River, constituted March 23, 1786, by Jonathan Mulkey and Isaac Barton, being twelve in number, with their names," etc. The church was constituted and for several years held its meetings at what was known as "Koonts' Meeting House," three miles northeast of Dandridge. Duke Kimbrough's name does not appear among the names of the constituent members; it is the twenty-fifth name on the membership roll; and, in July, 1793, he figures as a leading member of the church.

As soon as converted, like Saul of Tarsus, he began "straightway to preach Christ." He was called to ordination by the above church, "August, fourth Saturday, 1797," and Elders Richard Wood and Jesse Fears were requested by the church to act as a presbytery at the "following October meeting," the minute of which has perished. Elder Kimbrough became pastor of this old historic church in July of 1799, and continued pastor until his death, in September, 1849, a period of more than fifty years. As long as the old shepherd lived the church would have no other pastor, but when, by reason of the infirmities of age, Father Kimbrough was no longer able to attend his appointments regularly the church called first Elder James Kennon and afterwards Rev. William Rogers as "assistant pastor."

From 1803 to 1839 Elder Kimbrough was pastor of the Dumplin Church, Jefferson County. In the last year of this pastorate the church divided on the question of missions, conventions, and so forth, with protest and counter-protest. The pastor tried hard to hold the church together, and by his influence succeeded in postponing the split, but division was inevitable. The "antis" were in the majority. The missionary minority declared themselves "on constitutional principles to be the church," and as such resolved to hold their meetings on a different day. They also said, in their minute of May, fourth Saturday, 1839: "Father Kimbrough has declined being pastor for either party, but believing him to be in principle with us we invite him still to be our pastor." The invitation to remain pastor was declined, we cannot certainly say why, but most likely on account of existing complications, prejudices and "bad blood" incident to a church split, and with the hope, perhaps, that by a conservative and independent bearing he might be able to heal the breach in this particular church, and help to keep back other churches from a general denominational split. It is just to say, however, that, notwithstanding his conservative position, Elder Kimbrough was a missionary in sentiment, and affiliated with his missionary brethren.

Like most of the preachers of his day, Elder Kimbrough received little from the churches in the way of temporal support. One of his favorite sayings was that the "Missionary Society," from which he received his principal support, was his wife and children—a number of them stalwart and faithful sons.

Not only was he active and in demand as pastor; his labors in revival meetings were abundant and successful.

With great regularity, also, he attended the associational gatherings of the churches, and was often otherwise in the councils of his brethren. He seems to have been a popular preacher on such occasions, often preaching the introductory or other sermons.

"In the pulpit he was remarkable for earnestness, gravity, and unpretending dignity of manner." He had a deep, full voice, and was a natural orator. Years ago I visited the home of old Uncle Peter Bryan, then an octogenarian, and sat spell-bound for hours, listening to his reminiscent descriptions and his boyhood recollections of Elder Duke Kimbrough. He described him as having a "remarkable voice" and great "natural ability" as a speaker, expressing it as his "opinion" that if "Duke Kimbrough had been educated he would have been one of the greatest pulpit orators in the State of Tennessee." He told me also about his singing; how he loved to sing the songs of Zion, in family devotions as well as in the church; how happy he would sometimes get when singing; and how his voice, when singing, was as "clear as a girl's," even when it had become tremulous with age.

Practically, Elder Kimbrough was a man of only two books —Bible and hymn-book. These he kept with him and constantly used. To young ministers, especially, he was a "living concordance to the Scriptures."

In his old age the spirit of prophecy seems to have come upon Elder Kimbrough, and at times he seems to have had the vision of a seer. A notable instance is related by one of his sons and published in Borum's "Sketches." The father, when about 70 years of age, had a serious spell of sickness, and was given up to die. During this sickness he had uncom-

19

mon travail of soul, and predicted a glorious and widespread revival of religion, through which he would be permitted to live and preach, and in which his children would be converted. In confident anticipation of this event he would get happy and say: "The Lord has cut me down with one hand and raised me up with the other." Beginning to recover from his sickness he said to his wife, "Bring me my staff." She told him he could not walk; but he was sure "the Lord had sent his angel to bid him get up and walk, and he would obey the Master." He arose, therefore, and walked across the room, leaning upon his staff. He regained his strength and lived to see the "glorious revival" and preach through it, witnessing the conversion and baptism of a number of his children.

Following is the tribute of the Dandridge Church to the man who had been their shepherd for fifty years: "The piety and Christian character of Father Kimbrough were unsurpassed. He retained his mind to the last, and manifested a firm and unshaken faith in the Son of God. He felt that all was right. He had no doubts. His dying testimony was, "Grace! grace! It's all of grace!" And with those triumphant words upon his lips and a farewell tear in his eye, he passed without a groan beyond the veil, where, face to face, he could behold Him whom he had loved and preached for more than fifty years." (From the *Tennessee Baptist.*)

ANECDOTES OF DUKE KIMBROUGH.

1. In his old age Elder Kimbrough was quite bald, and was accustomed, when sitting in the meeting-house, to wear a cap or handkerchief on his head, for comfort. This he sometimes kept on even in the pulpit, till ready to begin the service. There happened, occasionally, to be in the congregation a certain brother who had a particular weakness in wanting to be recognized as a full-fledged preacher. He was a great admirer of Elder Kimbrough, and would have given his head, almost,

for the honor of sitting with the old Elder in the pulpit.   At length the coveted invitation was given and accepted.   The unsophisticated brother had observed the peculiar headgear of the distinguished pastor, and supposing it to be the proper style for the pulpit, pulled out his pocket handkerchief, bandaged his head, and took his seat in the pulpit, to the great amusement of the congregation.   My authority for this incident is the lamented Robert Reedy Bryan, erstwhile professor in Mossy Creek College, and principal founder of the same—a truthful man.   He used frequently to relate the circumstance, affirming that he actually witnessed the occurrence.

2.   As illustrating the confidence which worldlings and outsiders generally had in Elder Kimbrough's religion, take the following: At a certain place a Presbyterian meeting was in progress.   A proposition was made to a worldling, who was a Methodist by prejudice, to go to the meeting, and "get religion."   "No," said the worldling, "that is no place for me.   Those fellows won't do.   But if they will let Preacher Kimbrough examine them and he says they have got religion, I will take stock in the meeting."

3.   A peculiarity of Elder Kimbrough's preaching was a sudden and unexpected pause in his discourse.   The use of this surprise power, like the sudden stopping of a train of cars, was sometimes very effective.   On one occasion, however, the surprise came the other way.   The preacher was urging upon his members the importance of looking after their religion— "fencing it up"—and with the exclamatory statement that "circumstances alter cases," came to a sudden pause.   "Yes," broke in one of the sisters, "that's what I told John!   I told him if he planted the corn before he built the fence the hogs would root it up—and they did."

4.   In one of Elder Kimbrough's churches was a crooked preacher who had been excluded from the church a number of times, but, on making his confession, had been restored.   Finally the church refused to restore him.   What could he do?   Chang-

ing his tactics, he came before the church with a "new" experience, asking that he be received for baptism. He was deceived before; now he is all right. A motion was made to receive him and seconded. Elder Kimbrough, whose head had been hanging pretty low, straightened himself up in the moderator's chair, and said: "Brethren, it is my duty as your moderator to put the question to a vote. But I have no confidence in him. All who are in favor of receiving him say, 'I.' Nobody responded. The meeting closed and the congregation dismissed, the tricky preacher came out to where the old pastor was ready to mount his horse, and asked to be prayed for. "All right," said the Elder, "let us pray." The pastor knelt on one side of the stump and the hypocrite on the other, and the petition was, "Lord, if this man has religion, give me faith to believe it. If he has none, give it to him. Amen." (R. Newman, in *Borum's Sketches.*)

ISAAC KIMBROUGH.

Isaac, second son of Elder Duke Kimbrough by his second wife, a Miss Susan Hunter before her marriage, a daughter of Isaac Hunter, of Washington County, Tenn., was born in Jefferson County, Tenn., April 26, 1788. He made a profession of religion at the age of fourteen and, uniting with the French Broad (now the Dandridge) Baptist Church, was baptized, most likely, by his father, Elder Duke Kimbrough, who at that time was pastor of the church. Isaac Kimbrough served the church as clerk and deacon for a number of years and, as shown by the minutes, was often appointed on committees to 'wait on" delinquent and erring members. On Monday following the date of a regular meeting day, "March, fourth Saturday, 1842," invited ministerial brethren being present, to begin a "protracted meeting," the church "concluded to have Brother Isaac Kimbrough ordained, which was done by the following presbytery, day and date as above: Duke Kimbrough,

John Lockhart, Caswell Tipton, Robert G. Kimbrough." He
continued a member of the Dandridge Church for some years
after his ordination, frequently serving the church as a supply pastor and as acting "moderator" in the absence of his
father, the old pastor now nearing the termination of a fifty
years' pastorate of the church. In 1849 he moved to Polk
County, where he organized a church on his own farm, to
which he ministered efficiently for a number of years. Belonging to a family of preachers and living in an atmosphere
favorable to the development of preaching tendencies, it might
be considered natural, in a sense, that he should become a
preacher. In addition to this his brethren put him forward,
encouraged and used him, until the matter of preaching providentially assumed in his mind the form and character of duty
and a divine call to the ministry. He entered formally into the
ministry late in life, with little equipment except native ability and great familiarity with the Word of God. In his preaching he quoted, it is said, a great deal of Scripture, comparing
Scripture with Scripture, and so making his preaching strictly
biblical. He was a "living concordance" to the Scriptures.

He rode one year as a missionary of the Tennessee Association, preached to many churches, and did good work for the
Lord and the Baptists, but his most lasting work, perhaps, was
the foundation work which he did in the community where he
was brought up and the church of which he first became a
member.

He was married, in young manhood, to Miss Mary Randolph, a daughter, I assume, of James Randolph, a constituent
member of the Dandridge Church, and a sister of Henry Randolph, who became a Baptist preacher of ability, joining his
fortunes, in 1839, with those of the old school or so-called
"Primitive Baptists."

Isaac Kimbrough reared a large family of well-to-do chil-
dren, and has at least one grandson who is a preacher, Isaac
Z. Kimbrough, who has held good pastorates in Tennessee,
Arkansas and other states.

BRADLEY KIMBROUGH.

In the following sketch I follow Borum, Cathcart, and an obituary notice in the *Tennessee Baptist* (September 22, 1849), signed "W. R.," which I take to be William Rogers, the first president of Mossy Creek College. The facts thus gleaned and re-stated as compactly as possible will form the outline history of one of the largest and most interesting figures in the early history of Tennessee Baptists.

Bradley Kimbrough was born November 3, 1799, in Jefferson County, Tennessee, three miles from Mossy Creek (now Jefferson City). He was the oldest son of Elder Duke Kimbrough and his third wife, Eunice (Carlock) Kimbrough, of near Dandridge. He was born and reared on a farm. His father being a preacher, and away from home most of the time, and his four older brothers having married or gone to the War of 1812, and with a mother and several younger brothers and sisters to support, young Kimbrough, at the age of 12, was up against the necessity of taking the lead on the farm and supporting the family. This circumstance interfered with his getting an education. Nevertheless, when it was possible for him to be spared from the farm, he attended the neighborhood schools, and was an apt scholar. His father also sent him three months to a grammar school, five miles from home, then three months to the Dandridge Academy, and next to the Columbian Academy, where he made considerable attainments in science and philosophy, and studied Latin. This ended his schooling; but he and his brothers read and studied at home, and attended debating societies far and near, always taking a part.

In 1822 he commenced reading law with Judge Jacob Peck, who was then on the supreme bench with Haywood and White. Two years later the supreme court, which sat at Rogersville, gave him license to practice. He then located at Madisonville, where he practiced as a leading attorney for ten years.

As a representative of Monroe County, in 1834, he was a member of the State Convention which remodeled the Constitution of the State of Tennessee. The following year he refused to be a candidate for the legislature, choosing rather to be a preacher of the gospel, and was accordingly ordained to the ministry by the Madisonville Church in the year 1835. His first experience in preaching was a delightful seven months' missionary tour through Georgia and into South Carolina, preaching to churches and collecting his support as he went from place to place, making his circuit around through Hot Springs, North Carolina, to his father's home in Jefferson County, Tennessee, thence to Madisonville.

In December, 1836, he received an appointment as missionary under the direction of the Board of the Tennessee, or Middle Tennessee, Convention, operating mostly in Middle Tennessee and North Alabama. He continued two years in this work, with great opposition from brethren who did not much believe in missions, and were particularly opposed to conventions and general associations. However, he sowed the good seed, introduced the leaven of missions in the churches, created disturbance, excited discussion, aroused opposition, caused division, all of which was better than stagnation.

August 31, 1837, he was married to Martha H. Whitaker, a daughter of Deacon John J. Whitaker, of Mulberry, Lincoln County, Tennessee, a pillar of the Mulberry Baptist Church, and a liberal supporter of the Lord's cause. To this union were born five children, all daughters.

For the next few years he was pastor of churches. He served the church in Columbia twice a month for two years, giving one-fourth of his time to the Rutherford Creek Church, six miles north of Columbia, and the rest of his time to an interest in a school-house near his home, where a house of worship was afterwards built, as a result of his labors in connection with others. Not being able to give his whole time to the ministry here, for lack of support, he sold his farm and moved his family to Mulberry. His labors with this church and in the country round about, were blessed of the Lord. With the aid of other brethren he constituted a church at McMinnville, another at Winchester, another in Cornersville, and still another six miles from Shelbyville. His labors were extensive and abundantly blessed.

In 1845 an educational mass-meeting was held near Murfreesboro, for the purpose of taking steps toward the endowment of Union University. The society voted to endow the university with fifty thousand dollars, and appointed a committee to secure an agent to raise the money. The committee employed Elder Kimbrough, who gave himself unreservedly to the work, going on horseback from church to church and from house to house, completing the proposed endowment in less than two years. He now gave himself for a time to evangelistic work, holding meetings here and there, giving special attention to weak churches. But the Domestic Missionary Board at Marion, Alabama, offering him work, he accepted an appointment as missionary and served the board one year. He was solicited to serve the board at Marion longer, but having offers at the same time from the Bible Board and Union University, he chose the harder job, collecting the money due on bonds that had been given to endow the university. Railroads in this country in Kimbrough's day were few and far between—and riding thousands of miles on horseback, along unbeaten roads through dismal wilds, was no easy job. It took moral courage and physical energy and endurance.

In the course of his ministry Elder Kimbrough witnessed many remarkable religious revivals, and the Lord gave him many seals to his ministry.

He assisted in the organization of Liberty Association, was a member of the body thirty-eight years, and several years its moderator. He was also the honored president of the General Association or Convention of Middle Tennessee and North Alabama.

Elder Kimbrough had ministerial gifts of a high order, and they were wholly consecrated. He also had good native ability and a legally trained mind. All these were assets which guaranteed his success in whatever he undertook. He closed his earthly labors June 30, 1874, "falling on sleep" in Jesus the Lord, whom he had faithfully served.

Elder Bradley Kimbrough was a "bright and shining light in our beloved Zion. He had a stately form and a benignant face. He was courageous, but tender and humble as a child. He was quick and impulsive, reached his conclusions, at times, by intuition rather than by reason, but his conclusions were generally correct. He had a zeal for the Lord's work that knew no discouragement."

ROBERT G. KIMBROUGH.

Robert G., the youngest son of Elder Duke Kimbrough, by his third wife, Eunice (Carlock) Kimbrough, a daughter of Christopher Carlock, was born July 24, 1806, in Jefferson County, Tennessee. Young Kimbrough was brought up to farm-life, with such educational advantages as a preacher's son would have in the community where he was brought up, one hundred years ago. He tutored some in a Methodist college at New Market, having what studies he could carry in the meantime, but, finding there were objections to having a Baptist teach in the school, he resigned his position, at the same time ending his college days. The rest of his education he dug out at home and by dint of hard study in the school of life and experience. His first serious religious impressions were on this wise: His oldest brother, William (a half-brother), many years his senior, was on a visit to his father's home. He had just made a profession of religion and was all aglow with his new-found hope. By request of his father, he told before the entire family his Christian experience, which made a deep impression upon Robert. At the same time he heard Elijah Rogers preach "one of his soul-stirring sermons, which greatly increased his interest on the subject of religion." He stifled his convictions, however, and went on in his unbelief and indecision till he came under the influence of a great revival, at the age of twenty-five, when he fully resolved to "seek the Lord." The second Saturday in June, the darkest and the brightest day of his life, the light of God shined into his darkened soul. The following Saturday he was approved for baptism, and the next day was baptized by Elder Augustine Bowers into the fellowship of the Mill Spring Church, Jefferson County, Tennessee, with twelve other converts. Standing on the bank of the river, witnessing the scene, was a vast throng of people, and his venerable old father, whose deep-toned, solemn "Amen," to each immersion, made the occasion memorable. After some months of prayerful study and struggle of mind with reference to a call to preach, his impressions ripened into a decision, and he answered, "Here am I; send me." He was licensed to preach, December, the first Saturday, 1833; and at the July meeting (first Saturday), 1836, he was ordained to the full work of the ministry, by a presbytery consisting of Elders Duke Kimbrough, John Lockart, Augustine Bowers, and James Kennon.

January 23, 1836, he was married to Lemira A. Wheeler, a daughter of Thomas and Elizabeth Wheeler, of Campbell County, near Jacksboro, Tenn. They had seven children, four of them dying in infancy, two sons and a daughter living to become members of a Baptist church.

Elder Kimbrough's first efforts at preaching were in Jefferson County. But it was not long till he received an appointment, with Brother J. S. Coram, from the East Tennessee General Association, to do mission work and to preach to the destitute in the counties of upper East Tennessee. After another year or two these brethren were appointed by the same body to do similar work. He then left his native county, moving to Jacksboro, the county seat of Campbell County, where he taught for one year in the County Academy, and organized a Baptist church, which he served as pastor in connection with a small interest at Fincastle, a nearby village, where the anti-mission influence had reduced the church to a membership of five. Both these churches were built up and strengthened by his ministry, and he had the pleasure of baptizing something like a hundred persons during his one year's stay in the county, some of them being Methodists. In 1844 he moved to Knox County, and became pastor of two large country churches, Third Creek and Beaver Ridge. The last mentioned was the largest church in the Tennessee Association, having a membership in 1846 (Benedict) of 258; Third Creek being the third largest, with a membership of 226. These churches were blessed under his ministry, Beaver Ridge especially, receiving large accessions to her membership. In 1847 he accepted a commission to be an assistant to his brother, Bradley Kimbrough, in raising money to endow Union University, at Murfreesboro. He continued in this work about fourteen months, laboring mostly in East Tennessee and North Alabama. At one church he told the people the Baptists were wanting $50,000 for Christian and ministerial education, whereupon an anti-mission and anti-education preacher said: "I have now found where the missionaries' bank is; Bob Kimbrough has let the cat out of the wallet."

In 1848 he moved to Marshall County, locating at Cornersville, where he spent most of his remaining days, when not away from home on a missionary tour. He now accepted an agency under the appointment of the Foreign Mission Board, and was the first agent the board ever appointed for Tennessee and North Alabama. He traveled over most of this territory, generally on horseback, making his own appointments, preaching not only in churches but in schoolhouses, private houses, in groves, anywhere, in order that he might reach the people with his message. His desire was to preach the gospel to sinners wherever he might find them, and to stimulate the churches to send the gospel where it was not, that the whole world might hear it. Many churches and individuals responded to his appeals for money; some had their suspicions and doubts, and turned a cold shoulder. During his missionary operations he had frequent opportunities to help his preaching brethren in protracted meetings, in which line of work he had many seals to his ministry. After eleven years of seed-sowing, and a little reaping, in the foreign mission work, he returned to the pastorate, taking charge of the Mount Zion and Marshall churches. In 1868 he traveled as agent for the Home Mission Board. By request of the General Association he moved to Murfreesboro, and taught a class of young ministers for two years. In 1872 he took charge of the Marion Church, in Cannon County, witnessing a goodly number of additions to the church. In January of the following year he moved back to his farm in Marshall County, where he finished his course, dying peacefully at his residence, near Mars Hill, on the 22nd day of July, 1879, aged 73 years.

"Resolved, That our church has lost a devout and earnest member, the community a good citizen, and the cause of Christ a zealous and able minister of the gospel; that we regard Brother Kimbrough as a Bible Christian, sound in his doctrinal sentiments, unswerving in his defense of the gospel, etc. Done by order of his church." Signed by the moderator and clerk.

ANECDOTES.

1. During one of his missionary campaigns with Brother Coram, in Roane County, as they were on a still hunt for Baptists they chanced, one day, to meet up with a gentleman, to whom they made known their business. He informed them that the lady of the house near by was a missionary Baptist. They rode at once to the house, and at first found no one within, but soon they heard some one coming down stairs, who proved to be the lady of the house. They told her who they were, that they were Missionary Baptist preachers. She im-

mediately wept profusely, at which they were greatly surprised, but, calming herself, she told them that when she heard
them enter the house she was upstairs on her knees praying
to the Lord to send Missionary Baptist preachers to her house,
and that when she found two already in her house her prayers
were answered sooner than she expected, and she couldn't help
but weep. The husband was an elder in the Cumberland Presbyterian church, but was glad to help arrange for a meeting
in an old house near by. He took the preachers as his guests
and the meeting began and continued for some days. One
evening, when the man of the house was out, Brother Kimbrough, feeling a little mischievous, bantered Brother Coram
for a discussion on certain controverted points of doctrine.
"All right," said Coram, humoring the joke and himself wanting some fun. Said Kimbrough to Coram: "I suppose, sir,
you are a Baptist preacher?" He acknowledged that he was.
Then said Kimbrough: 'For the time being I am a Presbyterian preacher, and I attack you on your strange doctrine,
that only immersion is Scriptural baptism, your opposition to
the baptism of infants, and your close communion." So the
argument began, but as Coram was pressing the argument and
forcing his opponent, not unexpectedly, to surrender one position after another, the man of the house came in, and seemed
to want to help Brother Kimbrough to stand his ground; in
a little while, however, he turned the matter over to the com-
batants, to knock it out in their own way. Kimbrough got his
whipping all right, and enjoyed it immensely, as did also the
woman of the house.

2. As Elder Kimbrough was traveling in Alabama, in the
interests of Union University, he met up with a man by the
name of Kitchen, and inquired of him the way to Elder Roach's.
Mr. Kitchen was an enthusiastic Whig, and was more interested in politics than religion. So his first question to Brother
Kimbrough was, "Where are you from?" and his second,
"Whom are you for—how do you vote?" Dodging a little,

and wishing to give the conversation a turn, Elder Kimbrough replied: "I am for the Lord Jesus Christ; he is my candidate. I think we all might be for him. Are you a Christian?" "Yes, sir." "Are you a preacher?" "Yes, sir." "Well, light and come in. I just left the table; there is plenty, and you must eat." Brother Kimbrough insisted on being directed to Elder Roach's, but Mr. Kitchen positively refused to give him directions till he should "eat," insisting that it was his custom to "feed the preachers." He introduced the preacher to "the old woman," his wife, who would not hear to his eating a common dinner with the family, but directed him to a chair till she could make suitable preparations, saying: "I will not set the like of this before a preacher. I was raised to feed the preachers, and I glory in it. Take a chair. I will boil the coffee, sir." The dinner being replenished with coffee and other "extras," Elder Kimbrough sat down to a hearty meal. While he was eating Mr. Kitchen talked and walked around the table, expressing his gratification, wondering at and admiring the physical "build" of the preacher, for he was "put up from the ground." The dinner finished, Elder Kimbrough got his directions to Preacher Roach's, and went on his way rejoicing.

I. B. KIMBROUGH.

Isaac Barton Kimbrough, namesake of Elder Isaac Barton, of pioneer fame, was born near Madisonville, Monroe County, Tenn., February 10, 1826. His parents were William and Elizabeth (Molder) Kimbrough, of Jefferson County, Tenn. He was the seventh in a family of eight children. He had three uncles who were Baptist preachers of distinction and ability. His grandfather, Elder Duke Kimbrough, was among the early settlers of the new country, was nearly sixty years a minister and fifty years pastor of French Broad (now the Dandridge) Church. Young Kimbrough was left an orphan at the tender age of seven, and grew up without a father's coun-

sel or a mother's care. Thus early life became to him a battle
and a struggle. He was brought up on a farm, with few advantages of an education. July 29, 1847, at the age of twenty-
one, he was married to Miss Mary J. Henderson, of his native
county. At this time he could scarcely read intelligently. At
the age of twenty-four he was converted, and with the call to
Christ there came a call to preach his gospel. He was now

I. B. KIMBROUGH, D.D.

awakened to a sense of the imperative need of an education and, with both hands and an iron will, he took hold of the double task of making a living for "ween and wife" and preparing himself to preach. By "sweat of brow" by day he made the "living," and by sweat of brain by night (mostly by the light of a torch) he made an acquaintance with books, acquired a knowledge of the Bible and dug into the deep mysteries of theology.

He united with the Madisonville Church in the spring of 1850, and was baptized by Elder A. Stapp. He was ordained by Shady Grove Church in the autumn of 1852, Elders H. C. Cooke and T. J. Russell acting as a presbytery. For two years he served as missionary and evangelist in Monroe County, Tenn., North Carolina and North Georgia. He then became pastor, and served at different times the following churches: Spring Creek, Big Creek, New Hopewell, Tellico, Madisonville, Hopewell, Sweetwater, Mount Harmony, Eastanallee, Salem, Union, Fork Creek, and possibly other churches. At this early period of his life, as missionary and pastor, he baptized into the fellowship of Baptist churches more than 1,000 persons, who were converted under his ministry, constituted eight new churches, and afterwards had the pleasure of seeing several of his converts become Baptist preachers.

In 1873 he accepted an appointment as missionary under the auspices of the General Association of East Tennessee; his two years' work under the direction of the Mission Board, stimulating, enlisting, collecting, put missions among East Tennessee Baptists on higher ground.

In 1875 he moved his family to Mossy Creek, putting some of them in college, while he himself undertook the herculean task, as financial agent of the college, of raising money with which to provide larger and better quarters for the overflowing school. Just how many thousand dollars, in cash and bonds, he raised for the college cannot be accurately stated, since the college records were burned in the disastrous fire of

December 13, 1916, which destroyed our administration building; but a sum not less than from $16,000 to $18,000, funds
sufficient to secure the purchase of the Major Mountcastle
property, which was used for classroom purposes for several
years, then becoming Carson Hall, a dormitory for boys, at
present belonging to Jefferson City, and used for a public
school building. So active, insistent, persistent and ubiqui-
tous was I. B. Kimbrough as a financial agent and money-
getter, with his eye on every Baptist pocketbook, to collect the
Lord's dues, that Dr. T. T. Eaton, then pastor at Chattanooga,
was more than once heard to say of him: "When Kimbrough
dies it will have to be said of him, that the beggar died also."

I. B. Kimbrough was a good parliamentarian, knowing
well how to handle a deliberative body. He was ten years
moderator of the Sweetwater Association and three years president of the East Tennessee General Association. He was active in the organization of the Baptist State Convention. He
was one of the vice-presidents of the Convention, and ever
labored for the unification of Tennessee Baptists in co-operative effort. He was one of a committee appointed by the Convention to investigate and report on a suitable location for the
Southwestern Baptist University, locating it at Jackson.

Not the least of his services to the Baptists was that which
he rendered as their standard bearer in several public discussions, a dozen, perhaps, with Pedo-baptists, Campbellites and
Adventists. He was a skilled debater, an able defender of the
Baptist position. He carried the standard with a steady
nerve, never lowering the flag, and the cause of truth never
suffered in his hands. His premises were like the impreg-
nable rock of Holy Scripture upon which they were laid, his
arguments were logic linked and strong, his quotation of Scripture was a steady fire upon his opponent, his sarcasm was merciless, withering, unrelenting. It has been said that not one
of his opponents ever remained on the ground to fight to a
finish all the questions scheduled for discussion, but invariably

20

cut short the allotted time for debate, quitting the field before
the battle had been joined on all the questions at issue.

Elder Kimbrough was a Fullerite in theology, holding to
Andrew Fuller's theory of the Atonement. He read with delight and profit Abraham Booth's "Reign of Grace." He was
a great admirer of J. R. Graves, and was a "Landmarker" in
faith and practice.

His greatest endowments were a strong intellect and a
soul of fire. Next to these were a wonderful physique and a
powerful voice. His usual weight was 230 pounds; height,
five feet, ten inches; hair, a chestnut brown; eyes, a deep
blue; skin, fair; complexion, florid. He was a giant in strength.
His will was imperious, his imagination lofty at times and en-
trancing. Few men were more positive in their convictions,
few, if any, had more decision of character or had more energy
and perseverance. He was at times eccentric in manner, and
sometimes rough. His peculiar oddities of expression were
not always pleasing. He was educated but not polished, was
a diamond, but a diamond in the rough. I suppose it would
have been impossible to polish him. While his outstanding
characteristic was rugged strength, still he combined with that
a tenderness that was eloquent, at times, with feelings of sup-
pressed emotion, and strangely touching. In one sense he was
sui generis, a genius of his own order, distinctly original and
unique, without a duplicate, standing apart, and a law unto
himself. In another sense he was a fellow servant and a brother, a typical mountaineer, an East Tennessean, "to the manner
born," and proud of the fact that he had been born and reared
and had spent his life, to quote one of his favorite expres-
sions, "among the vine-clad hills and rock-ribbed mountains,
God's country, bounded by the Cumberland range on the north,
which is the backbone of the world, and the Alleghanies on
the south, a country including East Tennessee, the Switzerland of America." His strength was as the strength of the
mountains under whose shadows he lived; his eloquence as

the dashing streams and swiftly-flowing rivers of his native land, untutored, untrained, but having in it spontaneous, original and, sometimes, irresistible force.

As illustrating the more winsome and appealing side of his nature and as showing what grace can do in subduing, soften ing and refining the untamed nature of man, the writer dis tinctly recalls an experience of his schoolboy days. A protracted meeting was in progress. Elder Kimbrough, having come in from his travels and labors to take some needed rest, was out at the meeting, and it was at night. The war-worn veteran got up to talk. The spirit of exhortation came upon him with great power, and he was supremely happy. With walking stick in hand he walked the floor with as much liberty and ease as if he had been at home in the presence of his own family, talking to us eloquently of heaven, our future home. Gradually bringing his powers of imagination into play he carried us all, a vast throng, up with him through the gates into the city and had us walking with him on the streets of gold and looking with him upon the jasper walls. He intro duced us to the heavenly company and to the Saviour himself. It was a marriage feast, and many guests were coming in. But the time came when the door must be closed, and some who had been invited would be shut out and, hearing the words, "too late, you cannot enter now," would go away disappointed and lamenting their sad fate. It was a feat of sacred and really inspired eloquence, possible only to a gifted orator, under the enthralling power of the Holy Ghost, and the effect was electrically thrilling throughout the entire audience.

In the year 1876, perhaps, Carson College, in recognition of his ability and merit, conferred upon him the honorary title, Doctor of Divinity.

In 1879 Dr. Kimbrough moved with his family to Texas, settling in Collin County. He was pastor at McKinney, and organized several new churches in the surrounding territory. Later he was pastor at Weatherford, Plano, Henrietta and

Bowie, Texas. In 1890, following his missionary and pioneer impulse, he went to a remote unorganized district of the extreme western part of Texas. Here he organized many small churches at ranches, under trees (where trees could be found), and in other destitute places, throughout a large and sparsely settled section, since organized into counties and developed into a magnificent country. Under his ministry was built at Plain View the first church house within a radius of a hundred miles of that center. That section has since developed into a Baptist stronghold, óne of the denominational colleges being located in its center. In Texas, as in Tennessee, he was imbued with the missionary and pioneer spirit, labored for harmonious and organized denominational effort in carrying out the great commission, was active and outspoken for local and state-wide prohibition of the liquor traffic, and was not afraid to meet a religious opponent in public discussion. When the time came for him to put off his war harness and lay his armor by he was with one of his daughters at Barstow, in the Pecos River country. He had been preaching fifty-two years, was tired and wanted to rest. His mind wandered at times, but his faith in God was unfaltering. He died as he had lived, in the triumph of an overcoming faith, passing to his reward December 21, 1902. He was buried at Plano, Texas, beside his companion, who had preceded him to their new home above. On the tombstone of the veteran soldier is the inscription: "He fought the good fight, he kept the faith." The epitaph of his companion in early toils reads, by her own request: "A sinner saved by grace."

Out of a large family five are still living, three sons and two daughters, all living in Texas and all making good, I am told, in their several vocations.

DAVID KITZMILLER.

The death of Brother D. Kitzmiller (1898) was a distinct loss to the Baptists of upper East Tennessee. He was a pioneer of the mountains, a man of rugged strength of body, mind and character, as his face in the portrait shows. He was the son of David and Elizabeth Kitzmiller, and was born in Washington County, Tenn., March 31, 1833. His father was a man of piety and influence and, though not a preacher, was gifted in prayer and able in exhortation. He was also a strong Baptist, and lived to within three months of his 96th birthday. His grandfather, Martin Kitzmiller, was Pennsylvania Dutch, and lived to be upwards of 90. His grandfather on the maternal side, David Hughes, from Ireland, was almost in sight of his one hundredth birthday when he died. The subject of our sketch seemed to have been built for a full hundred years, but he was not proof against "neuralgia of the heart."

Brother Kitzmiller received the principal part of his education at the Fall Branch Academy in his native county. In his early manhood he was converted and, uniting with Buffalo Ridge Church, was baptized by Elder W. A. Keen. August 26, 1854, his church licensed him to preach, and in 1856 ordained him, Elders W. A. Keen, John A. Viers and M. V. Kitzmiller acting as a presbytery. He was married September 1, 1857, to Elizabeth C. Carriger, daughter of T. L. Carriger, of Watauga Valley, Carter County. This union was crowned with nine children, six of them still living.

Among the churches served by him as pastor we mention Blountville, Pleasant Grove, Denton's Valley, Cobb's Creek (now Holly Springs), Friendship, Edwards' Memorial, Chinquepin Grove, Poplar Grove, Bluff City, Harmony, Sinking Creek, Stoney Creek, and Watauga, in Tennessee, besides a seven years' term of pastoral service in Virginia. He was also a missionary of the General Association of Virginia for two years, preaching in Russell County, where he baptized hun dreds of people. Elder A. Routh, his successor on that field, said: "Brother D. Kitzmiller did a great work in Russell County. He was a strong man, sound in the faith, an able doctrinal preacher, and a successful evangelist."

He was forty-one years in the ministry, witnessed the conversion of some 2,000 souls and baptized about 1,600 persons, ten of the number becoming ministers of the gospel. Much of

D. KITZMILLER.

his ministry was given to weak and struggling churches and to destitute, out-of-the-way places. In his own community he was a main pillar and liberal supporter of his church.

He was a leading spirit in the Watauga Association, and for several years was the efficient moderator of that body. He was a zealous advocate of ministerial and general education, was a pronounced believer in missions, and always contributed to the enterprises of his denomination.

A marked peculiarity of Brother Kitzmiller was his powerful voice. He made the unrepentant sinner hear in its thunder tones the voice of doom, and with it aroused those "at ease in Zion" with a trumpet call to duty.

This faithful servant of the Lord was called to his reward May 30, 1898. His church (the Watauga), where he had lived and labored for twenty-four years, memorialized him in her minutes and in the *Baptist and Reflector,* paying worthy tribute to him as a "citizen, husband, father, Christian, and a faithful minister of Jesus Christ."

MARTIN V. KITZMILLER.

Martin V. Kitzmiller was born in Washington County, Tenn., January 25, 1825. He was a son of Henry and Elizabeth (Carr) Kitzmiller and a grandson of Martin and Mary Kitzmiller, who came from Pennsylvania and settled in Washington County, Tenn., about the year 1800. His maternal grandmother was Mary DeVault, M. V. DeVault, of Jonesboro, being a grandson namesake. The Kitzmillers are of German descent, or Pennsylvania Dutch, and are a numerous and noted family in this country.

Elder Kitzmiller was converted at the age of fifteen, and was baptized into the fellowship of the Buffalo Ridge Church, Washington County. Two years later, by authority of this church, he was ordained to the work of the ministry. He became an active and influential minister in the Holston Association, his name being prominent and of frequent occurrence in the minutes of that body. He was pastor of the Buffalo Ridge Church in 1845 (Benedict), and was also pastor of Harmony and Fall Branch, and perhaps other churches. He was a member of the council that officiated in the ordination (1856) of Elder David Kitzmiller.

In early manhood (April 29, 1847) he was married to a Miss Mary Crouch, of his native county, to which union were born eight children, five sons and three daughters. Losing his first companion he was married a second time (March 4, 1897) to "an old acquaintance of the family and a member of his church," Melvina Lightbourn, a daughter of James B. Lightbourn, "of the West Indies."

Leaving his native heath for the wider "west," a year or two before the breaking out of the Civil War, Elder Kitzmiller sustained his record of "pioneer" work in his adopted state of Illinois. Here he built up a number of new interests, notably the Girard and Auburn churches, serving one of them as pastor thirty years, the other eighteen. During his pastorate of the first named church he received into the fellowship of the church some 500 members, five of the number baptized by him becoming Baptist preachers. "Fully 1,000 persons were baptized by him" during his ministry. In addition to his pastoral and evangelistic work he served on the town school board, and in the year 1890 he was appointed postmaster at Girard, "a selection by President Harrison which met with universal approval."

Elder Kitzmiller died at his home, Girard Ill., at the age of 81. Several of his children survive him, living in the west. He has two living sisters, Mrs. Elizabeth Duncan, now 81 years old, and Mrs. John Robertson, who is 77 years of age. Dr. R. C. Kitzmiller, of Fordtown, Tenn., his only surviving brother, is now quite an old man and somewhat infirm, but is greatly interested in our Baptist history and rejoices in the success of the Baptist cause.

RICHARD KNIGHT.

Richard Knight was a son of William Knight. He was born May 3, 1800, in Buncombe County, N. C. He was married, when quite young, to Elizabeth Burke, a daughter of David Burke, of North Carolina. To this union were born five children, the youngest of them, Benjamin Knight, is still living, and upwards of 80 years old. His early educational advantages were limited. His wife taught him to read; in fact, he never got further in "book learning" than the Bible and hymn book, and Buck's Theological Dictionary. He was converted under the preaching of "Billy Baker," a colored preacher and a Methodist, both he and his wife uniting, at first, with the Methodists in North Carolina. He afterwards joined the Baptists, and was baptized in due form. About the year 1827 he moved to Tennessee, and settled on Grassy Fork, in Cocke County. In the organization of the Big Creek Church (at Del Rio), August 12, 1833, Richard Knight was one of the "constituent members." On the birthday of the church he was "ordained a deacon." October, fourth Saturday, 1838, the church "authorized Brother Richard Knight to preach from a text or exhort in the bounds of any of the churches where he may see proper."

June, fourth Saturday, 1853, he and Elder J. J. Stamps served as a presbytery in the constitution of Mt. Zion Church, Grassy Fork, Brother Knight becoming pastor and continuing in that relation as long as he lived.

Richard Knight in some respects was an extraordinary man, wonderfully gifted. I have often heard my father say that "Dickey Knight was the best natural orator" he ever heard. He was marvelously gifted in prayer and exhortation. When happy he would "shout" in spite of himself and of all conventional proprieties, and he could "beat anybody praising his Saviour." One of the earliest recollections of the writer is "Uncle Dickey Knight" and his fervent, soulful prayers, his shouting exhortations. There was an educated young preacher in the church for whom Brother Knight had great admiration and respect, but when the spirit of exhortation came upon him he would walk the floor and say, "I am happy tonight. When I feel like I now feel I would shout if the devil was at the door instead of you, Brother Jesse." Mounting as in a chariot above the earth and beyond the clouds, in one of his exalted and exultant moods, he addressed the pastor in a most familiar way, "Well, Jo, if one drop in the bucket is like this, what will it be to swim in an ocean of bliss up yonder?"

In a protracted effort at the Mouth of Big Creek, following a meeting of the association, there was preaching talent of a high order, one or two "doctors of divinity" helping in the meeting. But little interest was manifest, and the meeting was about to be closed without results, when it was decided to "preach Brother Knight." Approached upon the subject he refused at first, protesting that he could not preach. He finally consented, however, to "try." Taking a text he proceeded slowly and with some embarrassment for a little while, but the spirit of exhortation coming upon him he went all over the house, making personal appeals to the "boys" and to the "girls," telling them what the "devil was saying to them," to keep them out of heaven, and exhorting them to renounce the devil and all his works and come forward for prayer. Some forty persons came forward to the "anxious seat," and many of them were converted.

Brother Knight exhorted everybody to the narrow way and the better life as long as he "had breath." He believed in the Lord and in his brethren, but didn't believe much in the doctors. In his last illness he was urged to send for the doctor. "No," he said; "my time has come." There was a home-made medicine man who had done a good deal of free medical practice in the neighborhood. It was agreed that he might come to see him. It would "do him good to see him," but he doubted the "good of his medicine."

Everybody had confidence in Dickey Knight's religion. He fell on sleep January 11, 1859, and was buried on Grassy Fork, under the shadow of Mt. Zion Church. His epitaph, "Full of Faith and of the Holy Ghost," tells the true story of his humble but fruitful life.

PETER KUHN.

Elder Peter Kuhn was born in Pennsylvania December 1, 1793, and came with his parents to Washington County, Tenn., at an early period in the settlement of the state. Having lived in this county a number of years he moved to Sullivan County, where he spent most of his ministerial life. He was twice married and reared a considerable family, but the children, I am told, moved west and south, and perhaps none of them are now living. For many years he was a member of Muddy Creek Church, being also pastor of the church for a good many years. He was also pastor of Rocky Point Church in Sullivan County for a long time. Elder Kuhn went far and near to attend and hold revival meetings; his gifts were in that direction. He was an evangelist rather than a pastor. He preached the gospel in the demonstration of the Spirit and in power, and his preaching was effective in winning the lost to the Saviour. Like many other preachers of his day, his education was limited and most of his preparation for the pulpit was made between the plow handles, or while laboring in some way with his hands to support himself and family. Brother Kuhn, I am told, "had a sunny disposition, was a good singer, was well reported of by his neighbors, was a good man, and enjoyed the confidence and esteem of all who knew him." He lived to a good old age, making his exit from life as he neared the seventy-eighth milestone on the journey, and his body was laid to rest in the graveyard of the old Muddy Creek Church. His grave is marked by a neat tombstone bearing the inscription: "Elder Peter Kuhn, born December 1, 1793; died November 15, 1871. For forty years he was a faithful preacher of the gospel."

JAMES LACY.

James Lacy was born in Virginia about the year 1799. His wife, who before her marriage was Nancy Moody, a daughter of George Moody, was also born in Virginia, on the James River. At the time of their marriage both the families lived in Grainger County, Tenn. They became the parents of twelve children, nine sons and three daughters. About the year 1829 or 1830 Brother Lacy was ordained by the Blackwell's Branch Church, of which he was a member, Elders C. C. Tipton and H. Woodson Taylor acting as a presbytery. He served as pastor the following churches: Blackwell's Branch, Buffalo Creek, Central Point, Kidwell's Ridge, New Prospect, Sulphur Spring, Beech Grove, Locust Grove, County Line, Head of Richland, and others. He was a messenger of Blackwell's Branch Church to the Nolachucky Association from the year 1830 to 1855, rarely, if ever, missing a meeting. The next few years his name appears on the Association minutes as a messenger from the Head of Richland Church, where he continued to hold his membership as long as he lived. He was a successful missionary of the Nolachucky Association for a number of years. His report as missionary for the year 1851 was: "Labored forty-four days; preached thirty-nine sermons; baptized forty-two persons; assisted in the ordination of three ministers and one deacon; spent six days of my time in destitution." Another annual report reads: "Attended eleven protracted meetings; preached 113 sermons; baptized fifty-five persons; helped ordain three deacons and one minister; witnessed" so many conversions and "donated" so many days of labor. The minutes show that he preached the "introductory sermon" at three different times, his subjects indicating a practical turn of mind and a progressive spirit. His last sermon before the

body, in the year 1861, the year before his death, was from
the text: "For the weapons of our warfare are not carnal but
mighty through God to the pulling down of strongholds." He
was active in the Association and in many ways a most useful
member of the body. His good sense, tact and conciliatory
disposition made him a suitable member to serve on committees appointed by the body to adjust differences, etc., and so
promote the peace and harmony of the Association. In the
records of church councils, over a wide territory, one of the
familiar names is that of James Lacy, one of the rewards of
whose ministry was the benediction of his Lord and the brethren, "Blessed is the peacemaker." He was called to the pastoral care of the Mossy Creek Church in its infantile days,
"October, first Saturday, 1846."

"His style of preaching was exhortation and doctrine, revival meetings being his greatest delight. His associates in the
ministry were C. C. Tipton, H. W. Taylor, T. J. Lane, James
Greenlee and Samuel Jones."

He "departed this life August 21, 1862, being about 63 years
of age," the clerk of the Association further adding, "That
gospel which he had so ably preached for thirty-three years
was his stay and comfort in a dying hour."

He died in Grainger County, where he had lived most of his
life, and was buried in the family graveyard on the W. M.
Moody farm, near the Holston River. He has a large posterity, at least sixty-five grandchildren and a great number of
great-grandchildren. He had a preacher son, James K. Lacy, a
useful minister, who moved to Texas years ago, and from Texas
to Missouri, where he died. His youngest and only living child
is A. T. Lacy, of Lenoir City, now an old man and a brother
beloved.

TIDENCE LANE.

"FIRST MINISTER TO PREACH REGULARLY TO A TENNESSEE CONGRE-
GATION."

Tidence Lane, son of Richard and Sarah Lane, was born in
Maryland, near Baltimore, August 31, 1724. He was a grandson of Dutton Lane and Pretitia Tidings, and a great-grandson
of Major Samuel Lane, an officer in the King's service in the
Province of Maryland, in 1680. He was an older brother of
Dutton Lane, a "pioneer" preacher in Virginia, whom both
Semple and Taylor mention in their respective histories of Virginia Baptists and Baptist ministers as a minister of "prominence" and "influence." He was the honored father of Lieut.
Isaac Lane, who, under Colonel Sevier, performed patriotic
service at the battle of King's Mountain, October 7, 1780; who
also, in 1802, "gave the land on which was built the meeting-
house of the first Baptist church organized," it is claimed,
"in Claiborne County," Tenn., the church at Big Spring (now
Springdale).

The register of St. Paul's Parish shows that Tidence Lane
was *christened* "Tidings," from which it would seem that it
was his father's intention that his son should be the namesake
of his paternal grandmother, whose maiden name was Pretitia
Tidings. But later generations of the Lanes have thought
Tidence the preferable name, and have adhered to this spelling and pronunciation.

In early colonial times the parents of Tidence Lane moved
from their native state of Maryland to Virginia and thence to
North Carolina, where young Lane grew to manhood, and
where he married Esther Bibbin (or Bibber), May 9, 1743.
To this union were born nine children, seven sons and two
daughters.

About this time, perhaps a little earlier, young Lane was
convicted and converted in a most remarkable way, under the
ministry of Shubael Stearns, who had been "itinerating" ex-

tensively in Virginia and North Carolina, and preaching with wonderful success. Morgan Edwards describes him as a "marvelous preacher for moving the emotions and melting his audience to tears. Most exciting stories were told about the piercing glance of his eye and the melting tones of his voice, while his appearance was that of a patriarch." Young Lane had the most "hateful feelings toward the Baptists," as he confessed, but "curiosity" led him to make a horseback trip of some forty miles to see and hear the famous preacher, with the following result, in Elder Lane's own words: "When the fame of Mr. Stearns' preaching reached the Yadkin, where I lived, I felt a curiosity to go and hear him. Upon my arrival I saw a venerable old man sitting under a peach tree with a book in his hand and the people gathering about him. He fixed his eyes upon me immediately, which made me feel in such a manner as I had never felt before. I turned to quit the place, but could not proceed far. I walked about, sometimes catching his eyes as I walked. My uneasiness increased and became intolerable. I went up to him, thinking that a salutation and shaking of hands would relieve me, but it happened otherwise. I began to think he had an evil eye and ought to be shunned, but shunning him I could no more effect than a bird can shun the rattlesnake when it fixes its eyes upon it. When he began to preach my perturbations increased, so that nature could no longer support them, and I sank to the ground." (Morgan Edwards' unpublished manuscript.)

In regard to his call and ordination to the ministry I have no definite information. We find him, however, "among the first Baptists" to set foot on Tennessee soil. He has the distinction of being "the first pastor of the first permanent church organization" of any denomination in the state of Tennessee, Buffalo Ridge, in Washington County, constituted in 1779. Under this date Ramsay says: "Tidence Lane, a Baptist preacher, organized a congregation this year. A house for public worship was erected on Buffalo Ridge." (Annals of

Tennessee, p. 180.) The *Nashville American* (Sunday issue, May 16, 1897), among the one hundred "prize questions" submitted to its readers, had this: "Who was the first minister who preached regularly to a Tennessee congregation?" And the prize-taking answer was: "Tidence Lane, pastor Buffalo Ridge, 1779." The Presbyterians generously and frankly concede to the Baptists this priority of date in church building, claiming 1782 as the date of their first church organization, viz., that of New Bethel Church in the forks of the Holston and Watauga rivers. (Pioneer Presbyterianism in Tennessee.) Benedict (General History Baptists) places the date of Baptist beginnings in the state "about the year 1780." Ramsay's date is 1779. While Benedict was a painstaking and thoroughly reliable historian in matters of vital importance and while he visited in person (in 1810) the historic grounds of our Baptist people throughout the country, and had, therefore, opportunity to investigate their claims and traditions, nevertheless, Ramsay, in my opinion, would likely be more accurate in a matter of date, being in easy reach of all the sources of information, having access to all the records in the state, public and private, and having, as he did, a smaller field for study, less subject matter to investigate, more written documents to refer to, and a later date, with its better opportunities for historical research, than his predecessor had or could have at his early day.

Under date as above (1780) Benedict mentions by name eight Baptist ministers, who moved thus early into "the Holston country," all of them Virginians, "except Mr. Lane, who was from North Carolina. They were accompanied by a considerable number of their brethren from the churches which they left. Among the other emigrants there was a small body, which went out in something like a church capacity. They removed from an old church at Sandy Creek in North Carolina, which was planted by Shubael Stearns, and as a branch of the mother church they emigrated to the wilderness and settled on Boone's Creek (then in North Carolina, now in Tennessee). The church is now called Buffalo Ridge." Tidence Lane, as above stated, was its first pastor. With respect to our tradition that Buffalo Ridge came out from Sandy Creek Church (North Carolina) in an organized capacity and established itself in its new home as an "arm" of the mother church, with Tidence Lane as pastor, it may be said that Benedict in 1810 visited both these churches, mother and daughter, and made the record above given. Whether the record was made on the evidence of written documents or of verbal tradition, it is impossible at this distance to say; if the latter, the age of the record and the matter-of-fact way in which it is made, stamps, it seems to me, the tradition as *history*.

Tidence Lane has also the distinction of being "the first Moderator" of the first association of any denomination in the state, the old Holston, organized at "Cherokee meeting-house," in Washington County, on Saturday before the fourth Sunday in October, 1786, ten years before Tennessee was admitted into the Union.

After a sojourn in the "Holston country" for some four or five years Elder Lane pushed on toward the west into what is now Hamblen County, making a location on Bent Creek, near the present town of Whitesburg. Here he and Elder William Murphy constituted the Bent Creek (now the Whitesburg) Church, "June, the second Sunday, 1785," Elder Lane becoming pastor of the church and continuing pastor as long as he lived, some twenty-one years. At the organization of the Holston Association (1786) Bent Creek Church was represented by Tidence Lane, Isaac Barton and Francis Hamilton. Tidence Lane was chosen Moderator, and was elected to the same position in May and October of the following year.

Tidence Lane was active in the ministry, had good organizing and good preaching ability. To use Benedict's language, he was a preacher "of reputation and success." He was much sought in counsel by the churches. He was not so hard in doc-

21

trine as some of his brethren, his doctrinal belief being a modified Calvanism.

The writer has been searching for Tidence Lane's Bible, which he willed to his son Isaac, but it seems to have been lost or destroyed; its successor, however, to which has been transferred some of the entries, doubtless, of the old Bible, has been in the Lane family for more than a hundred years. It gives the dates of the birth, marriage and death of Tidence Lane, Sr., the subject of our sketch. The book is now in possession of Mrs. Crocket Williams, of Morristown, a descendant of Tidence Lane, Sr., about five generations removed, and has been handed down to the youngest child of each succeeding generation since 1812. According to this record Tidence Lane and Esther Bibbin (or Bibber, possibly a contraction of Van Bibber) were married May 9, 1743. To this union were born nine children, seven sons and two daughters. Elder T. J. Lane, for fifty-four years a member of the Bent Creek (Whitesburg) Church and forty years a Baptist minister, was a grandson of Elder Tidence Lane.

Mrs. S. B. Allen, of Williamsburg, Va.; Mr. R. A. Atkinson, of Baltimore, Md., and Mr. H. E. Lane, of Whitesburg, Tenn., all of whom have been interested in furnishing materials for this sketch, are direct descendants of Tidence Lane, of the fifth and sixth generations. Beside these are many others of his kith and kin scattered throughout Tennessee and elsewhere, who are justly "proud of their ancestor."

Having set his house in order and made his will, "the second day of July, 1805," Tidence Lane passed to his reward January 30, 1806.

NOTE.—Some years ago, on the farm of Brother George Smith, on Bent Creek, one mile from Whitesburg, the writer was shown a large elm tree, one hundred feet tall, perhaps, and with branches reaching full fifty feet in all directions, under whose shade, more than a century and a quarter ago, tradition says, "Tidence Lane and Isaac Barton preached to the people."

(See "Will of Tidence Lane" in Appendix to this volume.)

T. J. LANE.

Thomas Jefferson, son of Aquila and Agnes (Fitzgerald) Lane, was born in Jefferson (now Hamblen) County, Tenn., near Whitesburg, October 9, 1804, being the youngest of twelve children. He was a grandson of Tidence Lane, from North Carolina, one of the earliest settlers in upper East Tennessee, the first pastor of the first church (Buffalo Ridge) established in Tennessee, and first pastor of Bent Creek (now the Whitesburg) Church, the third oldest Baptist church in the state, having been organized, according to the records, "by Tidence Lane and William Murphy, the second Sunday in June, 1785," the former serving the church as pastor until his death.

The subject of our sketch, while yet in his eighteenth year, was married to Miss Vaney Pangle, a daughter of Frederick and a sister of old Uncle Clinton Pangle, now living (1896) and in his 87th year, well preserved in body and mind. This union was crowned with seven children, two sons and five daughters.

January, second Saturday, 1834, he related his Christian experience before the Bent Creek Church, and was baptized by the pastor, Andrew Coffman, a good and useful man. The same year he was made clerk of the church, and in June of 1837 was "ordained deacon."

His impressions to preach ripened in the forty-second year of his life, and on the "second Saturday" in June, 1846, he was ordained to the work of the gospel ministry by Joseph Manning and Woodson Taylor. For a long time before his conversion he was under "conviction" for sin, undergoing a state of warfare between a sense of sin and a sense of duty, and even after his delayed conversion was deterred from the ministry by a high sense of necessary ministerial qualifications and a sensible experience of his own lack of fitness. In the providence of God he had fallen heir to his grandfather's library, which he diligently devoured, thus supplementing his lack of education and laying the foundation for future ministerial usefulness.

Besides serving his home church, Bent Creek, as pastor for a number of years, he was also pastor of Liberty, Union, New County Line, Cedar Creek, Robertson's and Cloud's Creek, Morristown and Rogersville churches. In the interims of pastoral service he not infrequently labored as "missionary" for

T. J. LANE.

50 cents a day. As pastor, in common with most of the preachers of his day, he thought it "inexpedient" to stress the matter of pastoral support, and was not disappointed in receiving little or no compensation for his services. Right or wrong, these good brethren acted conscientiously, and made great sacrifices to preach to the churches without charge. As for Brother Lane, he had his sure support in his wife and children and a good farm.

In theology Brother Lane was a free-salvationist and combatted the hard, hyper-Calvanistic doctrine of predestination. He did his own thinking, but frankly acknowledged that he belonged to the "J. R. Graves school" of theological teaching, and was a "landmark Baptist." He was an uncompromising advocate of the independence and autonomy of local churches. He was jealous of the Baptist birthright of soul liberty and independence, and of individual and church rights. He magnified the church, next to her sovereign Head, and was afraid of overorganization and centralization, or anything like popish usurpation of power among Baptists. In the pulpit, and out of it, he was a man of vigorous thought, impassioned speech, and commanding presence. If there was anything he believed in and prided himself in more than anything else, next to loyalty to Christ and vital godliness, it was in being a *sound* and *consistent* Baptist. Hence, he was preeminently a doctrinal preacher and an enforcer of scriptural discipline in the churches in which he had an influence and a voice. If at any time he appeared stubborn or contentious it was not a fault of the heart, but the result of conscientious convictions, a naturally strong will and a constitutional inability to yield until convinced that he was wrong.

Among his associates in the ministry, or the preachers of blessed memory, "into whose labors he entered,' the Whitesburg church records contain the following venerable and venerated names: Isaac Barton, Caleb Witt, Pleasant A. Witt—the last two, good and strong men, but of the Primitive persuasion—James Bradley, Andrew Coffman, Woodson Taylor, Grant Taylor, Jeremiah Hale, Ephraim Moore, and Joseph Manning.

At the close of the Civil War ('65) he refused to be pastor of his home church, but gladly consented to serve as clerk, as in his earlier days, and to hunt up the scattered members of the flock for re-enrollment. Not the least of his self-denying and useful labors, during a long life, was his pastoral oversight of his home church and his continual presence and influence with it, to counsel and guide in the stormy days of war, and to conserve the integrity, purity and spiritual interests of the church in the no less perilous times of "piping peace."

In his extreme old age it was the writer's privilege to be in the home of Brother Lane and converse with him, on many occasions, about the things of the kingdom. He was well preserved in mind and memory to the last, and zealous for the cause of truth and righteousness. On July 3, 1888, in the 84th year of his age, he passed to his reward.

After writing the above sketch, twenty years ago, the writer happened upon the following incident, which is here given as a "sidelight" on Brother Lane's character. A good Baptist woman who, it seemed, had been converted in spite of her prejudice from hardshell sentiments to missionary views, in telling her experience said: "Old Uncle Tommie Lane could make things so plain you couldn't help seeing them. You just had to believe them, whether you wanted to or not."

(See picture of old Lane Bible in Appendix).

BENJAMIN LANGSTON.

Benjamin Langston, the son of Thomas and Louisa (Atchley) Langston, was born September 12, 1835. He was the oldest son of a large family and brought up in moderate circumstances, but with limited educational advantages. But he had a strong intellect, was a student and a close observer, and became a preacher of no mean ability. In his early manhood he made a profession of religion and joined Dumplin Creek Church, Jefferson County, Tenn. At different times he held his membership in Providence, Red Bank, Knob Creek, Marshall's Grove and Sevierville churches, all in Sevier County. He was a member of the last-named church at the time of his death, February 17, 1903.

On July 31, 1856, he married Mary H. Atchley, a woman of strong character, lovable disposition, genuine piety; she was a Christian indeed, a "helpmeet" for the Lord's servant in his ministerial labors and sacrifices. They had only one child, Sarah, who is the wife of H. H. Ogle.

In the Civil War B. Langston was a soldier in the Union army; he was sergeant in Company L, 9th Regiment, Tennessee Cavalry. Soon after the close of the war he was ordained to the gospel ministry by Providence Church. His ministerial activities were mostly confined to Sevier County. He was pastor of Shiloh, Gist's Creek, Rocky Valley, Zion's Hill, Antioch, Marshall's Grove, and other churches. He was a solid and instructive gospel preacher, and his pastorates were successful. He believed in progress and urged his churches to go forward in doing the Lord's will along New Testament lines. He was a missionary, a man of good judgment, was interested in his Association and the "Fifth Sunday meetings," was a good citizen and a useful minister of Jesus Christ.

His grandson, B. C. Ogle, one of our Carson and Newman boys, is a good Baptist and a coming lawyer in the city of Knoxville.

JAMES LANKFORD.

James Lankford (Langford, as now spelled) was born in Blount County, Tenn., April 4, 1805. In 1826 he was married to Ruth Gambol, which union was blessed with a family of ten children, four sons and six daughters.

He was ordained by Ellijoy Church, Blount County, April 28, 1833, Elijah Rogers, Joshua Frost, William Billue, and Eli Roberts constituting the presbytery. He was born, lived and died and was buried under the shadow of this church. He was moderator, assistant pastor and pastor of this church pretty much all of his ministerial life. September 26, 1839, he received a call to the Dumplin Church, and was pastor of that church at the time of his death (1845).

In 1841 he was assistant pastor to Elijah Rogers of the Boyd's Creek Church, succeeding him as pastor in '42, and continuing pastor till '44. He was founder of Hopewell Church, Knox County, about the year 1833, and was pastor till his death, a period of some fourteen years. He was doubt-less pastor of other churches also, but his gifts peculiarly fitted him for evangelistic work; he therefore gave his time and energy almost wholly to holding protracted meetings. In this work he was associated a good deal with Elder C. C. Tip-ton. The two were very unlike in disposition and gifts, but each was a supplement to the other. Tipton was strong, com-bative, rasping; Lankford was smooth, conciliatory, tender— "he was friendly and interested in everybody; he shook hands with sinners and had their confidence." (Peter Bryan.)

Speaking of James Lankford as an all-round man John S. Tipton said: "He is the best calculated of any man I ever saw to carry on a meeting by himself; he was a good preacher, a good exhorter, a good prayer, and a good singer. Back seats were no refuge for the sinner; he could reach the furthest back with his voice and put the audience under the spell of his influence more completely than any man I ever heard preach."

In holding meetings Elder Lankford's singing voice stood him in good stead, for many times he would have to lead the singing, even when doing all the preaching himself. He was particularly noted, however, as a tenor singer. During a re-vival at Dumplin Church, on one occasion, when the congre-gation was singing one of the grand old songs of Zion, "the tenor voice of James Lankford was distinctly heard, above and apart from every other voice, more than a mile from the church."

Three-quarters of a century ago few names on the records of Baptist churches in Blount, Knox, Jefferson and Sevier counties were more prominent or familiar than that of James Lankford.

He was pastor of Hopewell Church fourteen years, and received from the church during that time, it was thought, about $200. All that time he was noted for his punctuality, was never late getting to the church but once. One of the members, a Brother White, said to him, "Brother Lankford, you are a little late today." "Yes," said Brother Lankford, "my horse laid down and died last night. I had a hard time to borrow one, and it was too far to walk." "Boys," said Brother White, "let's buy Brother Lankford a horse"; and in thirty minutes they had raised $40 with which to buy their pastor a saddle horse.

January 25, 1845, Brother Lankford, still in the prime of life, not yet 40, was stricken with a new disease, which the doctors called "quinsy" (inflammation of the throat), and died suddenly, his wife having preceded him (dying of the same disease) to the better world by the space of two weeks. They were buried in the same grave at Ellijoy Church, where they sleep side by side till the "resurrection morning."

ASA M. LAYMAN.

Asa M. Layman was a son of Elder Daniel Layman. He was born in Sevier County, Tenn., November 24, 1818. Being the son of a self-sacrificing minister, who was away from his home most of the time, preaching to the churches mostly at his own charge, and therefore poor, young Layman's lot was hard work and constant struggle to help support the family. This necessity deprived him of school advantages and other means and opportunities of getting an education in his boyhood days. His early schooling was that of hard work and self-denial. He was greatly indebted to his parents, however, for moral training and a good example, which "kept him from being profane or reckless" as he grew to manhood.

He was married to Miss Jane Ferguson April 30, 1843, and to this union were born eight children. In the year 1845 he made a profession of religion and was baptized by Elder James Kennon, uniting with the Sevierville Church. Transferring his membership to Bethel Church, Sevier County, he served the church as clerk for some time. When Jones' Chapel was organized, close to where he lived, he became a member of that church, also church clerk. At the call of this church he was ordained to the ministry, October, 1856, Elders John Russell, William Ellis, Robert Atchley and Richard Evans acting as a presbytery. He preached his "first sermon" at Jones' Chapel from Amos 4:12: "Prepare to meet thy God."

He was pastor of Providence, Henderson's Chapel, Red Bank, Bethany and White Oak Flats churches. Most of his time, however, was given to revival and evangelistic work. He was devoted to his home church, Jones' Chapel, and made it a rule to be present on her regular meeting days, if possible, in order to worship with his family and the brethren with whom he stood in covenant relation.

He was a plain, practical and earnest preacher, adorning the doctrine he preached with a godly life. "He was a strong man and an uncompromising Baptist." (J. Russell.) "He labored successfully in protracted meetings, giving good heed to his ministry. He was a useful minister and church member, a kind husband, a faithful father, an obliging neighbor." (Minutes East Tennessee Association.)

He died March 17, 1867, aged 48 years, 8 months and 28 days, and was buried in the cemetery at Fair Garden.

F. C. LEWALLEN.

"F. C. Lewallen, born February 29, 1832; died February 12, 1900:

> 'The light has gone out of the home,
> And all is dark and drear;
> The children now are sad and lone,
> No father's love to share.'

(Inscription on tombstone here in Bethel Cemetery, near Clinton.)" So runs the "notebook" record.

Brother Lewallen was of Welsh descent. His father was Samuel S. Llewellyn, born in 1805, dying in 1870; his mother was Katharine Llewellyn, born in 1809, dying in 1883. In 1854 F. C. Lewallen was married to Miss Margaret Ann Smith, daughter of William and Cynthia Smith. Young Lewallen was brought up on a farm, with fair educational advantages, and in his younger manhood taught school for a livelihood and to improve his education. He made a public profession of faith in Christ and united with Bethel Church, Anderson County, September 8, 1866. Four years later his church, approving his gifts, "liberated him" to preach the gospel. The larger part of his ministerial life was spent in Anderson County, and mostly in his home community, where he was born and reared. He was pastor of Clinton Church from June 15, 1873, to October 15, 1877. He was a "strong preacher and an able defender of the faith; he ranked among the strong preachers and able leaders of the Clinton Association, and served many of her best churches as pastor." Brother Lewallen had only three children, a son and two daughters. His beloved companion preceded him to the better land just a year. He is survived by his son, Brother W. S. Lewallen, of Clinton, and a daughter, Mrs. W. H. Rutherford, wife of the Baptist pastor at Williamsburg, Ky. He was living with his daughter at the time of his death. "He was a kind and gentle spirit and every

one loved him. He left an untarnished record as a Christian
man and a gospel minister. The end came peacefully, and he
went away to receive the reward of those who are wise and,
by God's help, turn many to righteousness."

WILLIAM LINDSAY.

William, a son of William and Mary Lindsay, and an older
brother of Elder Jonathan Lindsay, was born in Carter (now
Johnson) County, Tenn., in the year 1821.

The family moved to Campbell County when William was
a very small boy. Here he grew to manhood, working on the
farm, spring, summer, and autumn, and at "the forge" during
the winter months. His educational advantages were limited.
At the age of twenty he was married to Miss Huldy Cooper.
To this union were born eleven children.

He professed faith in Christ in his twentieth year and was
baptized, uniting with the Indian Creek Church. Soon after
his conversion he began to preach, exercising his gift as opportunity offered, but was not ordained till about the year
1851. He was ordained by the authority of the Indian Creek
Church.

His ministry was in Campbell, Anderson, Morgan, Roane,
Scott, Union and Knox counties. He was well acquainted
with such "pioneer preachers" as Joshua Frost, William
Hickle, Jonathan Bishop, and Chesley H. Boatwright, and entered into and continued their labors.

He was the second and fifth pastor of Longfield Church
(near Coal Creek), serving the church from 1851 to 1881, and
from '85 to '87, a period altogether of some thirty-two or thirty-three years. He was also pastor of a great many other
churches, scattered over a large territory. He did a great deal
of protracted meeting and missionary work, and was said to
be "an able and successful evangelist." He was also a "strong
defender" of the Baptist faith and of "the true doctrines of the
Bible."

In 1868 he was chosen moderator of the Clinton Association.
He was faithful in his generation and made a good record
alike as a pastor and as an evangelist. In September of 1887
he died in the triumph of a living faith, at his home, about
four miles northeast of Coal Creek, in Campbell County.
Blessed be the memory of the just.

JONATHAN S. LINDSAY.

Jonathan S., son of William and Mary Lindsay, was born
in Carter County, Tenn., September 28, 1823. He was one of
a family of ten children. He had an older brother, William,
who was a Baptist preacher of influence and great usefulness.
The father, with his family, moved to Campbell County when
Jonathan was only six months old. His father worked in
iron—was a "forge builder"—and was in good circumstances
till young Lindsay was about fourteen years of age, when he
had the misfortune of losing his property. This providence
left the son largely on his own resources, to help make a living for the family and to get an education. Fortunately he
lived only three and a half miles from Jacksboro, where he
obtained a fair education. At the age of sixteen he had an
offer of a "free education" from the University of Tennessee,
provided he would teach in East Tennessee, when graduated,
as long as he had studied in the university. This appealed to
him, and he had his things "packed" ready to go, but his father
was in delicate health and prevailed on him not to go. So he
finished his education and made a little money by teaching
several schools in Campbell and Anderson counties.

At the age of twenty-four he was converted in a meeting
at Deep Ford, held by William Lindsay and J. C. Hutson, and
was baptized by Chesley H. Boatwright.

He was married October 3, 1850, to Katherine L. Keeney,
and their home was blessed with a family of twelve children,
six sons and six daughters. Four of his sons and two of his

daughters he educated at Mossy Creek (later Carson) College. He also gave the college a hundred dollars at one time and, at different times, helped poor boys to attend the college.

The first Baptist Sunday school in Campbell County was organized by Jonathan Lindsay at Indian Creek Church. He was ordained deacon by this church in 1851, and in '62 was ordained to the ministry (with C. L. Bowling), Elders J. C. Hutson, Wm. Lindsay, Levi Adkins and Powell Harmon acting as a presbytery.

He was pastor one year at Indian Creek, and some three or four years at Jacksboro. But he was not much inclined to take the pastoral care of churches. He was a substantial farmer, and felt like he could do more good making money and giving to the cause of education and missions and aiding his brethren in council than by assuming the responsibilities and duties of a pastor. He was a liberal supporter of his home church, and gave liberally to almost every church and school and worthy cause within his reach. He rarely failed to attend the public gatherings of his brethren, such as "associations, conventions and commencements," and always helped finance such occasions in a public-spirited way. For instance, when the East Tennessee General Association met at Morristown, and J. R. Graves was there, a collection was taken for some denominational enterprise, when Brother Lindsay gave all he had with him (about $20), and had to borrow money to get home on.

Jonathan Lindsay was a leading spirit in the organization of the Clinton Association, and was frequently urged to allow himself to be voted on for moderator, but he always answered he could "do more on the floor of the association than in the moderator's chair." He never failed to attend his church meetings or the meetings of his association, unless providentially prevented.

In 1885 he was one of a committee appointed by the Clinton Association to effect the organization of the New River

Association, which was done in due order, and that body was launched auspiciously.

For many years Brother Lindsay had advocated the founding of a high school for the boys and girls within the bounds of the Clinton Association, and when the Andersonville Baptist Institute became a reality he was jubilant, and, like Simeon of old, felt that he could "depart in peace," since his eyes had seen a long-deferred hope fulfilled.

From personal knowledge the writer can testify, with W. R. Riggs and a host of others, that Jonathan S. Lindsay was a man of "sterling worth, of high moral ideals, regular in his habits, faithful to his church and Sunday school, liberal with his means, a safe and wise counselor, a good minister and a good citizen, a man who believed in progress and who did a wonderful amount of good in his day."

February 26, 1902, he passed to his reward, honored and loved by all who knew him.

J. W. LIVINGSTONE.

John William Livingstone was born in Wilkes County, N. C., March 27, 1831. He was the son of Elder Cornelius Livingstone, a useful and beloved minister of North Carolina. He was married December 28, 1853; in 1860 was ordained to the ministry, and in the year 1878 he left his native state and came to East Tennessee, locating in Greene County. He traveled over several counties in upper East Tennessee as a missionary evangelist, preaching and organizing Sunday schools, looking after the interests of weak and backward churches, helping pastors in special meetings. His labors were mostly in Greene and Cocke counties, where he is affectionately remembered by many of the old people. He died near Corcord Church, in Greene County, in 1888.

His grandson, Brother D. N. Livingstone, pastor Gillespie Avenue Church, Knoxville, in a personal letter, makes this statement, which I add as a sort of postscript to my imperfect sketch of a worthy and self-sacrificing preacher of the gospel: "I have just had the pleasure of holding a meeting at Warrensburg, where my grandfather held a meeting before I was born. I was also called to Shelby, N. C., for a meeting, where my great-grandfather was pastor for several years."

SAMUEL LOVE.

The place where I am now standing is historic ground. Here in the cemetery of the old Washington (Presbyterian) Church, Knox County, rests the mortal remains of one of Tennessee's ablest and most lovable preachers, whose passing in the prime of life brought sorrow to many a heart. Three miles away is the brick house in which he lived and died, and here in the cemetery is a tombstone marked: "In memory of Rev. Samuel Love, a Baptist minister, who was born January 5, 1802, and died August 19, 1840: Whose praise is in all the churches."

Samuel Love was born in Jefferson County, Tenn., four miles east of Dandridge. His father, William Love, was of Scotch-Irish descent, but born in Virginia. His mother, Miss Lucy Chilton, before marriage, was of Welsh descent. The son inherited the sturdiness of his Scotch ancestors; from his mother he inherited the Welsh "fire and feeling" so characteristic of his preaching.

Young love was brought up on a farm, with fair educational advantages for his day, and was the subject of "early religious impressions." He was "approved for baptism" by the French Broad (now the Dandridge) Church, November, fourth Saturday, 1822. He was authorized to "exercise a public gift," October, fourth Saturday, 1823. He was further "liberated" at the April meeting of the following year. September 23, 1826, he was "ordained" to the full work of the ministry by a council composed of Elders Richard Wood, Henry Randolph and the pastor, Duke Kimbrough, Brother Wood preaching the ordination sermon. Simultaneous with his conversion, it would seem, was his "call" to preach, for the day he joined the church, we are told, "he delivered an earnest exhortation" to the people. With the call to preach also came the call to equip himself for the undertaking. His father's ambition was to make a lawyer out of his gifted son; failing in that, his next highest ambition was that he be a Presbyterian preacher. For a while it seemed that that was what he was going to be. Young Love had matriculated in a Presbyterian college or high school at Dandridge, in charge of Dr. John McCampbell. In the study of the Greek language it chanced that the pupil came upon the Greek word *baptidzo,* and he asked the president and professor what he understood to be the original and true meaning of that word. The frank reply was, that the word meant "to dip, to immerse." Said Love, with a smile, "If that be so, I can't be a Presbyterian." The teacher was greatly impressed by the evident sincerity of his pupil, and was afterwards heard to say: "That young man is a great *free* soul, and, knowing his convictions as I do, I would not urge him to be a Presbyterian for anything in the world." Love lived in Dr. McCampbell's home, used his library, attended his school for several months, becoming a good Latin and Greek scholar. He afterwards taught school to pay the doctor what he owed him for "schooling," and, after he had become a preacher, I am told, he often "supplied" Dr. McCampbell's New Market Church, when it was not convenient for the doctor to do his own preaching. Teacher and pupil always had very great respect and admiration for each other.

November 14, 1826, he was married to Elizabeth West, of Grainger County, Tenn. To this union were born four sons, one of them, James K. Love, becoming a preacher.

His field of labor was Anderson, Campbell, Grainger, Jefferson, Knox and Sevier counties. He was instrumental in building up Beaver Dam and Little Flat Creek churches, established the "mission" which afterwards became the Third

22

Creek Church, near Knoxville, held meetings in destitute places, ministered to weak churches, distributed Bibles, collected for missions. He labored under appointment of a number of our conventions and societies, North and South, and independently as well. "He was eminently useful, mingled in many glorious revivals and hundreds in our churches view him as the honored instrument of their conversion." Isaac Ellege, a venerable father in Israel, says of him: "Sam Love was a fine-looking man, fair-complected, medium size, was a genuine missionary and a great soul-winner. He preached a great deal of the hard doctrine out of the Baptists in these parts." Sister Nancy Johnson, an octogenarian, who grew up under his ministry, says of him: "Love by name and love by nature. He always preached with tears. No man was more loved by his brethren or more esteemed by the world than Brother Love." He was the "unwearied advocate of missions, Sabbath schools, temperance and education, in the midst of opposition. When church doors were shut against him he would preach in groves, barns or private dwellings. He breasted the storms of winter and the storms of persecution that he might preach the gospel of missions everywhere."

As a sample of the marvelous energy displayed and the prodigious amount of work done by our hardy pioneer fathers, in a given time, I submit the following extract from one of Brother Love's quarterly reports to the American Baptist Home Mission Society, dated "October, 1835": 'Miles traveled (horseback and on foot), 1,200; sermons preached, 80; lectures delivered, 35; families visited for religious conversation, 700; church meetings attended, 16; associations attended, 4; temperance societies attended, 4; baptisms, 3; times of administering the Lord's Supper, 3; attended a Baptist camp meeting in Monroe County, remained eight days, witnessed 25 professions of faith and 14 baptisms." '

The writer has heard many thrilling accounts of his wonderful power over an audience; how in sermon or exhortation he would bring his hearers to their feet and draw them about him in spontaneous "amens," in demonstrations and "shoutings" of joy, in "halleluiah" praises to God.

The candle of his life burned out all too quickly, less than fifteen brief years of ministerial labors, but the love light of his life left a glow in the hearts of the people he was leading in the heavenly way; his works follow, and he will never be forgotten. "The sublime tones of his heavenly-inspired eloquence are yet sounding in our ears." When nearing the end of life's journey he was visited by Elder James Kennon, a brother beloved, who spoke to him of his self-denying labors and the hardships he had endured. "Yes," he replied, "but, thank God! eternity will be long enough to rest in." "But what of the comforts of religion in a dying hour?" said Brother Kennon. "Oh, my brother!" was the reply, "there is a boundless fulness in Christ. It is all around me. It is all through me." Thus he passed from the glory here to the greater glory beyond.

E. J. LOVING.

Edmund J. Loving was born in Hawkins County, Tenn., made a profession of his faith in Christ and joined the Cloud's Creek Church in the year 1866. He afterwards moved to Spruce Pine Grove Church, where he was ordained to the ministry in the usual way, by vote of the church and the laying on of the hands of the presbytery. He then moved his membership to Rock Bridge Church.

Brother Loving never acquired a very extensive acquaintance with books outside of the Bible and hymn book. The writer has a very distinct recollection of Brother Loving when he came to Carson College (about 1874 or 1875), especially as he appeared, the first time, in the Philomathean Hall. He must have been 25 years old (was a married man, I think) and fresh from the mountains, with the dress and other peculiarities of the typical mountaineer. But he had good native sense, and a voice like a lion. We were partly amused and partly surprised; when he roared in debate we took notice, if it was not exactly with fear and trembling. He remained in school only a few weeks, I think. Twenty years later I stayed all night with him and was entertained at his home north of Clinch Mountain. He had done and was doing a great work. Besides being pastor of a great many churches in that region of country, he had been a wonderfully successful evangelist in many places, and had been missionary of the Holston Valley Association for four years. Before his death, which occurred March 11, 1904, he had baptized about 4,000 people into the fellowship of Baptist churches. That is a remarkable record. He died of blood poison, caused by a wound from a rusty nail. Judged by man's "feeble sense," that was a calamity. How many more he might have brought into the Kingdom if he could have lived out his allotted years! But these things are in the hands of the Lord, and whatever he does, or permits, is right. His servants fall but his work goes on.

Elder Loving was a member of a lodge at Tate Springs and, after funeral services had been conducted at the church, he was buried with Masonic honors.

LUNAH W. LOWE.

Elder Lunah Lowe was born in Grainger County, Tenn., about seven miles from Rutledge, November 26, 1820, and died at his home, one mile east of Rutledge, June 13, 1894. He spent the most of his life in his native county, and was known by almost everybody in the county. He made a profession of religion and was baptized early in life, casting his lot with the Baptists. Yielding to his impressions to preach the unsearchable riches of Christ he was ordained to the work of the ministry by authority of the Blackwell's Branch Church, and served as pastor, at one time or another, the following churches: Central Point, Head of Richland, Mouth of Richland, Little Valley, Puncheon Camp, Beech Grove, Blackwell's Branch, Kidwell's Ridge, Macedonia, Poplar Springs, Indian Ridge, Block House, Locust Grove, and perhaps another church or two. He was popular as a pastor and enjoyed the respect and esteem of the churches to which he ministered and of the community in which he lived. His moral character was above reproach. He was not only a pastor, beloved and respected, but was a successful revivalist. His Bible was his sole text-book, his only and all-sufficient rule and authority for doctrine and practice, which fact made him a pronounced Baptist. He believed in missions and pastoral support, thought that "the laborer was worthy of his hire," but, like many other preachers of his day, did not stipulate with his churches for a fixed salary. He had a number of striking sermons, prepared for special occasions, which he preached with great power and impressiveness, notably one on Faith, in which he was said to have reached "towering heights for a man of his education." At the time of his death he was a member of the Rutledge Church, to the upbuilding and advancement of which, for many years, he had devoted his energy and ability. He was buried in the Methodist burying ground at Rutledge.

In his young manhood he was married to Mary Ferguson, to which union were born four sons and two daughters. He is survived by his four sons (all of them now old men) and one daughter, his widow having followed her husband to the better country some years ago. Earth was made poorer but heaven richer by the passing of Lunah Lowe.

D. F. MANLY.

David F., son of Absalom and Winnie C. Manly, was born in Grainger County, Tenn., September 7, 1841. He obtained the rudiments of an English education from the public schools of his native county. Later he attended one term of a high

D. F. MANLY.

school. His education, for the most part, was dug out of men
and books, denominational papers and other literature from
the religious press. He was a diligent student and always
learning in the school of life and experience.

In the month of September, 1865, he was converted, and in
March of the following year was baptized, uniting with the
Sulphur Springs Church, near Powder Spring Gap, Grainger
County. In August, 1866, he was made deacon and served his

church in that capacity for ten years. February 1, 1876, he was ordained to the work of the ministry by the Oakland Church, Drs. Jesse Baker and N. B. Goforth, and Elder J. M. Carter constituting the presbytery.

He has served as pastor the following churches: Beaver Creek, Sulphur Spring, Big Valley, New Prospect, Sevierville, Alder Branch, Rocky Valley, Dumplin, Rogersville Junction, Concord, Union, Warwick's Chapel, Boyd's Creek, Pawpaw Hollow, Prospect, Knob Creek, Pleasant Grove, Piedmont, Oakland, Mill Spring, Poplar Spring, and possibly another church or two. As pastor he has trained his churches to support the ministry and to give to every good cause, has taught them their duty to support the gospel at home and abroad. As a result his churches not only supported him but gave liberally to missions and education. He is interested in Christian education, and is a member (1897) of the Board of Trustees of Carson and Newman College.

In addition to his heavy pastoral work he has held meetings in almost every county in upper East Tennessee. From the date of his ordination to the date of this writing (June 30, '97), a period of twenty-one years, he has "carried," says the record, "four churches at a time, and sometimes five, has conducted 140 revival meetings, witnessed about 3,000 conversions, and has baptized 2,500 persons" into the fellowship of Baptist churches.

Few of our preachers have more calls to officiate at marriages and funerals, or to make public addresses on special occasions.

He is a hard student and a laborious worker, has a voice of great power and endurance, a strong native intellect, is gifted with the orator's temperament, and has an impetuous and forceful delivery.

Considering the amount of pulpit work he has done, especially his excessive labors, over-exertions and exposures in protracted meeting work, he would have been broken down

long ago but for his wonderful constitution, his body of iron
and nerves of steel. Years ago the doctors told him he would
"kill himself preaching"; that unless he put on the brakes he
would not "live twelve months." However, he is still alive and
well preserved, is also sobering down, as he grows older and
wiser.

Speaking of Brother Manly's stormy delivery, I am reminded of an incident which illustrates a point, which also is a good
joke on both the parties concerned. In the first year of my
ministry I was helping Brother Manly in a meeting in Knoxville. It was with a congregation that afterwards became the
Broadway Church. We were taking it "time about" preaching, but Brother Manly, being my senior in the ministry and
more experienced, had charge of the meeting. One of the members, a good sister, who had been a regular attendant, dropped
out of the meeting, and the preachers, hearing she had become
suddenly ill, went to her home to see her. We found her in bed
but not seriously ill. We were soon engaged in a triangular
conversation, which centered upon the interests of the meeting, the good sister on the bed punctuating her remarks and
ours with an occasional expression of pain. The conversation, at length, drifting a little from the main subject to other
related matters, we discussed the different styles of preachers
and preaching, the different fancies and the unaccountable
tastes of people, some preferring sweetness and light in a
preacher, others being partial to the loud and noisy preacher.
The writer, using an illustration from nature, made the unfortunate remark, that it was the lightning, not the thunder,
that killed. Brother Manly said, "Yes, that is so." Our good
sister chimed in: "That's what they say. But I like to hear
the thunder roar. Brother Manly, I like to hear you preach."
We were both a little embarrassed but said nothing.

April 19, 1860, D. F. Manly and Katherine Hudson, daughter of James T. Hudson, of Jefferson County, were united in
marriage. These thirty-seven years she has "tarried by the

stuff," while her husband has continually "gone down to the battle."

He has been living at Dumplin for several years, is in his 57th year, and renewing his youth. At present he is pastor cf Piedmont, Mill Spring and Knob Creek churches, and is considering calls to other fields.

The above sketch, written and published in 1897, is a partial and imperfect record of the active and useful life of one of our most successful preachers, who fell on sleep, January 28, 1913, and was buried at Piedmont, where he had wrought heroically for a number of years in building up the Master's cause.

JOSEPH MANNING.

The subject of our present sketch, Joseph Manning, is

"One of the few, th' immortal names,
That were not born to die."

He was born in Cocke County, near the French Broad River, September 22, 1806. In his nineteenth year he was married to Lucinda Huff, by "Joseph White, minister of the Gospel." The second Saturday in October, 1828, he and his wife joined the Clay Creek Church, by experience and baptism. Just one year after uniting with the church he was "ordained deacon." The "second Saturday" in June, 1831, he was granted liberty to "exercise his gifts in the bounds of Long Creek and Clay Creek churches, either to exhort or to take a text, if it lay with weight on his mind." At the regular June meeting, a year later, he was fully liberated "to exercise his gift wherever the Lord might cast his lot." The following year the Clay Creek church "agreed to call a presbytery from West Tennessee and North Carolina, to ordain Ephraim Moore and Joseph Manning to the work of the ministry." Only one minister could be secured for the service. Accordingly, the first Saturday in May, 1833, these two brethren, Manning and Moore, were ordained to the full work of the ministry, Elder Garrett Dewees, of North Carolina, and some deacons, constituting the presbytery. Elders Manning and Moore were joint and alternating pastors of this newly constituted church, for several years, and Manning singly for a long term of service.

JOSEPH MANNING.

August 12, 1833, Elders Manning, Moore and Henry Hunt organized the Big Creek Church, at the mouth of Big Creek, on French Broad River; and, May 19, 1838, Manning and Moore, aided by Elder Garrett Dewees, organized the Pleasant Grove Church, six miles from Newport, on the Pigeon River, the church calling Elder Manning as her first pastor.

Elders Manning and Moore were also the leaders in the organizaiton of the East Tennessee Association, consisting at first of only three churches. During a long and useful ministry Elder Manning was pastor of the following churches: Concord, Greene County, 23 years; Dandridge, 14 years; Sevierville, 6 years; French Broad, Cocke County, 21 years; Pleasant Grove, 40 years; Big Creek (Del Rio), nominally, till his death, September 10, 1883—a period of fifty years.

Elder Manning never kept a record of the persons converted under his ministry, but over a large section of country, where he labored in meetings and was pastor, he was father to a greater number of spiritual children than any preacher of his day—among them, a number of preachers who became men of influence and of note.

He also preached more "funerals" and attended more Associations than any man known to the writer. Many times he would ride horseback a hundred or two hundred miles into Western North Carolina, as "corresponding messenger" to some Baptist Association; and sometimes would go horseback from his home, sixty miles east of Knoxville, to Middle Tennessee (a four weeks' trip), to represent his brethren in council.

He and his true yoke-fellow, Ephraim Moore, bore the brunt of battle over a large part of East Tennessee, in the antinomian and anti-mission controversy of the '30s and '40s. In this crisis in Baptist affairs Elder Manning thought it inexpedient to press the matter of ministerial support, and, consequently, received little pecuniary compensation for his ministerial labors.

His dependence for a living was a good little farm and a business life-partner who always claimed that "she herself supported one missionary."

In his preaching Elder Manning emphasized the doctrines of grace, particularly the atonement, the priesthood of Christ, and justification by faith. He was strictly a New Testament preacher, rarely ever, if at all, taking a text from the Old Testament. The writer of this sketch has vivid boyhood recollections of Father Manning's favorite pulpit themes and his frequent quotations from his favorite author, McKnight. I have in my possession McKnight's Commentary on the Epistles of Paul—a well-worn volume, with the well-marked familiar quotations, which I prize as the gift of James Manning, "in memory of" his father. One of Elder Manning's most valuable assets, as a preacher, was a voice of great pathos, flexibility and sweetness. Among my earliest recollections are the sweet-toned cadences of his voice and the melting tenderness of his exhortations, tenderness and tears, as I recall, that rarely failed to make a small boy weep, and feel that he was a great sinner.

Elder Manning was also a gifted singer. Even in his old age he loved to sing the songs of Zion, and would sing them with great unction and power. In his prime, I am sure, he must have been a wonderfully sweet singer in Israel. Years ago, "Uncle Malcolm" McNabb, then 84 years old, and a Methodist, but a life-long friend of Father Manning, told me how he had "heard Mr. Manning sing in his younger days, when he could sure-enough sing; and how he had many times seen him leading a double-file singing procession of members and new converts down to the edge of the river, where the crowds waited to witness the baptismal scene."

Hundreds of times I have heard the remark that "Joseph Manning never had an enemy; that nobody was ever heard to say a word against him." That was the rule, but the following is the exception. In the strife between the mission and anti-mission parties of his day a little bad blood would naturally be stirred up. And so it was said that some of his opponents would try to get even with him by circulating the vexing report, that when "sick" on one occasion, and thinking he might never get well, he showed great alarm, and was "afraid to die."

On the hill at the old home place, where flows the French Broad River, rests the mortal remains of him who was indeed to many a "father in Israel," his epitaph being the living and dying sentiment of his life—"only a sinner saved by grace." He rests from his labors, and his works follow. His memory is a benediction.

> "The memory of the just
> Smells sweet and blossoms in the dust."

ELISHA MARTIN.

Elisha Martin was born February 9, 1809, in Russell County, Virginia. He was converted when about fifteen years old. For a number of years he was a Methodist, a "class leader and exhorter." February 25, 1830, he was married to Emily Nelson, a daughter of James Nelson, and was blessed with a family of seven children. Having married a woman who was a Baptist, and with Baptist convictions, he commenced anew to read the Bible more carefully than he had ever done, that he might show his wife the error of her way and convert her to the faith of the Methodists. Instead of converting her, however, he was himself converted to Baptist views; and was accordingly ordained to the Baptist ministry, in Scott County, Virginia, May 29, 1841, "by fasting and prayer, and the laying on of the hands of the presbytery"—the presbytery being Elders David Jesse add Silas Ratliff.

He was pastor of Harmony, Limestone, Cherokee, New Salem, Flag Branch, Clear Fork, Stony Point, Gap Creek,

Concord and other churches. He revived the Warrensburg Church at the close of the civil war and led the church in building a house of worship. At the same time he and Jesse Hale were co-pastors of the Concord Church, working in harmony and holding the church together in the troublous days that followed the war. Brother Martin was a plain man and a plain preacher; was "kind, friendly, sociable and courteous in disposition—the kind of man that makes a good pastor. He held his churches together and saw them prosper in his hands."

Three or four Baptist preachers of prominence and note by the name of Martin have labored extensively in Tennessee, some of them coming from Virginia. Whether any of them were relatives of Elisha Martin or not I have not been able to discover. Most likely they were. Any way, Elisha Martin wrought nobly for the Lord and the Baptists for thirty-seven years, and his record is on high. He passed to his reward February 19, 1878, dying in the triumph of a living faith.

J. F. B. MAYS

J. F. B. Mays was born in Surry County, North Carolina, April 4, 1827. His parents, F. B. and M. (Tharp) Mays, were from Virginia, Pittsylvania County. His mother dying when he was an infant, his father took the infant son and returned to Virginia, where the child grew to young manhood, and was partly educated in the Lexington Military Institute. When eighteen years old he united with the followers of Alexander Campbell; but in studying systematic theology and prayerfully investigating the doctrine of justification by faith, as taught in the Scriptures, he became a Baptist, and united with the Baptist Church, Lexington, Virginia, January 1, 1853. In April of the same year he was licensed to preach, and preached his first sermon in a country church, "under the eye of" his old professor, Dr. Thompson. In 1854 he went to South Carolina, and served as a missionary of Union Association. The next two years he tutored and studied theology and the ancient languages under Drs. Boyce, Edwards and Royal, and in 1858 got an A.M. degree from Wake Forest College. Finishing his course of study at the Presbyterian Theological Seminary, Columbia, South Carolina, he was ordained the same year by the Greenville (South Carolina) Baptist Church, Dr. James C. Furman, President of Furman University, preaching the ordination sermon. Mount Moriah Church, Greenville, South Carolina, was his first pastorate. He undertook agency work, and raised money to build a house of worship in Columbia, and "paid his debt for tuition." In three months' time, in 1859, he raised in North Carolina from $12,000 to $15,000 endowment money for the Southern Baptist Theological Seminary. January 10, 1860, he was married to Miss Sarah R. Durham, of North Carolina. The same year he canvassed Mississippi and a part of Georgia for the seminary, raising for the institution, in bonds, about $1,000 a week. In 1861 he was called to the charge of Tuskegee Military Institute, Tuskegee, Alabama. The Civil War breaking out, the professors and students volunteered for service, and the institute closed its doors. Just at this time Elder Mays received a call to the church at Talladega, Alabama, where he had marked success in his pastorate, and preached a great deal to the soldiers.

In Talladega his first child was born, and his wife became a hopeless invalid, suffering greatly the balance of her life. At this time he held many protracted meetings in Alabama and North Carolina, having many glorious and never-to-be-forgotten revivals with the soldier boys in the camps of the Confederate Army. At the close of the war he was a Domestic Missionary in Beulah Association, North Carolina. He was next called to do agency work for the Southern Baptist Theological Seminary in Kentucky. During his campaign for the seminary he was called to be pastor at Jackson, Tenn., where he built up the church from a membership of fifty-two to 250. During his five-and-a-half years' pastorate here he organized the church for effective service in every department of its work, and did valuable pioneer work for the education of women, in the projection and establishment of a Female Seminary of learning. His presence and influence in the West Tennessee Baptist Convention was an inspiration and in every way helpful.

He was called to the First Church of Knoxville in January, 1873, and served the church as a devoted and efficient pastor till September 30, 1878. Near the beginning of his Knoxville pastorate he lost his first wife, to his great grief; but three years later (August 31, 1876) he married a second wife, Mrs. Mattie J. Shepherd, of Knoxville, Tenn., whom the writer knew as an excellent Christian woman and a splendid pastor's wife.

June, 1872, Union University, Murfreesboro, conferred upon him the honorary title, Doctor of Divinity. In the early years of his ministry he had read and pretty well digested Brown's Body of Divinity, Fisher's Catechism and Calvin's Institutes of the Christian Religion. He was a life-long student, and kept up a life-long acquaintance with the classics. The first time the writer ever met Dr. Mays was at a Carson College commencement, in the year 1873, I believe, on which occasion Dr. Mays gave the literary address. The address was exceedingly entertaining, instructive and impressive, an intellectual feast, made up almost altogether of striking beautiful passages from his rich stores of classical literature. The boys never forgot the eloquent address, or the speaker—and he never forgot them, but kept in touch with them and visited them as long as he remained in Knoxville. He was a member of the presbytery (1878) which ordained the writer, and preached the ordination sermon.

Dr. Mays was a self-reliant, self-made man. By his own exertions and perseverance he made his way through eight years of college work, educating at the same time a half-brother and a half-sister. He was always interested in ambitious young men and capable young women, who needed an education, and turned the steps of many such toward Carson College and other Baptist schools.

As to physique and mental and spiritual make-up Dr. Mays has been described on this wise: "He is about 6.2 in height, round and somewhat muscular; very erect, with dark curly hair (it was iron gray when I first knew him) and dark hazel eyes, which are rather small and deeply set; weighs 185 pounds; is sociable and agreeable in manners; is earnest and pious, full of energy and zeal; is an indefatigable pastor; has in him a rich vein of humor which flashes and sparkles at times, never failing to bring a smile."

Dr. Mays went to Florida for the benefit of the climate to his impaired health, and spent the last years of his life in that state. He was living in Apopka at the time of his death, December 21, 1883. The minutes of the Wekiva Association, for 1884, in announcing the passing of "Dr. J. F. B. Mays, pastor of the First Baptist Church of Apopka," bear this testimony: "Our brother enlisted in the service of his Master early in life, and illustrated in his life and death the loveliness there is in the religion of Jesus. All his life and in the dying hour his hope was clear and his faith unshaken. Living he lived for Jesus, and dying he rejoiced in his power to save. He fell in the forefront of the battle."

JAMES BOLIVAR M'CALLON.

A remarkable man was J. B. McCallon, of Meigs County. He was an "Old School" Baptist, for years a recognized leader of his association—the old Hiwassee. He was a great "commoner" among his people; and really there have lived and wrought among Tennessee Baptists few greater or better men

23

than J. B. McCallon. In 1896 it was the writer's privilege to
visit Brother McCallon at his home near Ten Mile, and stay all
night with him, and engage him for hours, far into the night,
in delightful conversation concerning the things of the kingdom and the history of his own life work.

My "note book" reveals the following: He was a son of
John McCallon and was born at Athens, McMinn County, Tennessee, November 23, 1827. His father was a "merchant, a
farmer, a stock-trader, a Democrat, and, in 1847 and 1848, a
soldier in the Mexican War." His grandfather, Andrew Mc-
Callen, and his great-grandfather were soldiers in the "War
of the Revolution." His great-grandfather lived to be 111
years old. His grandmother, on the paternal side, was a Carson, a near relative of Alexander Carson, of Baptist fame. His
father was a Scotch Presbyterian—a sure-enough believer in the
"hard doctrines." Missionary and Old School Baptists "don't
know anything about *predestination,* as the Scotch Presbyterians believed and taught it." It is easy to believe that Brother
McCallen's inheritance of Scotch blood and training had something to do with hardening his doctrinal beliefs and practices,
possibly beyond the Scripture warrant.

September 28, 1848, he was married to Miss Sarah Butler,
a daughter of Jacob M. Butler. October 19, 1853, he was converted. In September, 1858, he was baptized by Elder Micah
H. Sellers, being the last person this "father in Israel" baptized, uniting with the Concord Church, Meigs County.   In
February, 1859, he made his "first public talk." and the following month was "liberated to exercise a public gift." In May,
second Saturday, 1862, he was "ordained," Micah H. Sellers
and Asa Newport acting as a presbytery. Brother Sellers was
his spiritual father and his father in the ministry; his mantle,
like that of Elijah falling upon Elisha, in a sense, fell upon
Brother McCallen, who became his worthy successor in the
prophetic office of the called and anointed man, who, in New
Testament times, *speaks for God,* as well as the prophets of

the olden times. The faithful pastor and teacher is a true prophet of God, and ought to be honored for his work's sake.

J. B. McCallon was Moderator of the Hiwassee Association a great many years, and sometimes was clerk of that body. He organized several of its churches, Caney Ford and Haley's Grove, for instance; and was pastor, at different times, of Concord, Zion, Town Creek, Yellow Creek, Shiloh, Decatur, Kingston, Good Hope, Old Friendship, Ten Mile, Pisgah, Fellowship, and other churches. He not only "fed the sheep" of his own charge, but he evangelized his Jerusalem, baptizing hundreds of people in Meigs and surrounding counties; he then carried the gospel to the regions beyond, "preaching all over the mountain section of East Tennessee and Kentucky, holding many successful revivals."

On the occasion of my visit to Brother McCallon, referred to above, I was shown a Minute of the Hiwassee Association representing thirteen churches, with a constituency of 769 members and five or six ordained preachers. Brother McCallon was very frank in his confessions and statements. Speaking of Brother Sellers, he said he had often heard him say, that if he had his ministerial life to live over again he would preach more on "giving"; he exhorted Brother McCallon to indoctrinate the churches on that subject. But Brother McCallon frankly acknowledged that he "never quite had the courage to do his full duty" in this respect. He had received little from the churches in the way of compensation for his services. But if he could "begin again" his program would be this: "I would preach the gospel, and have me a good lot of deacons to serve tables—(1) a table for the poor of the church, (2) the table of the Lord's Supper, (3) the pastor's table."

The Hiwassee Association, by committee and resolutions, memorialized Brother McCallon as follows: "Our fallen brother and recognized leader was a remarkable man in many ways. He had a wonderful memory, able to quote readily any passage from God's Word, and knowing by heart the whole of the four gospels. He had a great intellect and matchless pulpit powers, being one of the greatest sermonizers of his day. He was rarely ever known to miss one of his appointments. Too much could not be said of his Christly walk, his faith and zeal as a Christian, his devotion to his family and friends. But he is no more with us. We shall no longer hear his matchless sermons and his earnest, eloquent prayers. His voice will no longer be heard in the councils of his brethren. His voice is hushed in death. September 11, 1914, at six o'clock, on Sunday evening, he departed this life. His funeral was held at Concord Church on Monday, Elders R. J. Gorbet and S. A. Waller officiating. His tired body was laid to rest in the old graveyard nearby, where it awaits the resurrection of the just. 'A prince in Israel is fallen.'

> " 'Servant of God, well done;
> Rest from thy loved employ.' "

P. B. M'CARRELL.

I am standing at the grave of the beloved and lamented P. B. McCarrell. On his monument here in the Mount Olive cemetery (Blount County) I read this inscription: "In memory of Rev. P. B. McCarrell. Born December 14, 1841. Departed this life August 6, 1887. A faithful Baptist minister, a worthy citizen, an affectionate husband."

Pleasant Baker McCarrell was the son of Joseph G. and Jane McCarrell, being one of a family of eleven children. His paternal grandfather, James McCarrell, was born in Scotland, but, coming to this country, settled first in Virginia, then moved to Tennessee, settling in Knox County. His grandmother came from Pennsylvania, but was of Irish descent, hence the Scotch-Irish characteristics of our subject. P. B. McCarrell belongs to a family of singers, and was himself a fine singer. His grandfather was educated for a preacher,

but discovering his real gift, decided to be a singer. When
Dr. J. R. Graves lectured and preached in Blount County he
had Brother McCarrell associated with him as his singer.
They were so well suited to each other, Dr. Graves said, "When
I get to be Moody, 'Bake' McCarrell shall be my Sankey."

Brother McCarrell never attended college, but got a good
working education from public and private schools and by

P. B. McCARRELL.

studying at home. In his youth the miscarriage of an axe unfitted him for labor on the farm and made it necessary for him to prepare himself in some way to live off his wits. Fortunately he had energy and ambition, along with a good mind, and so was enabled to master difficulties and rise superior to the circumstances of his birth and environment. He taught school, and in educating others educated himself—in studying school tactics, learned how to handle grown-up people and manage churches.

He was converted in his fourteenth year, in a meeting held at Mount Olive Church, by C. C. Tipton, Isaac Hines and J. M. Stansberry, and was baptized by Brother Hines into the fellowship of the Mount Olive Church. In his nineteenth year (May 1, 1860) he was married to Miss Sallie Johnson, a woman of rare good sense, piety and domestic virtues. She was a devoted wife, and though having no children of her own, was a true mother to the children of others.

By vote of Mount Olive Church, May, "second Saturday," 1867, he was licensed to preach. May 10 of the following year, at the request of Mt. Lebanon Church, he was ordained "to the office of an evangelist," and authorized to "exercise all the functions of a minister of the gospel." Signed by the presbytery, Wm. N. Carson, pastor; William Billue, late pastor; H. S. Hodge, elder; Wm. L. Cottrell.

As pastor he served the following churches most efficiently and with great satisfaction: Mt. Lebanon, Mt. Olive, Rockford, Gallaher's View, Stock Creek, Laurel Bank, Alder Branch, Pleasant Grove, Island Home, and Sevierville. He was pastor of five of the above churches at the time of his death. He was greatly loved by his churches, was popular with the people, and was well supported. This enabled him to buy and pay for a good home at Rockford.

As pastor-evangelist he had marked success. His brother-pastors sought his aid in protracted meetings, and many weak and pastorless churches were strengthened and put on their feet by his labors. "He was the leading man in revivals in this county. He held powerful meetings in Blount and Knox and Sevier counties, and built up the churches. He loved children, and had a great influence over them. He could get down among the people and have them to do anything he wanted done" (J. W. Hitch).

He was a strong advocate of temperance and preached it as a part of the gospel. He believed also in the legal prohibition of the liquor traffic. He was the chosen leader of the prohibition movement in Blount County, where he lived, and made his power felt not only for right living but also for righteous legislation.

The most marked characteristics of P. B. McCarrell, as I gathered them from many sources, were his studious devotion to the Bible, his unfailing energy, his punctuality (he made it a rule never to disappoint a congregation), his whole-hearted consecration to the Lord's work, his love for his own Baptist brethren, and his charitable and sweet-spirited disposition toward all Christians. One of his favorite Scriptures was: "Behold how good and how pleasant it is for brethren to dwell together in unity."

Dr. E. A. Taylor preached his funeral discourse in the presence of a vast concourse of grief-stricken friends, paying worthy tribute to the deceased.

GARNER M'CONNICO.

Garner McConnico was a native of Lunenburg County, Virginia, born in the year 1771, being the youngest of three brothers. His mother was a woman of unusual piety and firmness of character, who, like Solomon, believed "in bringing up a child in the way he should go." This characteristic crops out incidentally in the story of young McConnico's conviction and conversion, as related by James Ross (Life and Times of Elder Reuben Ross), as follows: An old Baptist preacher who had belonged to the British army and had remained in Virginia after the War of the Revolution was over, had made an appointment to preach in the neighborhood of the McConnicos. Garner's mother wanted to hear the preacher, and requested her son to go with her to the meeting. The boy, however, for reasons satisfactory to himself, didn't want to go; he hated the very name, Englishman, having been compelled, many times, by the British and Tories to leave his home and lie out in the woods, when the oppressors would be in that part of the country. Thinking it prudent to comply with his mother's wishes, her request now taking the form of a command, he decided to go, but was determined not to listen to a word the preacher might say. On reaching the place, however, he concluded to go just near enough to look at the preacher. Fitting the action to the thought, he found the preacher to be such a diminutive, unsightly dwarf of a man, that young McConnico felt some curiosity to hear him talk a little. He heard him as he had never heard mortal man speak before; the preacher seemed to "bring the very heavens and earth together," and when he came to himself he was standing near the old man in tears. From this time he never rested until he embraced a hope in Christ, uniting with the Baptist Church at Tusekiah, on the relation of his Christian experience. In his young manhood he was married to Miss Mary Walker, and soon began the exercise of his public gifts of prayer and exhortation, and received from his church a "license" to preach.

About the year 1795, hearing reports of the "extraordinary attractions of the beautiful valley of the Cumberland, as a place for settlement," and, like many others, being affected by the prevalent "western fever" of the times, Garner McConnico, with his young wife, "fell into the current of emigration that was setting westward," and soon found himself "beyond the mountains" in Davidson County, Tennessee. Here he remained for two years "in a state of great darkness," as he said, on account of a temptation to give up the ministry. In fact, when he left his native Virginia he was "fleeing from the Lord," trying to get rid of his call to be a preacher of the gospel. In the new country of the Cumberland he was, on a memorable day, in search of his horse, that had strayed off in the spring of the year. As he was walking along a narrow path cut through the tall cane, in deep thought on the subject of preaching, he saw a small, venerable-looking man advancing toward him—a man who looked, as he imagined, very much like the apostle Paul must have looked. When they met, after the usual salutations, the following dialogue took place: "What sort of a country is this we are in?" said McConnico. "A very rich, wooded country," answered the venerable-looking man. "Any religion in it?" questioned the younger man. "A few professors, scattered about here and there," responded the old man. "Any Baptist preaching in it?" "There will be Baptist preaching in it next Lord's Day." "And are you the preacher?" "I try to preach here sometimes for want of a better preacher." Here they parted. The old man proved to be Elder Dillahunty, a well-known preacher in that part of the country. "Next Lord's Day" soon rolled round; the old preacher was on hand to fulfill his engagement, and Mc-Connico was there. At the close of the sermon the preacher announced that he would preach at Richland Meeting House on a certain Lord's Day, when young McConnico, a bit nervous, rose to his feet and said. "And I will be with you there." "And who are you?" inquired Father Dillahunty. "The man you met in the canebrake." "A Baptist?" "Yes." "And a preacher?" "Why, yes, I *have* tried to exercise a little in that way." And now the "secret" he and his wife were going to keep so close is out, and it is really and embarrassingly known that he is a *preacher*. Preaching day came around. McConnico was present, according to promise, but tried hard to beg off. The old preacher, however, held him to his promise. The young preacher proceeded with the sermon, and when about half through the old man rose from his seat, took the young preacher in his arms, wept aloud, and thanked God that he had found a young Timothy on the frontier both able and willing to assist him in spreading the glad tidings in the wilderness (Reuben Ross, Chapter XV).

In the fall of 1797, Elder McConnico removed to the neighborhood of Franklin, Williamson County, where, in a beautiful spot of country, he lived for thirty-five years, and reared a large and most estimable family. His mansion, after the old Virginia fashion, was ever the scene of a profuse and generous hospitality. In it was found the best society then in the west; and especially was it the delightful resting place of way-worn ministers of the gospel of Christ (R. B. C. Howell). Here he built up the Big Harpeth Church, the third Baptist church planted (1800) south of Nashville. In this same year (1800) he was ordained to the ministry by the authority of this church, becoming its pastor the day of his ordination, and continuing pastor till the day of his death, a period of thirty-three years. He was largely, if not chiefly, instrumental in organizing (1803) the Cumberland Association, and was Moderator of that body many years in succession. The most noted church of this Association, the Big Harpeth, constituted with twenty members, and so long shepherded by Elder McConnico, became the mother of seven other churches. Benedict, exploring the country (1810) in the interests of his great History, found this church and Association in a flourishing condition, referring in a footnote, to the pastor and Moderator as a "distinguished preacher in the midst of his labors and usefulness."

Elder McConnico, though not a classical scholar, was, nevertheless, a diligent student of the Bible and had an extensive acquaintance with the standard theological works of his day. He prepared his sermons, it is said, with great care, and in his preaching clung with an unyielding purpose to the great doctrines of the cross. He was industrious and indefatigable in his labors, not only in his own church and com-

munity, but in sister churches, striving with true evangelistic
spirit to preach the gospel in "regions beyond."

Many professed faith in Christ under his ministry, and a
great number of churches were founded mainly through his
instrumentality. His popularity was almost unbounded. Of
his appearance and style, Dr. Howell gave the following description: "His figure was tall and commanding, and in every
movement there was a natural finish and grace, of which, however, he seemed himself to be utterly unconscious. His complexion was fair and ruddy, his hair black, his eyes were large
and dark, overshadowed by brows not particularly heavy but
distinctly marked; his forehead was broad, high and smooth;
an indescribable benevolent smile was ever playing about his
mouth; his voice was remarkable for its manly tone and musical sweetness, and his whole finely chiseled face, alike in conversation and in the pulpit, was lighted up by an unmistaka-
ble expression of intelligence. His piety was uncompromising.
His manner was dignified and attractive. Had you entered into
conversation with him or been one of his numerous auditors
beneath the deep shade of the gigantic primeval forest, where
he so often preached, you would soon have found coming over
you a strange feeling of reverence for his mighty mind. Like
an atmosphere, his intellect seemed to enclose you on all sides,
and his very modesty and deference to your judgment made
his conclusions so much the more resistless. His discourses
seemed alike effective with persons of every variety of culture
and of character. Though the details of his life have passed
into oblivion, his memory can never die."

ANECDOTE: Among the so-called religious phenomena of
McConnico's day was a peculiar exercise known as the "jerks,"
an affectation revived, of late years, among the "holy rollers,"
calling themselves The Church of God. Benedict says: "When
I was in this country—that is, the valley of the Cumberland,
in 1810, it so happened that I did not see this distinguished
preacher (McConnico), but heard much of his fame and minis-

terial success. The following anecdote of him I find in my second volume, page 256. During the great revival in that region, and the unusual gesticulations which in some cases attended it, one of the *jerkers* began his motions at one of his meetings. The preacher suddenly made a pause, and with a loud and solemn tone exclaimed, 'In the name of the Lord, I command all unclean spirits to leave this place.' The jerker immediately became still, and the report was spread abroad that McConnico cast out devils."

An Incident: The following incident, though almost unbelievable, is nevertheless vouched for by a trustworthy author as an actual occurrence. I give the exact words of the author: "Garner McConnico, who belonged to the Cumberland Association, used to come down now and then and preach among us. He was a large, handsome man. His voice was singlarly rich and powerful, and his talents of the first order. On one occasion he had an appointment to preach under some shade trees on the banks of Big Harpeth River, but there fell a heavy rain the night before, and when he reached the river it was past fording, consequently he could not join his congregation. He spoke to the people, however, from the opposite bank, telling them if they would seat themselves and be quiet they should hear what he had to say. This being done, he raised his voice a little above its usual pitch and preached a fine sermon, every word of which was distinctly heard, notwithstanding the distance and the dashing of the swollen stream against its banks. Elder Todevine used to say, when speaking of him, 'Brother McConnico has a voice like a trumpet.'" (J. R.)

"Elder McConnico died suddenly, full of faith and hope, in the year 1833, in the 62nd year of his age."

MOSES M'GINNIS.

The subject of this sketch, a son of Edward and Nancy McGinnis, was born in Smyth County, Virginia, July 16, 1779. He was of Irish, or Scotch-Irish, descent. His parents came to Tennessee, locating in Hawkins County, when Moses was a lad nine years of age. When a full-grown man he went to school to Elika Taylor, who "taught him grammar," and was afterwards proud to testify of his pupil that he was a "bright and talented man, and self-made." At the age of 40 he made a profession of religion and was baptized by Hughes O. Taylor into the fellowship of War Creek (now Flat Gap) Church. Soon after his baptism his church ordained him deacon. In 1835 he was "licensed to preach," and in the same year was "ordained" to the full work of the ministry.

In his young manhood he was married to Mary Wolf, a daughter of Charles and Susanna Wolf, a woman of Dutch parentage, industrious and capable. To this union were born seventeen children. One of his sons-in-law, "who lived on the same farm, had sixteen children, the youngest of them old enough to go to school" (Aunt Betsy Haynes). Whether or not any of the other children with like large families are written in the book of the generations of the McGinnises, the writer is not informed.

Brother McGinnis' field of labor was Hancock, Hawkins, Claiborne and adjoining counties. He was pastor of the following churches, and helped in the organization of a number of them: Duck Creek, Bean's Creek, Richardson's Creek, Flat Gap, and Cool Branch. He belonged to the territory of the Mulberry Gap Association and left a lasting impress upon all that section of country. Like his Master, he "worked while it was day," and his sun went down without a cloud. December 14, 1873, being in his 85th year, he fell on sleep. The testimony of his brethren, after his departure, was, that "he stood as a watchman on the walls of Zion for nearly forty years; that he was a zealous and faithful expounder of Bible truth, and had become deeply enshrined in the hearts of the people whom he loved and served; that he endured the pain and confinement of a protracted illness with Christian patience and resignation, often speaking to his brethren in the most glowing terms of his strong and abiding hope of a glorious future— a brighter land and a better home than we have ever dreamed of here below."

ELIHU MILLIKAN.

Among the familiar names in the old church-book and Associational Minute-records of East Tennessee Baptists is that of Elihu Millikan—"kan," as he wrote it; "ken," "can," "kin," as variously spelled by others; and "gan," according to the preference of most of his descendants.

The subject of our sketch was the son of William and Eleanor Millikan, and was born in Guilford County, North Carolina, December 6, 1785. At the age of seven he came with his parents to Jefferson County, Tennessee, the year this county was "erected" (1792), locating near where Morristown now is. Here young Millikan grew to manhood. In his twenty-third year (September 29, 1808) he was married to a Miss Nancy Hurst, and February 20, 1838, he was married a second time, to Miss Cynthia Lea. His first marriage was blessed with fourteen children; the second with two, one of them, Mrs. William Marshall, of Knoxville, being the only child now living.

In the battle of New Orleans (1814) he fought under Andrew Jackson, sharing with that famous general and obstinate fighter a most brilliant victory over the British.

Of his religious life we have no particular account until he appears before the public as a minister of the gospel. We only know that his father was a Quaker and his mother a Baptist, and that when he was converted he searched the Scriptures for himself and became a Baptist. But as to the time, place and circumstances of his conversion and baptism there is no preserved record. The presumption is, however, that, living in the neighborhood of Bethel South (now the First Church of Morristown), he united with that church and was baptized by Isaac Barton, the pastor. This church licensed him and Hughes O. Taylor, at the same meeting, to exercise a "public gift," and by the authority of the same church they

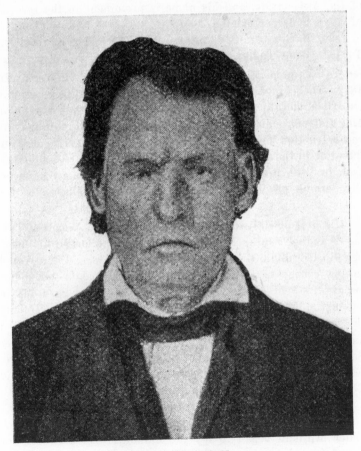

ELIHU MILLIKAN.

were ordained together (September 18, 1825), Elders Isaac Barton, Caleb Witt and Henry Randolph acting as a presbytery.

In 1830, Elihu Millikan and Hughes O. Taylor were delegates of Bethel South Church to the Nolachucky Association, in its "third" annual session. For several successive years he was an appointee of his church to attend the annual meetings of the Association, and his name is prominent in the records of that body, associated as it is with the familiar names of Isaac Barton, Andrew Coffman, Hughes O. Taylor, Woodson Taylor, Grant Taylor, T. J. Lane and other noted men.

He was Moderator of the Association for seven years. In 1839, the year of the split with the "anti" brethren, he was elected Moderator over Pleasant A. Witt, who was a popular and a strong man; and was continued Moderator through the reconstruction period that followed. He was active and influential in the Association, serving on important committees, and, in 1846, preaching the introductory sermon—a noteworthy sermon on the preacher's office as an "ambassador for Christ."

His first official work was as co-pastor with Woodson Taylor of Bethel South (Morristown). Later he moved his membership to Buffalo Creek (now Buffalo), Grainger County, and taking charge of the church, served it as pastor for about twenty-five years, resigning his charge the "third Saturday in October, 1859," on account of the infirmities of age. During this pastorate the church was visited with a great revival—a meeting in which Asa Routh did the preaching and Brother Sam Jones the exhorting, in which there were ninety-nine professed conversions, ninety-one being received into the Buffalo Church by "experience and baptism."

In the "thirties" of the last century, when Mossy Creek (now Jefferson City) was known as "Mossy Creek Iron Works," Elder Millikan began to lay the foundation of a church for this future Jerusalem of East Tennessee Baptists. Two and one-half miles northeast of Jefferson City he had charge of an "Arm" from Bethel South, at the old "Doctor Reese place,'" where one of the James brothers now lives. The building material gathered here he removed to Black Oak Grove, where (April 12, 1834) he was chiefly instrumental in founding a church. This church united with the Oakland Church, and together they constituted the Baptist Church at Mossy Creek, May 8, 1841. Elder Millikan was chosen pastor, and served the church efficiently for seven years.

He was also pastor, at one time or another, of Mouth of Richland, Head of Richland, Shady Grove, Blackwell's Branch, Indian Ridge, Powder Spring, Little Flat Creek, New Market, Bent Creek, Lick Creek, and other churches. Bent Creek and Lick Creek are now, respectively, the Whitesburg and Warrensburg churches.

Elder Millikan was frequently called in council in the ordination of ministers and deacons, in the settlement of church difficulties, the recognition of new churches, etc., as well as to attend, everywhere, "sacramental" and "protracted" meetings, and on "camp-meeting" occasions. In the records of the organization and recognition of the First Baptist Church of Knoxville (January 22, 1843), beside the well-known names of James Kennon, William Billue, Robert G. Kimbrough and J. S. Coram, is the no less familiar name of Elihu Millikan.

Twenty years ago Jethro Hill, of near Mossy Creek, bore this testimony: "I am in my 93rd year. I knew Elihu Millikan, and heard him preach, as far back as 1828. He was the principal preacher in this part of the country. He preached the missionary doctrine, and was an able man." The venerable brother, William Haynes, who was acquainted with Elder Millikan for years and from his boyhood heard him preach, said: "Brother Millikan was a strong doctrinal preacher, and was successful in revivals. Everybody had confidence in him. He had a good influence in the community, and few preachers, if any, built up the Baptist cause more than he."

24

Speaking of Elder Millikan's wonderful voice, "Uncle Sammy West," of Buffalo Church, assured me that he heard the sound of the preacher's voice, one night, from the church to his home, a distance of "two miles, air course." Winter had stripped the leaves from the intervening trees, the night was still, and the air frosty. Brother West lived on a ridge above the church. It is known that sound tends upward, and travels best at night. We may suppose, also, that a church door had been left open for a time. With these modifying conditions of the problem we may credit the seemingly incredible.

Brother Millikan was fervent and effective in prayer, and loved the old songs of Zion. It was his uniform custom, I have been told, to sing just before the benediction was pronounced:

"Dismiss us with Thy blessing, Lord;
Help us to feast upon Thy Word;
All that has been amiss forgive,
And let Thy truth within us live."

Before the Civil War Elder Millikan had a good farm and owned a few negroes. Visiting the old Millikan homestead, near Lee's Springs, Grainger County, a few years ago, I found old "Uncle Jerry," the colored man, who in other years had been "waiting boy" to Elder Millikan, currying and saddling his horse, and "such like turns," to get his master off to his appointments. Uncle Jerry was a staunch Baptist, and this was his testimony to the all-rightness of his former master: "He fed and clothed well, and had reasons about him."

From a tombstone in the family graveyard I copied this inscription: "Rev. Elihu Millikan. Died December 21, 1864; aged 79 years and 15 days. 'Them that sleep in Christ will God bring with him.'"

Just a little while before he breathed his last some friends were singing one of his favorite songs, "How Firm a Foundation." When they came to the words, "I'll never, no, never, forsake," he clapped his hands and said, "No, He never will! He never will!" and passed in triumph to the skies, the day above noted.

There are no preachers, I believe, among the descendants of Elihu Milligan. Leslie N. Milligan, a great-grandson, comes nearest to being a preacher of any of the connections I happen to be acquainted with. He is a deacon of the First Baptist Church of Jefferson City, is a teacher of the men's Bible class in the Sunday school, is strongly Calvanistic in his views of Bible doctrine, like the elder Millikan, is one of the best-posted laymen on the doctrines and traditions of Baptists known to the writer, and enjoys the distinction of having been moderator of the Nolachucky Association.

W. A. MONTGOMERY.

William Allen Montgomery is an only son of William H. and Sarah Montgomery. He was born in Jefferson County, Tennessee, November 16, 1829. His mother was a daughter of Chesley Jarnagin, of Welsh descent. His grandfather, William Montgomery, was of English extraction but born in South Carolina. The family into which he married, in North Carolina, was partly Irish. Coming to Tennessee at an early day he settled in Jefferson County, a little below Dandridge, where his son, William H., and his grandson, William A., were born. His grandmother, on the maternal side, a daughter of Elder Isaac Barton, was of Dutch and Huguenot descent. His great-grandfather, Isaac Barton, was one of Tennessee's earliest pioneers—a Baptist preacher who had the honor of giving to the United States Senate a gifted son and to the Tennessee bar a great-grandson of ability and distinction.

At the age of 14 young Montgomery professed faith in Christ and was baptized. In 1845, at the age of 16, he entered the University of Tennessee, graduating in his twenty-first year (1850), with the first honors of his class.

He read law with Hon. E. Alexander, judge of the Knoxville Circuit Court, and was admitted to the bar in the fall of 1851.

He was married May 9, 1854, to Miss C. E. Franklin, of Jefferson County, Tennessee, a daughter of Major Lawson D. Franklin, a wealthy planter and slave-holder of the antebellum days. In 1855 he went to Texas to raise cotton and

DR. W. A. MONTGOMERY.

make money. In 1861 he was a member, from Washington
County, of the Texas convention that voted for the "secession"
of Texas from the Union; and then entered the Confederate
service. In 1862 he was "licensed" to preach to the soldiers
by the Independence Church, Texas. In 1867 he returned,
with broken fortunes, to his native East Tennessee, and settled
down on the old Franklin homestead, near Leadvale. In 1868
the Leadvale Church ordained him, Elders Ephraim Moore,
T. J. Lane, S. H. Smith, and J. M. L. Burnett acting as a
presbytery.

As pastor he served efficiently the following churches:
Leadvale and Dandridge, from 1868 to 1872; First Church,
Lynchburg, Va., six years; First Church, Memphis; First
Church, Chattanooga; Greensboro, Ga.; Thomaston, Ga.; Leadvale, Rogersville and Hot Springs (N. C.); Mossy Creek (now
the Jefferson City First). In his Lynchburg pastorate he
did monumental work. The church, when he took charge,
numbered 400. During his pastorate there were added by experience and baptism 250, and others by letter; 200 were sent
out to form the College Hill Church; at the close of his pastorate the church was left 650 strong.

To his exceptional administrative ability as pastor Dr.
Montgomery added the rare gifts of an evangelist, as witnessed
by his wonderful meetings at Trenton, Milan, Jackson, and
other places in Tennessee and elsewhere. In his evangelistic
tour of West Tennessee and Mississippi there were 1,000 professed conversions under his ministry in a single year. This
was the year of richest harvest in his ministry, perhaps, but
his labors on other fields and at other times were signally
blessed of the Lord, and hundreds were added to the churches
through his instrumentality.

As Secretary of State Missions he did a most valuable work
in *unifying* the Baptists of the State. It was through his
efforts and influence, in large measure, that the East Ten-

nessee General Association was brought into organic union
and active co-operation with the Baptist State Convention.

As President of Carson College, and later of Carson and
Newman (1888-1892) and professor of metaphysics and theology, he showed himself a fine organizer and an able teacher.
It was during his administration that the marriage of Carson
and Newman took place and co-education became the order
of the day for East Tennessee Baptists. It was also during
his presidency that the magnificent new Administration Building, recently destroyed by fire, was erected for the larger work
of the college. On the occasion of his resignation as President
the Board of Trustees by resolution testified to "the great
ability, untiring faithfulness and unswerving integrity with
which the President had advanced the important interests
which had been committed to his charge," and to the gratifying fact that he had "devoted his fine talents and rare scholarship to the up-building of our beloved institution."

From Carson College he received his D.D. in 1870; from his
alma mater, the University of Tennessee, he received the honor
of an LL.D. degree in 1876.

As associate editor with Dr. J. R. Graves of the *Tennessee
Baptist,* the same with Drs. Jeter and Dickinson, of the *Religious Herald,* and as "staff" correspondent of the *Baptist and
Reflector,* by his crisp, pointed and pungent editorials and
sundry articles he contributed much to the enrichment of our
denominational literature.

It was as a *preacher,* however, that he *excelled.* Preaching
was his forte. He had preaching gifts in an eminent degree.
The marked elements of his strength were originality, a mind
trained to think, the power of clear, forceful statement, ability
to drive the plowshare of incisive propositions through a subject, laying out all its contents and exposing them to view.
He preached on great subjects, handling them masterfully,
his full-orbed mind illuminating them on all sides. He could
think on his feet, without notes, with a mental intensity that

was electrical in its effect. He gripped his subject and his audience alike—was alike master of subjects and "master of assemblies."

While never failing to emphasize the "doctrines of grace," he pressed home on the sinner with powerful argument and appeal his immediate and urgent duty and responsibility of accepting the divine offers of mercy and salvation, at the peril of his soul. He was not characteristically an expository or textual preacher, but uniformly chose subjects—great subjects, as already intimated—for pulpit treatment, and discussed them, not homiletically, as a rule, but logically and persuasively, with a view to immediate, practical results. He was not always at his best, but take him in a series of subject-sermons, say for a month or six weeks, every day, or twice a day, and the writer has never heard his equal as a sermonizer.

Perhaps his most intimate associate in the ministry, and one of his most confidential friends, was J. M. L. Burnett. They were like Jonathan and David, wholly unlike, but co-laborers in the Lord's work, and socially and otherwise were a self-constituted "mutual admiration society." They were both fathers in the ministry to the writer, and were greatly helpful to him in his early ministry, both of them serving in the council at his ordination, and Dr. Montgomery performing the ceremony on the occasion of his marriage. So the writer, reverencing Dr. Montgomery as a father and appreciating fully his great worth and eminent abilities, feels free to speak of him as he was and to mention his faults as well as his virtues. He was a noble "man of God" and a truly great preacher, but he was not perfect. He was not a Pharisee and made no claims to perfection. If he were alive, I doubt not he would have me paint him as he was. So, in candor I would have to say, he was always strong but not always sweet. He was not equally pleasing at all times, was not always gracious. He was sometimes caustic; he sometimes dipped his tongue or pen in the "waters of Marah." He was ambitious and proud and had an infirmity of temper which he, no less than his friends, deplored.

The writer has sometimes thought that the devil had a particular grudge against W. A. Montgomery, for sometimes, when he had preached like a seraph—preached as few men ever preached, and there was "glory all around," the hand as of some malignant spirit, appearing out of the darkness, would dash the feast with pitch from the sulphurous regions below. But it is exceedingly gratifying to know that this battle-scarred veteran soldier and distinguished leader, as he faced the setting sun, through trials and through grace abounding, became sweeter, tenderer, more gracious, and more sympathetic—chastened by affliction, sweetened by sorrow, mellowed by the frosts of adversity, ripened for glory. His last pastorate was at Decatur, Ga., during which he was President of the Pastors' Conference of Atlanta, respected and greatly loved by his brethren. The last two years of his life were spent in the home of his daughter, Mrs. A. C. Moore, of near Rankin, Tenn., not far from the old Montgomery home. It was here that he died, Dec. 16, 1905. His funeral sermon was preached by his pastor, Elder W. C. Hale, and his body was interred in the Beth Car cemetery, near Leadvale, Tenn. He was survived by his beloved companion, four sons and three daughters.

Dying Testimony: "Oh, thou God of universal peace, to whom all eyes must turn for everlasting salvation, blessed be thy high and holy Name! Amen!" "It is sweet to die." "What a glorious privilege to hear the music on the way home." "I shall see Jesus face to face, and walk the streets of the New Jerusalem." "Put on the plain marble slab above my grave—'A sinner saved by grace.'"

A Tribute:

"Deep teachings from the Word he held so dear,
    Things new and old in that great Treasure found;
A valiant cry, a new, strong note and clear,
    A trumpet, with no false, uncertain sound—
These shall not die, but live, his rich bequest
To that beloved church, whose servant is at rest."

EPHRAIM MOORE.

Three miles south of Morristown, on the brow of a hill overlooking the old Moore residence, now owned by W. G. Taylor, Esq., is a grave where sleeps the dust of one of East Tennessee's ablest and most noted preachers of a former day. The tombstone bears the inscription: "In memory of Rev. Ephraim Moore; born July 1, 1793; died August 5, 1875." He was born near Lancaster, Pennsylvania, was a son of Samuel and Ann Moore, and the oldest of four children. Elder Moore was of Scotch-Irish descent, a man of passionate nature and disposition but firm and uncompromising in principle. His face shows firmness of character and intellectual strength.

He was educated almost altogether in the school of experience, and was truly a self-made man. The loss of his father, in early life, put upon his shoulders the responsibility of supporting his widowed mother and the younger children, depriving him of the opportunity of attending school. While still an inexperienced youth he left his native state and came to East Tennessee to battle with the wilderness and build his fortunes. Here his mother married a second time, and young Moore went to live with his "Uncle White," near Bull's Gap, where, in his teens, he courted and married a Miss Nancy Lane, cousin of Elder T. J. Lane, a sensible, industrious and capable young woman, who became the mother of his ten children.

Soon after his marriage the adventurous boy-husband secured land in Jefferson (now Hamblen) County, near the present site of Morristown, where, according to family tradition, he left his young wife and child and went to fight the Indians, in the War of 1812, and where he afterwards lived and built up a handsome estate.

Young Moore was brought up in the faith of the old school Presbyterians, and observed to some extent the prescribed rules, but was not religious. His heart went after pleasure and folly. He often reproached himself for being a "fool's fool"; that is, a "fiddler." But it pleased God to arrest him in his pursuit of folly and fun and bring him to a better mind. The circumstances of his conviction and conversion are as follows: He was attending a Methodist meeting at the old Sulphur Spring camp-ground. The preacher, a Methodist, made some assertions that happened to cross his ingrained

EPHRAIM MOORE.

prejudices, and he found himself saying emphatically to himself: "It's a lie! It's a lie!" But the Holy Spirit was sending arrows of conviction through the "joints of the harness"
to rankle in his soul till he should cry mightily, "What shall
I do? What shall I do?" and turn to God and be healed by
the Great Physician. For months he groped in darkness and
was as the stricken deer. Restless and wandering he had
gone out into the field, he knew not why. Putting his hand on
an ear of corn as it hung upon the stalk, he stopped and stood
motionless for a minute, when something seemed to say to
him: "Go to the house and get the Bible and read it." He
did so, and at once his eyes fell upon John 6:28, 29: "What
shall we do, that we might work the works of God?" with the
Christ-given answer: "This is the work of God, that ye believe on him whom he hath sent." "Is not this for me?" he
said. "Then why can't I take it? I will." On that radiant
Sunday morning he passed out of darkness into light and ap-
propriated to himself the promised and offered blessing of salvation. · Reading the Bible for himself he soon settled his doctrinal and denominational difficulties and applied for membership and baptism at the hands of Bethel South Church (now
the Morristown First), and was baptized, we presume, by
Elder Isaac Barton, who was pastor of the church at that time.
He preached his first sermon, it would seem, without knowing
or intending it, on this wise: It was at a prayer meeting service. No one had been appointed to conduct the meeting, or
maybe the appointed leader was absent. The older brethren
present hesitated or dclined to take hold of the situation.
Brother Moore, however, took the Bible which, of late, he had
been diligently reading, and proceeded to read the parable of
the sower, making comments as he read. He had "liberty" as
he read and expounded the Word, and the people gave attention. The brethren soon told him he must "preach for them
again." So he had been "preaching" without intending to do
so, and was thus providentially led into the ministry. Doubt-

less he was licensed to "take a text" or "exercise a gift" in the usual way, but the church records covering this period are lost, and we are left to conjecture.

Just at this time, throughout the state, the question of missions and methods, the so-called "societies" and "institutions of the day," with the deeper question of the Atonement, whether limited or unlimited; that is, who and how many are entitled to have the gospel preached to them? was to the front among Batpists, and others as well, threatening to divide the denomination. Moore was preaching "free salvation to all who will believe the gospel" and world-wide "missions," and his zeal soon got him into trouble with his church and precipitated a "heresy trial," which had a far-reaching effect. The question at issue was: "Is salvation for the elect only? or, is there salvation for all?" It was a question, on the one hand, of the divine decrees, and, on the other hand, of "preaching the gospel to every creature." Moore was a redoubtable champion of the doctrine of a free salvation to all who will believe, against the so-called "hardshell" dogma of "particular, eternal and unconditional election and reprobation." The old school Baptist, the hyper-Calvinist, reasoned: "According to the Scriptures there is salvation only for the elect. It will avail nothing to preach to the non-elect. Therefore we will preach to the elect only, "feed the sheep," and God will do the rest." "A *nonsequitur,* a fallacy, a begging of the question," replies the moderate Calvinist, who has read the commission to "go preach" and believes in missions and the use of means to accomplish the divine purposes. But Moore believed that the germ of the fallacy in the anti-mission conclusion of his hardshell brethren was in their anti-Scriptural premise, namely, that the Atonement in Christ was limited, that God was a respecter of persons, and not the benevolent Being the Scriptures represent him to be. Moore's advocacy of these views being offensive to many of his ministerial brethren, and, presumably, to a majority of his church, it was decided to call a council to consider his offenses and advise the church. The accusations and rumors of heresy were brought forward and duly canvassed. Moore's defense of himself seemed unanswerable, and was almost satisfactory to the council till the question was asked: "Have you read Dewees' book? and do you endorse it?" The answer was: 'I have; and so far as I understand it, endorse it." This was enough. Dewees was suspected of leaning towards Arminianism, and his book was particularly obnoxious to Elder James Kennon, who was "prosecutor" in the case, a good man, but of strong predestinarian sentiments. His influence in the council determined the action of the body in the condemnation of Moore, who was accordingly excluded from the church. Justice requires it to be said, however, that the church as a body was not quite satisfied with its action in the matter, and finally, with the exception of a small fragment, came over to Moore's side of the question, and after a few years, through the influence of Woodson Taylor, the pastor, restored him to fellowship. Meanwhile, however, Elder Moore had been received into the Clay Creek Church, Cocke County, and was preaching to the church with entire acceptance. Following is a copy of his license to preach: "January, first Saturday, 1833. The Baptist Church of Christ at Clay Creek, now in session, do liberate and license our brother, Ephraim Moore, to take a text and exercise his gift wherever the Lord in his providence may cast his lot. Done by order of the church. Daniel A. Hurley, Clerk." The same year the church called for Brother Moore's ordination and sent a committee to West Tennessee, then to North Carolina, to secure a presbytery. Elder Garrett Dewees, of North Carolina, responded to the church's call, and accordingly "ordained Ephraim Moore and Joseph Manning to the full work of the ministry, May, first Saturday, 1833."

As pastor Elder Moore served Clay Creek for several years, Friendship about ten years, Warrensburg some twenty-five years, also other churches. But he did not seek the pastoral care of churches. He was a man of affairs, a great doctrinal preacher and expounder of the Scriptures, a man looked up to and prominent in the councils of his brethren. "As a theologian and a thinker he was a man of ability. He believed in grace, and could come as near as any man drawing the line between the extreme of Calvinism, on the one hand, and the point on the other hand, where Arminianism would subvert the doctrines of grace." (W. A. Keen.) He had a special fondness and ability for discussing at length the great doctrines of the Bible, sometimes prolonging the sermon two or three hours. Take, for example, this outline on "The Kingdom of God," which I find among his sermon notes: "A kingdom implies four things: 1. A King; 2. Subjects; 3. Laws; 4. Territory." The discussion of that subject, as Ephraim Moore would discuss it, would require from two to three hours. His famous sermon on The Dispensations of Law and Grace, or The Two Covenants, required four hours (generally two Sundays) for a full discussion. The "notes" I find on this subject correspond most strikingly with my boyhood recollection of "Uncle Ephraim's" three hours' discourse on the Abrahamic Covenant, with the stopping place in the discourse, the offering up of his son Isaac, and his promise to "resume" at that point in his next discourse.

The triumph of Moore's theology, in the "battle of the giants," particularly in East Tennessee, through the 30's and 40's, is seen in the deliverance of a joint convention of representatives of the Holston, Tennessee, Nolachucky and East Tennessee Associations, called to meet with the Pleasant Grove Church, Cocke County, August 25 and 26, 1843. In the revision by this body of our Articles of Faith, "Article 7" was made to read: 'That the blessings of salvation are made free to all by the gospel, and that nothing prevents the salvation of the greatest sinner on earth but his own voluntary refusal to submit to the Lord Jesus Christ, which refusal will subject him to an aggravated punishment, the final resolution stating, "that none of the above articles shall be so construed in their meaning as to hold with the doctrine of particular, eternal and unconditional election and reprobation." This was a large and widely representative body of East Tennessee Baptists, and its deliverance was unanimous.

Among Elder Moore's associates in the ministry I mention Elder Joseph Manning, a "true yoke-fellow." They were like the law and the gospel, each the complement of the other. Moore, for the most part, was an Old Testament preacher, representing the rigor and justice of the law; in Manning were united the sweetness and tenderness of the gospel. They labored together a great deal in protracted meetings and in other ways; together they founded the Big Creek (Del Rio), Pleasant Grove, and other churches, and were the principal founders of the East Tennessee Association. Many an association did they attend together, riding horseback long distances, even to West Tennessee, to meet with their brethren in council—talking together as they journeyed about the Master's kingdom. But their earthly toils are ended; they rest from their labors, and talk together up there, perchance, as they walk the streets of gold, of their toils and triumphs in the Master's cause on earth.

He had passed his eighty-second milestone when his travels and labors ceased. From the minutes of the East Tennessee Association (1875) I give the following brief extract: "Our association was organized with four churches and 169 members. The preaching of Elder Moore was very acceptable and very powerful, and though his sermons frequently lasted two or three hours they were attentively listened to, and 'believers were added to the churches, multitudes, both men and women.' Churches were organized and added to the association till the 'little one has become a thousand,' now numbering thirty-two churches and 2,540 members. In this Elder Moore had a great part. He was thirteen times moderator of the association, and a preacher for over fifty years." Signed by the committee: "J. Manning, A. A. Vinson, Sr., J. Kenyon."

Among the descendants of Ephraim Moore in the Baptist ministry in the State are his grandsons, Elders P. H. C. and J. F. Hale, two of our best preachers, and his great-grandsons, Tom and Arthur Hale, who are making good as younger ministers and pastors of Baptist churches.

DANIEL P. MORRIS.

D. Morris was a minister and messenger of Double Springs, in the Holston Association, in 1817. In 1843 he was a messenger of Buffalo Church, Grainger County, to the Tennessee Association. In 1852 he was pastor of Lost Creek and Rocky Valley Churches, Spring House being his postoffice address. In 1853 he attended the association as a "messenger" from Indian Ridge Church, Grainger County. In 1854 the association minutes show him to be pastor of Paw Paw Hollow. He baptized Elder John Day, and after Day had become a preacher was associated with him a great deal in ministerial labors. They were both successful in revival meetings, built up the churches, and witnessed many conversions under their ministry. Elder Morris was of a good family and widely connected; was near kinsman, I figure, to the Morrises who laid the foundations of Morristown, and gave their name to that city. He was a man of energy and activity in the ministry, reaching out here and there, and pushing into the fields beyond. From the incidental references to him in association minutes and church records I have a good impression as to his ability and force as a preacher; but so far have not been able to obtain definite data as to his family life or any considerable information as to his public or ministerial life.

PRYOR A. MORTON.

Pryor A. Morton was born in Union County, Tennessee, March 26, 1833. His father was David Morton; his mother's maiden name was Nancy James. He was one of a family of ten children. He professed faith in Christ at the age of four-teen, and united with the Methodist Church, and was a "class leader" in that denomination. But he married a Baptist woman, Margaret Shipe, an intelligent, well-posted Bible reader, who could always beat her husband in argument on controverted doctrinal points. Mrs. Morton's pastor was Elder J. S. Coram. Brother C. and Brother M. had many good-natured arguments over the questions that divide the Methodists and the Baptists; and in their discussions they made an agreement that if Coram ever decided to join the Methodists, Morton should sprinkle him, and if Morton at any time should become convinced that he was wrong and decided to join the Baptists Coram should immerse him. In due time Coram baptized him (at the age of 25) into the fellowship of the Milan Church, Union County. Dr. J. W. Jenkins, who relates the above incident, was baptized the same day and by the same hands. Brother Morton soon entered the Baptist ministry, and subsequently served as pastor the following churches: Locust Grove, some twenty years; Milan, Texas Valley, Nave Hill, Maynardville, Bethany, Alder Springs, Big Valley, Big Sycamore, Providence, Powell's Valley, and a score of other churches. For years he was moderator of the Northern Association, and was one of the strongest and most influential preachers in that body. He was a good moderator and a good preacher. He was distinctly a doctrinal preacher, emphasizing doctrine on all occasions. He had the shepherd's heart, and was a real pastor, taking care of the flocks over which he was overseer, healing, restoring and feeding the sheep.

During his ministry Elder Morton, it is said, baptized "ninety-nine" Methodists into Baptist churches.

25

"Elder P. A. Morton departed this life on the 19th day of April, 1892, aged 59 years and 23 days. He served more than thirty of our churches as pastor, one of which he served twenty years and another one seventeen years. As a defender of Baptist principles he had no superior in the association. He was a deep preacher and endowed with extraordinary reasoning powers, but with all his logical force and ability as a preacher he had genuine meekness and humility. In his death our association has lost one of its brightest lights." (In Memoriam, as published in minutes of Northern Association.) He had money "laid away" with which to purchase a plain marble slab for his grave, on which were to be inscribed, according to his request, his name and dates of his birth and death, with the added words, "A sinner saved by grace."

P. A. Morton had six children, two sons and four daughters. His oldest son, Elder J. W. Morton, is a Baptist preacher of standing in the Northern Association; his nephews, Elders G .W. and J. C. Shipe, are able ministers of the New Testament and among our best pastors.

The following story is told of Elder Morton and a young man, a school teacher who was attending one of Brother M.'s meetings and was a "mourner." The young man was a little eccentric but thoroughly in earnest. The preacher happening upon the young teacher and wishing that he might help him in his search for light and relief from his burden, thus addressed him: "Well, my young friend, how are you getting along in your seeking?" and so forth. The answer was a little unexpected: "I'm not through yet, but I'm expecting to come through with flying colors." He made a profession and was urged to join the church. But he had been raised a Presbyterian, had heard a good deal about the "perseverance of the saints," and wanted to be sure he had a religion that would "hold out" to the end. He wanted to "try" his religion of what sort it was. He had a stumpy piece of "new ground" to plow; he would try "Jack and Eleck" in that, and if he kept his religion—didn't "swear"—he would be "all right" and would "join the church."

Elder Morton, coming down from the pulpit, after preaching on a certain occasion, was accosted by one of his hearers, who frankly said to the preacher: "I don't believe what you preached today," and was answered as follows: "The Lord didn't commission me to make you believe the gospel, but only to 'preach the gospel' to you."

J. H. MORTON.

John Houston Morton, a son of John and Mary Morton, was born near Montvale Springs, Blount County, Tennessee, December 18, 1833. He professed faith in Christ December 29, 1851, and the following April was received for baptism by the Six Mile Church, near his home. He was educated at Mossy Creek (now Carson and Newman) College, graduating the first year of the Civil War. In the army he was chaplain of the Third Tennessee Cavalry, later was appointed second lieutenant of the 3rd Regiment, Company F, and at the close of the war was Captain of Company K, 3rd Regiment, Cavalry.

November 10, 1864, he was married by Elder Isaac Hines to Mary Jane Wade of Sevier County. May 19, 1867, he was married a second time, to Mary L. Parks. To this union were born six children, three sons and three daughters.

December 1, 1865, he received a commission from the Home Mission Society to do missionary work in eastern Tennessee, salary $500 a year, with a bonus of $200, to be collected on the field.

October, 1862, he was a messenger of Boyd's Creek Church to the Tennessee Association, and a member of the committee on resolutions. Returning from the war he gave himself to the Lord's work as much as the exigencies of supporting a family would permit, and as he had opportunity. He was pastor of Boyd's Creek, Six Mile, Maryville, Miller's Cove, Pleasant Grove, and other churches in Blount County and contiguous territory. He was a well-posted and instructive preacher; in his style of preaching was doctrinal rather than evangelistic; was better adapted to building up churches than holding meetings. "He had a good knowledge of Scripture, was a brave man and preached the truth in all plainness and boldness, but his delivery was not as good as that of some preachers who were less scholarly and not so well posted in the Bible." (J. W. H.)

In addition to his ministerial work he was farmer, county surveyor and county superintendent of public schools, Blount County, trustee of Chilhowee Institute, trustee of Carson College (Carson-Newman), and so forth. The last few years of his life he was active in the work of the Chilhowee Association, in which body he was a trusted counselor and whose progress and prosperity greatly concerned him. His death occurred July 17, 1892; he was buried in the cemetery at Piney Level Church, Blount County, Tennessee.

JONATHAN MULKEY.

A PIONEER OF 1775 AND THE FIRST PREACHER ON TENNESSEE SOIL.

In the old cemetery at Buffalo Ridge, Washington County, is a monument with the inscription: "In memory of Jonathan Mulkey, Sen.; born October 16, 1752; departed this life September 5, 1826, after having been a preacher of the gospel of the Baptist order more than fifty years."

Jonathan Mulkey was born in Virginia, and is of Welsh descent. Though there are missing links in the family record, it is reasonably certain that his father was a Philip Mulkey, whom Semple mentions, in connection with William Murphy, as an active pioneer preacher in Virginia, in 1756, and who, a little later, according to Benedict, was a "reputable and successful minister for many years" in South Carolina.

The dates of Benedict are somewhat confused, I think, with regard to Tidence Lane and Jonathan Mulkey, as are also Ramsey's dates with regard to Cummings (a Presbyterian minister) and Mulkey. There is no doubt but Lane was the first permanent pastor of the First permanent church (Buffalo Ridge, 1779) in Tennessee. This is now universally conceded, I believe. It is equally certain, I think, that Mulkey was the first preacher to plant his feet on Tennessee soil, to remain and engage actively in the Christian *ministry*.

Ramsey, in speaking of Col. Christian's expedition against the Cherokees, in the fall of 1776, mentions the Rev. Charles Cummings as the chaplain of the expedition, and says of him that he was the "first Christian minister that ever preached in Tennessee, a pioneer of civilization, of learning and religion —let his memory not be forgotten." (Annals of Tennessee, page 169.) The same author, however, in another place (p. 144), mentions "Mr. Mulkey, a Baptist preacher," with three others, as "pioneers in Carter's Valley," Hawkins County, "late in the fall of 1775," about a year earlier than Mr. Cummings and the Cherokee expedition. Cumming's work, mainly, was in Virginia; Mulkey's was in Tennessee.

A bold and spirited adventurer, Mulkey, in early manhood, left his native Virginia and came to what is now East Tennessee, to battle with the wilderness and the Indians. With his little company he made a settlement in Carter's Valley, a little west of where Rogersville now is. The settlers, while clearing their land and preparing for a crop, got their bread-corn from where Abingdon, Virginia, now stands, and for their meat "hunted buffalo." They had planted their corn and worked it once when the rumor of a Cherokee invasion reached them, and all was confusion. The little farms had to be abandoned. The families below the North Fork of Holston re-crossed that stream, and the women and children were conducted back as far as the present Wythe County, Virginia. (Ramsey.)

Among my "notes" I find the following "incident of Mulkey," vouched for by the venerable William A. Keen, and generally believed as a creditable tradition handed down by Mulkey himself: In one of these Indian raids, as Mulkey and his companion were trying to make their escape, the Indians overtook them, knocked down, scalped and left for dead Mulkey's companion, while Mulkey himself, slightly wounded by a bullet, leaped into the Holston River, swam across, and made his way to Heaton's Station. But imagine his surprise when, on arriving at that place, he found his companion, whom he had thought scalped and sure enough dead, very much alive. He had not been killed by the Indians, but had made his escape and by a shorter route had reached the station before Mulkey.

In October of 1786, at the organization of the Holston Association, in the meeting-house of the old Cherokee Church, the names of Jonathan Mulkey and Anthony Epperson appear on the minutes as "messengers" from Kendrick's Creek (now Double Springs) Church; of which church he was doubtless the founder and first pastor. He was also pastor of Buffalo Ridge, Cherokee, Sinking Creek, Muddy Creek, and other churches. He was a strong preacher of the true pioneer spirit, and more inclined to do active evangelistic work than to be pastor of churches. He was a leader in the Holston Association for many years; for seven years was its moderator.

James White, a Baptist deacon, living near the center of the "Mulkey dominion," I have been told, would go from seven to ten miles, about every Sunday, to hear "Father Mulkey" preach. He was pastor of Buffalo Ridge as long as he lived, and when too old and too feeble to preach standing, the church, it is said, made him a suitable and easy pulpit-chair, that he might sit down and pour out his soul in melting exhortations to a devoted people who would listen to his every word.

The reader, with the writer, will feel a sense of loss that there are so few memorials of the first real, resident pioneer preacher in what is now "fair Tennessee," but then, a wilderness portion of North Carolina; his ministry and adventurous life antedate the Declaration of Independence by eleven years.

It is gratifying to know that in the subject of this sketch and his descendants we have a goodly line of Baptist preachers. Jonathan Mulkey had a son, Isaac, who was a Baptist preacher, and a useful man.   Isaac had a son, Philip Mulkey, who was a preacher of the Baptist faith.   This Philip was the great-grandson namesake of the elder Philip Mulkey, mentioned by Semple and Taylor, and the great-grandfather, on the maternal side, of E. K. Cox, pastor at Sweetwater, and E. A. Cox, pastor at Watertown, sons of the venerable W. K. Cox, of near Jefferson City—all Baptist preachers of ability and very great usefulness.   To this list of inheritors of a favorite family name might be added the name of Philip Cox, a promising young son of pastor and Mrs. E. K. Cox (as above), who may himself, some day, with the Lord's blessing, become a Baptist preacher.

(See paragraph on Mulkey, in introduction; also snapshot picture of Mulkey's tomb, in Appendix.)

WILLIAM MURPHY.

William Murphy was born in southern or southwestern Virginia and was doing pioneer work for the Lord and the Baptists in Virginia long before Tennessee was a State.   The date of his first and his second birth are alike unknown.   We only know that he and his brother Joseph were converted when quite young, under the ministry of Shubael Stearns, both of them becoming active ministers of the gospel in their early Christian life.   They were popularly known as "the Murphy boys," and sometimes stigmatized by their persecutors as "*Murphy's boys.*"   The educational advantages of both these preacher-brothers were meager, but both of them were effective preachers of the Word, and did *pioneer* work. William was the abler of the two. His "natural powers of mind were good, his addresses attracted attention, and through him many were brought to a knowledge of the truth. His discourses were of a doctrinal cast, and were sometimes controversial. But it is believed that he was more ambitious to glorify his Saviour in the salvation of souls than to distinguish himself as an able polemic (Taylor, Virginia Baptist Ministers). He was also strongly Calvinistic in his doctrinal beliefs. When, for instance, in May, 1775, this query came up to his Association, and occupied the attention of the body for a whole day, "Is salvation by Christ made possible for every individual of the human race?" while most of the talent of the Association took the affirmative or the so-called "Arminian" side, Elder Murphy championed the negative. The Association divided over the question, each party electing its own Moderator; before final adjournment, however, by concessions on the one side and forbearance on the other, the calamity of a permanent division was happily averted (Semple).

Perhaps Elder Murphy's greatest single achievement under God, while still in Virginia, was the leading to Christ of one of Virginia's most prominent and useful Baptist ministers, Samuel Harris.

Some time before 1780 Elder Murphy emigrated to "the west"; that is, to North Carolina, first, settling a little later, it seems, in upper East Tennessee, where he became "one of the most active ministers in the Holston Association." He was one of the constituent members of that body, being a messenger of the Cherokee Church, where the Association was organized (1786), with Tidence Lane as Moderator and William Murphy as clerk. The following year (1787) William Murphy was "chosen moderator."

In 1785 (June 11), William Murphy and Tidence Lane organized the old "Bent Creek" Church (now Whitesburg). In

April, 1897, this church celebrated, with suitable ceremonies, its one hundred and twelfth anniversary.

September 14, 1798, William Murphy and Isaac Barton were a "presbytery" in the organization of the "Church of Christ on Lick Creek" (now the Warrensburg Church), with a constituency of "eighteen members," David Wisecarver, clerk.

Benedict, who gathered his information (1810) from near-at-hand sources, speaks in high terms of William Murphy's ministerial labors in the Holston Association, "which he assisted in raising up, and in which he was very active and much esteemed until his death, the exact time of which is not known, but it is believed to have been about 1800."

RICHARD MURRELL.

"Richard Murrell was pastor of the old Double Springs Church, for more than a third of a century. He was also pastor of Fall Branch, Beech Creek, Clear Fork, and other churches, in the early history of the Holston Association. He was a man of great piety and humility; was not a doctrinal preacher, like his great-grandson, R. M. Murrell. He dealt in experimental religion; he knew what that was, and used it with very great effect. He was a most wonderful exhorter. When the Holston Association met at Roberson's Creek Church, Brother Murrell followed the preaching brother in exhortation, according to custom. He exhorted with such power that all the great throng of people on the grounds was deeply moved as one man; some cried aloud, others could be seen holding to the saplings and bushes, weeping, greatly exercised and stirred with religious emotion." (Wm. A. Keen.) He was moderator of the Holston Association in the year 1808. In a sketch of R. M. Murrell in the *East Tennessee Baptist* (January 26, 1889) the author made this statement: "Brother Murrell comes of preaching stock. His great-grandfather,

Richard Murrell, for whom young Murrell was named, was a noted pioneer Baptist preacher in upper East Tennessee, and was pastor of Double Springs Church between thirty and forty years."

This fragment of a sketch is presented as a memorial to the name of one of our worthy pioneer preachers, pending further investigation of the records of a life which deserves more extended mention than is here given it.

GORDON MYNATT.

Gordon Mynatt was born in Knox County, Tennessee, March 20, 1811. He was a son of John and Elizabeth Mynatt. He was a grandson of William and a great-grandson of Richard Mynatt, who came from England and settled in Virginia in early colonial times. Gordon Mynatt was ordained by the authority of Bethel Church, Anderson County, November 8, 1835. He had an older brother, William, who was a preacher of ability. The two brothers understood and supplemented each other so perfectly that they labored together a great deal, and most successfully, in protracted meetings, both in Tennessee and Alabama. They held a great meeting in Talladega, where their brother-in-law, Dr. Matt. Hillsman, the pastor, had prepared the way. Gordon Mynatt married Mary Hillsman, a daughter of John Hillsman, of near Knoxville. Matthew Hillsman evened up with Gordon by marrying his sister, Ann Eliza. The Mynatt brothers were both strong men, and fairly well educated for preachers of their day. They did quite a good deal of evangelistic work in Alabama as well as in Tennessee, both of them dying in Alabama—Gordon, on November 4, 1884; William in April, 1881. Gordon Mynatt was pastor (in Tennessee) of Beaver Dam, Third Creek, Bethel, and Clinton churches.

Matt. H. Mynatt, son of Elder Gordon Mynatt, and clerk of Beaver Dam Church, promised to procure for the writer

the ordination papers and also a picture of his lamented father.
But he has passed beyond the bounds of time; maybe some
other member of the family will be able to confer this favor.

WILLIAM C. NEWELL.

William C. Newell was born in Jefferson County, Tennessee,
October 15, 1813. He was the first-born of John and Sibyl
C. (Gillett) Newell. At the age of twenty he professed faith
in Christ, uniting with the Concord Church, in Greene County,
Tennessee. By authority of this church he was ordained
(March, 1848) to the work of the ministry, and soon afterwards was appointed as a general missionary to labor in the
"destitute portions" of Greene and Hawkins counties. In 1857
he moved to Washington County, uniting with the Buffalo
Ridge Church, where he kept his membership for fifteen years,
serving the church as pastor most of that time.

He was married to Mary A. Price, November 23, 1847. To
this union were born two daughters, Adelaide and Cordelia.
Adelaide married Elbert H. Crouch, father of Dr. Austin
Crouch, of Murfreeboro, Tenn. Losing his first wife he was
married a second time, March 8, 1854, to Mary D. Kitzmiller,
a daughter of Henry and Elizabeth Kitzmiller, and a sister
of Elder Martin V. and Dr. R. C. Kitzmiller, who is still living
and in his "nineties." In October, 1872, with his family (a
wife and five children), he moved to Mt. Vernon, Arkanksas
(Faulkner County), where he lived the rest of his life, doing
ministerial work so far as his health would permit, but not
venturing to undertake the pastoral oversight of churches on
account of a "throat trouble," which would often annoy and
sometimes disable him in his efforts to preach. Elder Newell
died July 29, 1887, aged 73 years, 9 months, 14 days."

"W. C. Newell was a clear thinker, a sound Baptist and
an instructive preacher. He was well posted on Baptist
affairs, and was spiritual. There was not a blot on his char-

acter, and his conduct at all times was above reproach" (W. A. Keen.) He was a "good theologian, and a friend and wise counselor to young preachers. He was a fine conversationalist, rich in anecdote, and a splendid entertainer. In preaching he was generally deliberate and quiet, always clear-cut in his doctrinal statements, and never noisy. He was a good debater and gave at least one Campbellite preacher a genteel threshing in a public discussion. He was a strong force, and a valuable man, in any community or Association where he went. He was a saddle and harnessmaker when a young`man" (W. K. Cox).

Elder Newell was a practiced writer, and as clerk of the East Tennessee and Holston Associations made splendid minutes of the proceedings of those bodies. He was "correspondent" to Benedict in preparing the revised edition (1846) of his great work, "A General History of the Baptist Denomination in America and Other Parts of the World," and as a colleague of the great historian he traveled over pretty much all of East Tennessee, investigating conditions and gathering materials for a history of our people, from written and unwritten sources, furnishing same to Benedict. In his history of Associations in Tennessee, Benedict makes many complimentary references to and frequent quotations from his "correspondent" and "colleague," Mr. Newell, using, or carefully "preserving," original documents furnished him by his painstaking "coadjutor," for future reference. In a footnote to page 793 of this work is this statement by the author: "Mr. Newell has lately entered the ministry; he was a lay brother during most of his historical inquiries on account of my work. To use a term much employed in the South and West, in historical inquiries, he is an 'effort man' in full measure," meaning by that expression that his correspondent believed in world-wide missions, education, organization, and the use of all the machinery necessary to the successful execution of our Lord's command to "go into all the world, and make disciples," and train them for kingdom service. At this time (1846) there was sore need of "effort" to bring about better conditions, especially home effort; for, according to Mr. Newell's reports, there was "scarcely a Baptist Sunday school in all of East Tennessee; the first Baptist Church of Knoxville had preaching every Sunday, the Baptist Church at Jonesboro had preaching twice a month, while the other churches still held to the monthly system."

Some of the living descendants of Elder Newell are, Mrs. Etta Keathley, a daughter; Mr. E. K. Newell, a son, and a number of grandsons, all of Arkansas. Another grandson is Dr. Austin Crouch, one of Tennessee's ablest preachers. These and others revere the memory of W. C. Newell.

WILLIAM OGLE.

Bethel Church, Sevier County, "met in regular session, October, fourth Saturday, 1836. Item: "Examined Brother William Ogle touching his call to the ministry and the principles of his faith, and were satisfied, and set him apart for ordination on the fourth Saturday of November following, and chose Brethren Eli Roberts, Johnson Adams, Daniel Layman and Andrew Connatser to act as a presbytery." This event was in answer to the prayers of his mother and other devout women who lived many miles from a Baptist church. Sevierville Church (the Forks of Pigeon then), fourteen miles distant, was the nearest church to the Ogles at that time, and the ancestors of William Ogle wended their way to and from this church, Saturdays and Sundays, carrying their shoes in their hands. But the praying mother of William Ogle wanted a church and a preacher, after her own heart, nearer home; and, to consult the Lord about the matter, held prayer-meetings, with other good women, in a laurel grove, for years; then got her answer. William Ogle was distinctly a mountain preacher, who "preached the gospel to the poor," with little remunera-

tion. "Brother Ogle was a preacher of ability and of good
address in the pulpit" (J. Russell). He was an uncle of
Richard Evans, another famous mountain preacher. The Ogles
are a numerous and widely scattered family, and many of
them Baptist preachers of ability.

E. W. OGLE.

E. W. Ogle was born in Sevier County, Tennessee, May 8,
1847. He professed faith in Christ in his early teens, and
joined the Baptist church at Gatlinburg, in his native county.
August 29, 1867, he was married to Miss Sarah Reagan. Some
time after his marriage he was "ordained deacon," and served
his church in that capacity for a number of years, "using the
office of a deacon well."

June, 1878, he was liberated to exercise his gift in a public
way; and was ordained to the regular work of the ministry,
January 1, 1882.

He served as pastor the following churches: White Oak
Flats, Evans' Chapel No. 1, Lebanon, Shady Grove, Rocky
Grove, New Era, and Hill's Creek.

His associates in the ministry and the council that ordained
him were: Elders Richard Evans, J. B. Walker, and J. S.
Ogle.

He was greatly devoted to his home church, giving to it
his time, prayers, and means. "To him it was the dearest spot
on earth." He was one of the leaders in the movement to
build a church at Banner—was Moderator of the council at its
organization.

E. W. Ogle was a man who "always stood firm to his convictions. He would never compromise with sin. He was always outspoken against whatever he believed to be wrong."

After a service of more than forty years in his Master's
cause, he "fell on sleep," January 18, 1902. His last sermon,

and one of his ablest, just two weeks before his death, was
from Job 14:14: "If a man die, shall he live again?"

"He has gone where the sunlight of heaven has burst on his
never-dying soul, to bathe in the great sea of God's love, to
wear a crown of never-fading glory, and to walk the golden
streets of the bright home above" (Committee on Resolutions).

F. M. OTEY.

Frazier Madison, son of Frazier Otey, was born in Bedford
County, Virginia, in 1818. He was married to Miss Syrena K.
Newlee, of Christiansburg, Virginia, in 1841. To this union
were born eight children, five sons and three daughters. In
September, 1842, he made a profession of religion, and was
baptized by Absalom Dempsey, uniting with Mill Creek Baptist
Church, Bottetourt County, Virginia. In 1851 he came to Tennessee, settling at Cumberland Gap, Claiborne County. Here
he united with Salem Baptist Church, and was ordained by
the same to the full work of the ministry, about the year 1865.
Thus Brother Otey began his ministry rather late in life. But
he was a good soldier of Jesus Christ. He preached the truth
as he saw it, giving himself to the ministry of the Word, mostly
among the mountain people of East Tennessee. "Few of us
can appreciate the hardships and privations these early ministers and their families endured in carrying the gospel to the
people of the mountains, especially during the trying times
just after the war. If there be a seat of honor at the right
hand of the Father, I doubt not it is occupied by the old
soldiers who never feared or failed to declare the whole counsel
of God in times that tried men's souls."

Brother Otey was a good man and a useful preacher. He
lived his religion, and enjoyed the confidence and esteem of all
who knew him. F. M. Otey passed to his reward, September
8, 1908, and his body rests in Greenwood cemetery at Knoxville,
awaiting the resurrection of the just.

Elder Otey reared a large and respectable family. Those who survive him not only revere his memory, but honor him for his integrity and his work's sake.

One of his sons, Brother J. M. Otey, of near Jefferson City, is one of our most useful Baptist preachers.

J. M. PENDLETON.

Dr. J. M. Pendleton, *preacher, theologian, author,* and *pio-neer* TEACHER of *preachers,* was a son of John and Frances J. Pendleton. He was born in Spottsylvania County, Virginia, November 20, 1811. He was named for the "greatly admired statesman," James Madison, who was then President of the United States. His mother was a Thompson, before her marriage, a daughter of Charles Thompson, of Virginia, a woman of good blood and breeding, of "excellence of character and amiable qualities." Both of his grandfathers were "natives of Virginia and of English descent." His paternal grandfather, Henry Pendleton, was a "freeholder" of Culpepper County, Virginia, and became a "soldier in the Revolutionary War." When James was one year old, his father, who had been teaching and selling goods, decided to "seek his fortune in what was then the new State of Kentucky," and taking his family with him, went "west." His destination was Christian County, Kentucky, where he settled down on a farm near the present town of Pembroke. Here young Pendleton was brought up to farm life, after the manner of the times, being "mill-boy" for the family till large enough for harder work on the farm, and, through the winter seasons, attending school. There was no school building in the neighborhood, but his father knew the art of teaching. Resuming, therefore, his "former vocation of teacher," the elder Pendleton gave land for a community school building, and the neighbors built the house. It was a "typical schoolhouse" of the pioneer days, built of "rough logs, chinked and daubed with red clay, parts of the logs cut out to let in the light, and panes of glass so adjusted as to keep out the cold; the floor was of dirt and the chimney had a fireplace six feet wide and four feet deep; the benches were made of slabs, and had no backs—everything, it seemed, was so arranged as to keep the feet of the small children from reaching the floor." In this rude building, under the tuition of his father, James Pendleton got his start in his life-long pur-

DR. J. M. PENDLETON.

suit of learning, made attainments in the knowledge of "spelling book" and "reader," and in due time reached "the rule of three" in arithmetic and learned something of "geography" and "grammar."

For his early religious impressions he was indebted to his mother, who ever showed her concern for his spiritual welfare and talked to him often "about Christ and salvation," but not until he was fifteen years of age did he become really interested in religion. At this time he began in earnest to work out, in a legal and moral way, a "righteousness of his own," with the expectation of bringing God under obligation to save him on the ground of personal merit. But two years of unavailing struggle showed him the futility of his efforts, and left him still in spiritual darkness and unrest. In his search for light he chanced to get hold of a volume of sermons, by Samuel Davies, which he found in his father's library. The sermon which particularly attracted his attention was an exposition of I Cor. 1:22-24, where Paul represents himself and others as "preaching Christ crucified, to the Jews a stumbling block and to the Greeks foolishness, but to the called and saved, both Jews and Greeks, Christ the power of God and the wisdom of God." Something in the sermon gave him new light and a sense of peace. Elder John S. Willson, at this juncture, providentially becoming his spiritual guide, he was led in the way of salvation, and on the second Sunday of April, 1829, he related his "experience" of grace before Bethel Church, and was baptized, the Tuesday following, by Elder Willson, on a profession of his faith in Christ. In the warm glow of his "first love" he began to talk to sinners, tell his experience to penitents, pray in public, and exhort, on occasions. In February, 1830, his church "licensed" him to preach. The next two years he studied Latin grammar some, under an instructor in Russellville, taught school, and "accompanied different ministers on their preaching excursions." These preachers, Dr. Pendleton says, were not very "complimentary" in their remarks about his sermons. One of them said, "You certainly could do better if you would try." Another said, "You are scarcely earning your salt." The criticism of another was, "You say some pretty good things, but your preaching is neither adapted to comfort the saint nor alarm the sinner." But the last straw (suited to break the camel's back, but didn't) was a remark by a layman, "As God is omnipotent He, of course, can make a preacher of that young man." It is gratifying to know that young Pendleton survived these discouraging criticisms and made a preacher of rare ability. He was ordained at Hopkinsville, Kentucky, November 1, 1833, by a council composed of Reuben Ross, William Tandy, William C. Warfield and Robert Rutherford. He was pastor of Hopkinsville and Bethel churches for four years, dividing his time equally between the two churches. He became pastor of the Bowling Green Church the "first day of the year 1837 and continued there for twenty years, with the exception of a few months." His salary was $400 a year for all of his time. In January, 1857, he removed to Murfreesboro, Tennessee, to teach theology to the preacher boys in Union University, and to become pastor of the church at that place. These positions he filled with efficiency and honor until the breaking out of the Civil War (1861), when the university was suspended. The following year he became pastor at Hamilton, Ohio, remaining there three years. In November, 1865, he became pastor of the Baptist church at Upland, Pennsylvania. This was the church of the wealthy and liberal Crozers, here was the seat of the Crozer Theological Seminary, and here was a great opportunity for a preacher and pastor of Dr. Pendleton's caliber. This was his greatest pastorate, continuing through a stretch of nearly eighteen years, in which he witnessed, under his preaching, great and wonderful revivals, baptizing at one time 200 converts, at another forty. He resigned this pastorate in June, 1883, having gone beyond his "three score and ten" years of life, and having safely passed the traditional, imag·inary "dead-line" in the ministry.

Going back some forty-five years, on March 13, 1838, Dr. Pendleton was married to Miss Catherine S. Garnett, daughter of Richard Garnett, of Glasgow, Kentucky. The happy couple, we are told, took their principal *bridal tour* on horseback, visiting friends in different places and going as far as Louisville. This was before the modern conveniences of "honeymoon" travel were extensively known in Kentucky. To this union were born seven children, two of them dying in infancy. A promising son, John M., between whom and his father were conscientious differences as to the war between the States, became a Confederate soldier, but was killed by a fragment of a shell before he ever fired a gun. This was a great grief to his father. His oldest daughter, Letitia, became the wife of Dr. James Waters, one of Tennessee's scholarly and able preachers. His second daughter, Fannie, was married to Prof. Leslie Waggoner, of Bethel College, Kentucky. His youngest daughter, Lila, was married to Mr. B. F. Proctor, a lawyer of Bowling Green, Kentucky. His only surviving son, Garnett, was educated at Rochester University, New York, graduating in 1875; took a law course in Philadelphia, and is now a prominent lawyer and Baptist in Chester, Pennsylvania.

As a preacher Dr. Pendleton had an analytical mind, was clear· in his statements, forcible in his thinking; was methodical, always following a prearranged, well-defined plan; was a model sermonizer. He was distinctly and eminently a doctrinal preacher and a teacher of the Word of God. He had a fertile brain and was a prolific writer. He was a constant writer for the denominational press and for local papers. He was the author of a number of books, pamphlets and tracts. His first book, "Three Reasons Why I Am a Baptist" (1853), was received with great favor by the denomination. Then followed "Sermons on Important Subjects," a "Church Manual," "The Atonement of Christ," "An Old Landmark Reset," "Christianity Susceptible of Legal Proof," "Church Discipline," "The Lord's Supper," "Christian Doctrines, a Compendium of Theology," "Brief Notes on the New Testament," etc. For several years he was one of the editors of the *Tennessee Baptist*, and for six years was one of the editors of the *Southern Baptist Review*. He was a painstaking but a very rapid writer, rarely, if ever, rewriting a paragraph or even a sentence. He wrote "Brief Notes on the New Testament" in exactly eight months. His last book, "Reminiscences of a Long Life," a book of more than 200 pages, was written 'without notes," being reproduced from memory, in two months; he "began to write this on his seventy-ninth birthday, November 20, 1890, and finished it January 20, 1891."

The writer has read most of Dr. Pendleton's published works, and with interest and profit, and so has many another preacher and layman in Tennessee and the Southland. His Church Manual is a standard among our churches. His "Notes" on the New Testament are found in the libraries of many of our preachers and Sunday school teachers. His ablest work, I dare say, is his "Christian Doctrines," a work that will never perish, "concise, yet comprehensive, simple, lucid, logical, Scriptural, "supplying a long-felt want in the curriculum of theological education and in the libraries of Christian households."

Dr. Pendleton was a hard student, and systematic in all his work. As to physique and personal character he has been portrayed as of "medium height, well proportioned, firm of step as of convictions, a sincere friend, generous to every good cause according to his ability, unostentatious and affable with his friends, reserved among strangers, and cautious of his associations. His integrity of character and honesty of conviction were absolutely above suspicion, and were due to his abiding, unshaken trust in God" (J. W.).

As a student and interpreter of Scripture it was his habit to rely more upon the original writings of the New Testament than upon *versions* or *commentaries*. He read the New Testament through in Greek twenty-seven times and more than once in Latin and French. The impact of his thinking upon American religious and political thought earned for him a national reputation.

In the year 1865, Denison University, of Ohio, conferred upon him the honorary title of Doctor of Divinity.

Dr. Pendleton had an ambition to be an "accomplished debater"—and he was, claiming nothing unjust, yielding to nothing unjust, his "grand supreme purpose being the establishment of truth." More than most men he had reason to be gratified in seeing, before he reached his journey's end, his ambition and efforts crowned with success.

Toward the evening of life his sky was overshadowed by a dark cloud of sorrow: His beloved companion lost her eyesight, becoming permanently and hopelessly blind. But "nothing in their later years was more touching or beautiful than the lover-like devotion of the old man to one who, though stricken with blindness and the infirmities of age, ever remained to him the bride and the love of his youth." On the occasion of the celebration of their golden wedding (in the Baptist church, Bowling Green, Kentucky, where formerly he had been pastor so long), at the close of an address, in which he had briefly surveyed the bright mountain peaks and dark valleys of their married life, he turned to his wife with these words, pathetic and strangely touching: "Now, dearest one, it is fitting that I speak a word to you. There is no earthly object so dear to my heart. You are not as you were fifty years ago tonight. Then, with elastic step, you walked with me to the marriage altar, and we pledged to each other our vows of loyalty and love. I do not recognize that elastic step now. Then your face was fresh and blooming; now the freshness and bloom are gone, and wrinkles have taken their place, while gray hairs adorn your head. Then, and forty-six years afterward, the expression of your mild blue eyes was always a benediction; now that expression is no longer seen, for blindness has taken the place of sight. But, with these changes in you, my love has not changed. Bodily affliction has not eclipsed the intellectual and spiritual excellences of your character. You are the same to me, and no kiss during half a century has been more deeply expressive of my love than the one I now give you."

Incidentally I have mentioned the fact that Dr. Pendleton was one of the editors of the *Tennessee Baptist*. Dr. J. R. Graves had long published that paper in Nashville; in 1858 Drs. J. M. Pendleton and A. C. Dayton became joint editors with him. He was already engaged to supply two columns a week for the paper, was a correspondent for other papers, was pastor of the Murfreesboro church, was theological professor in Union University, and giving four hours a day besides in teaching other classes, and working on his farm for recreation. He differed with his friends, Graves and Dayton, materially and radically, in regard to the war, particularly on the doctrine of States' rights. When they found it impossible to adjust their differences they parted company, but parted as friends, Dr. Pendleton adhering to the Union, Drs. Graves and Dayton going with the Southern Confederacy. In justice to Dr. Pendleton it ought to be said, that he never was an "Abolitionist," meaning by that that slavery was in itself a sin to be abolished by force, regardless of consequences, but was an "Emancipationist," believing that slavery ought to be done away with gradually and justly, according to State Constitution and law.

After a strenuous and successful life of nearly sixty years in the ministry, rapidly succumbing to capillary bronchitis, on March 4, 1891, Dr. Pendleton, the battle-scarred veteran, closed his eyes and peacefully and painlessly made his exit.

"Life so sweetly ceased to be,
It lapsed in immortality."

His dying testimony was: "It is grace, grace, from first to last. My hope is just what it was sixty years ago, and I go into eternity with the one hope and plea, that Jesus Christ died in the place of sinners."

Memorial services were held, March 6, in the Baptist church of Bowling Green, Kentucky. By request of the deceased, Dr. T. T. Eaton, the funerals of whose father and mother Dr. Pendleton had preached years before, delivered the funeral address. Dr. W. H. Whittsitt, an old-time student, paid a just tribute to the memory of his former instructor. Others took part, and the choir in plaintive notes gave expression to the mingled feelings of sorrow and hope in the bosoms of a vast concourse of friends gathered to do honor to the dead. His mortal remains were deposited in the Fairview cemetery, one mile from Bowling Green. The Philadelphia Conference of Baptist Ministers, of which Dr. Pendleton had been so long a member, placed on record its deep feeling of loss in the passing of a "great and good man," who had been a "pillar of strength, a column of beauty, in the conference and in the denomination." The Board of Trustees of the Crozer Theological Seminary memorialized their "late colleague" in resolutions of appreciation of his "eminent worth" as a Christian and a minister, making special mention of his "indefatigable devotion as a trustee" to the interests of the institution. Also a memorial service was held in the Baptist church at Upland, Pennsylvania, where Dr. Pendleton had been pastor for nearly a score of years, Pastor Williams, his successor, paying him a beautiful and just tribute, weaving, of polished, beautiful and eloquent discourse, of true and tender sentiments, a "fitting chaplet to lay upon his grave."

JONATHAN QUARLES.

Jonathan Quarles, a son of Nathan and Priscilla Quarles, was born August 10, 1819, in Jefferson County, Tennessee. His parents were poor but hardworking people, and honest. His father, I have been told, was a professional "flax-breaker," in the days when Southern country folk made their own every-day summer wear of flax and cotton. He was mostly "raised as a bound boy" by one of the McGuires, and was sometimes taunted as a "flax-break" (Uncle Jere. Green) by his rude companions; but he had in him genuine stuff, and felt as Pope did, that—

"Honor and shame from no condition rise;
Act well your part—there all the honor lies."

July 20, 1837, he was married to Miss Mary Green, sister of the above Jere. Green, of Jefferson County. To this union were born nine children, five sons and four daughters. In a three days' meeting (August, second Saturday, 1843, and following days) he and his wife Mary were "received by experience" for membership in the Mossy Creek Baptist Church, and were baptized, most likely, by Elihu Millikan, the pastor. In December, 1848, he was dismissed by letter, to unite with the church at Mansfield Gap, where he kept his membership the rest of his life.

He preached a good deal to Mansfield Gap, Friendship, Dandridge, Dumplin, Mossy Creek, and other nearby churches, and was pastor of most of them. He did considerable missionary and evangelistic work in the Cumberland Mountains and in western North Carolina. "He was spare-made, weighed 140 pounds, had a clear voice, was a close arguer, and had no foolishness about him, in the pulpit or out of it. In conversation, on all occasions, he was ready to propose some subject for serious discussion. I would go forty miles to hear him preach, if he were alive" (Uncle Jacky Line).

He rarely failed to attend the annual meetings of his Association (the Nolachucky), representing his church in that body,
and frequently volunteering as a fraternal messenger to bear
the greetings of his brethren to some "corresponding Association." He was a substantial, "straight-out" man, a safe and
wise counselor. Having few advantages in his early life, his
education was limited. He and his son "Wash" attended school
together at Mossy Creek, and were "in the same class, ambitious to excel each other"—so said the President, Dr. Sam
Anderson. He was a hard worker, a good railmaker, a hard
student, and a good preacher. He attained a position of influence and usefulness in the community and in his denomination by energy, devotion and persistence. He was always a
close Bible student and faithfully served his day and generation.

He fell in the harness before reaching the prime of life,
and passed to his reward, July 22, 1858. He was buried in the
old Branner graveyard at Mossy Creek. On behalf of the
Association the clerk (G. G. Taylor) memorialized him on
the records as a "strong man" fallen, "great" in industry and
devotion and in "ability to confront opposition and demolish
error," a brother "beloved."

I close the sketch with the following incident given me by
Brother W. A. Bowers: Elders Jonathan Quarles and T. J.
Lane were holding a meeting in the old brick meeting house
at Mossy Creek, when Jefferson City was "Mossy Creek Iron
Works." The two brethren were taking it "time about"
preaching. One young man, who afterwards became a prominent lawyer, had been converted. It was Quarles' turn to
preach. He read the Scriptures and announced his text, but,
overcome with emotion and turning deathly pale, he was not
able to proceed. Unable to say a word of his sermon, he sat
down, groaning out, that "God only could save the people and
do the work needed to be done." It was the psychological

moment. The appeal had been made. Seventy to eighty persons surged forward for prayer and instruction in the way of life, and there were mourners everywhere in the building.

HENRY RANDOLPH.

In the cemetery of the old Friendship Church, Jefferson County, Tennessee, is a tombstone bearing this inscription: "Sacred to the memory of the Reverend Henry Randolph, pastor of the Primitive Baptist Church at Friendship; born July 4, 1778; died February 15, 1849. This tribute of affection (the monument) was erected to his memory by his friends." He was born in what is now Jefferson County, Tennessee—what was then Washington County, North Carolina. He was a son of James Randolph, whose name occupies the second place in a list of the "twelve constituent members" (1786) of the French Broad, or Dandridge, church. The same year also this same James Randolph was a representative of his church (Lower French Broad) in the organization of the Holston Association. The writer has made diligent but unsuccessful search for the old "family Bible," which, if it could be found, would doubtless give something of the genealogy of the Randolphs we should like to know. In the absence of family records I give this statement of Brother Wilson C. Witt, now more than 100 years old, who knew Elder Randolph well and whose information and recollection are remarkable: "Henry Randolph was a son of James Randolph, and had a son James, who was the father of Judge James H. Randolph, late of Newport, Cocke County." According to this bit of genealogy, which is entirely trustworthy, the subject of our sketch was the grandfather of Judge Randolph, the great-grandfather of Mrs. Ben D. Jones, of Newport, and the great-great-grandfather of the wives of ex-Governor B. W. Hooper and James R. Stokely, of Newport, all of them Baptists.

The fourth Saturday in April, 1814, Henry Randolph was received by "experience" for baptism and membership in the French Broad (now the Dandridge) Church. The fourth Saturday in August, 1817, he was "liberated" by the church and encouraged to exercise his ministerial gifts. In 1818 he was a messenger of his church to the Tennessee Association. The fourth Saturday in December of the same year the church granted him a "letter of dismission," and the following year we find him in attendance upon the Association as a "messenger of Friendship Church." The second Saturday in October, 1819, Friendship Church called him to the "improvement of his gift," and the first Saturday in March, 1823, he was "ordained" to the full work of the ministry, Elders Caleb Witt, Isaac Barton and William Wood acting as the ordaining council. He was a messenger of Friendship Church to the Tennessee Association some twelve to fifteen years, rarely missing a meeting. He represented Friendship Church in the Nolachucky Association from 1834 to 1839, when the Association (meeting with Concord Church, Greene County) divided. In the division Elders Henry Randolph and Pleasant A. Witt, with about one-third of the constituency of the Association, withdrew from the body, left the house where the body was in session, and went to the grove, where they organized, "on the fourth Friday in September, 1839," what they called "the Old School Nolachucky Baptist Association," with Henry Randolph, Moderator, and Pleasant A. Witt, Clerk. In separating from their missionary brethren they declared in strong terms "non-fellowship for the societies and institutions of the day." It is said that Elder Randolph, as he went out of the house, with his company of adherents, stopped at the door, turned around, and, putting his hand upon the door-facing, said in the hearing of all in the house: "Whichever side is right will live and prosper; the side that is wrong will go down."

Glancing over the minutes of the Nolachucky for 1836 I see that the introductory sermon was preached by Elder Henry Randolph, from the Book of Revelation, 22:9, last clause, "Worship God." It was doubtless a characteristic sermon, emphasizing the divine prerogative to bestow mercy, receive worship, and be Sovereign of the Universe.

Elder Randolph held the extreme Calvinistic views of most preachers of his day. He was a thorough believer in the doctrines of grace. "Salvation is of the Lord," was a favorite theme with these old preachers, and anything that smacked of Arminianism was to them an "abomination." Being a strong predestinarian in his doctrinal belief, he did not subscribe, of course, to a gospel of "free salvation to all who will believe"—the doctrine preached by his missionary brethren. The popular charge brought against him and his associates of the old school persuasion, that "they preached infants to hell," he stoutly denied. The "charge" was the result of a natural and easy inference on the part of his opponents, but was not, he contended, a justifiable or necessary conclusion from his premises.

"Uncle" Wilson Witt, who is a thoroughly competent judge, pays this fine tribute to Elder Randolph as a man and a preacher: "Brother Randolph was a strong denominational man and had a wide influence. He was able in the pulpit and wonderfully gifted in prayer. His voice and manner were unusually impressive. He was as firm in principle as he was hard in doctrine. He had a reputation for firmness, honesty and integrity of character. Everybody had confidence in him as a man and a minister, and that gave him great influence with the people."

ELI RATLIFF.

One of the most effective preachers of the Holston Association was Eli Ratliff, a man small of stature and insignificant in personal appearance, but when "in the Spirit" and aroused, a great and commanding preacher. Before entering the ministry he was a surveyor, and a good one, it is said. He had good and sufficient reasons, as he thought, to "fight his impressions" to preach, and for a time stoutly resisted the Lord's call to him to preach his everlasting gospel. It was only when the Lord took hold upon him with a strong hand, bringing him near to death's door, that he yielded. In a critical illness, in which for days he swung like a pendulum between life and death, not knowing what the issue would be, he had time and opportunity to think and pray. Like a convicted sinner he saw the fiery flames of torment reaching up from beneath, and eager to devour him, felt that nothing but the hand of mercy held him up out of the horrible burning pit, and that he ought to perish, if he didn't make God a promise in good faith that he would preach His gospel the very best he could. Then, like Nehemiah, he turned himself to the wall, prayed, accepted the will of God, made his vow of consecration, and from that hour began to recover his strength and to get well. When he enlisted in the ministry he enlisted for active service, and gave much of his time and energy to self-denying evangelistic labors, in which the hand of the Lord was with him, making him a power for good. He was pastor of Fordtown, Harmony, Fall Branch, Double Spring(s), and other churches.

Elder Ratliff, from the account I have of him, was diminutive in size, thin, and considerably stooped, but was a bundle of nerves, a veritable galvanic battery; when he preached it was a common thing to see his entire physical frame tremble, to hear his feet "clatter on the floor," and to feel a tremor or vibratory movement in atmosphere, audience and building.

As a result of his peculiar nervous organization he was subject to alternating moods of feeling, high and low. In his high moods he would preach like a seraph—preach as though inspired indeed; then his spirits would drop and he would be like Elijah under the juniper tree.

The following incident, related by Elder W. K. Cox, is strikingly characteristic of Eli Ratliff in the ups and downs of his Christian and ministerial experience: The brethren of Fordtown Church, of which Brother Ratliff was pastor, were wanting a protracted meeting; they thought the church and community were "ripe" for it. With a little hesitation on the part of the pastor the meeting was commenced on Saturday, that being the regular business meeting day. At every meeting, from the very first, the brethren would encourage the pastor to call for "penitents" to come forward. But Elder Ratliff's reply would be: "There is not a penitent in fifty miles of here." On Wednesday, however, perhaps at the evening service, not wanting to discourage the brethren, at the close of the sermon he gave an invitation to any who might want to be prayed for to come forward, when about fifteen persons presented themselves as objects of prayer. The preacher was more than surprised; he looked as though he was actually "scared." The meeting went on gloriously, resulting in some forty or fifty conversions and many additions to the church.

J. W. REED.

John Wiley Reed was born on Powell's River, near where it empties into Clinch River, in the year 1840. He was a son of John Reed, commonly known as "Sonny John," and was of 'black Dutch descent." He professed faith in Christ at New Salem Baptist Church, in Anderson County, Tennessee, in a revival meeting conducted by Brother Azariah Herrell, assisted by Elder Frazier Demarcus. Uniting with New Salem Church, he was baptized by Elder Herrell, October 18, 1866. His church licensed him to preach, or exercise a "public gift," the second Saturday in October, 1869, and shortly afterwards ordained him. He was at once called to the care of Zion Church, which he served as pastor for four years. He was also pastor, at one time or another, of New Salem, Pleasant Hill, Longfield, Macedonia, Cedar Hill, Island Ford, Island Home, Coal Creek, Beech Grove, Indian Creek, Jacksboro, Grantsboro, Murrayville, Newcomb, Big Spring, in fact nearly every church in the Clinton Association. He was pastor of Longfield Church, near Coal Creek, from 1883 to 1887, and again from 1896 to 1910, altogether a period of seventeen years. He was unusually popular as a pastor, and generally had more churches on his hands than he could properly care for. In addition to his work as pastor he held a great many protracted meetings, and baptized hundreds of people.

He served one or more years as Moderator of the Clinton Association, was a member of the General Assembly of Tennessee, one session, and was a member of the State Senate also. He was a good presiding officer, had varied gifts, a splendid physique, a good voice, and was a popular and able speaker. His educational advantages were limited to the common schools of the country, but he was a constant reader, and by reading "acquired a fund of varied and general knowledge, so much so that the public scarcely detected in his speaking any indication that he was not well educated."

With a strong mind and fine physical frame, J. W. Reed "possessed a great gift of speech, and was one of the best and most logical reasoners on doctrinal and theological questions of any of the preachers in this part of the country. He was also among the foremost in defending Bible teaching and practice and the distinctive doctrines of the Baptists" (W. R. Riggs).

J. W. Reed, in young manhood, was married to Miss Manda Caroline Coatney, a daughter of John Coatney. The issue of this marriage was ten children, five sons and five daughters —eight of the family still living.

March 27, 1910, at three score and ten, Elder Reed passed from his earthly home, four miles east of Coal Creek, to his heavenly home in the better land.

May the good seed he has sown in the Clinton Association, and elsewhere, bear much fruit in the years to come.

JESSE RIGGS.

"Rev. Jesse Riggs: Forty years a Baptist minister; born August 22, 1792; died January 27, 1869"—tombstone inscription at Double Springs Church.

Through the representations of Elders W. A. Keen and W. K. Cox, the subject of this sketch seems to the writer like an old acquaintance. Nevertheless, he has to confess that he has been unable to secure data and definite information for a sketch at all worthy of his subject. The scene of his labors, however, was in upper East Tennessee, the upper Holston country. He was about forty years pastor of the Double Springs Church, which was the largest church representing in the Holston Association in 1845, reporting that year 223 members. Brother Keen always regarded Jesse Riggs as his spiritual father and his father in the ministry—always spoke of him as Father Riggs. In a great meeting held by him and William Cate (1841) with the Fall Branch Church, during Brother Riggs' pastorate of that church, Brother Keen (with seventy-five others) was converted, and was led down into the water and baptized by Father Riggs.

He was married to Mary Ann Barron, August 12, 1813, and to Hannah Humphreys, November 4, 1858.

In Minutes of the Holston Association for 1869 is a published obituary of Elder Jesse Riggs, "a beloved and much respected minister of the Association for forty years, and pastor all that time of Double Springs Church." It spells something for a man to be pastor of a church continuously for forty years.

27

Jesse Riggs, it is said, when thoroughly stirred, was a powerful exhorter; but steadfastly believed some very hard doctrine—in fact thought that whatever was to be would be sure to come to pass, and that the Lord didn't very much need human help to carry on His business. So, in the meeting above referred to, he had a suspicion at first that a good deal of the so-called "revival" was "fox-fire," and was about to shake off the dust of his feet against the place and leave the meeting. Brother Cate said to him, "Brother Riggs, how long have you been pastor of the church? How long have you been praying for these sinners?" "All the time," was the reply. "Now, Brother Riggs, why should you be so scared when the Lord so marvelously answers your prayers?" Brother Riggs saw the point, and broke forth in a most wonderful exhortation.

ELI ROBERTS.

Eli, son of Phillip Roberts, was born in Sevier County, Tennessee, October 23, 1801. His mother, whose maiden name was Margaret Coonts, was his father's second wife. His father was a native of England, but coming to this country in colonial times and settling in Sevier County, at a time when the county was still largely an unsubdued wilderness and subject to the raids of hostile Indians, he had the misfortune to lose his wife, the mother of his children, through the hostility and treachery of these savages—the two children, by a good providence, escaping the fate of their unfortunate mother.

March 24, 1823, he was married to Elizabeth Gobble, who became the mother of his ten children, four sons and six daughters.

The first Sunday in March, 1825, he was accepted as a candidate for baptism by the Forks of Little Pigeon Church (now the Sevierville Church) and was baptized the same day by Elder Richard Wood. He was granted license by his church to "exercise his gift in public," in November, 1832, and in

May, "first Saturday," 1833, he received his ordination at the hands of Elijah Rogers, Noah Cate, and Johnson Adams, who constituted the presbytery. He was often Moderator of this his home church during the pastorate of "Father Rogers," and succeeded him as pastor in 1840, serving the church for five years. He was also pastor of Red Bank, White Oak Flats, Wear's Valley, Sugar Loaf, Bethel, Dumplin, and other churches.

Like most of the preachers of his day, in this part of the country, Elder Roberts had a limited education. The 'three R's," however, in which he was proficient—"reading, writing, arithmetic"—gave him good business qualifications; and the citizens of his county (Sevier) made him Trustee, after he had become a preacher, and continued him in office for six years.

Bible and hymn book were his preaching outfit. He got very little from the churches in the way of material support. He was a good farmer, however, and made a good living for his family. However, in his later years, he had the misfortune of having to pay "security debts," and was entirely "broken up" at the time of his death.

"Eli Roberts was the ablest preacher for his culture I ever heard; and was one of the first preachers to take a firm stand on missionary ground in this part of the country. He was a doctrinal preacher; and didn't weave in much exhortation— when he preached he preached, expounding the Word" (J. Russell).

Eli Roberts had in him the poetic instinct, and wrote quite a good deal of poetry, religious and otherwise. He wrote out in verse a pretty fine speech for his son Mark to commit to memory and recite. The subject of the speech was "Learning," and the first lines:

> "Good learning seek and strive to gain,
> Though it may cost great care and pain."

From that proposition, and good advice, he proceeds with a practical, utilitarian argument in regard to the doctor, the lawyer, etc., reaching in the last lines this conclusion:

> "Then, learning is the thing for boys—
> It makes them men upon the stage,
> And has done so through every age."

A sentiment like that, clothed in poetic garb, is calculated to stir the ambition of a boy and give him a start in the right direction. The poem, therefore, is worth while. His religious poems are much after the style of the old-time poetry of the oldest hymn books, and served for ornament in religious discourse as well as teaching.

Reviewing his life and anticipating his death he said to "Uncle Dicky Evans": "I'd love if possible, to preach one more sermon; if I had the whole world in one congregation, I would like to tell them of Jesus and His love." In his last sickness he was patient and submissive to the Father's will. To the loved ones gathered about him he said, "Weep not, I am going where the wicked cease from troubling and the weary are at rest."

During the latter part of his life he held his membership with the Red Bank Church. In one of his last preaching services he prayed most earnestly that one of his sons might be a preacher, and a little later Mark Roberts entered the ministry. This "father in Israel" had two brothers, one son and four grandsons who became preachers.

Having fought the good fight, our brother received his discharge, August 9, 1859. He was buried at Middle Creek Methodist Camp-ground, three and one-fourth miles across the country from Pigeon Forge, Sevier County. For the funeral discourse Elder George Sims took for a text: "For we must needs die, and be as water spilt on the ground, which cannot be gathered up again; neither doth God respect any person:

yet doth he devise means, that his banished be not expelled from him" (II Sam. 14:14). A striking and suggestive text, that; I have no notion that the sermon conformed to the homiletical rules laid down in Dr. Broadus' "Preparation and Delivery of Sermons," or to the strict laws of Scripture interpretation— nevertheless, one can see how Brother Sims, from that text, could give his hearers a helpful and an edifying discourse. Don't you wish you could have heard it? I do.

MARK ROBERTS.

Mark Roberts was a son of Elder Eli Roberts, one of the ablest of the older pioneer preachers of the country. He was born in Sevier County, Tennessee, February 16, 1835. He was married to Maleta Drinen, a daughter of James Drinen, of Sevier County, April 8, 1858. The issue of this marriage was eleven children—four of them dying in infancy. Three sons and four daughters are still living, all members of Baptist churches. Brother Roberts was converted early in life, but did not unite with any church till after his marriage. In August of 1858, being in his twenty-fourth year, he was received by experience and baptism for membership in the White Oak Flats Church, where he kept his membership as long as he lived. July 3, 1875, he was licensed to preach, and was ordained August 6, 1876.

In a ministry of thirty-seven years he was pastor of sixteen or more churches: Gatlenburg, Wear's Valley, Bethel (Blount County), Antioch, Evans' Chapel, Marshall's Grove, Olive Springs, Rocky Grove, New Salem, Laurel Grove, New Era, Oldham's Creek, Shady Grove, Ogle's Cross Roads, Banner, Sugar Loaf, and perhaps others.

Brother Roberts was a faithful minister of Jesus Christ. He was strictly a Biblical preacher. His sermons always abounded in Scripture quotations; he preached the Word, and

that only. To him the Bible was the solution of all problems
and the answer to all questions of importance. All sorts of
questions would be put to him by his neighbors. Some of them
he would answer directly, some of them from the pulpit, but in
either case the answer would come from the Bible. "He lived
a humble, consecrated, devoted life." His motto was, Be right

MARK ROBERTS.

and do your duty—leave results to God. His belief in the Bible
and in the right was as firm as the great mountains, among
which and under whose shadows he preached.

August 4, 1912, Brother Roberts preached the funeral discourse of a leading citizen and member of his church, following
the Sabbath discourse with two other sermons, on Monday and
Tuesday. These were his farewell discourses. He fell on sleep
November 1, 1912. "Brother Roberts was an exemplary Christian and an able preacher of the gospel. He was a faithful

and true servant of the Lord, and his labors were greatly blessed. We mourn his loss. But he had fought the good fight, had kept the faith, and has gone to his reward." (From resolutions adopted by the church.)

J. P. RODDY.

Jesse Preston Roddy, son of James and Margaret Roddy, was born in Rhea County, Tennessee, August 10, 1823. He was the oldest of a family of eight children. The loss of his father by death was a providence which placed upon him, at the age of seventeen, the responsibility of caring for a widowed mother and a lot of fatherless children. This stern necessity deprived him of all educational advantages. September 6, 1841, he professed faith in Christ, and was baptized by Elder Chas. Taliaferro into the fellowship of Bethel Church. February 6, 1842, he was married to Miss Emily McClane, to which union were born nine children. At the call of Bethel Church he was ordained, October 2, 1867, by a presbytery composed of J. B. McCallon, Asa Newport and R. T. Howard.

In his early ministry he was associated with Elder McCallen in missionary work in the old Hiwassee Association. Later, in September of 1875, he was a leader, together with Z. Rose, Allen King, W. A. Selvedge, Horace Sturges, and others, in the organization of the Big Emory Association, and became the first missionary of that body. He served in this relation a number of years, laboring mostly in the mountain districts of Roane and Cumberland counties. He also labored extensively in Rhea and Meigs counties. He was a great lover of the "hill country," where he was greatly loved by the people, and where he was successful in planting new churches and building up struggling Baptist interests.

He was a good organizer, an untiring worker and a successful evangelist. He was "at all times fully in the gospel har ness, and at work. No man would overcome more difficulties in order to fill his appointments. He rode over mountains as no other man, visiting the poorest hovels to tell of Jesus and his love. He attracted crowds to hear him preach, and by his earnestness and sympathy held them and influenced them for good as no other man. He labored successfully and built up a good interest in the destitute places of our mountain country." (Wm. Whitlock.)

ELDER JESSE P. RODDY.

Leaving his native East Tennessee, in 1892, he went to Texas, locating in Dallas County, where he served as missionary of the Dallas County Association, also as pastor of the Prairie Valley Church, until physical disabilities compelled him to give up his work. The clerk of the church bore testimony to the high esteem in which the church held their beloved pastor.

This servant of the Lord wound up his life's work, and died at his home, near Landcaster, Texas, January 13, 1898, in his seventy-fifth year. Friends and loved ones prayed earnestly for his recovery, but it was the Master's will for him to rest from his labors.

At the first meeting of the Big Emory Association, after his death, beautiful and tender words of testimony were spoken by Elder Joseph Wilson, Brother S. J. Martin and others, in regard to the character and life of Brother Roddy as a "pioneer of the mountains" and the bringer of glad tidings to the poor.

The committee appointed by the association to memorialize Elder Roddy, in a "biographical obituary" (Minutes, 1898) pay worthy tribute to him as a "citizen, father, friend and faithful servant of the Lord—now gone to his reward, and to hear the welcome:

> " 'Servant of God, well done!
> Rest from thy loved employ!' "

ELIJAH ROGERS.

I am now standing on historic ground—the ancient site of the Forks of Little Pigeon (now Sevierville) Church, the first Baptist church of Sevier County, constituted in 1789. Just out there stood the old meeting-house, where the Baptist saints worshipped, and where Richard Wood and Elijah Rogers preached the gospel and ministered to them as pastors for more than fifty years. And here in the old cemetery is a tombstone bearing the inscription: "Sacred to the memory of Elijah Rogers; born May, 1774; died May, 1841."

Maj. E. E. McCroskey, a descendant of Elijah Rogers, says the Rogers family is originally from Wales. In its later history it was identified with the Puritan stock of Plymouth Rock fame. Two brothers of this name came from over the waters in the "May Flower" with the goodly company of the Pilgrim Fathers. One of them located in Massachusetts, the other in Virginia. The members of the family in the New England states have an unbroken family record back to the year 1300.

Elijah, the son of Henry Rogers, was born in Fauquier County, Virginia, but at the age of 15 came with his father and other members of the family to Sevier County, Tennessee, then a part of the "western territory" of North Carolina. This county at that early date was largely an unsubdued wilderness, infested by the Indians, whose hostile aggressions, for a number of years, involved the races in perpetual warfare or vigilant watching on the part of the settlers against the sudden raids of the hostile and suspecting natives. In all this young Rogers was an "active participant." (S. C. Rogers, in *Borum's Sketches.*)

Elijah Rogers lived before the day of public schools in Sevier County, or even private ones. But his battle with the wilderness developed in him strength of character as well as strength of muscle. He was in every sense a self-made man. His education, from first to last, was secured by hard digging and persistent application. He possessed the talent of self-helpfulness and acquired in large measure the virtue of self-reliance. In his early ministry and even on toward middle life, though not lacking in masculine strength, he was "raw and awkward and unpromising," we are told; yet by dint of effort and perseverance he became, in time, a fairly polished speaker, for his day.

At the age of 20 Elijah Rogers was married to Miss Katherine Clack, daughter of Spencer Clack, a Baptist, and a prominent citizen of Sevier County—one of a delegation of "five members," elected to represent his county in a convention called by the Governor (William Blount) to meet at Knoxville, January 11, 1796, to formulate the first constitution for the government of the new State of Tennessee (Ramsey's Annals, p. 651) ; and was also a member of the legislature for a number of terms. This union was blessed with a family of ten children, five sons and five daughters.

In 1796 he and his companion united with the Forks of Little Pigeon (Sevierville) Church, and were baptized, it is supposed, by Elder Richard Wood, who was then pastor of the church. Subsequently this church licensed him to preach, but he was not ordained to the full work of the ministry till he had reached his thirty-sixth year.

In 1810 Boyd's Creek Church called for his ordination, and he was accordingly ordained, in the usual way, as we may suppose, by the laying on of the hands of a presbytery, presumably by the authority of the old Forks of Little Pigeon Church, of which he seems still to have been a member.

He served Boyd's Creek, Alder Branch, and Sevierville as pastor the greater part of his ministerial life. Of Boyd's Creek he was pastor more than thirty years. He was the first pastor of Alder Branch, he and Augustine Bowers being the joint-founders of the church. He was successor to Elder Richard Wood in the pastorate of the Sevierville Church. For more than fifty-two years these two faithful under-shepherds took care of the Baptist flock at Sevierville, each serving the flock faithfully to the close of his life.

These men were present at the baptism of John Hillsman (August, 1825) in the Tennessee River at Knoxville, in the presence of 3,000 people, Elijah Rogers being the administrator. This was the first baptism in the city of Knoxville, and the beginning of Baptist history at this now Baptist city. (Old record.)

These two men were the chief pillars of strength to the Baptist cause in all their part of the country for years, serving the churches, for the most part, at their own charge. They, with other Baptists, had seen and felt the injustice of a compulsory religious (?) tax to support the state church, and the pendulum had swung the other way. Right or wrong, following the Baptist custom of the times, they said little about pastoral support, and "farmed" for a living. "Preacher Rogers" was held in repute as a farmer, and was said to be the "best corn-grower" in Sevier County.

Elijah Rogers was moderator of the Tennessee Association twenty-four years in succession—a fact in itself showing unusual influence and popularity, and an honor rarely duplicated in the history of deliberative bodies.

He was a pioneer in missions, and a John the Baptist preparing the way for a missionary movement, even while he was held in fellowship by his anti-mission and anti-effort brethren. While the leaders of the anti-mission school gave their time and energy to discussing "fixed fate, free-will and foreknowledge absolute," Elijah Rogers was one of the first to break the shell of fatalistic belief and declare for missions. His contention was for "free salvation," or a salvation available for all men, a universal commission, and the obligation of the churches to give the "gospel to every creature." In the war with the so-called "Ironsides" he was able and distinguished as a fighter. He had an appointment, I am told, on one occasion, to preach a special sermon on the points of difference between the "missionaries" and the "antis." The appointed day came round, the multitude gathered, the sermon—a "great sermon"—was preached. It was a great triumph for the cause of truth. The opposition was not entirely quieted, but to a great extent was disarmed. The friends of missions were encouraged, and furnished arguments for the defense of their cause. The controversial spirit, however, was not natural to him. He was inclined to be conservative and conciliatory, rather than combative. Churches, rent asunder by strife over the question of missions, sent for Elder Rogers, far and near, to help them settle their troubles; and few men could do more by tact and prudence than he to restore peace and unity to a divided church.

I close the sketch with the relation of the following anecdote, which is vouched for by good authority. Elder Rogers had a small Testament which he was accustomed to carry about with him in one of the hind pockets of his coat. While getting ready to start to one of his Saturday appointments he happened upon a pack of cards about the barn, which some of his boys, as he supposed, had been playing on the sly, and had forgotten to "hide," as they intended to do. He put the cards in the same pocket in which he had previously put his Testament, and went on to church, intending to give the boys a lecture, on his return home. When the time to begin the preaching service had arrived he had forgotten all about the "cards." Imagine his surprise, when, putting his hand in his pocket for his Testament, he pulled out the cards instead, in plain view of the audience. As soon, however, as he could recover himself from his embarrassing perplexity, he explained the situation and proceeded to give a moral lecture on the wickedness and folly of "card-playing."

WILLIAM ROGERS.

Pioneer of higher education and first President of Mossy Creek (now Carson and Newman) College.

William, the son of Vincent and Abigail Rogers, was born April 3, 1817. He was converted early in life and identified himself with the Baptists. He was educated at Maryville College and the University of Tennessee.

In May, 1846, he was called to ordination by the Pleasant Grove Church, Sevier County, and was soon thereafter ordained to the full work of the ministry by Nails Creek Church, of which he was a member.

From 1849 to 1851 he was pastor of the Dandridge Church, successor to Elder Duke Kimbrough.

February 11, 1851, in connection with C. C. Tipton, he was appointed by the "Baptist Educational Society of East Tennessee" financial agent for the "Mossy Creek Baptist Seminary," and instructed to raise money to "complete building, purchase library and apparatus, and also for endowment." August 7 following he reported "three and a half months' labor, and $2,386.50 in bonds, notes, books and cash in hand" for the college; also the "favor and goodwill of many friends," a spirit of "improvement" among Baptists, a sentiment in favor of "educating the ministry," and some "difficulties to contend with."

August 7, 1851, he was elected first president of what is now Carson and Newman College, with Robert Reedy Bryan as "associate professor."

In September of 1851 the college opened its first session in the Baptist church building, and in November following President Rogers died.

William Rogers was a man of scholarly attainments, fine executive ability, and a commanding speaker. His death was a great blow to the infant college.

In early manhood Elder Rogers was married to Miss E. J. Williams, daughter of Captain Wm. B. Williams, who lived on Little River. To this union were born two sons.

A tombstone in the old Mossy Creek Cemetery reads: "Sacred to the memory of Rev. William Rogers, President of the Mossy Creek Missionary Baptist Seminary, member of the Dandridge Church: Born April 3, 1817. Died November 24, 1851. An exemplary member of the Baptist church, a useful minister of the gospel, humble and persevering in the cause of Christ. He sacrificed property, health, and life for truth's sake."

So costly a sacrifice may have been necessary in laying the foundations of a great denominational school. We cannot tell. The decrees of God and the ways of Providence are inscrutable, and it is not for us to say to Jehovah, "What doest thou?" But it is possible for short-sighted man to take things out of the hands of Jehovah and make a providence of his own, that is not for the best. And the sacrifice of so promising a life, at the age of 35—a life that promised in every way to be a tower of strength to the cause of higher education among East Tennessee Baptists—seems, to the feeble sense of man, at least, to be a distinct loss to the denomination, and a calamity greatly to be regretted.

ZACHARIAH ROSE.

Zachariah, son of Francis and Elizabeth Rose, was born in Buncombe County, N. C., July 2, 1809. His parents were very poor in this world's goods, and the death of his father, when young Rose was but a boy, left a widowed mother and six children for the oldest to look after and provide for. This necessity, in the providence of God, cut off for young Rose all opportunities for an education till he was grown. Moving, with his mother and the younger children, to McMinn County, in East Tennessee, he had his .first introduction to school life in Forest Hill Academy, near Athens, where he vigorously prosecuted his studies for six months. So rapid was his advancement that he soon became a teacher in the academy. By close application, both in school and at home, he at length became a good English scholar, and acquired a working knowledge of Latin and Greek. In his fourteenth year (September, 1822) he professed faith in Christ, and uniting with New Providence Church, Monroe County, was baptized by Elder George Snider, August 7, 1823. On December 23, 1832, he was married to Mrs. Sarah Burch (nee Miss Cate), to which union were born nine children, eight of whom he was permitted to see grow up and become Christians in very early life.

Z. Rose, I have been told, was chairman of the first county court of Polk County, helped to lay out the county, and taught the first school in the county.

He was ordained by the Ocoee Church, Polk County, November, second Saturday, 1841, Elders Jason Matlock, Clemence Sanders, and Elijah Clayton acting as an ordaining council. Soon after his ordination the Lord graciously visited the Ocoee Church with a wonderful revival, as a result of which Elder Rose baptized into the fellowship of that church 100 new converts. His labors were similarly blessed at other places. The first thirty years of his ministerial life were spent, almost

entirely, in protracted meeting, or evangelistic work, in East
Tennessee, eastern Kentucky, north Georgia, and Texas.   In
this work of evangelism his labors were greatly blessed of the
Lord.   He labored three years in Texas, organizing and foster-
ing new interests, and strengthening weak interests in Eastern
Texas Association.

ZACHARIAH ROSE.

For more than a quarter of a century Elder Rose was clerk of the Sweetwater Association. He was largely instrumental in the organization of the Big Emory Association, which he considered necessary to the development and increased efficiency of the Baptist people of that section.

Elder Rose was a man of more than ordinary organizing and executive ability, not only in the Lord's work but in business affairs. He lived and labored, at one time and another, in seven different counties in East Tennessee, residing in some of these a second or third time. In the meantime, and as an accompaniment to his moving, he sold and bought, and bought and sold, and "swapped," farms, any number of times; built fifteen grain mills, several sawmills, and quite a number of church-houses and school-houses. He was a many-sided man. He was a sound doctrinal preacher, but was not as "hard" in his doctrinal belief as some of his ministerial brethren. He had a number of discussions with the champions of other faiths, and was considered one of the ablest debaters in lower East Tennessee. He was a good writer and contributed many valuable articles to the religious press; was a great admirer of Dr. J. R. Graves, and wrote for his paper—not always agreeing with the editor. He wrote a pamphlet on election and predestination, which was widely read. He was a strong man, an uncompromising Baptist, and left a lasting impress on his day and generation. He labored and prayed earnestly for harmony and co-operation among all true Baptists, "missionary, anti-missionary, so-called, and omissionary," along the lines of Baptist evangelical teaching and evangelistic endeavor for the salvation of a lost world. I find in my "notes" this tribute from Dr. N. B. Goforth: "Elder Z. Rose was a strong preacher of a pure gospel, and might be classed with Ephraim Moore, T. J. Lane, Woodson Taylor, John Scruggs, and other strong and militant Baptists of his day. Give him a place of honor, let his name stand prominent on the roll of worthy Baptist names in our East Tennessee Zion."

In 1875 Elder Rose lost his first wife, and in the following year he married the widow Neil, of Meigs County. In September, 1886, after a lingering illness, Elder Rose fell asleep in Jesus, and was buried in White County, Tennessee.

Among the living descendants of Zachariah Rose is Pastor W. N. Rose, of Jonesboro, Tennessee, who possesses in good measure the spirit and worthily wears the mantle of the elder Rose, his grandfather.

Since writing the above the following incident has come to me, being vouched for by good authority: Just before the Civil War Elder Rose held a four days' debate with a Methodist preacher at Rhea Springs, in Rhea County, where the Methodists had held their annual camp meetings for a number of years. On camp meeting occasions it was a popular and prevalent custom, I believe, in those early days, to sprinkle babies; it sometimes happened also, on such occasions, that the usual revival was enlivened by denominational thrust and counter-thrust and throwing out challenges for public debate. On the occasion here referred to there were present some fifty ministers, among them three preacher-brothers of note and ability, vast crowds of people being in attendance. The preachers were proclaiming their doctrines boldly, sprinkling infants, as usual, and challenging discussion and refutation. Elder Rose accepted the challenge, and one of the three "preacher-brothers," who was considered the ablest debater, was appointed to engage him in public debate. It was a battle royal, continuing four days, resulting, it is claimed, in complete victory for the Baptists, and the establishment of the Rhea Springs Baptist Church. It is also said that the Methodists broke camp and never had another meeting at Rhea Springs, and that for twenty-five years after the debate a case of baby sprinkling in that community was not heard of.

REUBEN ROSS.

Reuben Ross was born May 9, 1776, in Martin County, North Carolina, near Williamston, the county seat of said county. He was the youngest of six brothers and the ninth in a family of ten children. He was a son of William and Mary (Griffin) Ross, both of North Carolina. His grandfather, whose name also was William, at an early day, emigrated from Roanoke, Virginia, to Martin County, North Carolina. The Ross family is of Scotch descent, several persons of this name, as tradition has it, having left Scotland together, in very early times, crossed the Atlantic and settled in Virginia—their descendants emigrating to Maryland, Pennsylvania, and other parts of the country. Of the six brothers of this family, three—Martin, James and Reuben—became Baptist preachers, and three became soldiers in the war of the Revolution. To win the independence of the colonies William Ross, the father of Reuben, was patriotic enough to sacrifice his entire property. "Poverty is generally regarded as a calamity, but Reuben Ross rejoiced in his youth, in his manhood, and in his old age, that his father became poor by cheerfully surrendering his estate to help forward the Revolutionary contest. When an old man he was heard by the writer to say: I was always proud that my father became poor by spending his estate to carry out the principles of the Declaration of Independence." (J. M. P.) This deprivation was a handicap to young Ross, in a way, making it impossible for him to go to school much in his youthful days. "Nine months of schooling, interspersed through a period of seven years, a few days at a time," constituted the sum total of his education in the school-room. But Reuben Ross had "superior intellectual endowments, and ambition, which enabled him to throw off encumbrances and rise above the circumstances of his lot—to become in time a preacher of distinction, popular alike with the learned and the unlearned." He had also the inestimable advantage of piety and religious instruction in the home, both his parents being exemplary Christians and Baptists. He never knew anything but to believe in the truths of the Christian religion, and was often the subject of religious impressions; his mother's night-time "whisper-prayers," overheard by the lad, never ceased to haunt him. But he never gave himself to God until after his marriage. In his twenty-second year he was united in mar-

REUBEN ROSS.

riage to Miss Mildred Yarrell, who as a bride became a member
of the Ross family, and in the providence of God soon obtained
a joyful hope in Christ.   The young husband strangely discouraged his wife from making a public profession of her faith.
He had become fascinated with the dance and other worldly
amusements, and while believing in a general way in the Bible
and in Christianity he had come to look upon religion as something "solemn and gloomy, suited, not to young persons, but
to those in the declining years of life, no longer able to enjoy
the gaieties and pleasures of the world."   Just at this time
the sudden death of a boon-companion set him to thinking about
the uncertainty of life, the danger of procrastination, and the
awfulness of death. judgment and eternity, to one out of
Christ; and on his knees he earnestly implored God in his great
mercy to spare his life and give him a chance to repent, believe and be saved.   Long and bitter was his struggle with
doubts and darkness and the fatalistic beliefs that had been
instilled into him from his youth.   But at last the light dawned
and peace came, and with him "old things had passed away,
and, behold! all things had become new."   He related his experience of grace before the brethren of the neighborhood
church, of which his wife had already become a member, was
approved for baptism, and was baptized by the pastor, Elder
Luke Ward.   He was soon "licensed" to preach, and in 1807,
just before emigrating to Tennessee, he was ordained to the
full work of the ministry by a council composed of Elders
Joseph Biggs, Luke Ward and James Ross.   The young preacher
having decided to seek a home in what was then considered
the "far West," the brethren of the church said, "He must,
at once, be set apart and ordained to preach the gospel, that
he may be qualified to build up churches and administer the
ordinances in the land whither he is about to journey."

He commenced his journey westward "toward the distant
Cumberland," with other emigrants, May 6, 1807, and on the
4th day of July, 1807, he reached the town of Port Royal, in

Montgomery County, Tennessee, where he "preached his first sermon west of the mountains, to an audience seated on the ground under the widespreading branches of a shady tree." Here he taught school for three months, and joined the Red River Church.

April 2, 1808, Spring Creek Church, formerly an arm of Red River Church, or the Fort Meeting-house Church, was organized as a separate and independent body, and extended a call to Elder Ross to become pastor. This call was accepted, and in March, 1810, a twenty-nine years' pastorate was begun. He and his wife uniting with this church, held their member-ship here a great many years. About the year 1837 this church joined the Red River Association, of which Elder Ross became moderator, and continued as such for several years. This association, and the churches composing it, becoming more and more Calvinistic and non-missionary, preaching only to "elect sinners"—the sheep already in the fold, and neglecting or ig-noring the Lord's command to "go into all the world and preach the gospel to every creature"—and Elder Ross becom-ing more and more evangelic in his views, and evangelistic in practice, it was finally agreed that there should be a peaceable division of opposing and belligerent elements, the result being the organization (October 28, 1825) of the Bethel Association. Of this association Elder Ross was moderator from its origin to the year 1851, when the "infirmities of age prompted him to tender his resignation."

In a very fine address delivered in the chapel of Bethel College, Russellville, Kentucky, May 9, 1861, and reported for the *Louisville Courier-Journal,* and quoted in Borum, and else-where, Dr. Samuel Baker pays Reuben Ross this high tribute: "The wide influence which he secured by his great powers of expounding the Scriptures seemed like a magic charm. As a preacher he was earnest, devout and solemn. His enunciation was peculiarly dignified, and his expositions, his expostula-tions, his entreaties, and his appeals were framed after the best

models of those good men who, in primitive times, declared in
our own tongue the wonderful works of God. With an untiring hand, for almost forty years, he bore the ark of God into
the darkened corners of Logan, Todd and Christian counties, in
Kentucky, and Robertson, Montgomery and Stewart counties,
in Tennessee—and wherever the ark rested there was a blessing from God. When such a man has moved before the public
eye, engaged their understandings, warmed their hearts for
forty years, his exit from the world must cause a deep sensation in all ranks. And it was so. In the full possession of his
faculties, in the eighty-fourth year of his age, amid the most
hallowed and triumphant sentiments of his faith, he was called
to resign his soul into the hands of his Redeemer. He died
in 1860, and was buried at his old home, in Montgomery County, Tennessee. As a mark of respect and veneration the Bethel
Association has erected an appropriate monument to his memory, and his son, James Ross, of Montgomery, Tennessee, is
engaged in writing his biography."

(This promised "biography"—Life and Times of Elder Reuben Ross, with Introduction and Notes by Dr. J. M. Pendleton—was published in 1882, and reads like a romance. The
author has greatly enjoyed its perusal.)

Years after the funeral obsequies and the above address,
at the suggestion of a ministers and deacons' meeting, a large
number of the relatives and friends and acquaintances of the
loved and lamented Father Ross met at the old homestead, in
order to hold some befitting memorial service in connection
with the monument which had been erected to his memory.
"The occasion was one of deep and impressive solemnity, full
of heart-touching reminiscences, which found utterance in the
silent tear, rather than the pomp of ceremony. It was a congregation of mourners, composed of the children and grandchildren of brethren and friends of life-long acquaintance, met
together to pay the last earthly tribute of respect and veneration to a father in Israel." (*Western Recorder,* July 1, 1871.)

Dr. J. M. Pendleton, in his Introduction to the Life and Times of Elder Reuben Ross,. uses these finely descriptive and eloquent words: "There was in the expression of his eyes and in the features of his face a union of intelligence, gentleness, solemnity, greatness, majesty. In his sermons were combined exposition, argument and exhortation. He had no knowledge of the languages in which the Scriptures were originally written, but the Spirit who indicted the Holy Oracles dwelt in his heart, sanctifying his large common sense and making him a great interpreter of the divine word. He was a born logician. His appeals were generally fine specimens of impassioned eloquence, and at times their power was transcendent and irresistible. They carried everything before them.

The intonations of the preacher's voice were melting, finding their way to every heart; his deep emotion was seen on the quivering lip and in the tearful eye, while the whole face was in a glow of ardent excitement. I have seen the wonders of Kentucky's great cave, the thousand objects of interest in our centennial exposition, the magnificent scenery of mountains and vales, the wild, dashing, thundering waters of Niagara, and I have stood on the shore of the Atlantic, where wave after wave has rolled in majesty and power; but I do not remember anything that has impressed me more deeply than a sight of Elder Reuben Ross, with a countenance full of dignity, solemnity, anxiety, tenderness and love, entreating sinners to accept Christ and salvation."

ASA ROUTH.

Twenty years ago, in a published sketch of Asa Routh, the writer characterized the subject of his sketch as "the grand old man eloquent, now in his seventy-ninth year, and, though deaf and stooped with age, still preaching the glorious gospel he has preached so well these fifty years."

Asa, son of Stephen and Sarah Routh, was born July 23, 1818, in Clinch Valley, Grainger County, Tennessee, four miles north of Rutledge. His father was born in Sevier County, Tennessee, and was a soldier in the War of 1812. His paternal grandfather's name was Isaac, of Welsh descent. His mother, whose maiden name was McCluskey, was Irish, as the name indicates. It is from these sources our subject inherits his two most marked characteristics, Welsh fire and Irish wit.

Elder Routh was converted in his twenty-sixth year, at the Powder Spring Gap Church, Grainger County, in a meeting held by Elders James Kennon, William Hickle, and Joel Aldridge, the last-mentioned baptizing him into the fellowship of the above church. In his twenty-eighth year (1846) he was called of the Lord to preach the gospel and was licensed by the Puncheon Camp Church to exercise his preaching gift, and, a few months later, was ordained by the same church to the full work of the ministry, Elders James Greenlee and Daniel P. Morris constituting the presbytery.

In Tennessee Elder Routh was pastor of the following churches: Elm Spring, Puncheon Camp, Buffalo, Tazewell, Little Sycamore, Rob Camp, Independence, Blountville, Holston Valley, Bluff City, Bethel, Johnson City First (which he organized), Old Union, Boon's Creek, Fordtown, Beech Grove, Chalybeate Spring, Liberty and Friendship. In Virginia, he was pastor of Clear Spring, Wallace, Castle Woods, Sulphur Springs, Independence, Bethel, Oak Grove, Mendota, and Lebanon churches.

In 1860 he sold his home at Little Sycamore, and moved to Lebanon, Virginia, where he spent thirteen years of active ministry: First, as missionary pastor of the Lebanon Church, under the Virginia State Board of Missions, and afterwards under the auspices of the Home Mission Society, of New York. Scarcely had the pastor begun work on his new field when the terrible war between the States broke out and the Virginia board could no longer carry on its mission operations.

It was at this juncture that the old soldier needed the courage
of a hero. In the midst of the perils and hardships incident
to war, dropped by the board which could no longer help him,
anxious about the support of his large family, and without resources, he thought he would have to go back to his old home
and friends in Tennessee, to keep the wolf from the door. But
the heroic little "mission" church said, "Stay with us. As

ASA ROUTH.

long as we have bread and meat you shall have part." At the close of the war the Home Mission Society came to his relief with a supplement to his salary of $300 a year for three years. For this timely help Brother Routh makes the following grateful acknowledgement: "But for this aid I don't see how I could have kept above the waves. I shall never forget the generosity of those northern brethren."

Though the churches served by Brother Routh prospered, as a rule, under his pastoral oversight, it was not as pastor that he was most uniformly successful. Evangelism was his forte. He was instrumental in the conversion of more than 5,000 people. He baptized more than 3,000 converts into the fellowship of Baptist churches. In his palmy days he would not unfrequently witness more than 100 conversions in a two or three weeks' meeting. In a great meeting with Rev. B. G. Manard, at Bristol, there were 138 converts. At Buffalo, Blountville, Sodom, and Watauga, he enlisted more than 400 soldiers for the King. As missionary of the East Tennessee General Association, his report of work done within the "bounds of the Mulberry Gap Association" shows, among other items, "number of baptisms, 161; number of conversions, 314." In the early struggles of Baptists for a foothold in Knoxville Brother Routh held at least three successful meetings, assisting Drs. J. F. B. Mays and T. C. Teasdale and Rev. J. M. Walters in establishing Baptist churches in that gem city of the mountains.

Thus gifted as an evangelist and successful as a revivalist and soul-winner, with a limited education, and with little or no opportunity for wide reading and painstaking study, Brother Routh rather regretted in his old age, especially in the light of God's signal blessings upon his soul-winning ministry, that he had not "given himself wholly to the work of an evangelist." He recognized that holding meetings was his "particular calling." In "pastoring churches," as he put it, he was always sensible of a "loss of energy." "If I had my ministry to live over again," he would say, "I would never take the pastoral care of a church."

Among his associates in the ministry I mention Elders W. A. Keen and Thomas Gilbert. Brother Keen was his fellow-missionary under the appointment of the East Tennessee General Association, and was his fellow-helper in protracted meetings on various occasions. He and Brother Gilbert also were a strong team in many a good meeting.

How do we account for Brother Routh's success? What is the secret of his power? Several things must be taken into the account. 1. The hearer is impressed that he is in the presence of a God-called and God-sent man, bearing a message. 2. The messenger is an original, abrupt, John-the-Baptist sort of man—a striking figure, a unique personality. Who that ever saw the preacher could ever forget the piercing eye, the rugged face, the commanding voice? 3. The directness of his appeals. 4. His consecration to the work of the ministry. He magnified his office as a preacher. "Asa Routh's power," says W. A. Keen, "is in his directness, in his searching, matter-of-fact style of preaching, and his consecration to the work." 5. His generalship. Rev. J. H. Moore, characterizing Brother Routh as a preacher, says: "Asa Routh is a wonderful commander, a great strategist. If he had been trained at West Point, he would have made a Lea or a Jackson." 6. A combination of gifts and graces, which the writer has described elsewhere as follows: He is thoroughly sincere, perfectly honest. He has convictions, and produces conviction in his hearers. He knows the human conscience and is acquainted with the hiding places of guilt, and when he has found the sinner he fearlessly says to him, like Nathan to David, "Thou art the man." He preaches the law as well as the gospel, and has a unique personality. His small black eye pierces you, his trumpet-voice awakes and startles you, his pungent speech takes hold of you—he holds the sinner over the flame till he can smell the brimstone. But to the awakened and alarmed

soul, anxious to escape the wrath to come, he can preach like
a seraph, telling the wonders of redeeming love. 7. A marked
element of power in Brother Routh was his pathos. The first
time I ever met him was at the East Tennessee General Association, more than forty years ago. The place of meeting was
the Mouth of Big Creek (Del Rio). Brother Routh preached
in the grove. His text was, "For God so loved the world,"
etc. The entire discourse was in a pathetic strain, and had a
fine effect. I cannot recall a single division of his sermon.
but I have never forgotten the bit of poetry the preacher quoted
and the story of its composition. The verse is this:

> "Could we with ink the ocean fill,
>   And were the sky of parchment made,
> And every stick on earth a quill,
>   ' And every man a scribe by trade,
> To tell the love of God to man,
>   Would drain that ocean dry,
> Nor could the scroll contain the whole,
>   Though spread from sky to sky."

8. Another by no means inconsiderable element of power in
Elder Routh's preaching was his quaint humor and sober wit,
which was an enemy to dullness in the pulpit and served to
keep his hearers on the alert. Elder Routh was not a "professional" evangelist, counting numbers. On the contrary, he
utterly despised hypocrisy and shams. But after his great
meeting with the Buffalo Church, Grainger County, in which
there were 112 "professions" and ninety-nine approved for baptism, he was heard to say that "if a right respectable hypocrite
had offered to join, he might have been tempted to take him
in, just to make an even hundred."

On the subject of pastoral support Brother Routh thought
he knew a few things, "from not being supported himself."
So, when that matter was being discussed before the Holston

Association, he told the brethren he had a "staked and ridered" sermon on that important question and would "deliver" it in any of their churches, if they needed it.

Brother Routh had a kindly feeling toward young preachers, and, on a certain occasion, said he would like to "write a book" for their special benefit—a book of "advice." He thought he could say all that would be necessary in "one chapter."

Brother Routh was married three times, and was the father of twenty-nine children. "How many children have you?" I inquired. "I have booked my twenty-ninth," was the reply. He had been "in pretty close places" on account of having so large a family to support, and was "crowded" at times, but could always "find room for one more." The following anec-dote is vouched for by good authority: A stranger once upon a time stayed all night with Brother Routh, it being Sat-urday night. On Sunday morning the twenty-nine or more children and grandchildren were all together in the family circle. The stranger, surveying the group, inquired of the venerable patriarch, "Who is superintendent of this Sunday school?" "I am, sir," was the laconic reply.

In conversation with the writer Brother Routh made grate-ful mention of the fact that he had lived seventy-eight years and had never had a "woman tale to follow him." He was quite popular with the "sisters," however, as the following in cident will show. He was pastor of a church in what was called "the Dutch Settlement," where the women spun their own cotton and wool yarn and wove their own cloth. It so happened that the "good sisters" of the church made him pres-ents of thirteen jacket-patterns of their homespun check-cotton and turkey-red. His wife made him about two jackets from the turkey-red patterns, and suggested the propriety of her piecing together some of the other patterns to make him a pair of pants to wear, "one time," to the Dutch Settlement, as an object lesson to the sisters, that they might understand that their beloved pastor needed something besides jacket patterns of turkey-red. The wife's plan, however, was not carried out —the husband protesting that he would have been "too distinguished," and that it would not be "in good taste" for a preacher to be arrayed in such gorgeous apparel.

In his early ministry Brother Routh, with W. A. Keen, held a meeting at a place called Sodom, in the extreme upper corner of Hancock County, north of Clinch Mountain. The place was noted for its whisky-drinking, card-playing and rowdyism. There were but two Christians in the community. The Methodists had tried to hold meetings there, but had been run out. So when the Baptist meeting was announced many Baptist friends said, "Don't go." But Routh said, "I will go; the appointment has been made. If they whip me, I'll know how it feels to be whipped for preaching the gospel. I'll not be the first Baptist preacher that has been whipped for preaching." The people had good farms and were good livers, but were rough and profane, and there was no meeting-house in the neighborhood. So that, as they were building the arbor in the woods for the coming meeting, they would swear and and jest, and say, good-naturedly, "Let the preachers come on; they'll soon get tired of us." At last the preachers came—and they stayed. A mighty work of grace was wrought there. Sinners, under conviction, cried aloud for mercy. Strong men bowed in submission to the Lord Jesus, and accepted him as Savior. The power of the whisky business was broken. Decks of cards were burnt in great numbers, or scattered along the highways in all directions. Eighty persons were baptized and a Baptist church was established. It must have been this wicked "Sodom" that he referred to in a sermon afterwards. He told his audience about holding a meeting in a very wicked place, which, he said, was so "near to hell it seemed that he could smell the brimstone." Taking dinner that day with one of the members, a matter-of-fact sort of man, who took everything in a most literal way, his host and old-time friend said to him, in all seriousness, "Asa, did you really think you smelt the brimstone?"

Brother Routh's grim humor would break out in unexpected flashes of wit, on the most solemn occasions. For instance, in telling about his experience at the "mourners' bench," he said he felt like he was a great sinner, still, his conviction, he thought, was not great enough. Hearing one of his fellow-mourners praying for himself and for everybody else, he listened a while, and then said to himself, "Well, old fellow, if you felt like I feel you couldn't pray that way; I've got more than I can do to 'tend to myself."

Elder Routh didn't particularly admire a "fighting" preacher; but, in the providence of God, he was called on to "flog" several Pedo-Baptist preachers, one Campbellite, and one "Anti-mission" Baptist preacher, in public debate. In his debate with the Campbellite, his opponent, affirmed, as usual, that "the Spirit spent himself in giving the Word," and is no more; but, in the opening prayer, forgetting himself, he prayed twice for the Spirit's help in the discussion—Routh in the pulpit behind him taking notes. Routh proved his opponent's position false, first from the Scriptures, and then from his opponent's prayer, which he had noted down. His opponent denied that he had prayed for the help of the Spirit; but Routh threatening him with the "vote" of the audience to decide the matter, his opponent "wilted." Ordinarily Brother Routh was peaceable enough, but when it was necessary for him to put on his war clothes and defend the Baptist cause, he was a "hard fighter."

Brother Routh was greatly handicapped, socially, by an almost total deafness, which he contracted by exposure and excessive ministerial labors during the winter of 1852. To communicate with him you had either to write your message or speak through an ear-trumpet. The saving clause in the unfortunate situation was the fact that, although you could not make him hear you without the trumpet, he could hear himself speak with considerable distinctness. His public speaking, therefore, was not seriously injured by his deafness.

March 10, 1899, in the eighty-first year of his life, Asa Routh passed off the earthly stage of action. A year or two before his death the writer visited Father Routh at his home near Piney Flats, and found him comfortably situated on a farm of his own, consisting of seventy-nine acres.

About the last preaching he did he mentioned in a personal letter to the writer, as follows: "My dear Brother: I am just home from Russell County, Virginia. During October I was on my old field of labor, where I spent thirteen years of my ministry. I preached twenty-two sermons during the month, and had good, happy meetings. I was well paid at nearly every place, and my health improved all the time."

In those brief lines, and the facts back of them, is a gleam of sunshine for old age—an expression of appreciation that must have been gratifying to the battle-scarred veteran of many a hard-fought field.

THOMAS J. RUSSELL

Thomas J., son of William Russell, was born July 27, 1800, in Wilkes County, Georgia. His father was a native of Virginia, and of Irish descent. His mother's maiden name was Sallie Moreland, a native of Maryland. His father left Georgia soon after his son Thomas was born, moving first to South Carolina, then to East Tennessee, settling in Jefferson County. Here young Russell, in his nineteenth year, was married to Miss Jennie Green, of Dandridge, a daughter of John Ossian Green, who was a native of Scotland. The issue of this marriage was nine children—two of whom, J. S. Russell, of Athens, Tennessee, and William T. Russell, of Georgia, were able Baptist ministers.

29

ELDER T. J. RUSSELL.

Soon after his marriage, T. J. Russell, attracted by the out-look of the "Hiwassee purchase," moved to Monroe County, where, in his twenty-third year, he was converted and obtained a hope. His parents were Methodists and his wife was a Pres-byterian, but the study of the Bible and the preaching of George Snider made him a Baptist, and he was baptized by Elder Snider into the fellowship of Hopewell Church.

He was ordained to the work of the ministry in 1839, tak-ing charge of "country churches," and beginning his course of needed preparation for an effective ministry by earnest study of the Bible and Bible "helps." In youth and early manhood he had not enjoyed the advantages of an education beyond the limited curriculum of the common schools of his day. But wise reading and the mastery of a few good books gave him a good command of language, and made him a graceful and forcible speaker.

In 1842, in co-operation with the Sweetwater and Tennes-see Associations, he was appointed by the State Convention a "general missionary" for the territory between the Tennessee and Hiwassee Rivers and in Blount and Sevier counties, south of the Holston and French Broad. He continued in this work, under difficult and trying circumstances, for about four years, with marked success—holding many revivals, indoctrinating, stimulating and enlisting the churches, collecting for missions, preaching missions in groves and in front of "closed doors" (in anti-mission communities), and baptizing hundreds of people. A single church, Mount Harmony, in McMinn County, received for baptism at one time, it is said, about ninety of Elder Rus-sell's converts. During this four years' missionary campaign he organized and established many new churches. He organi-zed a Baptist Church in an old Methodist meeting house at Chatata, in Bradley County, another at Shady Grove, and an-other at Cane Creek, in Monroe County, and still others in dif-ferent parts of his field of labor, which, for the most part, became strong and efficient churches and still stand as monuments of his energy and zeal for the Baptist cause.

Having organized and set on foot a number of new churches "throughout the Hiwassee and Ocoee Purchases," he devoted himself for the remainder of his life to the pastoral service of some of these and of others of the older and more established churches. He was pastor of Shady Grove Church for twenty-five years, and of Zion Hill, his home church, he was pastor as long as he lived, or was able to preach. In all his ministry he "held the truth with an uncompromising spirit of loyalty to Christ and with love for the souls of men, and was greatly influential in "moulding Baptist sentiment" and in turning the tide of battle against the anti-mission forces of the '30s and '40s of the last century.

Of the character and quality of his personality and style his biographer says: "His reasoning was always clear, forcible and persuasive; his memory, even in extreme old age, was remarkably retentive; his imagination was fertile and in the heat and passion of delivery was lofty and unfailing. His voice was deep, full and musical. His manners were unassuming, and his character was marked by the utmost simplicity. He was kind as he was honest, provided bountifully for his family, and liberally educated his children."

Near Ten Mile, Meigs County, some years ago the writer visited and staid all night with a distinguished Primitive (?) Baptist preacher, the influential leader and Moderator of the Hiwassee Association (Primitive Baptist so-called)—a true and good man he was. In commenting on the Russells,, T. J. and J. S., father and son, he bore this testimony: "J. S. Russell was very much like his father, T. J. Russell, in personal appearance, and in other respects. Both were strong and good men. Both of them knew the Scriptures, and were effective as preachers. Both were powerful in exhortation. J. S. was fiery and dashy—greatly in earnest. T. J. was smoother, more argumentative, had a more musical voice." Speaking further of the elder Russell he said, "Father Russell had plenty of warmth and feeling, and was sympathetic, but had great self-control, and never cried." His tears were in his voice, not in his eyes. He also added, that the elder Russell was a most "approachable man, easy to get acquainted with, good-natured and genial, and never had the blues." He also spoke highly of the "missionary spirit and courage" of the two men, and frankly acknowledged that he himself never quite had the courage to preach "money, missions and ministerial support" as he ought to have done, and "would do, if the battle had to be fought over again."

After an "eventful career" in the service of his Master, in which he was greatly blessed and honored of God, Elder Russell, the faithful old soldier of the cross, with his aged and faithful companion, having "settled himself down for life on his beautiful farm in the quiet valley of Middle Creek, near Athens, Tennessee," fell to sleep in Jesus whom he had faithfully served, in the eighty-sixth year of his age. And on a monument which stands on the old home place is an inscription which reads: "Elder T. J. Russell; born July 27, 1800; died November 17, 1885—fifty years a minister of the gospel."

His praise is in the churches he served and built up.

JOHN RUSSELL.

One of our stalwart veterans and oldest living representatives of our East Tennessee Baptist pulpit is Elder John Russell, of Sevier County, now in his eighty-first year, sweet with age, youthful in spirit.

The subject of our sketch was born in Jefferson County, Tennessee, near Leadvale, December 18, 1845. He is the youngest of a family of ten children. His father, William Russell, was a native of Virginia, but came to Tennessee during the war of 1812, and married Miss Sarah Moreland. His grandfather, John Russell, was a soldier in the war of the Revolution.

In his eighteenth year, under the preaching and influence of Elder Layman Jones, one of his earliest teachers, and the man for whom Jones' Chapel was named, he was convicted of sin. Not long afterwards, on the north bank of the French Broad River, alone with God, the new light shined into his heart, and he was baptized by Dr. Thomas Hill into the fellowship of Hopewell Church. In his seventeenth year, September

JOHN RUSSELL.

4, 1832, he was married to the "wife of his youth," a Miss Nancy Patterson, of Sevier County, who was his companion for fifty-five years and the mother of his twelve children.

In 1838 he began to preach, his church having voted him "liberty" to exercise his "gift" in a public way. He preached his first sermon at Providence Church, taking for his text John 3:14, 15: "As Moses lifted up the serpent in the wilderness," etc. June 18, 1845, he was ordained by the Hopewell Church to the full work of the ministry, accepting the pastoral care of the church. The preaching of a "missionary" sermon, however, soon got him into trouble with his church, and serious charges were preferred against him. He was charged with "preaching for and associating with other denominations," and with "not answering the calls of churches to attend their communion seasons." The matter coming to a vote, there was a "tie," and the Moderator cast the deciding vote in favor of the accused. Bethel, in the exercise of her rights as an independent church, opened her doors, and on the relation of his Christian experience received him into full fellowship, confirming his "ordination." As a specimen of Baptist ecclesiastical documents of fifty years ago I give a full *verbatim* copy of his credentials from the Bethel Church: "March 17, 1849: Know all whom this may concern: On the day and date above written, John Russell came forward and joined us, the United Baptist Church at Bethel, he being previously a member of the Primitive Baptist Church at Hopewell, and was by them legally ordained to the gospel ministry. We therefore receive him as such, and think a re-ordination unnecessary; believing him to be orthodox in faith and pious in life, and qualified to serve in the ministry. We, therefore, by the power in us inherited, do ratify and confirm said ordination, thereby securing unto him all right and privilege to act as an ordained minister, where God in his providence may cast his lot. Done by order of the church. Eli Roberts, Moderator; Asa Layman, Clerk."

Brother Russell has been preaching fifty-eight years. He has been pastor of the following churches: Bethel, Red Bank, Walnut Grove, Henderson's Chapel, Boyd's Creek, Antioch (Sevier County), Antioch (Jefferson County), Alder Branch, Powder Springs, Pawpaw Hollow, Shady Grove, Millican Grove, Pleasant Grove (Cocke County), Union, Providence, Dandridge, Sevierville, and, for thirty-eight years, his home church, Jones' Chapel. He was missionary of the East Tennessee Association for four years, and two years its Moderator. He has taught twelve schools, married forty couples, and preached about 100 funerals.

In common with the men of his day his educational advantages were poor, but through life he has availed himself of all available materials for the building of a man. Webster's "blue back" was his speller; his reader the New Testament. Grammar was not taught in his neighborhood; this he drew from books, "like bees," as he put it, "suck honey from blossoms." He studied arithmetic and penmanship, and, long afterwards, Hedge's logic, which he thought was "calculated to cure 'most anybody of the big-head, if he had sense enough to be cured at all."

He was a man of two books, the Bible and hymn-book. My note-book styles him "the poet-preacher." Not unfrequently he would use hymns of his own composition in the public worship; and sometimes would close his sermon with a spontaneous outburst of poetic fire that would move and thrill his audience.

Here is a little poem which he composed for the dedicatory hymn of a new house of worship for the Jones' Chapel Church —the hymn to be sung to the tune of Old Hundred:

> It's in this house we meet today,
> The place to preach, and sing, and pray;
> May many souls in it be found
> To hearken to the Gospel's sound.

May those who labored here to rear
A house to offer fervent prayer,
See all their children and their race
Become the trophies of God's grace.

May love among the brethren dwell,
And oft of Jesus may they tell;
And live in peace, in union be,
Then happy through eternity.

On the fly-leaf of the old family Bible I find lines in the same poetic strain, "written by John Russell, July 6, 1864, for the benefit of his children," some of whom were then unsaved:

"This Bible is the book I love—
It points me to a world above,
Where I shall rest my weary head,
When I am numbered with the dead."

Another verse appeals to his children to "take his place," and in a third verse he prays for his "companion" and their children:

"That all around God's throne may meet,
Where all their joys should be complete."

As a preacher Elder Russell was always Scriptural and methodical, but was a little shrinking, especially at Associations, and on state occasions. If there was "talent" present, or preachers that knew more than himself, he would always let the other man do the preaching. As he grew older, however, he learned, he said, that an educated and sensible audience was more appreciative, and could "make allowance," better than an ignorant audience. The writer heard him preach in his eightieth year. His memory was remarkable. The sermon was fine. It was the essence of the gospel. It was Scripture heaped up, Scripture logic, "linked and strong."

Brother Russell has lived a life above reproach. One of the very greatest assets of his long ministry has been the unbounded confidence the people have always had in his piety and integrity. His word was his bond. He has also grown sweet with the years. Though he felt constrained, some six or eight years ago, on account of advancing age, to give up the pastoral care of all his churches, he is not soured or discontented. He has the spirit of resignation, has an abiding peace, and never "doubts the promises." He has largely acquired the virtue of self-control, and does not get excited and "off his balance" as he once did. He has also realized the desire expressed in the simple couplet:

"I want to live a *Christian* life,
Free from *envy, hate* and *strife.*"

His old age has been greatly blest by his marriage, June 5, 1888, to Mrs. Mary Thomas, whose considerate and helpful kindness to him has been a constant benediction.

(The above sketch, in substance, was published in the E. T. Baptist, February 14, 1896).

NOTE: Among the handful of "fragments," gathered by the writer at the Sevier Association and sent to the Baptist and Reflector (October 31, 1901), was this: "Our greatest pleasure was in seeing old Father Russell and hearing him talk and pray. He is in his eighty-sixth year, and has lived above reproach as a minister for sixty odd years. His memory will be a benediction for years to come." The following year he passed to his reward.

JAMES STERLING RUSSELL.

James Sterling, son of Thos. J. Russell, was born in Jefferson County, Tennessee, October 10, 1822. His grandfather, William Russell, was born in Virginia, but in an early day moved to Georgia, thence to South Carolina, and about the beginning of the last century moved to Tennessee, settling in Jefferson County. His great-grandfather, John Russell, came over from Ireland in the times of "persecution" in the old country, and fought as a soldier in freedom's cause in the Revolutionary War. His grandfather, on the maternal side, was a Green, a native of Scotland. The subject of our sketch, therefore, is of Scotch-Irish descent.

While still an infant James Russell moved with his parents to Monroe County, where, in his fifteenth year, he was converted under the preaching of Elder George Snider, and was baptized by him into the fellowship of Hopewell Church.

In 1842 he was married to a Miss M. C. Cate, daughter of Gideon Cate, of McMinn County; and in 1891 was married to Mrs. Maggie McCarter.

Young Russell was brought up on the farm, acquiring a taste for farming, trading and handling live stock, enjoying such educational advantages as were common to farmer boys in the community where he was reared.

Shortly after his marriage he moved to McMinn County, settling down, in 1850, near the town of Athens, where he built up a "handsome estate," consisting of some seven hundred acres of valuable land and "bank-and-woolen-mill stock" to the amount of several thousand dollars.

His "call to preach" was to him an occasion of considerable perplexity and trouble of mind. He had a "taste for making money," and thought his "talent" lay in that direction. After some resistance and delay, he finally yielded to the impressions of the Spirit and his convictions of duty, and in 1856 answered the call "Here am I, send me," and commenced preaching. He was ordained by Zion Hill Church, the third Sunday in April, 1857—Elders John Scruggs, H. C. Cooke, T. J. Russell and H. M. Sloop serving as the ordaining council.

His first charge was the Chestua Church, Monroe County, which he served as pastor for eighteen years. He was also pastor of Spring Creek, in Polk County, and Mount Harmony, Zion Hill, Shady Grove and other churches in McMinn and

J. S. RUSSELL.

Monroe counties. For twenty-six years he was pastor of Shady Grove Church, successor to his father, Elder T. J. Russell— father and son serving the church for a pastoral period of fifty-one years. He was also successor to his father in the pastorate of Zion Hill Church, where he long held his membership and in whose cemetery he was buried, when his life work was ended.

Though entering the active ministry rather late in life, Elder Russell proved to have more than ordinary "preaching

gifts," as well as a "talent to make money." In a ministry of
nearly forty years he was instrumental in building up many
good churches and witnessed the conversion of hundreds of
souls.

He was generous and open-handed to the poor, and gave liberally of his means to all good causes. In the erection of a
house of worship for Zion Hill Church he was a leader, and
the largest contributor to the building fund. He was chiefly
instrumental in building the new Baptist meeting house in the
town of Athens. He superintended the burning of the brick
and the erection of the building, kept the accounts, paid the
bills, and turned over the house when finished to the church
"free of debt," and in his "will" gave to the church the full
amount of the claim he held against it—some $2,500.

As a speaker he was "fluent, fiery and forcible. He was
earnest and sympathetic, more of an evangelist than a doctrinal
preacher. His manners were simple, his actions lively and energetic, his principles firm; his character was solid, his life
consistent. All who knew him had the utmost confidence in
the integrity of his character and the purity of his motives."
In doctrinal belief he counted himself a "landmark Baptist,"
and did not affiliate with men or countenance measures not
bearing the distinct stamp of the Scriptures.

May 3, 1895, being in his seventy-third year, he closed his
earthly career, dying as he had lived, securely "sheltered in the
Rock." His funeral services were conducted by Brethren Calvin Denton, Joseph Janeway and Dr. N. B. Goforth, who bore
beautiful testimony to the character and life of a "fallen
friend and brother, and the affectionate devotion of his
churches to him as their pastor". His memory is cherished, and
the grass grows green over his grave at Zion Hill, where his
body rests till the resurrection morning.

The honored and lamented W. T. Russell, of Jefferson City,
erstwhile Professor of Mathematics in Carson College, for

twenty-five years Superintendent of Mossy Creek Baptist Sunday School, for many years Senior Deacon of the First Baptist Church of Jefferson City was a son of Eld. J. S. Russell.

JOHN SCRUGGS.
GREEK SCHOLAR, FARMER, MINISTER AND DEBATER.

John Scruggs was the second son of Richard and Eliza (McMahan) Scruggs. He was born in Grayson County, Virginia, March 14, 1797. In the early settlement of the new country his father came to Tennessee, settling near Warrensburg, in Greene County. He studied under Dr. Samuel Doak, founder and first President of Tusculum College, a Presbyterian school near Greenville, but took his degree (A.M.), September 25, 1824, from Greenville College, under the presidency of Charles Coffin. He was a classical scholar, knew the dead languages quite well, and read New Testament Greek fluently. He was a pioneer among Baptists in this part of the country, so far as the study of Greek is concerned. "John Scruggs was the first Baptist preacher I ever heard read Greek. He read it, and understood it, and was looked up to as an authority," (Elika Taylor). For a short time after graduation he taught school in Rogersville and was a good teacher.

September 7, 1824, he was married to a Miss Theresa Newell Carter, a daughter of Francis J. and Esther Crocket Carter, of near Newport, Cocke County, and a first cousin of the celebrated Davy Crocket. To this union were born fourteen children. In 1833 he moved to Monroe County, where he purchased a large body of land on Chestua Creek at $1.50 an acre. At one time he owned 1,700 acres of land, and at his death, after selling off and dividing up with his children, was still the owner of 700 good acres—a right handsome estate for a Baptist preacher. He was ordained by the authority of Chestua Church—Elder Robert Snead preaching the ordination

sermon from Paul's charge to his son Timothy, "I charge thee
before God, etc., *preach the Word.*" He was the founder of
Mount Harmony Church, also its pastor for more than twenty
years. He was also pastor of Chestua, Zion Hill, Madisonville
and other churches. He contributed toward the new brick
meeting-house of the Chestua Church more than one-third of
the entire cost of the building. He bought and sold horses, at
the same time was an "independent colporter," selling books
for the J. R. Graves Publishing House all the way from Indiana to South Carolina. Wherever he "traded" he sold books
and preached the gospel. Alike at home and abroad he received little for his preaching. He preached for one church for
seven years regularly, I have been told, and received $7.00 for
his services.

It is worth while for an association to have an efficient
clerk, and it ought to be considered a providence when good
timber in any religious body is furnished to hand for the making of a first-class clerk. The Sweetwater Association was
fortunate in having John Scruggs as clerk for a great many
years; the minutes speak for themselves.

Elder Scruggs was a close Bible student, a fine reasoner,
clear-headed and logical, a forcible doctrinal preacher, a man
of talent, and an able debater. He had a number of public
discussions with Pedo-Baptist opponents. He was "competent
and able in discussion," and in his day and place was the recognized standard-bearer of the Baptists. In matters of history,
church polity or Baptist usage, John Scruggs was the commonly accepted referee, and his judgment was greatly deferred
to throughout the association. At the funeral of Brother
Scruggs the testimony of the venerable Robert Snead, a co-
laborer and by some years the senior of Brother Scruggs, was:
"About the finest preaching I have ever heard in all my life was
a fifteen or twenty minutes sermon delivered by our deceased
brother, John Scruggs, before the Sweetwater Association."
This is high praise indeed. And I suppose that for incisive

statement and clear, forceful presentation of the great New Testament doctrines, John Scruggs was unsurpassed, if equaled, by any of his associates in the ministry.

November 11, 1867, marked the passing of this faithful servant of the Lord and valiant defender of the Baptist cause. He was buried in the graveyard of the old Chestua Church.

A SIDELIGHT: In a recently published "History of Sweetwater Valley" the author, Mr. W. B. Lenoir, recalls the preachers of his boyhood recollection and the marked, particular thing about each of them that had remained with him through life. With one of them he had ever associated the word and doctrine of "Faith," with another "Love," with another "fire and brimstone," and so on, but the one word associated in his mind, from youth to old age, with the strong and scholarly Scruggs was the Greek word *"baptizo,"* which the preacher, he says, insisted always meant "to plunge or immerse," and could not "by any implication or indirection in the remotest degree mean anything else." The incident is a strong sidelight on the character of a faithful defender of the New Testament Scriptures, and has its lessons: What we *are*—where we place the emphasis, our bearing and manner—counts for much; the preacher *lives on,* embalmed in memory and reproduced in the lives of others—his words, his thoughts, echoing through the world and down through the corridors of time.

A. D. SEARS.

Dr. A. D. Sears was born in Fairfax County, Virginia, January 1, 1804. He was of English descent, his paternal and maternal grandfathers both coming from England and settling in Virginia at an early day. Leaving his native State, he went to Kentucky and settled in Bourbon County in the year 1823. In 1828 he married Miss Annie B. Bowie, whose native State was Virginia, but whose ancestors were from Maryland. To this union were born four children, two sons and two daughters, all of them dying in infancy, except one daughter, Marietta, who married John N. Major, of Christian County, Kentucky.

Dr. Sears was brought up, religiously, under the handicap of "deistical influences," and as he came to grapple in his own strength with the problems and mysteries of life, providence

A. D. SEARS.

and destiny, he was naturally, though perhaps unconsciously, influenced by the "pride of life," or the fancied wisdom and self-sufficiency (?) of the natural man; thus he became "skeptical" and greatly prejudiced against the Bible. "Denominational differences," in evidence about him, further aroused his prejudice, and as for the Baptists, he could scarcely tolerate them, especially their practice of immersion, which he considered vulgar and indecent. He had also brooded long and gloomily over the death of his two infant sons, which had been taken from him, as he thought, by some ruthless hand, "in the space of twenty-four hours." Thus musing and murmuring, as in a wilderness of doubt, as in a *Gehenna* of horrible darkness and unspeakable agony, he met a Methodist minister with a Bible in his hand, who, greeting him, said: "A. D., there is comfort for you here." Replying to the minister, he said: "I need it; for if this world were a keg of powder, I would strike a match to it, and we would all go to hell together." About this time, in his thirty-third year, he became interested in the subject of religion, and began to read the Bible and along with it the writings of Andrew Fuller, and without ever having heard a sermon from a Baptist preacher decided that a Christian is one who is "born again," also that Scriptural baptism is the "immersion of a believer in water." He and his wife "rode twelve miles on horseback to the nearest Baptist church, but neither of them had ever seen anyone join a Baptist church, and had to ask a man in the churchyard how to join." (A family tradition.) And so it came to pass that on the 19th of July, 1838, following his new light and his convictions of duty, he was immersed by Elder Ryland T. Dillard "in the waters of Elkhorn," at Bryant's Station, Kentucky," his wife being baptized at the same time.

From the day of his baptism he had "solemn impressions of mind" on the subject of preaching the gospel and the needful preparation for that duty. He did not mention his "impressions" to anyone, however, but was unexpectedly called on to lead in public prayer, was soon "licensed" to preach, and in a few months was "ordained" by the church he had joined—the ordaining council (Elders R. T. Dillard, Edward Durnaby, Josiah Leake) meeting at David's Fork on "Saturday before the third Sunday in February, 1840," and on that day solemnly setting him apart to the full work of the ministry. By the following Thursday he had become engaged in a protracted meeting with Elder James M. Frost at the Forks of Elkhorn, Franklin County, Kentucky. Plunging into evangelistic service he held meetings at Frankford, Georgetown, and Flemmingsburg. He served as a supply-pastor at Stamping Ground and the Forks of Elkhorn. He became missionary of the Bracken Association, and with Flemmingsburg as his place of residence he held protracted meetings and itinerated here and there, looking after the destitution of three or four counties. In the first year of his ministry he preached 366 sermons and baptized many converts. In April, 1840, he held a meeting at Shelbyville, Kentucky, witnessing 149 professions of religion. He held other successful meetings, with smaller churches in the country. On invitation he visited the First Baptist Church of Louisville, and, the last week in July, 1842, he commenced an eight weeks' meeting, baptized 125 persons, accepted a call to be pastor of the church, served the church as pastor seven years, baptizing into its fellowship upwards of three hundred persons, and resigned the care of the church July, 1849. He became general agent of the General Association of Kentucky, and held meetings at Henderson, Hopkinsville and other places, baptizing something over 250 converts. In July, 1850, he accepted the care of the Hopkinsville Church, remaining with the church up to the Civil War, and baptizing into its fellowship about 300 persons. During the war he spent four years in the South, supplying different churches, and, under the auspices of the Southern Board of Missions, preaching to the Confederate army.

Dr. Sears became pastor at Clarksville, Tennessee, in January, 1866. He continued pastor of the church a little more than a quarter of a century, doing monumental and lasting work. During his pastorate the church grew from a membership of twenty-five to a membership of 350, and erected a handsome and commodious building in which to worship, at a cost of $25,000. Clarksville was his third and last pastorate; Louisville and Hopkinsville were the others. The twenty-fifth anniversary of his Clarksville pastorate was celebrated with appropriate ceremonies, in January, 1891. The speakers of the occasion were his old-time friends, Dr. W. H. Whitsitt and Dr. T. T. Eaton. Another occasion of interest, during this remarkable pastorate, was the celebration of the golden wedding (1878) of the pastor and the pastor's wife. "The venerable pair received many attentions and valuable presents; the occasion was one of festive joy."

Both as a pastor and as an evangelist, Dr. Sears has had marked success. He baptized more than 2,000 persons, and witnessed considerably more than that number of conversions under his immediate ministry. He had an analytical mind, was a conscientious and industrious student, was a painstaking and methodical sermonizer, was a straightforward and lively speaker; his style was clear, crisp and pointed; his sermons were short but meaty. He was a good organizer and a devoted pastor, had a sunny eye, refused to grow old, or rust out or die at the top, or at the center. When the writer last saw him, at the age of 82, perhaps, he was erect, vigorous, still in his palmy days, preaching twice a Sunday without fatigue. Five years later he was still virile, and his "popularity with his people as great as ever." In the spring of 1891 the church remodeled their church home. Looking over the work being done, Dr. Sears twisted his foot on a small piece of lumber lying in the way and fell, breaking his hip. He died from the effects of this injury, June 15, 1891, being 87 years, 7 months and 15 days old. Dr. W. H. Whitsitt conducted the funeral services, the Knights Templars, in which order he had been Grand Commander of the State, having charge of the services at the grave. He was buried in Greenwood Cemetery, Clarksville, Tennessee. His beloved companion survived him several years, dying on Christmas day, 1894, at the age of 97, having lived "within the term of office of every President of the United States from Washington's last term to the first term of President Cleveland." His daughter, Mrs. Major, fell asleep in 1898, and was buried beside her beloved father. His living descendants are: W. H. Major, D.D., pastor Capitol Avenue Baptist Church, Atlanta; Mrs. John S. Nisbett, missionary of the Southern Presbyterian Church, in Korea; Charles Lee Major, manager American Baptist Publication Society's business, Chicago; Clarence Riley Major, business man, of Clarksville, Tennessee.

HOMER SEARS.

The following record marks the first appearance of Homer Sears in the State, so far as the writer has been able to discover: "March 23, 1844—It is unanimously resolved to call Rev. Homer Sears to the pastoral care of this church for the ensuing twelve months." (Records of the Baptist Church of Knoxville, now known as the First Church.) In this same year, one year after its organization, the Knoxville First Church represented the second time in the Tennessee Association, by her appointed messengers, Elders Homer Sears and William Rogers. In an old number of Dr. Howell's paper, *The Baptist,* dated Nashville, November 21, 1846, is found an editorial notice of a "new periodical in Tennessee, called the *Christian Magazine,* and monthly, located in Knoxville, with Rev. H. Sears, pastor of the church in Knoxville, as the editor, assisted by the Rev. William Cate, of Jonesboro, and Rev. J. A. Scruggs, of Madisonville, as corresponding editors." This makes Elder Sears a pioneer in Baptist religious journalism in Tennessee, especially in the eastern end of the State. During his six years' pastorate in Knoxville he was an active and influential preacher throughout the State, but more especially in East Tennessee, and particularly in the Tennessee Association, of which he was the efficient moderator for the years 1847 and 1848. As to his success in laying Baptist foundations in Knoxville and the appreciation in which he was held by his church, the following record is evidence: "Brother Sears, having offered his resignation of the pastoral care of our church, to take effect January 1, 1850, the church, in reluctantly accepting his resignation, desires to express her feeling of kind regard toward her late pastor; therefore, resolved, that Brother Sears in laboring with us five years (nearly six), under difficult circumstances, and in completing one of the best houses of worship in Tennessee, has manifested an unusual degree of self-sacrifice and of Christian faith and perseverance. Resolved, that we cordially commend Brother Sears to the favor of the denomination, believing that he will prove a faithful and successful laborer in whatsoever field Providence may cast his lot. Resolved, that this expression, etc., be published in the *Tennessee Baptist.*"

JOHN SEIBER.
(An Autobiography.)

The following interesting sketch is condensed from the author's manuscript, entitled "The Autobiography of Elder John Seiber." I preserve the author's words and original style, as far as possible, which will add interest to the sketch.

"I was born April 28, 1816, in Anderson County, Tenn., ou the headwaters of Poplar Creek. Was maried January 28, 1840, to Alvina Kincaid. We have raised a family of seven girls. To keep a supply for my family I have had to work every day, when at home, and every hour of the day, either on the farm or in the blacksmith's shop. This necessity was a great hindrance to my ministry. I professed faith in Christ September 4, 1848, and was baptized the second Sabbath of the same month. The following month, at the "Arm" of Zion church, Elder Joshua Frost called on me to pray in public, which was the beginning of my public life. This "Arm" was in the midst of destitution of some 15 or 30 miles' extent. I met with this little band monthly and held prayer meetings. In 1849 I was liberated by the "Arm" to exercise my gift. At a night meeting in the neighborhood my mind was impressed with a text and the Lord helped me to preach my first sermon, which was blessed to the salvation of four souls. The revival continued, there were other converts, and we sent for an ordained minister to do the baptizing. The next year we were constituted a church, known as New Bethel (Roane County), W. DeRossett and S. Hendrickson acting as a presbytery. I was then invited to the Robertson schoolhouse, a small house made of round logs, where Mt. Zion church and Roane College now stand. On Sunday Brother Agee came, and later Brother E. B. Walker. A revival started, and Mt. Zion church was the result. A little afterwards I went to another log schoolhouse, three miles north of Kingston. The Lord was with me, and we had a revival that was the beginning of Sugar Grove church. Meanwhile I had again been licensed to preach, this time by Zion church.

In February, 1852, I was ordained; in 1855 I was called to the care of New Bethel and Mt. Zion churches. In March of 1856 I was invited to Poplar Creek, three miles below Oliver Springs, where I had the privilege of preaching to the companions of my youth. Here I labored and was pastor once and again, baptizing nearly all the people in the neighborhood.

In 1866 I went to the X-Roads, near Lea's Ferry, and preached in a schoolhouse. Ten converts were baptized. Mt. Zion extended an "Arm" here, and in a short time New Hope church was constituted. In 1867 I bought land in East Fork

Valley, where I now live. There was no house of worship in
the neighborhood. I commenced to hold meetings in my dwelling house, and in 1869 we built a log-house where East Fork
Church now stands, and a church was constituted. In 1887
I was chiefly instrumental in rebuilding the old church at
Robertsville, constituting that church anew (by permission of
the East Fork Church), in May, 1888.

As pastor I preached several years at Zion and several years
at Poplar Creek. Have preached some in Clinton and some
in Kingston. I do not know how many persons I have baptized. I have baptized in every stream of note from Morgan
County to Knox County, in the lower end of Anderson and
the upper end of Roane, not only in creeks but in branches,
and in Clinch River from Lea's Ferry to Kingston, and across
the river, in Beaver Creek and in Bull Run. I have baptized
all my children, except one, and several of my grandchildren.
I have been instrumental in establishing seven churches, and
have had more destitution right at my door than I could possibly supply. I have helped ordain several ministers and deacons. As pastor I have received very little for my work. I
did not justify the churches in this, but did the best I could.
I had the anti-mission spirit to contend with and was called
"money-hunter," without getting the money. In my labors as
a missionary on destitute fields I have never received more
than 25 cents a day. I have been in many close places and have
had to endure hardships, but the Lord has been with me.

I have now passed the seventy-third milestone in my pilgrimage. I am admonished by the state of my health that
the time of my departure is near at hand. In the language
of another, I expect soon to pass through the valley of the
shadow of death upon the "car of salvation, which runs upon
the iron track of God's predestination, with the Holy Spirit as
the engineer and Jesus Christ as the conductor who has never
missed connection."

May 25, 1891, Elder Seiber died as he had lived, in the
triumphs of a living faith.

MICAH H. SELLERS.

Micah H. Sellers was born in North Carolina, January 13, 1786. In his seventeenth year he professed faith in Christ. With his conversion came impressions to preach, but he struggled against his impressions of duty for several years. In 1809, or thereabout, after a protracted delay and painful kicking against the goads, he began his ministry, with little education and under very "unfavorable circumstances," but with a keen sense of responsibility and a fixed purpose to qualify himself as best he could by the study of the Scriptures for his high calling as a minister of Christ. Little is known of his early ministry, which was in North Carolina, but we are told that he had a "strong mind, an indomitable will, great energy, and ardent zeal for the cause of Christ; that he was an original thinker, and at length attained to a great knowledge of the Bible."

Somewhere between 1812 and 1815 he came to Tennessee, settling in the Hiwassee district. He was ordained in 1820 by Little Emory Church. He was instrumental in gathering and organizing most of the older churches of the Hiwassee Association, south of the river, and is credited with baptizing the first convert ever baptized in the Hiwassee district before its purchase from the Indians.

At the organization of the Hiwassee Association at Pisgah meeting-house, "May, the fourth Saturday, 1823," Micah Sellers was clerk. In 1829 he was chosen Moderator, and was reelected Moderator of that body for thirty-eight consecutive years (till 1867), with the exception of two years. As a presiding officer and as a preacher his manner and bearing were dignified and impressive. His language was chaste and his style attractive—all acquired from the classic English of the King James' version of the Bible, which was his daily companion.

The theme with which "he melted the hearts of his hearers and moved them to tears was Christ and Him crucified." At the close of life he realized the truth and power of the promise: "Thou wilt keep him in perfect peace whose mind is staid on thee; because he trusteth in thee."

November 23, 1870, Elder Micah H. Sellers, in his eighty-fifth year, finished his earthly course. The Association of which he had so long been a standard-bearer appointed Elders Z. Rose, Jesse P. Roddy and J. B. McCallon a committee to memorialize him before the body and in its minutes. The committee, in its report, spoke of him in terms of appreciation and affection as an able minister of the New Testament and as a Father in Israel: "He labored with us in the ministry more than half a hundred years, and enjoyed the affection of the entire brotherhood, and shared the unbounded confidence of all who knew him."

G. G. SIMS.

G. G. Sims, son of Elliott and Joanna Sims, was born September 10, 1813. His father was a native of South Carolina; was a first-class mechanic and millwright, and brought up his son George to the art of building and repairing mills. November 24, 1833, young Sims was married to Miss Mary Fine, a daughter of Abraham Fine, of Cocke County. To this union were born seven children, three sons and four daughters. Making a profession of religion he was baptized, December 28, 1843. He was licensed to preach the first Saturday in April, 1846; was further liberated in May of 1847, and was ordained by Antioch Church, Jefferson County, November 8, 1847. Elder Sims did most of his preaching in Sevier, Jefferson, Blount and Cocke counties. His name appears frequently in the Minutes of the Tennessee, the Nolachucky and the East Tennessee Associations as "correspondent," "messenger," or "visitor." He was pastor of Antioch, French Broad, Jones' Cove, New Salem,

Wear's Cove, Tuckaleechee, and other churches. He held his membership with Antioch Church pretty much all his life, from the time of his conversion, and was pastor of the church a great many years, representing it in the Association, either the Nolachucky or the East Tennessee, almost every year to the day of his death.

Brother Sims was a thoroughgoing Baptist; the Bible was the "man of his counsel," his all-sufficient rule of faith and practice. On the flyleaf of his well-worn Bible is this inscription: "This is my articles of faith, covenant, and rules of decorum.—G. G. Sims." One of his favorite Scriptures was the thirteenth chapter of First Corinthians. He admired the graces of meekness, sincerity, love and charity, especially in a minister, and never tired of condemning the loud and loveless proclaimer and hypocritical professor as "sounding brass or a tinkling cymbal." I have been told that Brother Sims preached the funeral discourse of Elder Eli Roberts, the poet-preacher, from the text: "For we must needs die and be as water spilt on the ground, which cannot be gathered up again," etc. (2 Sam. 14:14), a striking text of Scripture, furnishing a theme, doubtless, for an edifying discourse. Just a short time before his death he preached at Wilsonville, Cocke County. The theme of his discourse was Death and Judgment, based on John 5:25-29. It was a "feeling and impressive sermon, moving many hearts and never to be forgotten" (S. A. Sims).

He fell on sleep February 13, 1872, and was buried in the Sims' family graveyard, three miles from the Jones' Chapel meeting-house in Sevier County.

The following story of Elder Sims is vouched for by good authority: In holding protracted meetings and doing missionary work he would necessarily have to be away from home a good deal. Ordinarily the "latch-string" would be on "the outside" to him, and he was welcome to visit the brethren at his pleasure and enjoy their hospitality. But on one occasion he failed to get an invitation to go home with anybody. He stepped up to a gentleman, after waiting for an invitation, and said to him, "Come and go home with me." "How far is it to where you live?" said the man. "About thirty miles," said the preacher. Taking the hint the man said, "It is only a mile and a half to where I live; you had better go with me." "All right, I believe I will," agreed Brother Sims, and went home with the gentleman, who proved to be a member of the church where he was beginning his meeting, and enjoyed a good dinner.

THOMAS SMITH.

One of my earliest recollections is of old "Uncle Tommy" Smith, a preacher of the "old school" type, in Cocke County. He lived to be 102 years and 2 months old. He preached his "last sermon' on his one-hundredth birthday, at the old Slate Creek Church, near Parrottsville. It was an occasion of a life-time. The people talked it for weeks before and after, with excited interest. The place of preaching was ten miles away from my boyhood home—too far for a small boy to go. The writer has often regretted that he was not old enough to join the horseback crowds of youngsters and older people that thronged the roads from every distant neighborhood. Many times I have heard my father and others speak of the occasion as something out of the ordinary. The preacher's text was from Judges, fifteenth chapter, fourteenth, fifteenth and six-teenth verses—the record of Samson's feat in slaying "heaps upon heaps" of the Philistines with the "jawbone of an ass." A vast crowd had gathered in and about the old meeting-house, curious to hear the venerable patriarch preach, on the occasion of the one-hundredth anniversary of his birth. I have never heard anybody say how he treated his text, but "he preached in his way" to a crowd of people that never forgot the occasion, the preacher or the text.

Elder Smith, so far as family records are concerned, is like Melchizedek, "without father, without mother, without descent, having neither beginning of days nor end of life." But he was a noted preacher in his day, and a good man. He was a member of Slate Creek Church, and pastor of the church for many, many years. He was a representative of his church, along with other messengers, in the Holston Association, as far back as 1818. Slate Creek was one of the churches dismissed from the Holston to form the Nolachucky Association, and was represented in this body at its organization (Bent Creek, 1828) by her "messengers, Thomas Smith and Simon Smith." For the next ten years he was a regularly appointed messenger to the Nolachucky, rarely missing one of its annual meetings. In 1837 he preached the introductory sermon, magnifying, like most of the preachers of his day, the love and sovereign mercy of God. His text was Eph. 2:4, 5: "But God, who is rich in mercy, for His great love wherewith He loved us, even when we were dead in sins, hath quickened us together with Christ (by grace ye are saved)."

In 1839, Slate Creek and her pastor, with other churches and pastors, withdrew from the Nolachucky Association, meeting with Concord Church, Greene County, declaring "a non-fellowship" for State Conventions, missionary and secret societies and other "institutions" of the day. The church never came back, and I have no further record of her pastor, Brother Smith.

W. L. SMITH.

William Landrum, son of John and Cynthia (Wyatt) Smith, was born August 30, 1822, "on the Bend of Chucky" (Nolachucky River), Jefferson County, Tennessee. He was the oldest of a family of eleven children. His father was of Irish descent, his mother German. "Irish fire, Dutch patience," is the way he characterized himself. His father moved to Campbell County when William was 12 years old, and died about one year afterwards. The next move was to Claiborne County, where he lived for some years; his last move was to Anderson, locating three miles below Andersonville, where he lived the rest of his life.

He was converted in his twenty-second year at Blue Spring schoolhouse (now Blue Spring Church) in a meeting held by Chesley H. Bootright and William Hickle. Reading the New Testament through twice, he was converted from Methodist to Baptist views on the question of the church and its ordinances,

W. L. SMITH.

and was baptized by Brother Bootright, the second Sunday in February, 1842, into the fellowship of Blue Spring Church, Union County. The second Saturday in November, 1847, his church licensed him to preach, and the second Saturday in April, 1849, ordained him, C. H. Bootright, Mark Monroe and Anderson Acuff acting as a presbytery. His first pastorate was the Blue Spring Church, beginning about the time of his ordination and continuing twenty odd years. He was also pastor of Milan, Providence, Liberty, Longfield, and other churches.

Brother Smith spent his life largely in missionary and evangelistic labors in Union, Anderson, Campbell, Claiborne and other counties in Tennessee; in Lee County, Virginia, and in southeastern Kentucky. He witnessed about 5,000 conversions and baptized about 2,000 persons into the fellowship of Baptist churches. In his evangelistic labors he was associated a good deal with Asa Routh, C. H. Bootright, William Hickle and the Acuffs.

February 19, 1856, he was married to Elizabeth Ann Sharp, a daughter of Isaac Sharp, of Claiborne County. Their home was blessed with ten children, nine of which they were permitted to "raise." Brother Smith never got a great deal of pay for his preaching: "Elizabeth" (his wife), he said, "is chairman of the mission board from which I have drawn my salary. I have gone to the war mostly at my own charges, and have never regretted that I enlisted."

Inquiring about his educational advantages and his schooling, I was told: "I am not a college graduate. They used to call me 'Pineknot Bill Smith,' from the fact that I had to do most of my studying by pineknot light, but I thought that was better than to be ignorant. However, I did go to the public school a little, and attended a good school at Clinton one summer, after I commenced preaching. I got far enough along to parse nouns and worry with verbs, and that, with my pineknots, has helped me a good deal in studying the Bible."

"What about helping preacher-boys to get an education?" I asked. The answer was: "I believe in that. But there has been a great deal of money and time wasted in educating preachers. Some of them can't preach, and some of them won't. But when a man will preach, I believe in giving him a chance. It takes three things to make the best preacher: Good sense, God and the schools." Brother Smith helped to ordain "four preachers who turned out all right." He expressed regrets that he had not kept a diary or journal of his "travels and labors," as he ought.

W. L. Smith was a genius in many ways and had a wonderful constitution. He was not lacking in strength of mind or of body—was a diamond in the rough. I heard him tell a Mossy Creek audience once that there were men like himself that the "professors couldn't polish very well; that he was made of weavers' beams, handspikes and crowbars—made for endurance, not for polish."

Brother Smith had a number of bouts with the Methodists on the subjects of apostasy and the perseverance of saints, and "kept a standing challenge" for the Campbellites to debate with him in public their theories of "water salvation" and "falling from grace."

W. L. Smith was the fourth pastor of Longfield Church, was a member of Blue Spring Church until 1849, at which time he went into the organization of the Andersonville Church, of which he remained a member till his death, April 8, 1909, having been an ordained minister of the Baptist faith for sixty years.

ROBERT SNEAD.

"Brickmason, farmer, minister of the gospel, railroad director and capitalist."

The subject of the following sketch was born in Hanover County, Virginia, April 20, 1801, and is of Scotch-Irish descent. He was converted in the twenty-second year of his age and joined a Presbyterian church in Richmond, Virginia, January 9, 1823, he was married to a Miss Frances Henley. This union was blessed with a family of ten children, four sons and six daughters. To settle the church-and-baptism question, his wife, being a Baptist, proposed that they read the New Testament together, marking the passages *pro* and *con*. The husband assenting, the critical reading contest was begun. At the close of almost every chapter "Frankie" would score a point against her husband and in her own favor. The husband, a little discouraged but not despairing, kept thinking it would be "better further on," especially in the Acts, where he expected to find comfort from the baptism of the jailer and his household. On reaching that point, however, it did not read just as he expected to find it, and as he had so often heard it quoted. It was a "household," it seemed, of gospel *hearers* and *believers* that was baptized. He took the passage to his pastor, who, reading it carefully and with looks of surprise, confessed that the passage favored the Baptist position. For some time the unequal contest went on, but finally the surrender was made—"Frankie" and the truth had triumphed. The husband joined the Neriah Baptist Church, Rockbridge County, Virginia, and was baptized by Volentine M. Mason.

In 1826 he came to East Tennessee, bought government land at $1.50 an acre, and settled down in Sweetwater Valley, uniting with the old Sweetwater Church, then under the pastoral care of Elder Eli Cleveland. For some years he served as *deacon* and *clerk* of the church, but in 1833 he was ordained to the larger work of the gospel ministry, becoming a "true

31

yoke-fellow" with Elder Cleveland, who was twenty years his senior. Both of them were well-to-do farmers, owning fine property, and liberal with their means. Each of them contributed $500 toward building the old Sweetwater meeting-house, besides furnishing negroes to help in the building enterprise, boarding the hands, making the brick, and each with his own hands putting a large portion of the bricks into the

ROBERT SNEAD.

walls of the building. Brother Snead also gave liberally of his means towards the establishment of the Cleveland, the Jonesboro, the First Knoxville, and other churches, while those churches were yet struggling for an existence.

He served faithfully as pastor the following churches: Pond Creek (now Sweetwater), some twenty years; Madisonville, Riceville, and Liberty, a number of years; Old Sweetwater (after the death of the old shephord, Father Cleveland), for a time, and an "Arm" of the last mentioned church established at Philadelphia. Though frequently urged by Father Cleveland to take charge of the old Sweetwater Church, he would not consent to do so as long as the old shepherd was able, even in a feeble way, to get about among the members of his devoted flock.

As a self-made man Robert Snead is a striking example of the power of invincible will and persistent energy in overcoming difficulties and surmounting obstacles. With few advantages of an education in early life and with only the help of books and newspapers in later life, he forged his way to success. Beginning with the English Bible as his only text-book and library, he read and mastered that—reading slowly, as I have been told, as if spelling each word. But, with a giant mind and a regal will that triumphed over difficulties and made stepping stones of obstacles in the way, he rose to eminence, self-educated, and able to grapple the profound questions of theology and the great problems of human life and destiny. He was a great student of the Scriptures. His delight was in the law of the Lord. It was his habit through life to rise at 4 o'clock in the morning, to read and meditate upon the Holy Scriptures.

Broher Snead, it should be said, was a great *missionary spirit*. Sent out by Pond Creek (Sweetwater) Church, he traveled at his own expense, one whole summer, making a campaign of the churches in the interest of missions, indoctrinating backward churches, stimulating them to greater liberality, and enlisting the unenlisted in missionary endeavor.

As a speaker and reasoner, Elika Taylor says of him: "He was a masterly reasoner and strong debater. His command of the English Bible was perfect. By reading and close study he had acquired a good use of grammar and a fine command of language. His style of pulpit discourse was such as few speakers attain to."

As a doctrinal preacher he was unsurpassed. He had an analytic mind and was a profound thinker, yet he was as simple as he was profound. His mental force, his strong grasp of the truth, his simplicity, made him "mighty in the Scriptures." Dr. W. A. Montgomery's testimony was: "There was not a brainier man or a more profound thinker in the State. An abler doctrinal preacher I have never heard. I have heard a number of our great preachers, but have never heard a sermon that had such a profound and overwhelming effect upon a congregation as Robert Snead's sermon on the Judgment, at Philadelphia, Tennessee. His text was Eccl. 11:9: 'Rejoice, O young man, in thy youth; . . . and walk in the ways of thy heart and in the sight of thine eyes,' etc. 'Why not?' said the preacher. 'Doesn't the Bible say so? And what harm can it be? But as the sinners of his congregation were giving a loose rein to fancy and were high up in the seventh heaven of sensual delight and picturing to themselves still greater pleasure in sinning, the preacher broke in, 'But I have quoted only a part of my text. Will you hear the rest?' 'But know thou that for all these things God will bring thee into judgment.' Sinners tumbled from their seats, all over the house, and cried for mercy, as though the day of doom were already come and they had been brought before the judgment bar of an offended God, to give an account for the deeds done in the body."

As a presiding officer of deliberative bodies he was able and distinguished. He was fourteen years Moderator of the

Sweetwater Association, was Moderator of the East Tennessee General Association, more than once, we believe, and for years was prominent in the councils of his brethren. Only once was it the writer's privilege to look upon Brother Snead in a public gathering of representative Baptists—he towered like Saul in the midst of his brethren. To see him was to be impressed by the massive strength of his physique and the intellectual mould of his face.

As a debater, it is said, he showed himself not only a master in argument, but a skilled strategist in the use of military tactics. The following anecdote will illustrate: After a pub- lic debate with a Pedo-baptist opponent, in which he had adroitly baited his adversary into a trap—having gotten him so completely committed that he couldn't back down from his posi- tion—he was talking to a friend about the matter, and used this illustration: When he was a boy, he said, he used to kill snakes about old mill-ponds and other places. Very often, he said, in killing a snake he would strike too soon, before the snake had got its head well out of the hole, and so would miss it. He learned by experience to wait till the snake got so far out that he couldn't get his head back before he could give him a whack with his stick. In this way he would get his head every time. From the art of snake-killing he had learned a lesson in debating. He would wait till his opponent got well out of his hole before striking. Take off the head of error he would, and although the act involved the meta- phorical beheading of his oppenent, he didn't consider that he had thereby made any breach of the law of charity, which "rejoiceth not in iniquity, or error, but rejoiceth with the truth."

Having lost his first companion, Brother Snead was mar- ried, a second time, December 7, 1852, to Samantha M. Mc- Reynolds. This union brought one other child to the home, a daughter, now Mrs. S. E. Young, of Sweetwater.

The last year of his life Brother Snead was a great sufferer.
He was afflicted with cancer of the mouth, an incurable disease.
To obtain the best medical skill available he moved to Knoxville, but it was only a matter of time when his strong physical
frame would have to yield to the fell destroyer. From his
residence in Knoxville, March 29, 1878, the heroic sufferer
went up to the realm where there is no "night" of pain, no
"shadow" of death. All the days in which death was approaching with steady step the victorious sufferer was constantly
repeating the ever blessed fourteenth chapter of John, "Let not
your heart be troubled. . . . In my Father's house are
many mansions. . . . I go to prepare a place for you.
. . . I will come again and receive you unto myself," etc.—
the text from which his pastor, Dr. J. F. B. Mays, preached
his funeral discourse. "Why should I complain?" he would
say, "knowing that tribulation worketh patience; and patience,
experience; and experience, hope." Feebly uttering as his last
words, "Glory to God!" he sunk into the painless sleep of
death,

> "Calm as to a night's repose,
> Like flowers at set of sun."

GEORGE SNIDER.

The subject of the present sketch was born in Shenandoah
County, Virginia, January 1, 1769. He was the son of a
farmer, and had few advantages of an education in early life.
His father moved to Tennessee while young Snider was still in
his teens. In the fall of 1790 he was married to a Miss Mary
Walker and settled near Little River, in Blount County. This
happy couple, like "Isaac and Rebecca," lived and toiled
together for nearly fifty-six years.

In 1797 he professed a hope in Christ and united with the
Presbyterians, in which connection he continued about fifteen

years, leading a pious and consistent life. He had never studied the question of baptism, however, and upon a careful examination of that question he joined the Baptist Church at Miller's Cove, and was baptized, June 27, 1812, by Elijah Rogers. August 21 of the same year he was "ordained dea con." He was licensed to preach, March 27, 1813, and March 25, 1814, was ordained to the full work of the ministry by a council composed of Richard Wood, Thomas Hudiburg, Dr. Thomas Hill and Elijah Rogers.

In 1817 he was called to be pastor of Miller's Cove, and, a little later, of the Six-Mile Church. In the fall of 1821 he moved to Monroe County, and settled on a beautiful farm in the "Hiwassee Purchase." Here he spent the remainder of his life, serving as pastor, for many years, Hopewell, Big Creek, Chestua, and Tellico churches, the last named becoming the Madisonville Church, March, fourth Saturday, 1828, having the recognition of the "presbytery, Elders George Snider and James Myers." From July of the same year this church, for four years, had the services of George Snider and Daniel Buckner as co-pastors.

Brother Snider "had revivals in all his churches," it is said, and he was instrumental in finding and bringing into the Lord's service several useful ministers.

The first introductory sermon before the Hiwassee Association (1824, one year after its organization) was preached by Elder George Snider. The same year he was chosen Moderator of that body, and served in that capacity as long as the body had an existence, some five or six years. He was Moderator of the Convention (1830) which created the "Sweet water United Baptist Association," and served as Moderator of the new body from fourteen to sixteen years—up to within a year of his death. When the Association divided (1837) on the question of missions, Brother Snider stood firm for the "cause of missions," and rejoiced to "suffer persecution" for being loyal to the truth. Up to this time he had never been "evil

spoken, of," and two of his deacons had said to him, "Brother
Snider, we have come to the conclusion that the Lord's woe has
been pronounced upon you—all men speak well of you." A little puzzled, he replied, "Well, I don't know that I do have an
enemy in the world." But a few days later, meeting one of the
same deacons, he said to him, with an air of relief, "Well, I have
got rid of the 'woe' you spoke of."

In the cemetery of Hopewell Church is a monument erected
by the Sweetwater Association, bearing the inscription: "In
memory of Rev. George Snider; died August 31, 1846, in the
78th year of his age," with the added words, "I have fought
a good fight," etc.

In a "biography of Elder George Snider," published by his
Association (Minutes for 1846), are these fine words of recognition and worthy tribute: "His appearance in the pulpit was
manly, serious and affectionate. His preaching was generally
plain, engaging and impressive, reaching the hearts and con-
sciences of his hearers. He was pious and zealous, an excellent
and eminent minister of Christ. The topic on which he delighted most to dwell was salvation through the blood of
Christ. His affectionate exhortation to his brethren, in his
later years, was: 'Dear brethren, I must soon go the way of
all living. Be faithful and follow on. I hope to meet you in
heaven.' August 31, 1846, in the 77th year of his age, and the
thirty-fourth of his ministerial life, he fell on sleep. He had
no fear of death, and his sun went down without a cloud."

J. M. STANSBERRY.

Elder J. M. Stansberry lived near Mt. Olive Church, Knox
County, and was a useful minister in Knox, Blount and Jefferson counties. He was a member of the Mt. Olive Church, and
a messenger (1856) of the church to the Tennessee Association.
In 1859 he preached the introductory sermon before the Association from a rather difficult prophecy contained in Rev. 3:

1, 2, 3. The Association had met with the New Market Church, a new and weak church, on whose house of worship there was a considerable debt. Brother Stansberry was appointed by the Association as agent to visit the churches and raise funds with which to pay off the debt. He started his work by securing a cash collection of $161.25 before the Association adjourned. We presume the debt was raised. But the church, for many years, had a struggle for existence. In the following year (1860) Elder Stansberry was agent for the Bible Revision Association, actively and usefully employed in distributing Bibles and doing missionary work. Elder Stansberry was pastor of Mt. Harmony and other churches, was held in high esteem by the churches and enjoyed the respect and confidence of the people generally. He was pastor and inspirer to every good work, of W. L. Cottrell; was influential in leading him into the ministry, and was a member of the council which ordained him. Cottrell was a strong preacher and fine teacher in Knox and Blount counties; he taught P. B. McCarroll, who became a great preacher, and whose praise is still in the many churches he served. Thus Elder Stansberry, a faithful and true minister, though dead, yet lives in W. L. Cottrell and P. B. McCarroll, and still lives in the lives of those whom McCarroll influenced for good. That is immortality of influence; "blessed are the dead who die in the Lord, they rest from their labors, and their works follow."

MOORE STEVENSON.

(The following is practically a third edition of a sketch which appeared January 12, 1899, in the *Baptist and Reflector,* and later in Grime's History of Middle Tennessee Baptists. It is an interesting sketch, and I give Rev. J. H. Grime, "lover of history," credit for all the facts and most of the sentences. —ED.)

The name of this man of God is interwoven in the early history of Middle Tennessee Baptists. He was born in Northhampton County, North Carolina, in December, 1762. He was married to Sarah Perry in September, 1779. This union was blessed with ten children, from whom have descended many of the best citizens of Middle Tennessee, while many have moved to the great West. He, in company with the ancestor of the Rutland family, emigrated to this section of country in 1790, before Tennessee was a State, and settled in Sumner County. They soon afterward moved to Wilson County, and were among the first white settlers of the county. Elder Stephenson settled on Cedar Creek, near where Little Cedar Lick Church now stands, and became its founder. He was baptized before leaving his native State of North Carolina by Lemuel Burkitt, who afterwards became an eminent minister and historian of the old Kehukee Association. On coming to Tennessee, Elder Stephenson most probably attached himself to Station Camp Church, since it was the only church in his section at that time. Under the tutorage and influence of Elders James Whitsitt, Patrick Mooney and John Dillahunty, he entered the ministry in the year 1800. To his ability as a preacher Elder Whitsitt pays this tribute: "Elder Stevenson was a sure preacher; he seldom failed to rise high, and had perfect control of himself in the management of his voice. The doctrinal parts of his discourses were well studied and delivered in a deliberate manner, without much fatigue, and by the time he was through with his doctrine his feelings were generally up, and he would launch into exhortations, which were most admirable. He seldom sat down when his congregation was not in tears. His forte was repentance, faith and baptism. On baptism he excelled. He drew in a number of Pedo-baptists by his skillful management of that point. He did not ascend into the more sublime or strong points of divinity, and yet he was a strong believer. He did not hold with systematic preaching, and yet he had a system. He showed divine sovereignty in the new birth, for he was very experimental. His motto was, "Play the man, and 'the Lord do that which seemeth him good.' Like most other preachers of his day he was Calvinistic in his sentiments."

He did pioneer work and was the chief instrument in founding and building the following churches: Big Cedar Lick (Mt. Olivet at Leeville), Little Cedar Lick, Spencer's Creek, Barton's Creek, Bradley's Creek (then known as Philadelphia), and Bethesda. He was also father in the ministry to Elders Jacob Browning, Joshua Woolen, John Simpson, Edward Willis, James T. Tompkins, Elijah Maddox, William White and Micajah Estes. He and Cantrel Bethel served as a presbytery in the constitution of Round Lick Church at Watertown, July 2, 1803. He was also present and took part in the formation of Cumberland and Concord Associations.

Elder Stephenson was well educated, for his day, and was a man of fine address and pleasing appearance. He lived to see flourishing churches on his field of labor, where, in the beginning of his work, there was nothing but a wilderness with only a few pioneer settlers and not a single minister. His ministry was mostly in Wilson County. He was in easy circumstances, had a managing and industrious wife and overseers to look after his temporal affairs, so that he was able to give himself to the ministry, which he did. He died in the prime of life, at 59 years of age, passing from earth to glory March 18, 1818. His wife survived him many years, living to the ripe old age of four score and four years. Their dust sleeps together in the old Rutland graveyard, one mile from Rutland Church. The Concord Association memorialized him in her minutes for 1818, making mention of his "usefulness," commending his "piety and zeal" as a "great and good man fallen in Israel," and praying that the Chief Shepherd would "supply his place in the field below."

JAMES B. STONE.

James Bell, son of John and Elizabeth Stone, was born in Grayson County, Virginia, September 2, 1814. His father moved to Tennessee and settled in Carter County, in the early settlement of the country. Here also he died when James was only eight years old. The family afterwards moved to Washington County.

April 1, 1833, he was married to Freelove Duggar. In October of his twenty-fifth year he was converted and was baptized by Elder Rees Bayless, uniting with Buffalo Ridge Church. February following he was given verbal license to preach "within the bounds of the church." But breaking over the "bounds" prescribed by his license, by preaching at an Association, he came before his church and made his "acknowledgments," and was "liberated" to preach wherever he might have opportunity. May, fourth Saturday, 1841, he was ordained to the full work of the ministry, Elders Rees Bayless and Peter Kuhn constituting the presbytery.

His first ministerial work was as a missionary of the Holston Association, in Johnson County. At that time there were only three Baptist churches in the county, and they were very weak: Cob's Creek, with a membership of twenty-five; Pine Grove, with fifteen members, and Roane's Creek (Mountain City), with twenty members. Of Cob's Creek Church he was pastor for sixteen years. He was also pastor, at different times, of the following churches: Taylorsville, Pleasant Grove, Little Doe, Crab Orchard, Stoney Creek, Watauga, Antioch, Indian Creek (Erwin), Limestone, and Cherokee.

Brother Stone was the first "missionary" in Johnson County, and had some tough experiences. The missionary Baptists were few and feeble; the "Antis" were strong and bitter in their opposition. As showing the temper and the absurdity of the opposition, for instance, an excluded deacon "presented" Brother Stone and three of his deacons to the "grand jury," on the charge of "breaking the Sabbath" by taking collections, receiving pay for preaching, etc. Nothing came of the action, however, and the Sabbath collections, in fact, were not for the preacher, but for meeting-house repairs and for missions.

Brother Stone's tactics, as a missionary among a people largely anti-missionary, was "first to get hold of the children, and through them to reach the parents." Only in this way could he make progress.

J. B. STONE.

Brother Stone's advantages in his boyhood days and his opportunities for getting an education were very poor indeed. He never attended school "as much as nine months" in his life. His literary course consisted, principally, of spelling and reading, in a twenty-four days' term—twelve Saturdays and twelve Sundays—under a teacher whose ability to "pronounce" correctly was not extraordinary. The teacher gave assurance that, on Sundays, he would "keep the children out of mischief," but would have no "pay" for his work—on Saturdays he would expect "double pay."

One who knew Brother Stone well, and labored with him in the ministry, describes him as a "plain, unlettered, old-fashioned gospel preacher, a good reasoner, and a minister who could make the plan of salvation plain."

Brother Stone was also a good singer. He not only sung the gospel that he preached, but made himself useful by teaching "singing schools," as he had time and opportunity. His greatest sermon and sweetest song was a life above reproach.

We close our sketch of a good and faithful servant of the Lord with the following "tribute" of the Limestone Church, of which he was a member the greater part of his Christian life. "Our dearly beloved brother, James B. Stone, departed this life, June 24, 1897, having lived to the good age of 82 years and 9 months. He preached the gospel of missions and ministerial support in the midst of great opposition, when missionary Baptists were persecuted for preaching their doctrines. Nevertheless, he stood firm, true to his convictions of duty, and proclaimed the truth of the gospel, 'as delivered once for all to the saints,' not fearing what man could do. He stands side by side with the worthy defenders of Baptist principles, his name untarnished, his integrity unimpeached." Done by order of the church, and signed by "the committee."

ALVIS STOOKSBURY.

Alvis, son of Jacob and Huldah Stooksbury, was born April 20, 1845, near Loy's Crossroads (now Loyston), Union County, Tennessee. His grandfather, Robin Stooksbury, came from Virginia to Tennessee, with his family, early in the last century. His great-grandfather, Jacob, was the son of Wm. Stooksbury, who was the only son of Lord Stooksbury, of England, and came across the waters to seek a home in the new world before the War of the Revolution.

The subject of our sketch was brought up on a farm, and in early life had few educational advantages. In fact, the only school education he ever received was obtained at two or three short sessions of the public schools of his native county; the rest of his equipment he got from the school of life and experience. In this school he acquired the virtue of self-reliance and self-help.

In August of 1862, in a meeting held by Elder Reuben Green, he professed faith in Christ, and was baptized, uniting with Big Springs Church, Union County.

July, 1871, his church licensed him to preach, and December 20, 1873, ordained him. He was pastor of this, his home church, twelve years. He was also pastor of Alder Springs, Liberty, Big Valley, Loy's Crossroads, Powell's River, Fincastle, and Maynardville churches, for a number of years, serving them faithfully and well.

In addition to his pastoral work, he obeyed Paul's injunction to his son Timothy, "did the work of an evangelist." This he did extensively and successfully, not only among his own churches but on destitute fields and assisting his fellow-pastors. There were few more successful revivalists than Alvis Stooksbury. He was a tender, winsome, persuasive preacher; popular with all denominations, popular at funerals, popular with the young people.

REV. ALVIS STOOKSBURY.

In October, 1865, he was married to Elizabeth Duke, a daughter of William Duke, of Union County. To this union were born seven children, five sons and two daughters, all of whom were converted and became working members of Baptist churches. One of his sons, Prof. W. L. Stooksbury, at one time professor in the American Temperance University, at Harriman, later a professor in Carson and Newman College, and now of Knoxville, is one of our most successful educators; and another of his sons, Dr. J. M. Stooksbury, is a successful physician.

That Alvis Stooksbury was a trusted citizen and had the confidence of the people was evidenced by the fact that he was elected Trustee of his county (Union) and served in that capacity from 1872 to 1874, with entire satisfaction to the people of the county. For six years he tried his hand and head at the mercantile business, along with preaching, but did not succeed, for the reason that his heart was divided—he was not wholly following the Lord. He gave up the "goods business" and gave himself wholly to preaching the gospel. This brought him peace of mind and a good conscience, and the Lord "added the living," which had been previously withheld.

September 1, 1892, he was made a "Master Mason," and was "chaplain" of his lodge at the time of his death.

February 15, 1895, he left home for an evangelistic campaign. He was preaching in a successful revival at Sharon Church, Knox County; on the second Sunday of the meeting he preached three times, and at night was stricken with pneumonia, from which he never recovered. Lingering nine days on the border-land between earth and heaven, he passed to his reward May 5, 1895. His body was taken to his home in Campbell County, where "hundreds of friends from Campbell, Anderson, Knox and Union counties thronged to see the face of and pay the last tribute of respect to one whom they had loved in life and now delighted to honor."

The love of Christ constrained him, and his consecration deepened to the end. His life-motto still speaks from above his grave: "The longest talks and the longest walks I ever made were for Jesus."

> Through heat and cold he often went,
> And wandered in despair,
> To call poor sinners to repent,
> And seek the Saviour dear.

The last sermon he preached was a fitting close to his life: "Thou shalt guide me with thy counsel, and afterward receive me to glory" (Ps. 73:24).

This sketch may fittingly close with the following tribute by Brother U. S. Thomas, who knew Elder Stooksbury intimately and was converted in one of his great meetings: "Brother Alvis Stooksbury was a noble man of God, a close student of the Word, and a magnetic and eloquent speaker. He was never at a loss for a word. He stuck close to the Bible and his sermons were always fresh and meaty. He was a man of commanding appearance. He had a wide influence, and the people came from far and near to hear him. Above all, he was full of the Holy Ghost, and led many to the Saviour."

CHARLES TALIAFERRO.

The Taliaferros, as the name indicates, are of Italian descent. According to a family tradition, the first Taliaferro who came from Italy to England (in the time of William the Conqueror) was a soldier. This brave Italian saved the life of his commanding officer, and as a reward was "knighted," so to speak, or given a nickname which stuck and became the family name, "(I)talia-ferro," two Italian, or Latin, words, which, liberally translated, mean, "Sword-bearer of Italy." Three brothers, descendants of this first Taliaferro, came from England to this country in early colonial times. From these have sprung the different branches of the large Taliaferro family.

Charles Taliaferro was born in North Carolina, March 5, 1799. He was a son of Charles and Sallie (Burrows) Taliaferro. His grandfather's name was John, of Albemarle County, Virginia. The subject of our sketch was one of six brothers, three of whom—Charles, Richard and Hardin—became Baptist preachers. Charles was married to Miss Jennie Whitlock, of his native State, about the year 1820, and soon after their marriage, groom and bride, enamored of the "west country," as of each other, "rode horseback" from Surry County, North Carolina, to McMinn County, Tennessee, several miles west of Knoxville, when there was practically no roads and the country through which they traveled was much of a wilderness. To this marriage were born three sons and two daughters. He was married a second time, October 22, 1839, to Elizabeth Eldridge, to which union were born six children, four sons and two daughters.

As to his conversion, baptism, call to the ministry. or ordination, the writer has no definite information; but at the organization of the Hiwassee Association (1823), Charles Taliaferro was present as a delegate from the Tennessee church, from which time he was a prominent figure in the Association for a third of a century. He began his ministry, it is thought, with Prospect Church (near Loudon), which he founded and built up to be "some three hundred strong in membership," and was his "home church" as long as he lived. When the Association divided (1836) over the question of the State Convention, etc., Charles Taliaferro stood with the more liberal and progressive element, though only four churches, out of a hitherto large body, stood with him.

In 1836 he was chosen clerk of the Association, and served in this capacity for a number of years, not only keeping the records of the body, but doing a vast amount of clerical work besides—writing "protests," letters of "correspondence," "circular letters," etc. In 1847 he was elected Moderator of the Association, and was re-elected to that position annually for several years. In 1848 he preached the introductory sermon from II Tim. 2:15, "Study to show thyself approved unto God, a workman," etc. In 1850 his text for the introductory sermon was Daniel 2:44, "And in the days of these kings the God of heaven shall set up a kingdom," etc. In the following year his text was, "Take heed unto thyself, and unto the doctrine," etc. (I Tim. 4:16). The Association had been fostering a weak interest in Chattanooga, with more or less failure and discouragement, and in 1851 appointed Charles Taliaferro, with others, to look after that interest and "reorganize" the church, if possible. In 1853 the Association "was organized by choosing Elder Charles Taliaferro, Moderator, and Wm. Wall, clerk. On motion, appointed C. Taliaferro to preach a missionary sermon on Sabbath of our next Association." 1842, "On Sabbath, Archibald Fitzgerald and C. Taliaferro preached to a large and well-ordered congregation." Almost every year Charles Taliaferro was appointed by his Association to go as a corresponding messenger or to write a letter of correspondence to some "sister Association." He was particularly fond of the Sweetwater Association, and nearly always attended the anniversary meetings of that body.

Relative to the division of the Hiwassee Association, above referred to, is a reference in the records worth noting. The Association minutes of that year (1836) are headed after this style: "Minutes of the minority of the Hiwassee Association of United Baptists: Opened and held in the woods near Concord meeting-house, Meigs County, the third Saturday in September, 1836. Whereas, we, a part of the Hiwassee Association, believe that the majority have left the ground upon which we were constituted, etc.; we, the undersigned churches, consider ourselves properly the Hiwassee Association, upon constitutional principles. Therefore, resolved, that we have no more correspondence with those that have departed from the United Baptist principles," etc. John Farmer, Moderator; C. Taliaferro, clerk. Then follows the "reasons" for their action, "set forth in circular form," with the "circular" appended to the Minutes.

Elder C. B. Martin says of Charles Taliaferro: "He was an able and earnest minister, a great and good man." His only living son, now of Oklahoma, writes: "Father spent nearly his entire life away from home, preaching. He was the means of organizing Providence Church, near which he lived and reared his large family. He also organized New Providence Church in a log house, the old Hotchkiss home. The first man received into this church by baptism became a deacon. He preached his last sermon in this church from a favorite text, characteristic of the spirit of his ministry, "Let brotherly love continue." Just a few days later he took pneumonia fever and died at the home of his daughter, Mrs. Albert Eldridge. His death occurred May 23, 1856. In the Hiwassee Association Minutes for this year he is memorialized by report of committee on deceased ministers as follows: "With emotions of inexpressible grief we present you as our only ministerial bereavement this Associational year the name of our much-lamented and fondly cherished brother, Charles Taliaferro. In this bereavement we bow to the high behest of heaven, mingle our tears with those of the afflicted widow and orphaned children, and proclaim to the world that a faithful and devoted watchman has been stricken from the walls of Zion. He died about the 57th year of his age."

R. H. TALIAFERRO.

Richard, popularly known as Dick Taliaferro, was born in North Carolina about the year 1800. He was a son of Charles Taliaferro, and his mother, before her marriage, was Sarah Burrows. In the early settlement of the "Hiwassee Purchase" he was a preacher and an evangelist. He was a messenger of the old Sweetwater Church to the Hiwassee Association in 1827, and, as shown by the Minutes, was a "licensed" preacher. The next year he attended the Association as a delegate from Prospect Church, a new church which he had doubtless helped in founding. The next year this church was represented in the Association by Charles Taliaferro, and in 1830 by the two brothers, Charles and Richard; a third brother, Hardin, was also a preacher. In the Sweetwater Association Minutes for 1835 the name of R. Taliaferro appears in the list of "ordained ministers," and as a member of Sweetwater Church. In 1837 he attended the Hiwassee Association, and the record of the Sunday service is: "On Sabbath, at 10 o'clock, R. H. Talia- ferro led four willing converts down into the water and bap- tized them in the good old way. J. H. R. G. Gardner and C. Taliaferro preached to a large and well ordered, and seemingly well affected congregation, and R. H. Taliaferro closed by exhortation, calling for the anxious, and several, both men and women, came forward and bowed before the Lord." In 1880, Elder C. B. Martin, of Philadelphia, Tennessee, contributed this brief paragraph sketch of R. H. Taliaferro for Borum's "Sketches": "Elder Richard Taliaferro, familiarly known as Dick, was a brother of Charles, and was equally as good and useful a man. Dick was an evangelist, traveled extensively and held revival meetings. His success was wonderful. He was a fine exhorter and a splendid singer. He baptized a greater number of converts, perhaps, than any other minister who has ever labored in East Tennessee. He moved to Alabama a few years before his death, and died there during the Civil War."

HARDIN TALIAFERRO.

Hardin, the youngest of the three preacher-brothers— Charles, Richard and Hardin—was born in North Carolina. He was a son of Charles and a grandson of John Taliaferro. He began his ministry in Prospect Church, Roane (now Lou- don) County, Tennessee, and for some years was a preacher in the Hiwassee Association. He was a preacher of "talent and depth of thought," well educated, and a good writer. His Asso- ciation (the Hiwassee), in 1851, passed the following resolu- tion: "Resolved, that in view of the importance of an edu- cated ministry and of the liberal offer of Union Universtiy, at Murfreesboro, we will endeavor to sustain Brother H. Talia- ferro at that institution, and recommend to all our churches that are in favor of that arrangement to send to our next an-

nual meeting whatever they may think proper for that object."
He spent some of the best years of his ministry in Alabama,
where he labored in the pastorate, and was associated with
Dr. Samuel Henderson in editing the *Alabama Baptist*. He
not only did editorial work on the *Alabama Baptist,* but contributed a good deal to the denominational press, and was an
author of no little distinction. He moved back to Loudon
County, Tennessee, a few years before his death, locating at
Loudon. He spent his last years in active ministry among the
churches, and at the time of his death (1876) he was Moderator of Providence Association. "He died at his home, full
of years and in the faith" of the gospel he had preached to
others for more than forty years.

WILLIAM TARWATER.

William Tarwater was born in Knox County, Tennessee,
August 23, 1820. He was a son of Jacob Tarwater, a "full-
blooded German." His mother's maiden name was Margaret
Dozier. He received his education, for the most part, from
the district schools of his native county. He was converted
in the year 1843 under the ministry of Samuel Love, in one of
his great meetings, and was baptized by him, with thirty-two
other "candidates," in the French Broad River, eight miles
above Knoxville. He was married April 24, 1845, to Miss
Catherine King, a daughter of William and Elizabeth King,
and to this union were born seven children. In regard to his
married life he told the writer, some years ago, he and his
wife had "lived together forty-four years and had never had a
jar." He had been preaching in his "way," when these notes
were taken, some thirty-five years, but as an "ordained
preacher" only about ten years. He was pastor, or had been
pastor, of Caney Ford and Hopewell churches. He was not
called so much to be pastor of churches as to do missionary
and general evangelistic work.

Brother Tarwater was a thorough-going, uncomprising and enthusiastic Baptist. He "would be a Baptist, though all the world opposed." If there was just "one Baptist," he would be that "one"—and a "preacher," to make more and better Baptists. His line of reasoning was this: "The first preacher we read about in New Testament times was John the Baptist, a Baptist preacher. He had a commission from heaven to baptize, and baptized the Saviour. Christ and the apostles, and all the people baptized by John, were Baptists. The preachers sent out by Christ to preach and baptize were Baptist preachers. These preachers were commanded by their Lord to teach baptized disciples to observe all of Christ's commands. That is the way to make Baptists—and that is the church I belong to." The statement has in it truth and logic, though not put in categorical form or stated in the exact style in which the modern polemic would state it; and the common people, to whom he preached, would gladly hear an argument like that and feel the force of it.

Elder Tarwater died August 13, 1903, at Rockwood, Tennessee.

HUGHES OWEN TAYLOR.

Hughes Owen Taylor, son of James and Ann (Owen) Taylor, was born October 19, 1778, in what is now Henry County, Virginia. His grandfather, William Taylor, was also a Virginian. James Taylor purchased land in Virginia, Pyttsylvania County, May 30, 1771, but, September 2, 1797, sold out and came to the then new country, Tennessee, settling in Grainger County, one mile east of Crosby Station, on the K. & B. Railway. Here on the old Taylor homestead, a farm which has been owned by four generations of the Taylors, is a monument inscribed: "James Taylor, February 28, 1731—April 4, 1815. A private in the Revolutionary Army. See records of the Virginia House of Delegates, Document 44, page

47; and his wife, Ann Owen, September 25, 1733—April 12, 1814. Erected, 1912, by the James Taylor Memorial Association."

Of the date, place and circumstances of the conversion and baptism of Hughes O. Taylor there are no preserved records. From the Minutes of the Holston and Nolachucky Associations he is shown to have been a member of Bethel South (now the Morristown First Church) from 1820 to 1837. Elika Taylor is very positive in the statement that his father was a member of Bethel South from its organization (1803), that he was baptized by Isaac Barton the pastor; that he was also a co-laborer with him in the ministry for many years. He is also authority for the statement made elsewhere, that Hughes O. Taylor and Elihu Millikan were the same day "licensed" to preach by the Bethel South Church, and were afterwards (September 18, 1825) "ordained" to the full work of the min istry on the same day, Elders Isaac Barton, Caleb Witt and Henry Randolph acting as a presbytery. It is also likely that Hughes O. Taylor was pastor of the Morristown or Bethel South Church after the death of the old pastor, Isaac Barton, in 1831, but the church records have been lost and we can only conjecture.

Along with Elihu Millikan and the venerable Isaac Barton he represented Bethel South in the Nolachucky Association from its organization (1828) to the time of his death, March 10, 1837. In the Minutes of that body for the year 1838, the eighth item reads: 'The biography of Hughes O. Taylor, presented to this Association by Bethel South, accompanied with five dollars to defray the expense of annexing said biography to our Minutes, which was ordered to be done." But the "order," for some reason, was not carried out, and the "biography" has been lost.

Elder Taylor preached to Richardson's Creek, War Creek, and other churches north of Clinch Mountain, where "Moses McGinnis, John Day and other ministers grew up under his preaching and influence." He began his active ministry rather late in life, but he was well posted in the Scriptures and on the theological issues of his day. He believed in human depravity, free will, free grace, general atonement and the obligation of the churches to give the gospel to every creature. He was a "peacemaker" in his neighborhood and church, and was "frequently called on to help settle church difficulties."

August 28, 1800, he was married to Elizabeth Kennon, of Jefferson County, a daughter of Thomas and Rachel (Walker) Kennon. To this union were born eleven children, three of them—Woodson, Grant and Elika—becoming Baptist preachers of note and ability. He was not a golden-mouthed preacher like Woodson, nor so able a sermonizer as Grant, nor so well read as Elika. He was an "arguer rather than an orator," and was able in debate. He was a "natural mechanic," it is said, and taught his boys all manner of practical mechanic arts, such as making plows, building houses, blacksmithing, tanning hides, shoemaking, etc. The girls were taught by their mother the domestic arts of the day; they knew how to cook, spin, weave, sew, milk the cow and make butter.

Among my scattered "notes" of reference to Hughes O. Taylor, I find the following: "The church appoint the third Sunday in May for a sacramental occasion and invite John Kidwell, James Kennon and Hughes O. Taylor" (records of Buffalo Church); "received a corresponding letter from the Holston Association by their delegates, Isaac Barton, Caleb Witt and Hughes O. Taylor" (Minutes, Tennessee Association, 1821), which date makes me doubt the accuracy of the date above given (1825) for Hughes O. Taylor's ordination. That lost and lamented "biography," if it could be found, would doubtless supply data for a more satisfactory sketch.

One other reference. Among the many polemical bouts of the '30's and '40's, between the ultra-Calvinists, on the one hand, and the Fullerites, on the other, I find this record, vouched for by good authority, of a private debate between

Caleb Witt and Hughes O. Taylor. Witt: "Man in his natural state is helpless and desperately wicked; can the leopard change his spots?" Taylor: "True, but he is responsible." Witt: "He has to be knocked down before he will submit or come to his senses." Taylor: "Even so, but he is justly accountable to God." Witt: "He is more to be pitied than blamed." Taylor: "If not to be blamed, how can he be sent to hell?" Echo answers, How?

HUGHES WOODSON TAYLOR.

"Farmer, shoemaker, blacksmith, surveyor, minister; member of Bethel South (now the Morristown First), fifty-three years; messenger of his church to the Nolachucky Association forty-nine years, six years clerk, one year assistant clerk, twenty-three years Moderator, pastor of this church for many years." (Col. T. H. Reeves, Centennial Celebration, First Baptist Church of Morristown, 1803-1903.)

Hughes Woodson Taylor was born in Grainger County, Tennessee, September 22, 1803. He was a son of Elder Hughes Owen Taylor, a Virginian by birth, born in Henry County. His mother, Elizabeth Taylor, was a Kennon (or Cannon) before her marriage; of Irish descent and transmitting to her gifted son some of the blood and peculiar characteristics of that noted people. His grandfather, James, who was a son of William Taylor, both of them Virginians, came to the "new country," settling in Grainger County, Tennessee, in the fall of 1797 or the spring of 1798, when Woodson's father, Hughes O. Taylor, was about nineteen years of age.

Woodson Taylor was converted in the fall of 1822, while teaching school at Macedonia, near Morristown, but did not "join the church" until some years afterwards. February 2, 1823, he was married to Miss Alis G. Grantham. This union was blessed with a family of seven children, two sons and five daughters. After the birth of their third child both father and mother were led down into the waters of Holston River and together were buried with Christ in baptism (1826), becoming members of Bethel South (South of Holston River), now the First Church of Morristown. As to who baptized him, his call to the ministry and the date of his ordination, I have no information, since the church records for forty odd years were lost or destroyed, it is thought, during the Civil

WOODSON TAYLOR.

War. His aged widow, who in her ninety-third year, twenty
years ago, furnished me many of my "notes," remembered that
two members of the ordaining council were Joseph Manning
and Elihu Millikan. Of course, she could have told me who
baptized her and her husband, but if she did my "note" of same
has been lost.

Like most preachers of his day, Woodson Taylor had a limited education. This he improved greatly, from the beginning
of his ministry, by close application to study. During the
early years of his married life he would teach school through
the fall and winter months, devoting the "crop season" to
farming, which was his chief means of support throughout his
ministerial life.

Among the churches served by him as pastor I note the
following: Antioch, Cedar Creek, Friendship, Prospect, New
County Line, Warrensburg, Sweetwater, Bethel South, or the
Morristown First, Mossy Creek, now the Jefferson City First.
With Isaac Barton and Hughes O. Taylor he pioneered the
way for Baptists at Morristown. He was the first pastor that
ever received a salary on that field—$50. More than any one
man he tided the church over the difficulties incident to the
doctrinal and party strife of the '30's and '40's. From 1847—
the date of the church's earliest preserved records, to near the
close of his life—his name is prominent and of frequent occurrence in the records of the church among a score or more of
other noted and familiar names. Prominent on the records
of other churches also is the name of Woodson Taylor, who
had been called to "help" in a meeting, to attend a "sacramental occasion," or to "sit in counsel." A chief element of
his strength, the open secret of his popularity and success, was
his conservatism. He was not an extremist; was not rash.
Conservative and conciliatory in disposition and bearing, he
was enabled to heal many a wound made by the unhappy
division of denominational sentiment on the question of "missions" and the "societies of the day," as well as the hurts in-

flicted upon the churches by the ruthless hand of civil war. But notwithstanding his peaceable disposition and his habitual avoidance of controversy, he was a faithful defender of what he considered sound doctrine and the true principles of the Baptist faith. He saw and deprecated the evil consequences of extreme views of election and predestination. So, vexed and worried by the report, constantly circulated, that "Brother Randolph," and other preachers of the "old school" persuasion, had over and again "preached infants to hell," he proceeded to take Brother Randolph to task over the report, resulting, I have been told, in a spirited "tussle" between the two brethren. Brother R. denied that he had preached such doctrine. Brother T. protested that the ultra-Calvinism of Brother R. and of the "old school" brethren, to say the least, placed infants dangerously near the brink of that fearful place "prepared for the devil and his angels."

In a sense Woodson Taylor was a born preacher. His father before him was a preacher of no mean ability. The son, in particular, had the orator's tongue and temperament; was fervid and fluent; impassioned in manner; persuasive in speech. He was courtly and sympathetic. The last twenty-five years of his life he suffered from a chronic throat trouble, but even with this affliction and with the infirmities of age upon him, his quiet and subdued eloquence was impressive and effective. Both in manner of speech and in personal appearance, as I recall, he reminded one of the aged and silver-tongued ex-Governor Joseph E. Brown, of Georgia, as he appeared before the Southern Baptist Convention.

H. W. Taylor's tombstone, in a cemetery near Morristown, publishes the fact that during his ministry he baptized 1,406 professed believers into the fellowship of Baptist churches.

One of Brother Taylor's most intimate and valued friends was Elder James Gilbert, of the Mulberry Gap Association. In compliance with Elder Gilbert's request, that "Brother Taylor visit" him and his Association as long as he lived, or was able to get away from home, in the fall of 1887, Brother Taylor had the pleasure of visiting for the last time this Association, meeting with Cloud's Creek Church, and of preaching, on Sunday, what proved to be his last sermon. The following summer, June 5, 1888, he passed to his reward, leaving behind two of his children, and his aged widow, whom the writer, years ago, found at her home, "hale and hearty," at the age of 93. On Sunday before the summons came for him to depart to be with Christ, he was visited by his old-time friend, Elder T. J. Lane. "You'd like to have been too late," were the first words of greeting from the dying patriarch, as he "rounded the cape" in his 85th year. They recounted their labors and sacrifices, talked of the kingdom of God, the goodness of the Father, the promises of the Bible, and their heavenly home. As they quoted Scripture after Scripture and promise after promise, if one missed or failed to recall a word, the other would supply it. Happy meeting! grand converse this in the evening glow of life! But they have met above. Both are now in the "land of the cloudless sky," quoting Scripture, perchance, and recounting their earthly toils, while they "rest from their labors and their works follow."

E. A. TAYLOR.

Elika Adams, son of Hughes O. and Elizabeth Taylor, was born in Grainger County, Tennessee, July 30, 1811. His father was born in what is now Henry County, Virginia. His grandfather, James Taylor, and his great-grandfather, William Taylor, were native Virginians. His grandfather moved to Tennessee and settled in Grainger County when that part of the country was entirely new.

March 20, 1830, he was married to Miss Elizabeth Mays. This union was crowned with a splendid family of eight children, five sons and three daughters. In his twentieth year, soon after his marriage, he made a profession of religion, but did not unite with the church until some years afterwards.

February 14, 1837, attracted by the newer and greater "west," he left Grainger County and moved to Sweetwater Valley, then a wilderness, bought land four miles west of the present town of Sweetwater, lived in a cabin for a year, burnt brick and built him a substantial dwelling house, where for

ELIKA A. TAYLOR.

sixty-five years he lived in peace and comfort, till in his ninety-second year he was welcomed to his home on high, "a house not made with hands, eternal and in the heavens."

Soon after settling in his new home, yielding to his convictions of duty, Brother Taylor decided to obey the Lord in the ordinance of baptism, and was baptized by Elder Robert Snead, uniting with the Pond Creek Church. With the new work of grace in his heart he recognized a "call" to preach the gospel and was "licensed" by his church to exercise his "gift," which he proceeded to do. We might say in this connection that his church urged his ordination, but he never would give his consent to be ordained. He was, therefore, what might be called a "lay-preacher." He never accepted the care of a church, but gave a great deal of his time to preaching to weak and pastorless churches, settling church difficulties, helping his pastor, and ministering in many unofficial ways, as he had opportunity.

This "lay-preacher" superintended the building of the first church in Sweetwater, and also the first school house; he introduced the first two-horse wagons, the first threshing machines, and built the first machine shop, in this section. When he came the country was new, and farmers used the old-fashioned reap-hook to cut their wheat. But he has kept up with the times; in fact, has been a leader in all progressive movements. His memory goes back to the days before there was ever a railroad thought of, or a telegraph line, for this part of the country, or any modern improvement. It is very interesting to hear a man talk who has witnessed the introduction of so many new things, and note the keen interest he takes in them all."

Brother Taylor never enjoyed a classical or even a high school education. But he had a good mind and was thorough in the branches of study taught in the "old-field school." Most of his life, till upwards of sixty, he was a hard worker on the farm by day and a hard student by night. He burned the midnight

33

pine-knot, instead of the "midnight oil," to get his stores of knowledge, especially in studying the Bible. He was always a great student of the Scriptures.

He believed in education, and tried to give his children better advantages in that respect than he himself had enjoyed, "emptying his purse in their heads," according to Benjamin Franklin's advice, where it could "not be stolen." He also gave liberally of his time and means for the promotion of Christian education and the upbuilding of Baptist schools. He worked hard and traveled for the Sweetwater Seminary, soliciting girls and funds for that institution; and though the school could never be put firmly on its feet, he talked Christian education in many a home and church, sowed the good seed, and left an indelible mark for good upon many a young mind and heart. Though not educated in the broadest sense, yet he was a man of culture and refinement, was a high-toned Christian gentleman, a man of fine social qualities, always welcome to the best homes and the most refined circles.

He was given to hospitality. His home was always a home for preachers. The fireside talks and religious discussions in the presence of the family were always impressive and uplifting, and never to be forgotten. In his business transactions and his mixing with men he rarely failed to introduce the subject of religion. His charatcer and life were above reproach, and his influence was a benediction wherever he went.

Brother Taylor kept himself thoroughly posted on all the current issues of the day, and was a fine conversationalist. He was a great advocate of temperance, and personally was a teetotaler. He never failed to take an interest in politics, holding that it was the duty of every citizen to cast an intelligent vote. He cast his first vote for William Henry Harrison and his last (at the age of ninety) for William Jennings Bryan. He was clerk of his church for fifteen years, for many years one of her active deacons, and always ready to serve as assistant or supply-pastor. He belonged to a family of preach-

ers. His father, Hughes O. Taylor, was an influential preacher
of the early days. His brother, Woodson, was a fine preacher
and silver-tongued orator. Grant Taylor, another brother,
"the best investigator of us all (E. A. T), was an able pulpit
man. But Elika was second to none of them in ability as a
thinker, in personal force and genuine worth, as a Christian
and as a minister, though not a practiced and skilled speaker
like his father and preacher-brothers.

At the time of his death—May 10, 1902, in his ninety-second
year—he was a member of the First Baptist Church of Sweetwater, of which he had been a member (since September, 1842)
when it was Pond Creek Church in the country, which he had
been influential in moving to town, for its greater influence,
and of which he had been a pillar for many years. His "faith
in his Savior was unwavering" to the last, and upon the monument which marks his last resting place in the Sweetwater cemetery is this inscription: "In God is my trust."

GEORGE GRANT TAYLOR.

George Grant Taylor was born in Grainger County, Tennessee, March 18, 1816. He was a son of Hughes O. and Elizabeth Taylor. He was one of a family of eleven children. He
was brought up to farm life, and in his boyhood and early
manhood days was favored with fairly good educational advantages. August 11, 1840, he was married to Elizabeth Ann
Lane, a daughter of Elder T. J. Lane, of near Whitesburg.
This happy union was blessed with an issue of nine children.
I have not been able to find any record of his conversion and
baptism. The probability is that the first church with which
he identified himself was Bethel South, which was the nearest
church to his home, and where Isaac Barton had been pastor for many years, and where his father, Hughes O. Taylor,
and his brother, H. Woodson Taylor, had been and were still
ministering. Probably one of these servants of God baptized

him into the fellowship of what has since become the First
Baptist Church of Morristown. We find him a messenger of
this church to the Nolachucky Association in the years 1841,
1842 and 1843, and a messenger from Liberty Hill, a newly
constituted church, from 1843 to 1862, missing only one or two
meetings. He was for ten years clerk of the Association and
four years its Moderator. He preached three introductory
sermons: In 1851, from the text, "Go teach all nations"; in
1855, from the text, "The church of the living God, the pillar
and ground of the truth"; in 1867, from the text, "I am doing
a great work." He was also missionary of the Association for
a number of years. The character of his work as missionary is
indicated by his report to the body for the year 1851: "Labored ninety days, twenty-two of which are donated; preached
seventy-five sermons; baptized thirty-seven persons; witnessed
about 145 professions of faith; assisted in the ordination of
one deacon and the constitution of one church; spent twenty-
eight days of my time in destitution. G. G. Taylor, missionary." Elika Taylor, an older brother and a thoroughly competent judge, himself an unordained preacher, has this to say
of his brother Grant: "He had the best talent there was in
the family. He was a deeper man and a better investigator
than either of his preacher-brothers. He was also a very
earnest speaker. In preaching he was alive all over; his
gestures and his whole body spoke with energy and force. He
was one of the strongest debaters in the country, and was good
in protracted meetings, especially when he could have a good
gospel singer and a live exhorter to supplement his gifts and
reinforce his efforts. He lacked the melody of voice and
smoothness of speech of his brother Woodson."

In the war between the States Grant Taylor was a "Union"
man, but when the war was over he was a great pacificator,
lending his influence to conciliating men of different war
views, thus helping to unify divided churches and communities. In not a few of our churches, at the close of the war,

there were conscientious but strongly partisan Baptists who insisted that "rebel" members make "acknowledgments" to the church or be turned out. But Grant Taylor, I am told, always counseled moderation and charity, and at his own charge made trips to Knoxville, where a Federal Court would be in session, to intercede for his 'rebel" brethren and friends and help them out of their troubles.

January 26, 1869, at the home of Joel Dyer, near Buffalo Church, Grainger County, Grant Taylor fell in the harness, and passed to his reward. He was in the midst of a meeting with Buffalo Church, one of the churches of which he was pastor, but succumbed to overwork, exposure and pneumonia He was taken home and buried in the family burying ground on the old Taylor homestead, where sleeps the dust of four generations of the Taylors. "A watchman has fallen. The summons of death was served upon Elder G. G. Taylor, January 26, 1869." (Record of clerk, by order of the Association.)

C. C. TIPTON.

Caswell Cobb Tipton was born in Blount County, Tennessee, in the year 1810. He was a son of John Tipton and a near relative of "Col. John Tipton," a prominent and resourceful politician, who, on the "third Friday in August, 1786," was elected Senator from Washington County, to represent that county in the "General Assembly of North Carolina," who was also a member of the Territorial Convention which met at Knoxville, January 11, 1796, and who, in the early struggles of some of the eastern counties for independence and statehood, was a conspicuous and spirited rival of John Sevier.

The subject of our sketch was converted April 26, 1833, and was baptized by Elder James Lankford into the fellowship of Ellijoy Church, Blount County. This church "liberated" him, August 25, 1835, called him to ordination, July 1, 1838, and in the following month (August 24) he was ordained, Elders

William Billue, James Lankford and William Hodges acting as an advisory and ordaining council. January, 4th Saturday, 1841," Ellijoy Church voted to "solicit Brother Caswell C. Tipton to act as an assistant Moderator" to the pastor, Elder Billue.

In 1842 Elder Tipton was married to Miss Lucinda Brooks, to which union were born four sons and four daughters.

C. C. TIPTON.

In the same year he came to Mossy Creek (now Jefferson City), studied grammar under a teacher at Black Oak Grove, and by private study at home acquired a working knowledge of the Greek language.

At the founding of the Mossy Creek Missionary Baptist Seminary (1851) Elder Tipton became financial agent, and raised some $4,000 for buildings, apparatus and library. In 1855 the seminary became a college by charter, and in 1856 Elder Tipton began a joint agency work for Mossy Creek College for boys and the Jonesboro Female College, raising nearly $7,-000 for the two institutions. These were days of small beginnings, educationally, for Baptists in this part of the country, but it was a time of sowing for future harvests.

Among the churches of which Elder Tipton was pastor we might mention Mill Spring, Rocky Valley and Dumplin. But he was not built for the pastorate, so it would seem. His nervous energy and restless spirit made it necessary for him to be constantly on the go. His forte was agency and mission work. He would have been equally successful in evangelistic work, perhaps, if he had given himself more to that kind of work. Sixty years ago, when the Tennessee Association was in session at Alder Branch, Sevier County, William A. Keen, corresponding messenger from the Holston, in a speech on missions, made this statement: "When the Holston Association was doing little and many of her churches had closed their doors against the missionaries, two men from the Tennessee Association came into our borders and kindled a fire which burned like stubble. They were C. C. Tipton and Layman Jones."

Few men of his day were better posted on the distinctive doctrines of the Baptists than C. C. Tipton, or more fearless in preaching them. He was also familiar with the faith and practices of other denominations. Besides, he had a fondness for religious disputation, and was a skilled debater. He didn't hesitate in the least to cross swords with his own Baptist brethren, but nothing could please him better than to have an oppor-

tunity to try his good Damascus blade on some disputer of another denomination; and, from what I have heard said of him
and from my youthful recollection and impressions of his appearance and voice and manner in fireside conversation, I am
wont to feel very much, "Woe be to the hapless Pedo-Baptist
opponent, exposed to his pitiless logic, biting sarcasm and withering denunciation of wrath upon the wanton perverters of the
right ways of the Lord!" Speaking of the Tipton-Bogart debate
at Sevierville old Uncle John Russell said to the writer: "The
Methodist brother was completely demolished, if ever opponent
was demolished in debate." Mixed with his constitutional penchant for debate was a bit of grim humor; he enjoyed a practical joke. To Elder Russell I am indebted for the following
incident: C. C. Tipton, on his good saddle horse, was making
his way through the mountains over into North Carolina, to
have a public discussion with some Pedo-Baptist preacher,
whose name I have forgotten. By chance he fell in with a certain family who told him about a "debate" which was to take
place the next day in a distant neighborhood, and prevailed
on him to stay over night with them, and go along with them
to the debate the next day. He consented. With an early
breakfast and a good start they were soon well on their way,
and in due time reached the place appointed for the battle of
the giants. Imagine the surprise of Elder Tipton's traveling
companions to see him rise up before the vast crowd of people
assembled and proceed to open the debate.

The so-called "Primitive" or "hard shell" brethren came in
for their share of his knocks. I find in my "notes" this bit of
history, one of Elder Tipton's favorite illustrations: The anti-
mission brethren, he said, are like Wayland's mill, a noted
old-fashioned community water-mill, which ground one grain
at a time, especially when the water was low. One of the neighbors took a "turn" of corn to the mill and waited for his meal,
another neighbor being ahead of him and the water being low as
usual. As the mill proceeded with its work, grinding away, the

"rattle-staff," turning slowly, seemed to say, "It is hard work, hardly worth while, this particular election, grinding all day a grain at a time, there are few that be saved—the sheep must be fed—the dogs take the goats—no missions in mine." The man (in the parable) passed on, attended to other business, but returning, later in the day, after a good shower of rain had fallen, found the mill revived and in good spirits, humming with delight as it did its work, the "rattle-staff" fairly singing, 'Everybody, everybody, God loves the world, give everybody a chance, go into all the world, whosoever will may come." The parable was self-explanatory and struck home, doubtless, with good effect.

Elder Tipton was a faithful witness for the Baptists and the cause of truth, was a foundation-builder for our East Tennessee Zion, in education and missions and co-operative effort. He carried his campaign of Baptist education even to New York City and Charleston, South Carolina, and secured from both these places funds for our two schools, Mossy Creek College and the Jonesboro Female Institute. His labors were abundant throughout East Tennessee, covering a period of more than twenty-five years. He was a man of "fine personal appearance, thick set, heavy built, weighing about 180 pounds, of medium height, firm in manner and purpose, and thoroughly independent. He was a good speaker, and graced a pulpit handsomely." He was strong-minded, bright, energetic, ambitious. He worked best in the lead; didn't want to "take anybody's dust." He inherited his blood and passion and militant disposition, and could not well be anything other than his natural self. Far and near he was sought for in council, and few names are more prominent in the records of East Tennessee Baptists than that of C. C. Tipton.

At the close of the Civil War he moved to West Tennessee, and preached a year or two in that part of the State; then moved to Rolla, Missouri, where his death occurred in the year 1872. The writer is not aware that any of his immediate family are still living. He may have a son Joseph in St. Louis, and possibly another son and a daughter or two somewhere in the West. John T. Mullendore, of Texas, is a grandson, and Mrs. K. H. McNelly, Talladega, Alabama, Mrs. J. M. Catlett, Jefferson City, Tennessee, and Mrs. M. F. Nickols, Sevierville, Tennessee, are granddaughters—and were old enough to remember their grandfather when he was living. These, and many others, cherish the memory of a veteran soldier of the cross, who fought hard to win, and who, some day, we assuredly believe, shall wear the victor's crown.

MONROE TRENT.

Monroe Trent was born October 7, 1847; was married to Nancy C. Cope, September 11, 1887. He professed faith in Christ in October, 1867, uniting with a Baptist church on Clinch River. Afterwards he moved his membership to Trent Valley. In 1906 he became a member of Richardson's Creek, continuing his membership with that church till his death, August 12, 1914. His ordination to the ministry took place, January 6, 1877. Brother Trent was considered by his brethren one of the "best Bible-read" men of his Association—the Mulberry Gap. He was a "doctrinal" rather than an emotional or sentimental preacher. He was a man of good intellect and native strength, both of mind and of body. He was plain, outspoken and fearless. "He would preach what he thought the Bible taught, regardless of feelings. He was a zealous advocate of the truth as the Baptists see it and gave the best part of his life to the Lord's cause, with little remuneration from the churches. He preached to one church for two entire years, walking ten miles to his appointments, his only remuneration being one pair of home-knit yarn socks. It was the love of Christ and the advancement of his cause, not the hope of financial reward, that caused him to go through heat and cold, rain and snow, to preach to the needy and the lost the unsearchable riches of Christ."

Brother Trent accomplished great and lasting good in the field covered by the Mulberry Gap Association. For a number of years he was Moderator of the body. He fell in the harness, on day and date above given, and passed to his eternal reward in the heavens.

JAMES TUNNELL.

James Tunnell was born near Fredericksburg, Virginia, in the year 1777. He was a son of "Rev. Stephen Tunnell, a Methodist minister, who reared a large family, nine sons and one daughter." His grandfather, William Tunnell, was born in France, about the year 1703, being the oldest child of his parents, who were "godly people," the religious faith of the family, it is said, being "pronouncedly, pugnaciously Calvanistic." With William as a "babe in arms," his parents, fleeing from religious persecution, like many another Huguenot family, came to Yorkshire, England, where the infant son grew to manhood, and married Anne Howard—"Lady Anne," she was called, because the daughter of a "gentleman," the title clinging to her as long as she lived. This couple, about the year 1736, emigrated from Yorkshire, England, to Virginia, settling in Spottsylvania County, near Fredericksburg. Stephen Tunnell, father of James, was a soldier in the war of the Revolution. In 1789 he left his native State of Virginia, and came to Washington County, Tennessee, when James was a lad of twelve years of age, and settled near Jonesboro. At the age of twenty-one James Tunnell married a Miss Jane Ball, and settled on Beech Creek, in Hawkins County, where he lived the greater part of his life. In his old age he was married a second time, becoming stepfather to a second family of children. He owned a farm and considerable property, but "lost most of his estate," it is said, by the Civil War. He was a member of Double

Springs Church for half a century, perhaps. I have no account
of his ordination, and there is little record or written history of
his ministry. As to physique and temperamental make-up he is
described as being "above six feet high, slim, active, pugnacious,
fearless; before his conversion he would walk six miles before breakfast, any morning," it is said, "to lick a man who had
insulted him." He retained his fiery, vehement disposition to
the end of life, but controlled himself better after he became a
preacher. I doubt if he was pastor of many churches, but he
is said to have been "zealous and earnest and powerful in a revival." He was not a "Primitive or Old-School" Baptist, but,
like some of them, would "sing out" his sermons, I have been
told, after the approved fashion and popular and effective style
of preaching, in many parts of the country, at that day. Dr.
Broadus used to say that the "sing-song" habit of some of the
dear old men was a by-product of out-of-door speaking, and
being restful to the "overstrained vocal chords," was natural.

The Tunnell family is notably a family of preachers. Steph-
en Tunnell, father of James, was a Methodist minister, as we
have already noted. William Tunnell, an uncle of James, was
a Baptist preacher, of Anderson County, Tennessee. John Tunnell, another uncle, was a Methodist Elder of the Holston Circuit, and "one of the celebrities of the first Conference west of
the Alleghanies," held May 13-15, 1788, in Washington County,
Virginia, fifteen miles east of Abingdon. "On Sunday, the 11th,
Mr. Tunnell preached an excellent sermon with great effect.
Powerful exhortations followed. Under this sermon and these
exhortations Mrs. Elizabeth Russell—known in history as
Madam Russell, a sister of the illustrious Patrick Henry—was
convicted, and her conviction led in a few hours to her conversion" (Dr. Price, Holston Methodism). Robert M. Tunnell,
a great nephew of James Tunnell, is a Congregationalist minister in Kansas. Dr. Spencer Tunnell, of Morristown, one of
our best preachers and pastors, is a grandson; he has signal-
ized his present pastorate by building and paying for a magni-

ficent house of worship and baptizing in Holston River (May, 1913) 96 newly made converts in fifty-eight minutes in the presence of 5,000 witnesses gathered on the banks of the river. Another grandson, W. M. T., and older brother of Dr. Tunnell, dying at the age of thirty-seven, was a "brilliant and gifted, but timid preacher, pastor of his grandfather's old church—Double Springs.

Elder James Tunnell died near Robertsville, Anderson County, Tennessee, about the year 1865.

WILLIAM WEBB

William Webb was born in Virginia in the year 1800. His father came to Tennessee and settled in Anderson County when William was a small boy. He professed faith in Christ, and joined Zion Church the second Saturday in November, 1832. He was one of the members who went into the organization of the Clear Branch (now the Longfield) Church in 1834. He gave the land on which the Longfield Church was built, and helped to build the house of worship. He was a leader in all the progressive movements of the church, and stood as a firm and faithful advocate of missions in the troublous times (1834-39) when his church was much disturbed and divided over the matter of missions, conventions and other mooted questions of the day. He did much to advance and establish the "mission cause in Anderson, Campbell and Morgan Counties, and few men of his day and community equaled him in Christian philanthropy and benevolence." He was ordained to the full work of the gospel ministry, May, 4th Saturday, 1861, by the Longfield Baptist Church.

April 23, 1877, he died at his home, two miles northeast of Coal Creek, Tennessee, where he had lived in the confidence and affection of the people for many years. For these brief notes I am indebted to the kindness of Brother W. R. Riggs.

JOHN WEBSTER.

The two Websters, John and William, father and son, had the pioneer spirit and were active and influential ministers in the Clinton Association in the seventies and eighties of the last century. John Webster came from North Carolina near the close of the Civil War. He preached in Knox County for a while, then bought a farm near Clinton and settled down on it. He was pastor of New Bethel Church in Roane County, New Salem and Poplar Creek churches in the Clinton Association, and did a great deal of protracted meeting work with weak churches and in destitute places in the region round about. He died about the year 1875 or '76, leaving his impress upon the churches and the people within the scope of his ministry. His son, William, took up the work he left off, and was his successor in a sense. He became pastor of New Salem, New Hope and other churches, and with the spirit of evangelism went into destitute fields and out-of-the-way places to declare the counsel of God and invite men to be saved upon the terms of the gospel. He passed to his reward about the year 1884 or '85. Both of these men were good soldiers of Jesus Christ, and deserve a place in history. They sowed where others are now reaping. They preached the great doctrines of grace with great force. They visited the homes of the people and are gratefully remembered for having turned many to righteousness and for having led some who were nigh unto physical and eternal death to the Savior, and down into the waters of baptism and into the blessed fellowship of the people of God. Happy are such spiritual guides and watchers for souls; they have many stars in their crowns.

JOSEPH WHITE.

Joseph White, in the first quarter of the last century, was a prominent minister in the Holston and Nolachucky Associations. He lived near Warrensburg, in Greene County. His labors were mostly in Greene, Hawkins, and Cocke counties. He was an uncle of Elder Ephraim Moore, whom he took into his home as a lad, becoming a father to him, after young Moore had had the misfortune to lose his own father. In 1820 Joseph White appears in the minutes of the Holston Association as an "ordained" minister, and a messenger from the Lick Creek (Warrensburg) Church. He and Thos. L. Hale represented this church in the organization of the Nolachucky Association, in August of 1828. In his young manhood Elder Joseph Manning, a pioneer of Cocke County, was married to Lucinda Huff by "Joseph White, minister of the gospel." For four successive years he was a messenger of Warrensburg Church to the Nolachucky Association. After that his name disappears from the Association records, and he drops out of sight. In the early thirties he left Tennessee and went to the State of Missouri.

J. W. WHITLOCK.

In the year 1873 the subject of this sketch began a promising career as a missionary evangelist and pioneer preacher in the newly opened up territory along the Cincinnati Southern, northeast of Chattanooga, in Rhea, Roane and adjacent counties. In the midst of useful and abundant labors he was cut down before he had reached the maturity of his powers or had fairly entered upon the prime of his ministry. John Wesley Whitlock was born January 18, 1847; he died February 13, 1886, lacking five days of being thirty-nine years and one month old. He was buried at Jonesboro. His first pastorate was at Cedar Ford, Grainger County; his last pastorate was Jonesboro and Johnson City, where he did good work, laying solid foundations for more solid building in the future.

Brother Whitlock was scholarly, although he never attended college. He had a good common school eduaction. His book learning, especially in the classics, he dug out at home. He was a hard student, taught school, learned Greek and Latin, without a teacher, and taught Professor Mason, Superintendent of the Morristown High School, the mysteries of these dead languages.

Brother Whitlock was twice married. March 9, 1872, he was married to Miss Mary Nance, a daughter of Prior Nance, of Grainger County. His second marriage was to Miss Sallie Jarnagin. Both of his wives were excellent women—"helps meet for him," not only in domestic life, but also in the ministry, to which he had consecrated his life. A severe bladder trouble, baffling the physician's skill, brought him and his labors of love to what seemed to him an untimely end. It was a great struggle for him to be reconciled to an overruling Providence, which permitted his ministry to come to so sudden a close. But thinking and praying over the matter, and trusting all to the Great Father's infinite wisdom and love, he finally became reconciled, and passed peacefully to the rest that awaits the people of God.

JAMES WHITSITT.

James Whitsitt was a son of William and Ellen (Maneese) Whitsitt. He was born January 31, 1771, in Amherst County, Virginia. At the age of ten he moved with the family to Henry County, Virginia. He was born and reared in the Episcopal Church, at that time the established or state church of Virginia, but he knew nothing of an experience of grace. In 1789, in the providence of God, there was a great revival of religion in the neighborhood of the Whitsitt family, conducted by Elder Joseph Anthony, a Baptist minister of evangelistic fervor and spiritual power. Young Whitsitt came under the influence of the meeting, was converted, and, making a profession of his faith, was baptized by Elder Anthony. On the occasion of his examination and baptism he made an address, it is said, which was "characterized by great fluency, appropriateness and fervor." He entered into the revival with great zeal for the salvation of others, praying, exhorting and holding prayer meetings, with such marked success that his church in a very short time voted him a formal "license" to preach. He was then in his nineteenth year. About this time there were glowing reports from the "great West," and the family of an uncle and a part of his own family had moved to the "valley of the Cumberland," in what is now known as Middle Tennessee. James had been left behind to wind up the business. This done, he, too, following the migratory instinct so common to the people of those early days, set out for Tennessee, and at the end of a hard and perilous journey found himself in the bosom of his family. Here he met, courted and married his cousin, Jane Cardwell Maneese, a daughter of James Maneese, a most estimable and godly woman, who became the mother of his eleven children. By this marriage he came into possession of a large body of very fine land on Mill Creek, which he well knew how to cultivate and upon which he established himself for independent living the rest of his days.

Before leaving Virginia young Whitsitt, like many another youth, yielding to the pressure of unfriendly environment and anti-Baptist views, allowed himself to drift into skepticism and to doubt his religion, even going so far as to request exclusion from the church. But now, with a change of environment and a renewal of his hope, he writes to his former pastor requesting restoration to fellowship in his church, and a letter of dismission. His membership was transferred to the little church on Mill Creek (1794), where he was ordained to the gospel ministry, in which he labored with untiring faithfulness and distinguished success for more than fifty years. "From this time

34

onward, till near the close of his life, the history of Elder Whitsitt's labors would be the history, in large measure, of the Baptist denomination in the valley of the Cumberland." He took
the pastoral care of four churches: the church at Mill Creek,
Concord Church, in Williamson County, and Rock Spring and
Providence churches, in Rutherford County, exchanging Rock
Spring for Antioch Church, when that body had been organized, in order to locate his work nearer to his home. He continued his labors with these churches from thirty to forty years,
up to the time when the infirmities of age compelled him to give
them up, one by one, and confine his ministry to his home
church.

Elder Whitsitt was present at the organization (1796) of
the Mero District Association, the first association formed in
the Cumberland Valley, including all the churches in Tennessee, west of the mountains, being five in number. Mero District
is but another name for the territory now known as Middle
Tennessee. Upon the organization of the Cumberland Association (1803) Elder Whitsitt and his churches were transferred
to that body. Later (1810) at least two of his churches were
constituent members in the formation of the Concorn Association, composed of twenty-one churches lying east of Nashville.
This body, for the year 1812, reported 866 baptisms, 350 of
which were performed by Elder Whitsitt. In a list of twelve
"prominent ministers" who were in the organization of this Association, all men of "ability and sterling worth," the name of
James Whitsitt stands at the head. For years his influence in
the Association was paramount, and the proceedings of the
body bear much of the "impress of his views and opinions."

After the death of his first wife he was married to Mrs.
Elizabeth Woodruff, a member of his Mill Creek Church and a
mother in Israel. For four years his life was brightened by
her ministry and devotion—he was then left to live with his
youngest son, to whom he gave the homestead. The infirmities
of age were now pressing heavily upon him. Mill Creek, the

only church of which he was now pastor, allowed him an "assistant," but the relation soon became unsatisfactory to the old pastor, who resigned his charge, and, taking a letter of dismission, united with the First Church at Nashville, where he retained membership till the close of his life. After retiring as pastor he continued to preach funeral and other sermons, here and there, supplying for his preacher-brethren, occasionally, writing articles for the religious press, and rendering other service, as his strength would permit. He supplied the Second Church in Nashville, in the absence of the pastor, to the edification and delight of the church. On the second Lord's day in October, 1848, he was with his church in Nashville at their communion. His address on this occasion was peculiarly tender and affecting: "And now, brethren and sisters, farewell. This is our last interview. I am old and rapidly failing. The winter is almost upon us, and I can not be with you. Before spring comes I shall be gone, Farewell." This, indeed, was his last meeting with them. He died in perfect peace on the 12th of April, 1849, in the seventy-ninth year of his age.

Elder Whitsitt was a man of "striking personal appearance and manners—frame tall, combining elegance and strength, hair black, eyes dark, calm and shaded by heavy brows, countenance regular, manly and intellectual, uniting great benevolence and unyielding firmness; his whole demeanor evinced a dignity which repelled every light reproach and a self-possession which never forsook him. He was a man whom no one could imitate, and whose style and manner could never be forgotten by those who had once heard him. He was the uniform and earnest friend of missions, and had a primary agency in originating and sustaining the missionary operations of our State. He left a broader mark upon his generation than almost any of his associates in the ministry" (His pastor, Dr. R. B. C. H.).

"As a minister of the gospel he held a very high rank. His sermons were always able, and had the appearance of being elaborately prepared. His conceptions were clear and accurate. His reasoning faculties were unusually strong, and no metaphysical subtleties ever confused him. In the latter part of his life his sermons became less argumentative and more practical. He was also occasionally intensely pathetic, and the effect of his utterances at such times was well-nigh overwhelming" (Reporter to Cathcart).

I am citing a foot-note to Benedict's History of the Baptists, which will be of interest on account of its local reference and coloring as well as its touch and thrill of sentiment always to be found in the mutual friendship and admiration of two great souls, such as existed between the author of our great denominational history and one of the great makers of that history; and with this citation our sketch must close. Speaking of "Elder James Whitsitt" Benedict says: "I am pleased to put *Elder* against such ancient names. The hospitable mansion of this old friend was my home while I was exploring this region in 1810. He resides on the same side of the Cumberland River on which Nashville is situated, a few miles up that noble stream, and but a short distance from the seat of the late Gen. Jackson. Then there was no more appearance of a Baptist Church in Nashville, than as if the old English *Five Mile Act* had been in full force, which forbid all dissenters from settling within that distance of any city, town, borough, etc. At my instance, this aged minister has given me a brief statement of his pastoral services and relations, which I will relate in his own language: 'Since I saw you (1810) I have aided in building three brick meeting houses for the three churches I attended last; they are all on Mill Creek. The one nearest me, and where my membership is, is one of the best in the country; it is 60 feet by 40, with galleries on three sides, and is well finished. The other two are of the same dimensions, without galleries. The first one named (Mill Creek) is far the oldest church now standing on the south side of Cumberland River. This church has branched out into five respectable churches; for the main body, I officiated as pastor forty-eight years; I have now re-signed the pastorship of all the churches formerly under my care. I am now (1846) in my seventy-sixth year, having been in the ministry more than fifty years.' "

WM. A. WHITSITT.

Elder Whitsitt was born in Williamson County, Tennessee, July 25, 1816. He professed faith in Christ in his eighteenth year, and was baptized by Elder Peter S. Gayle into the fellow-ship of Mill Creek Church, Davidson County. His church made him clerk and deacon, which offices he held as long as he lived in the bounds of the church. In 1839 he was married to Miss Nancy Jane Morton, a daughter of Dr. Samuel Morton, and settled on a farm given to his wife by her father, near Con-cord Church, in Williamson County. Uniting with this church he continued to fill the two-fold office of clerk and deacon as he had formerly done at Mill Creek. Having embarked in the profession of teaching he pursued that calling for a time. But his church urged upon him the more important work of calling sinners to repentance. Accordingly, in the fall of 1843, he was licensed to preach. The following year the church called for his ordination, which took place on Saturday before the second Lord's day in July, 1844—Elders James Whitsitt (his grand-father), John Morton and R. W. January constituting the coun-cil. His venerable grandfather, who had been for many years the pastor of Concord Church, was now bending under the in-firmities of old age and was wanting to place the burden of caring for the church on younger shoulders. The new situation furnished him the opportunity he had been looking for to resign his charge and have his grandson for his successor. So the Concord Church, for twenty years, became the field for the younger Whitsitt's labors and usefulness. He was also pastor of Rock Spring, in Rutherford County; of Arrington and Har-peth, in Williamson County; of Antioch, McCrory's Creek,

Gethsemane, Smith's Spring and Old Mill Creek, in Davidson County. In nearly all these churches he had glorious revivals.

His first wife died in the tenth year after their marriage, leaving an only daughter. On the 14th day of January, 1850, he was married to Miss Malinda Weatherly. No children were born to the second marriage.

Elder Whitsitt, like many other ministers of his day, was not adequately sustained by the churches to which he ministered. Some of his churches at times would support him well; at other times the same churches failed to minister to him in temporal things as they should have done. The last churches served by him as pastor were Antioch and Smith's Spring, and it was his purpose to spend all his Sabbaths within the bounds of those two congregations. When old and decrepit with age his desire was still strong to be a watchman upon the walls of Zion, and his earnest prayer was that his last days might be his holiest and most useful ones. (Condensed from Borum).

MOSES WILBURN.

Moses Wilburn was born March 19, 1827, in Hancock County, Tennessee. He was a son of James Wilburn, a poor, but honest and hard-working mountaineer, unable to give his children educational advantages. The boy Moses was brought up to farm-life, and learned hard work rather than letters. At the age of sixteen he professed faith in Christ and was baptized into the fellowship of what is now known as the Sneedville Church. His church by the laying on of hands ordained him deacon, in which capacity he served his church, some two or three years. He was licensed to preach, June 8, 1851, and was ordained to the full work of the ministry August 9, 1852. He was pastor of many of the churches of the Mulberry Gap Association, and at different times was the Moderator of that body. A partial record of his ministerial life gives, "days labored, 1,456; sermons preached, 1,718; persons baptized, 779; couples married, 88." Moses Wilburn was a man of "great moral and religious worth, and though uneducated was an able expounder of Bible doctrines. Wherever he preached or ministered in any way, his labors and his influence were greatly blessed of the Lord." He was instrumental in bringing into the ministry a number of useful and noted preachers—among others, Dr. S. E. Jones and Elder D. L. Manis, both of whom he baptized. Dr. Jones says of him: "We could not call him an orator, yet his pulpit ministrations were powerful and there was an effectiveness and fluency about his speech which betrayed his wonderful pathos of soul, the pious fervency of his heart, and the living zeal of his nature. With unfeigned tears he sowed the precious seed; the harvest will wave, mature and golden, in eternal fields. He died July 4, 1878." For more than a quarter of a century he stood as a watchman upon the walls of Zion, faithfully warning the people. When, worn with watching and protracted illness, he fell asleep, he was buried in the Lawson graveyard in his native county, where the dead in Christ shall some day hear the summons, "Saints, arise!"

Brother Wilburn was married twice; first to Nancy Grimes, to which union there were born four children. His second marriage was to Sarah Grimes. Both of his companions preceded him to the better land.

CALEB WITT.

Caleb Witt, a son of Charles and Lavinia Witt, was born September 2, 1762, in Halifax County, Virginia. His father was also a native of Virginia, born about 1730, and perhaps in the same county as his son. Caleb Witt's mother has never been satisfactorily identified, her maiden name still being a matter of conjecture.

Caleb Witt was in the Revolutionary War; was "drafted from Dobey's Old Store," was in the Yorktown campaign, and saw Cornwallis surrender his sword. After his death (January 27, 1827), his "widow applied for a pension." (Miss Lucy M. Ball).

In 1783, while Tennessee was still the "State of Franklin," the Witts settled near Witt's Foundry, in what is now Hamblen County, Tennessee. Some of the farms in this neighborhood have been in continuous possession of the Witt family for 132 years.

September 2, 1784, the subject of our sketch was married to Miriam Horner, a daughter of William and Elizabeth Horner, and a native of Randolph County, North Carolina. This union was blessed with a family of eleven children. Coleman Witt, the youngest of the family, far up in his 80's when I saw him some twenty years ago, rendered the writer valuable service on a number of his sketches, for which acknowledgment is hereby duly made.

Caleb Witt had at least two brothers, Elijah and Joseph, who came to Tennessee in the early settlement of the country, and two sisters, Patsy, who married Capt. Thomas Jarnagin, and who was the great-grandmother of Dr. W. A. Montgomery, and Lydia, who married William Maze. Wilson C., son of Daniel Witt, is a near relative of Caleb Witt. He was ninety-nine last June, and promises me a picture of himself, on his one hundredth anniversary, should he live to see it. Elijah Witt, though not a preacher, was a student of the Bible, especially of the "prophets," and wrote a book, or pamphlet, entitled, "The Beast With Seven Heads and Ten Horns."

I have been told that when Caleb Witt and his wife, Miriam, commenced housekeeping for themselves their household effects consisted of a few pounds of feathers for a bed, a board for a table, stools for chairs, a broken pot for boiling vegetables, and a flat rock for baking bread. In addition to these necessary furnishings he had his "little black mare" with which to plow the fields.

He was a member of the old Bent Creek (now Whitesburg) Church, constituted in 1785. He was likely baptized by the long-time pastor, Elder Tidence Lane. This church licensed and ordained him to preach, and was served by him as pastor for a number of years.

Caleb Witt was a man of plain personal appearance, rather sharp features, high, shrill voice, passionate nature, and high temper; but a man of good spirit and splendid ability. In doctrine he was a thorough-going predestinarian, a strong advocate of the doctrine of "particular election." He was "hard" *a plenty* in his doctrine, but was not "anti-missionary." Luther Rice's "list of collections for Judson in Burmah showed Caleb Witt's name as one of the contributors of Bent Creek Church to Foreign Missions. I saw the list, and remember distinctly the name, but not the amount of the contribution." (W. A. Keen).

For a number of years Caleb Witt represented his church (Bent Creek) in the Holston Association, and was fourteen years the Moderator of that body.

He was a stalwart defender of Bible-and-Baptist doctrine, as shown by the following bit of history. Miller and Dodge, "Stone-ite preachers" from Kentucky, claiming to be Baptists, had sown the seeds of dissension in the Buffalo Ridge Church (a church with a membership of 350), subverting the faith of many and carrying them away to the Arian heresy as taught by Barton Stone and Alexander Campbell (both of whom denied the deity of Christ)—reducing the church to fourteen members. There was war in the camp and on the field; no political campaign was ever hotter. The Holston Association had met with the Cherokee Church. There was a large gathering of the Baptist hosts, and Caleb Witt was to preach the sermon. His text was Isaiah 9:6, 7: "Unto us a child is born, unto us a son is given; his name shall be called wonderful, counsellor, the Mighty God," etc. His theme was the "Deity of Christ," a doctrine which the enemies had assailed. The sermon was logical and compact, a solid mass of Scripture quotation, exegesis, and argument on the one point in dispute—the divine and eternal sonship and Godhood of the Second Person in the Trinity, the adorable Redeemer and Almighty Savior. Many lawyers were present, and their verdict was that Caleb Witt's defense of a great Scripture doctrine was complete, that his argument was the most convincing and unanswerable argument on that subject they had ever heard from a pulpit. It was a great triumph for the Baptist cause in the old Holston Association. The sermon went a long way toward discrediting the popular Campbellite heresy in the eyes of Baptists, and other denominations as well, and had a powerful influence in unifying the Baptists of the Association and establishing them in the fundamental doctrines of their ancient faith. (W. A. Keen).

As illustrating the divergent views of 'predestinarians" and anti predestinarians in the popular mind, Dr. W. A. Montgomery told me the following story of his great-grandmother, a Mrs. Jarnagin, who was a sister of Caleb Witt. Expressing herself in regard to the doctrine of election, on one occasion, she said: "Brother Caleb says, if a body isn't one of the elect, it's no use for him to try; he may weep his eyes out and pray forever, but it won't do any good. I reckon that's so, for Brother Caleb says so. But somehow or other I can't help but feel that everybody ought to try and strive to enter in."

This story comes to me from my correspondent in Illinois: Tradition says, that Caleb Witt went into a trance, on one occasion, and was laid out for dead. But, "coming to," he raised himself up and said that he had been to heaven and had heard a song that had never been sung on earth: "Live many years more; increase in store; and preach the gospel to the poor." The vision and the song made a lasting impression upon him, and he did live many years to "preach the gospel to the poor." He died January 20, 1827, near Russellville, and was buried in the old Bent Creek cemetery at Whitesburg.

My attention has been recently called to the will of Charles Witt, father of Caleb. He died in the year 1780, in Halifax County, Virginia, where his will is of record. He willed to each of his children a "cow" and so many pounds "sterling."

PLEASANT A. WITT.

Pleasant Alred Witt, son of Elder Caleb and Miriam (Horner) Witt, was born in Jefferson County, Tennessee, February 18, 1800. He was the sixth child and fifth son in a family of eleven children. He united with the Bent Creek Church, near Whitesburg, in the year 1817. He was married to Elizabeth Haun, daughter of Christopher Haun, of Jefferson County, October 13, 1818. To this union were born ten children. May, 2nd Saturday, 1823, Bent Creek Church "agreed that Brother Pleasant A. Witt should have license to go into all the world and to preach where God in his providence" might call him. In 1825 County Line Church "requested" his ordination. May, 2nd Saturday, 1826, his church ordained him—Daniel Howery, Henry Randolph, Elihu Millikan, Joseph White and Caleb Witt (the pastor) acting as a presbytery. April, 2nd Saturday, 1833, "church agrees to take Brethren Andrew Coffman and P. A. Witt jointly for their pastor for twelve months"; the following year the call is repeated; and the next following year they were continued co-pastors indefinitely, or "till a dissatisfaction arises."

Pleasant A. Witt was a messenger of Bent Creek (Whitesburg) Church to the Nolachucky Association from its organization (1828) to the year preceding the disruption (1839) of that body, without missing a single session. The Bent Creek record of "June, 2nd Saturday, 1839," is as follows: "Took up the Institution (s) named in our minutes, and decided we will not make them a test of fellowship: Vote, 38 to 27. The minority rent off from this church and hold their meetings on a different day, claiming to be the old Bent Creek Church, but call themselves by the name of Primitive Baptists." Elder Witt went out with the "minority," or seceding party, declaring "a non-fellowship" for all societies, organizations and affiliations not expressly mentioned in the Scriptures. His name no longer appears on the church records. He had been preacher of the Introductory sermon before the Nolachucky body in 1835, and in '37 and '38 had been the body's Moderator. He became a leader in the anti-mission movement.

In personal appearance Pleasant A. Witt was a good deal like his father, Elder Caleb Witt—figure lean and lithe, weight 130 to 140 pounds, eyebrows heavy, eyes piercing, features sharp, voice high-keyed and shrill. He was a fluent and forceful speaker, of a fiery disposition, controversial, combative, and a little rasping—not so "smoothe and popular" as his father, I have been told. This last statement ought to be taken with a grain of salt, perhaps, inasmuch as Caleb Witt died before the war of missions and methods was fairly on and his son, Pleasant A., was in the hottest of the fight, giving and receiving blows. In a situation like that, to be "smoothe and popular" with both sides, or with all of either side, would doubtless have been an impossibility. That he was honest in his views, I have no doubt. That he advocated them ably, there is no question. That he was unduly biased by the hyper-Calvinism of his day—by extreme views of "foreknowledge absolute, election, predestination, and reprobation," is equally certain.

Pleasant A. Witt passed to his reward February 1, 1872, and was buried at old Friendship, "the mother of churches," near White Pine, and his wife, Elizabeth, by his side. The tombstone inscription tells us he was an "Elder of the Primitive Baptist Church for fifty-two years"—adding the sentiment which had doubtless animated and inspired him in many a struggle and conflict of life:

"Father, I give my spirit up;
I trust it in thy hand.
My dying flesh shall rest in hope,
And rise at thy command."

Elisha F. Witt, of near Talbott, one of the best pastors in the Nolachucky Association, is a grandson of Pleasant A. Witt, and a great-grandson of Caleb Witt, one of the first preachers to sow "the good seed" in the virgin soil of the new State of Tennessee.

WILSON CARROLL WITT.

(Baptized July 29, 1917, aged 100 years, one month, one day.)

The following sketch was prepared by the author and published by request in the *Baptist and Reflector* of August 16, 1917. It is reproduced here, partly on account of the novelty of the situation, partly as a supplement to the sketches of Elder Caleb and Pleasant A. Witt, but most especially because of the fact that "Uncle Wilson" Witt is a concrete expression of conditions and influences that obtained widely and had to be reckoned with in many places, eighty and a hundred years ago. I reproduce *verbatim:* Friends and Brethren of the *Baptist and Reflector* Family: I am pleased to introduce to you and let you look on the kindly face of my friend and brother, Uncle Wilson Witt, son of Daniel Witt, who was a son of Elijah Witt, who was a son of Charles and a brother of Caleb Witt, one of Tennessee's earliest pioneer Baptist preachers, born in Halifax County, Virginia, September 2, 1762, was a soldier in the War of the Revolution, took part in the Yorktown campaign, and saw Cornwallis surrender his sword in 1781. Wilson C. Witt was born June 28, 1817, five miles south of Morristown, Tennessee, in what is now Hamblen County. The picture which graces this sketch was promised me more than a year ago, to go in my book of "sketches" and to represent the "Witt family," who were never fortunate enough to have a good picture made. The condition of the promise was, "provided we both should live" to see Brother Witt reach the one hundredth milestone on his journey of life and he should be strong enough to go to the photographer's gallery on the one hundredth anniversary of his birth. The picture herewith presented was made June 28, 1917, according to promise, and the mercy of God. Brother Witt is hale and hearty as he "turns a new leaf," takes up his long-neglected duty, and enters the threshold of a second century of natural life, walking in the Lord's appointed way. He has been "sick in bed," he says, only "once in life;" that was in his eighty-first year. He eats two meals a day, does not shun

WILSON C. WITT.

work, sleeps well, keeps on good terms with his conscience, and is well preserved in body and mind. He has been a great help to the writer in sketching the old-time preachers, with many of whom he was well acquainted.

Last Sunday afternoon (July 29), in the presence of a thousand or two thousand people, with two hundred automobiles and other vehicles innumerable, standing around, Brother Witt, along with his oldest daughter, a Mrs. Smith, seventy-six

years old, and two other ladies, was baptized into the fellowship
of the Witts' Foundry Church by the pastor, Dr. J. M. Anderson, of Morristown. Standing in the water beside Brother Witt
Dr. Anderson made, in substance, the following address:
"Friends, I think you will agree with me that this is a most extraordinary occasion. Uncle Wilson Carroll Witt, today one
hundred years, one month and one day old, has come to be bap-
teized. Brother Witt has had a sense of sins forgiven and has
entertained a hope in Christ since he was a young man. He
tells me that my grandfather, Rev. William Anderson, seventy-
five years ago, urged upon him the importance of being baptized. He now regrets exceedingly that he did not submit to
this holy ordinance in early life, and here in the presence of
the people makes confession of his dereliction of duty in this
regard, and sues for pardon at a throne of God's abounding
mercy and grace. But may I state in his behalf, that there are
mitigating circumstances; and however far he may have gone
afield and however many may have been his delinquencies, he
comes today, strong in faith and brave of heart, ready and
willing to obey his Lord's command. And may this, the crowning act of a long and eventful life, a life abounding in good
cheer and kindly deeds, be well pleasing in the sight of God and
a lasting benediction to us all!"

In regard to the "mitigating circumstances," above men-
teioned, it will not be amiss, I think, to offer a word in explanation. Brother Witt grew up under the strongest Calvinistic
influences, in an atmosphere created by the teachings of Elders
William Anderson, Henry Randolph, both of the elder Witts,
Caleb and Pleasant A., father and son, and Dr. Thomas Hill, all
strong men and nearly or quite fatalistic in their religious beliefs. They often visited Brother Witt's home and labored
with him as a young man quite a good deal to "show him the
right way." But with all the light they could give him he still
had a vague notion that there was "something more" in the
divine plan for man to do than the preachers of the "old school"

persuasion were accustomed to "give to the people." This explains his delinquency in the matter of being baptized and taking upon himself the obligations of a church member. Growing up as he did in an atmosphere of controversy and sometimes of bitterness, his non-committal attitude, under the circumstances, was not unnatural—he grew up between the two "schools" of Baptists. Though entering the vineyard, in a sense, at the "eleventh hour," Brother Witt, through the years, has been moral and upright, a splendid citizen, public spirited and intelligent—is indeed a very admirable and lovable man, now a "brother."

Brother Witt had nine children, and has lived to see all of them married and living within a radius of six miles of Morristown. He has seven living children, one hundred grand and great-grandchildren, and eight great-great-grandchildren.

It is interesting to note that in 1783, while Tennessee was still the "State of Franklin," the Witts settled near Witts' Foundry, in what is now Hamblen County, Tennessee. Some of the farms in this neighborhood have been in the continuous possession of the Witt family for 132 years. The lot on which stands the meeting house of the Witts' Foundry Baptist Church is a gift to the church of Wilson C. Witt.

DAVID WOLFE.

Elder David Wolfe was born September 13, 1817, one hundred years ago; and died at his residence in Hancock County, Tennessee, June 30, 1886. He professed faith in Christ October 5, 1845, and was baptized into the fellowship of Richardson's Creek Church by Elder Jesse D. Berry. After exercising his gifts in public prayer, exhortation and preaching he was ordained to the full work of the ministry, September 1, 1855. He was a faithful servant of the Master who had called him to preach the glorious gospel of the blessed God and to warn sinners to flee from the wrath to come. He stood as a watchman on the walls of Zion for more than thirty years, during which time he was pastor of a number of churches, serving them, for the most part, at his own charges. He was considered to be a successful evangelist for his day and time, and baptized a great many people. His education was limited, like most of the preachers in his part of the country, but he was familiar with the Bible; had the confidence of the people, and won many of them to the Lord. Brother Wolfe was conscientious and faithful to declare the Word of the Lord, was a good citizen and a peace-maker. He preached peace and good will wherever he went. "He was one of the most careful men I ever saw about doing or saying anything that would cause offense, give trouble, do harm, or put a stumbling block in the way of any man. The blessing belonging to the peace-maker was his." (G. H. Cope).

RICHARD WOOD.

I am now standing (1896) on the former site of the old Providence Church, Sevier County, a place made sacred by the sleeping dust of Elder Richard Wood, the "first preacher," it is thought, to preach the gospel, as Baptists believe and preach it, in Sevier County. He is the first preacher whom Elder John Russell, now upwards of eighty, among his first recollections, remembers to have seen and heard preach "when a very small boy." The old meeting house is no more, the church having long since gone down and been revived and established in another place. But the graveyard is still here, and a tomb-stone, bearing this inscription: "In memory of Rev. Richard Wood: Died, A. D., 1831; aged seventy-five years." Solitary and alone he pioneered the way for the Baptists over a large territory in Sevier and Blount counties, as far back perhaps as 1785 or '86. He gathered the materials for and was the founder (1789) and first pastor of the Forks of Little Pigeon (now the Sevierville) Church; and continued the pastor, actively and nominally, till his death—a period of forty-two years.

35

He was present at a "conference of nineteen churches" (a messenger from the Forks of Little Pigeon) assembled at Beaver Creek meeting house, on the 25th day of December, 1802, at which time the Tennessee Association was organized. In 1804 he was Moderator of that body. He was elected and served as Moderator of the body at eight of its annual meetings; and preached the "introductory" or "annual" sermon at seven different sessions of the body.

The ordination of Elijah Rogers, in 1810, brought to his help a true yoke-fellow and compaion in the ministry. These men of God held meetings together over the country, witnessing many gracious revivals, organizing churches, and baptizing multitudes of people. The first baptism ever witnessed in the city or neighborhood of Knoxville was that of John Hillsman, a convert of these two preachers and a first fruit of Baptist work in what is now known as a Baptist city. He was baptized in the Tennessee River in the presence of 3,000 people, in the month of August, 1825.

Since writing the above I find Richard Wood memorialized at length in the Tennessee Association minutes for 1834. By appointment of the Association the "biography" was prepared by Brother Samuel Love. I condense from the same as follows: Elder Richard Wood was born in Mecklenburg County, Virginia, in 1756. His parents were poor, but respectable people, belonging to the Episcopal or State church of Virginia. Young Wood had sufficient education to carry on his vocation as a farmer and mechanic. At the age of nineteen he was converted, under the preaching of some Baptist evangelists and missionaries from the North. He commenced preaching at once, in spite of persecution, which was the portion of Baptist preachers of that day. In his twenty-first year he was married to Mary Price, who had been converted in the same revival as himself. The war of the Revolution was on and he became a soldier, "facing with settled resolution the frowns of British tyranny and oppression, fighting manfully, that the American

people might enjoy the fruits of political and religious liberty."
In 1784 he moved to South Carolina, where he was ordained,
and preached for a while with great success to country churches.
At the close of the Cherokee war he emigrated to Tennessee,
locating in Sevier County. He planted churches on the creeks
and in the coves of Sevier and Blount counties. Two of the
churches he established, the Forks of Little Pigeon and Providence, had each extended three "arms" that had become separate and independent churches before he died. In old age he
had become heavy and was afflicted with rheumatic troubles,
but in spite of pain and the infirmities of age, and when he had
to have help to get on and off of his horse, he would go and
preach. One of his faithful old members testified: "Brother
Wood was entirely devoted to the ministry. His talents were
of a respectable order, which, being assisted by his great zeal
and earnestness, made him an interesting and a useful preacher. But his talents and zeal were not all. Behind these was a
consistent and devoted life, which the world could not gain-
say." February 4, 1831, "his ransomed spirit returned to God
who gave it." He left a widow and a large family of children
—all of them members of Baptist churches, two of his sons being ministers of the gospel.

WILLIAM WOOD.

In the minutes of the Tennessee Association, for the year
1834, is an obituary notice of the life and labors of Elder Richard Wood, of pioneer fame. The obituary ("biography" rather) states that Richard Wood had a "large family, all of them
members of Baptist churches, and two of them ministers of
the gospel." One of these "ministers," doubtless, was William,
and the other, most likely, was Joseph P., whose name I have
seen in association and church records. William Wood was a
member of the Forks of Little Pigeon (now the Sevierville)
Church during his youth and young manhood. In 1816-17-18

he was a messenger of his church to the Tennessee Association, being a "licensed" preacher, and serving the Association as "clerk," these three years. Under date of "first Saturday in August, 1818," is this item in the records of the Forks of Little Pigeon: "The matter in respect to Brother William Wood's ordination is taken up, and unanimously agreed to"—but there is no record that this agreement was carried out. He was likely ordained by Friendship Church, since his name appears in the Tennessee Association minutes for 1819, as an "ordained" minister of that church. In the same year, though not clerk, he is requested to use his clerical gifts in "writing a history" of the Tennessee Association, which he did, and was paid "four dollars" for his work. He was a messenger of Friendship Church to the Tennessee Association in 1821, and also the following year, when he was appointed by the Association to write the "letter of correspondence" to the Powell's Valley Association, and with other brethren was sent as a "corresponding messenger" to that body. At the same meeting "Brethren Richard and William Wood," father and son, are appointed to write the customary "circular letter" on some vital topic, to be appended to the minutes.

In 1824 he is found operating in the Hiawassee Association; in this year he represents that body as a "corresponding messenger" to the Tennessee Association, and is appointed, with Elijah Rogers and Duke Kimbrough, "to fill the stand on Sunday." In this same year Elder Wood baptized Hezekiah C. Cooke, into the fellowship of Connessauga Church, McMinn County, and, in 1830, gave his daughter Mary in marriage to young Cooke, who afterwards became a zealous and useful preacher of the gospel and an able advocate of Baptist principles. In 1826 he was appointed a "corresponding delegate" to the Caney Fork Association and to write a "corresponding letter" to the Tennessee Association; he was also appointed, with Elders Duke Kimbrough, William Jones and Samuel McBee, to preach on Sunday, which they did, "each of them delivering a sermon to a very large, respectable, and seemingly well affected congregation." In 1828 he is a messenger from Connessauga Church, and is appointed to write another letter to the Association of his first love, the Tennessee. When the Sweetwater United Baptist Association was formed (1830), Elder Wood cast his lot with that body, and served as clerk of the Association for the years 1833-34-35. In '34 he preached the Introductory sermon from the text, "What is the Almighty, that we should serve him? and what profit should we have, if we pray unto him?" (Job 21:15). This year, according to the minutes, he is an ordained preacher of New Providence Church; the year following he is a messenger of Tellico Church. He was appointed by the Hiwassee Association (1830) to write a "letter of correspondence" to the Mud Creek Association, to serve on a committee to receive the "contribution from the churches," and to "preach on Sunday," with Elders Richard Wood and Duke Kimbrough. In 1851 William Wood and H. C. Cooke were messengers to the Sweetwater Association from Connessauga Church. Elder Wood was appointed as one of the delegates to the General Association, also to preach the Introductory sermon the following year, when the body should be convened with Hopewell Church. The next year, however, Elder Wood was not in attendance, consequently another brother was called on to preach the sermon. His failure to attend is explained, perhaps, by the fact that at this time he was laboring to keep a weak interest alive at Chattanooga, which interest he represented, this year (1852), at the Hiwassee Association. At this meeting he was appointed to serve on two important committees, to "preach a missionary sermon on Sabbath," to attend the Sweetwater Association and also the General Association.

J. N. YADON.

Elder J. N. Yadon was born in Union County, Tennessee, May 3, 1823. He was a son of Joseph and Phoebe Yadon. Attending a meeting in a "still house" he was converted, at about the age of twenty-one. By experience and baptism he became a member of Hickory Valley Church. He was married, when eighteen years old, to Salena Conder, of Union County. To this union were born nine children, seven daughters and two sons. His ordination to the ministry was authorized by Hickory Valley Church, Elders William Hickle, Mark Monroe and other ministers taking part in the ordination ceremonies. He was pastor of Hickory Valley, Nave Hill, Cedar Grove and other churches in reach of his home. At the time of his death he was pastor of Head of Barren, Straight Creek and Cedar Ford churches, and was greatly beloved as a "father in Israel" by all who knew him, many of them his children in the gospel. He was Moderator of the Northern Association and a leading light in that body for many years; he was its Moderator at the time of his death, 1902, in his eighty-second year. Elder Yadon was a good minister of Jesus Christ, a workman approved unto God and honored of men. The writer met him once at an Association, and found him a man of great influence and of sterling worth. One of his living daughters is Mrs. W. A. McDonald, of Sweetwater, a good Baptist sister, who has fed and entertained many a Baptist preacher the last twenty or thirty years.

APPENDIX.

THE LOST STATE OF FRANKLIN.

The State of Franklin has received from historians such scant attention that its existence, to many, seems almost as mythical as that of the fabled Atlantis, an imaginary prehistoric continent or island supposed to have been engulfed by an earthquake and swallowed up by the Atlantic Ocean. But the State of Franklin, bounded on the east by Asheville, North Carolina, and on the west by the future Knoxville of East Tennessee, lying under the shadow of the Great Smokies, had an actual, historic existence for three years (1785-1787), with legislative, executive and judicial departments, a respectable militia, and a population of several thousand mountaineers in a remote wilderness, "infused with the principles which inspired the Revolution," with John Sevier, an ideal frontiersman, as Governor. This sturdy, patriotic people, at their own request, had been annexed to the State of North Carolina (1776), and with that State had shared the fortunes of the American Revolution. After the war, however, the territory of the future State of Franklin, without the people's consent, had been ceded to the Federal Government. This act was resented, and the people set up a government of their own. North Carolina re-annexed the State of Franklin as "Washington District." But a breach had been made which could not be easily healed. The old State asserted its right of jurisdiction and the new State its right of independence. The population was divided into two factions, one favoring the new State, the other opposing it. Elections were held and appointments to office were made under the laws of both states. Two sets of officers, therefore, claimed authority, and each nullified the acts of the other. One faction would steal the public records of the other, only to be treated in like manner in turn. The courts were in a chaotic condition. Wills could not be proved, titles perfected, nor justice administered. No taxes were paid. Marriages performed by officials of one faction were not recognized by the other. Thus matters went on, with plot and counter-plot, till the brave supporters of the Franklin government, overcome by the superior numbers of the opposition, with little or no bloodshed, reluctantly submitted to the authority of North Carolina, and the reign of chaos was ended. Sevier was arrested and prosecuted. But during his trial a hot blooded Franklinite and hero-worshipper rushed into the court room with dramatic demonstrations and references to the popular idol, when Sevier, taking advantage of the uproar that followed, walked out of the court room, made his escape, and was not again molested. This bit of early history gives a flash-light view of the conditions and difficulties with which our pioneer preachers had to contend in laying the foundations of Baptist history in the State; but the enduring strength of those foundations may be inferred, in part, from the following extracts from the "constitution or form of government" of the State: Section 2: "The House of Representatives of the freemen of this State shall consist of persons most noted for wisdom and virtue," and (Sec. 3), "no person shall be eligible or capable to serve in this or any other office in the civil department of this State, who is of an immoral character, or guilty of such flagrant enormities as drunkenness, gaming, profane swearing, lewdness, Sabbath breaking, and such like; or who will, either in word or writing, deny any of the following propositions, viz.: 1. That there is one living and true God, the Creator and Governor of the Universe; 2nd, That there is a future state of rewards and punishments; 3rd, That the Scriptures of the Old and New Testaments are given by divine inspiration; 4th, That there are three divine persons in the Godhead, co-equal and co-essential." It was also proposed to put into the constitution—"that no person shall be a member of the House of Representatives who holds a lucrative office, etc., or a minister of the gospel or attorney at law or doctor of physic," but there is some doubt as to whether this proposed article was made a part of the constitution. The Franklin legislature "ceased its functioning" (September, 1787), it is said, by enacting a law fixing the salaries of officers, nine in all—"1,000 deer skins" for His Excellency, the Governor, on down to "one mink skin" for the constable for "serving a warrant."

FIRST MINUTE OF THE OLD SCHOOL NOLACHUCKY BAPTIST ASSOCIATION, BEARING DATE OF SEPTEMBER, 1839.

This time-yellowed, but well preserved four-page document was purchased from a countryman by a curiosity hunter of antiquarian instincts for one dollar, and published in the Sunny South, March 21, 1902. There is a *reason* as well as "a time" for everything under the sun. I make copious extracts from this remarkable minute, in order to exhibit fully the point of view of our so-called "anti-mission" brethren. The Minute is sufficiently frank and plain in its utterances, to show that our Primitive brethren did not use language (according to a Frenchman's definition) "to conceal thought."

"Proceedings of the twelfth anniversary of the Old School Nolachucky Baptist Association, held at Concord meeting-house, in the woods, Greene County, East Tennessee, on the fourth Friday in September, and following days."

"1. The Association proceeded in the usual order and read the letters. The Institutionist side nominated a Moderator and clerk, and violently rushed into the stand, over the head of the old moderation, and commenced reading their letters again, and we retired to the woods and proceeded to our business there. 2. Read letters from thirteen churches. Two not hav-

554 Appendix.

ing letters were represented by delegates, and the following accounts taken, etc." Names of churches and their delegates are recorded.

"Received a corresponding letter from the Old School Tennessee Baptist Association by the hands of its delegates, . . who took their seats with us."

"Reasons for declaring a non-fellowship with the institutions of the day, falsely called benevolent, viz., Baptist State Conventions, tract and missionary societies, Sunday School unions, theological seminaries, home missionary and abolition societies, and tributary branches to the present plan of missionary operation now in use in the United States."

Items: "1. One article of the constitution of all Baptist churches reads thus: 'We believe the Scripture of the Old and New Testament is the Word of God and the only rule of faith and practice.' We find neither precept nor example in the Word of God by which the institutions are supported."

"2. We are directed in 2 Cor. 6:14, not to be 'unequally yoked together with unbelievers," and by reference to their own documents we think all will see that the society system, introduced and carried forward, is a practice diamentrically opposed to and in violation of that passage of sacred writ.

"3. We believe that theological seminaries are calculated to aid and abet in the corruption of the church by offering an inducement to designing characters to seek after and obtain the advantages to be derived from same; and through their influence as false teachers corrupt the church, of whom the Lord made us beware.

"4. Our Lord, in his infinite wisdom, placed the light on the candlestick (or church), and we are bound to believe that it is a more advantageous station, and conspicuous, than the temperance society, which is an amalgamation of professor and world and Christian and drunkard. And to say it is not is degrading to the divine character and a direct reflection on his infinite wisdom.

"5. And thus is fulfilled that prophetic passage which says, 'And through covetness shall they with feigned words make merchandise of you.'

"6. The introducing and advocating of societies has been the source of much trouble and distress to the people of God.

"7. The fact does exist that in the northern section of the United States there is a direct connection existing between the Society system Baptists and the abolitionists. Now, if there are four out of five of the Northern Baptists (who are) abolitionists, is it not obvious that they control some of the most important societies with which the Southern Baptists are united and for which they are going such lengths to support? And is it not also obvious that the money drawn from the pockets of the Southern people through the medium of the Triennial Convention and otherwise, under color of sending the gospel, etc., goes directly into the pockets and for the support of those whose aim seems to be to undermine the very pillars of the Constitution?"

The above items, or "reasons," are followed by a number of Scripture quotations, concluded by the words: "If you will not believe from these passages that we are justifiable in what we have done, we say, would you believe though one arose from the dead?" Signed by the moderator and clerk.

WILL OF TIDENCE LANE (DANDRIDGE COURT-HOUSE).

"In the name of God, amen, the second day of July, 1805, being sick in body, but sound in mind, thanks be to God: Calling to mind the uncertain estate of this transitory life and that flesh must yield to death when it shall please God to call, do make, constitute, ordain and declare this my last will and testament in manner and form following, revoking and disannulling by these presents all wills heretofore by me made and declared either by word or writing and this is to be taken only for my last will and testament and none other. And first, being sorry for my sins past, do most humbly desire forgiveness for the same. I give and commit my soul unto God my Saviour and Redeemer, in whom and by the merits of Christ Jesus I trust and hope to be saved and to have full remission of all my sins and that my soul with my body at a general day of the resurrection shall rise again with Joy and, through the merits of Christ's death and passion, possess and inherit the kingdom of heaven prepared for his elect and chosen; and my body to be laid in such a place where it shall please my Executor hereafter named to appoint. And now for the settling of my temporal estates and such goods, chattels and debts as it hath pleased God far above my deserts to bestow on me, I do order, give and dispose the same in manner and form following, viz., First, I will that all my debts and dues I owe in right or conscience to any person whatever shall well and truly be paid, or ordered within convenient time after my decease by my Executor hereafter named. Item, I give and bequeath to my son John one Book entitled Boston's Fourfold State. Item, I give and bequeath to my daughter Sarah one calico habit, a petticoat, apron, handkerchief and cap. Item, I give and bequeath to my son Acquilla one cow, two sheep, two Books, one entitled, 'every man his own lawyer,' the other the 'Baptist confession of faith.' Item, I give and bequeath to my son Richard one cow and calf, two sheep, my big plough and one hoe. Item, I give and bequeath to my son Joseph or heirs one Dollar. Item, I give and bequeath to my daughter Senea one striped habit, a skirt, apron, handkerchief, cap, necklace and hurssa. Item, I give and bequeath to my son Tidence one spotted cow and one steer, two sheep, my old Bible and testament. Item, I give and bequeath to my son Tidence's wife, Mary, one feather bed and two sheets. Item, I give and bequeath to my son Dutton one black three-year-old steer and a Book, Willson on the Sacraments. Item,

I give and bequeath to my son Samuel all my land whereon I now live and also my Negro Man Jack and my two horses and two feather beds and furniture and my hogs, together with all the rest of my household furniture and utensils and all my iron tools of every kind not heretofore mentioned.

I do further constitute and ordain my beloved son, Samuel, my Executor, to see this my last will and testament executed.

In testimony whereof I have hereunto set my hand and seal.

TIDENCE LANE.

Signed, sealed and done in the presence of
Test.,
CALEB WITT,
WILLIAM HORNER.

FRAGMENTS OF CHURCH HISTORY, OR "FLASH-LIGHTS" FROM CURIOUS OLD RECORDS.

Bent Creek (or Whitesburg) Records: Church organized "on Bent Creek and Holstein River" by William Murphy and Tidence Lane, "June, second Sunday (11th day of the month), 1785." . . . July 30, same year, "chose Tidence Lane as pastor. . . . January following, second Saturday, church "censures a brother for the transaction of fighting." At the next meeting in course the brother is "restored to fellowship in the church when (just so soon as) he feels satisfied with himself." . . . At the December meeting the church "excommunicates" a brother; and at a later meeting, "laboring" with a sister to no purpose the church votes to "excommunicate her out of our fellowship." . . . Received into the church William Murphy, Sen., and wife "by recommendation." . . . A brother "offering his impressions of mind" in regard to the ministry is "tolerated to preach upon trial"; six months later, however, says the record, "under consideration of some difficulties subsisting" between this brother and other members of the church, "we suspend the public improvement of his gift till further labors." . . . Church "declares a distress" with a brother "for not attending our church meetings for some time past," and appoints certain brethren to "cite him to attend the next regular meeting," to give an account of himself. His "reasons give satisfaction"; nevertheless the church is constrained to pass some resolutions and "agree that the non-attendance of members shall debar them from a seat" till they appear and 'render a reason." . . . Church appoints a "special meeting on Lick Creek" (with an Arm of the church) "in order to look into their ripeness for constitution." The church considering the brethren "ripe," agree to "give up twenty members south of Bay's Mountain for the constitution of Lick Creek (now Warrensburg) church." . . . Church "deposits a subscription of five pounds in the hands of our deacon for the support of our elder sister—for this year." . . . Church "agrees to recommend to the Association of churches (i. e., the Holston) the reprinting the Baptist Catechism for the use of the respective churches in the instruction of children." . . . It is "agreed to admonish Sister ——————— for the dispersion of Sister ——————'s character." . . . Making a mistake in hastily authorizing a brother to preach, the church makes correction as follows: "As the church licensed Brother ——————— to preach, they now call in his license and give him the privilege of exhortation." . . . The church "censures the conduct of Brother and Sister ——————— in making a frolic." . . . The church appoints certain brethren to "cite Sister P. to our next church meeting, to give satisfaction for not taking her seat in the church." . . . A committee reports, "We consider Brother ——————— ripe for excommunication," but the "church through kindness postpone the business till our next meeting." . . . In reference to the rights of members and the incompetency of outside witnesses, the church puts itself on record as follows: "In case of a difficulty in the church, this church will not call on the world for testimony." . . . The church recalls Brethren Coffman and Witt as co-pastors, this time *indefinitely,* or "until a dissatisfaction arises." . . . Church agreed that "they would race out" from their abstract of faith the sentence that refers to the "Philadelphia Confession of Faith," and substitute therefor "the Old and New Testament." . . . The church, "by request of Brother and Sister K., agrees to release them from the office of deacon and deaconess." . . . June, second Saturday, 1839, "Took up the institution(s) named in our minutes (referring to State Convention, secret societies, etc.) and decided we will not make them a test of fellowship: Vote, 38 to 27. The minority rent off from this church and hold their meeting on a different day, claiming to be the old Bent Creek Church, but call themselves by the name of Primitive Baptists."

French Broad River, otherwise Lower French Broad, or Dandridge, Church Records: Church organized by Jonathan Mulkey and Isaac Barton, March 25, 1786, with "twelve constituent members." The following items make interesting reading: Brother ——————— "is taken under dealings for his making a shooting match"; church "labors with him" for same, and finally "excommunicates him for the sin of gaming and refusing to hear the church." . . . Another brother is "taken under dealings for drinking too much liquor." . . . Church "agrees" that Sister ——————— shall be "excommunicated for speaking disrespectfully of a sister member of the church and contradicting her own words, and refusing to hear the church." . . . On the *second probation* or *universal salvation* "heresy" the church makes this deliverance: "It is the mind of this church that if any member shall avowedly profess his belief to be that a damned soul could ever have admittance into the realms of eternal bliss, after receiving his awful doom, he shall have no fellowship with us." . . . A certain brother "having shot a deer on the Sabbath day was laid un-

der censure of the church," but "before the church arose," the
brother "made acknowledgment of his crime," and was "forgiven." . . . Another brother making "satisfactory acknowledgment for his errors and crimes for which he had been
excommunicated, was restored to fellowship." . . . A
charge is preferred against a female member and the church
"cordially agree to excommunicate her from our fellowship."
. . . Paw Paw Hollow "directs a letter to this church,"
asking the church to "enjoin" one of her members to "pay" his
just and honest debts. . . . "Sabbath day, June 28, 1846:
Pastor ———————— this day delivered a very able sermon on
the subject of baptism, after which, with a short intermission,
a Presbyterian minister "delivered a sermon on the same subject, advocating sprinkling to be the true mode of baptism.
The meeting was then dismissed." . . . To settle a personal
difficulty between two prominent brethren, the church "concluded to send for help," viz., Isaac Barton and Tidence Lane,
or either of them, "respecting the debate between" the two
members. The "help" sent for came, and at a call-meeting of
the church "advised" that both of the contending brethren "are
worthy of censure, and that the church should tenderly deal
with both of them for their crimes." . . . A brother with
an infirmity of temper or lacking in self-control "is called in
question for fighting." . . . Following is a specimen of
church and committee proceedings of early days, in grave
offenses, such as "flirtation," "breach of promise," and the like.
The case slightly borders on the sensational, but has a serious
aspect, involving the honor of two lovers and affecting, somewhat seriously, the fellowship of two sister churches. The
bit of history also has its lessons, and is evidence that at least
six Baptist preachers could be found in this section, a hundred
years ago, with "business sense" and practical wisdom, who,
acting as judge and jury in a sort of ecclesiastical court, and
dealing with a difficult case, knew how to render a verdict and
fix a penalty. I condense as much as possible a series of

records in the case, and find the facts to be these: A brother in the French Broad Church had a daughter who was being courted by a member of Bethel Church (Bethel South, now the Morristown First). He was in the family a great deal, paid particular attention to the daughter, was considered a suitor, and was encouraged. The courtship went on smoothly for some time, but finally came to a standstill and was broken off, to the surprise and chagrin of the family. The father brought his trouble to the church. The matter was taken up with Bethel Church, where the alleged delinquent was a member. With due deliberation Bethel "agrees on a plan," which is consented to by the two "grieved brothers," viz., to refer the matter to a committee of six brethren (each church selecting three), and "nominates" her three ministers, who are "notified to meet" on neutral ground on a certain day. "Our church concurs," says the record, and "nominates" three ministers to meet with Bethel's representatives. Both churches agree that the "action of the committee shall be final." The report of the joint committee as "ordered of record," is as follows: "State of Tennessee, Jefferson County, Friendship Church, 4th of April, 1822: We, Richard Wood, Thomas Hill, Elijah Rogers, Joseph White, Charles Kelly and Lewis Reneau, chosen by the joint choice of Bethel and French Broad churches to hear and determine a matter of controversy subsisting between Brethren —————————— and ——————————, having convened and taken upon ourselves the final decision of said matter in dispute: Whereupon (the distressed brother) came forward and charged Brother —————————— with having for a considerable time paid addresses to one of his daughters, under forms and circumstances that authorized him and his family to believe that he intended to marry her, and having expressly solicited his daughter to give her consent to join him in the matrimonial contract, and after having obtained sufficient encouragement, both from her, himself and his family, and after so far succeeding in gaining the approbation and consent of his said

36

daughter, himself and family, abandoning his suit and treating his said daughter, himself and family with entire inattention and contempt: To which charges so made as aforesaid the said Brother ——————— was evasive in his reply, neither admitting nor denying the fact of his telling the said daughter directly and positively that it was his wish to marry her, but admitted of having for some time visited the family, paid particular attention to the daughter, talked to her about marriage, and was well treated by the family: Whereupon Brother ——————— (the accuser) read a copy of a letter by him sent to (the accused) Brother ——————— relative to said subject, and one sent by the accused in reply, and a third from the accuser, rejoining to said reply. After the reading of which said letters several witnesses were introduced and gave evidence relative to divers facts relative to said charge exhibited against the accused. After hearing of which and having retired to consider of the said charges and having considered the whole of the testimony, are of the opinion: First, That the brother bringing the charges erred in his mode of dealing with the accused, in deviating from the rules laid down in the 18th chapter of Matthew, (we) do determine that he receive a public reproof, and that Brother Rogers deliver it. Second, We are unanimously of the opinion that the accused is guilty to the full extent of the charges exhibited against him, and for such his offense in willfully, wickedly, falsely, maliciously and deceitfully imposing himself on Brother ———————, his family, and particuarly on his said daughter, by pretending a wish to marry her without having any such intention, he (ought to be) and is hereby excommunicated from the fellowship of the church. Signed by order of the committee."

HOLSTON ASSOCIATION RECORDS.

This body was organized at "Cherokee Meeting House," in Washington County, five miles south of Jonesboro, on Saturday before the fourth Sunday in October, 1786, ten years before Tennessee was admitted into the Union. The following churches, seven in all, were represented in the organization: Kindrick's Creek (now Double Springs), Bent Creek (Whitesburg), Beaver Creek, Greasy Cove, Cherokee Creek, North Fork of Holston, Lower French Broad (now the Dandridge Church). Tidence Lane was the Moderator, William Murphy, the Clerk. The body was "not an association of ministers, but of churches," organized, not to "legislate but to give counsel, each church being an independent body." The Association answered "queries" sent up by the churches, and gave advice on such matters as, "points of doctrine, church discipline, the duties of deacons, qualifications of deacons' wives, the laying on of hands, foot-washing," etc. One of the ministers, Jonathan Mulkey, was a pioneer preacher "of the Baptist order" (1775) before the Declaration of Independence. Buffalo Ridge, the oldest church in the State (1779), was organized three years after the Declaration of Independence and four years before the end of the Revolutionary War.

The Association was *missionary* from the beginning. The third Introductory Sermon (1790), preached by William Murphy, from Matthew 28:19 ("Go ye therefore"), was a missionary sermon. "This was twenty-four years before the American Baptist Foreign Mission Society was organized, fifty-five years before the Southern Baptist Convention began work, and twenty-two years before Adoniram Judson was ordained as a Foreign Missionary." (Dr. S. W. Tindell.)

In 1802, the year before the body was divided (that the Tennessee Association might be formed)—that is, in a period of sixteen years from its organization—the body had grown "to 36 churches and 2,477 members."

THE FAMOUS BOONE TREE.

An old beech tree, formerly standing near Boone's Creek in sight of the stage-road leading from Jonesboro to Blountville. Twenty-two years ago the writer saw the tree still standing, and copied from it these words: "D. Boone CiLLED BAR On Tree 1760." For picture of this old historic tree, now fallen down, I am indebted to the courtesy of Elder W. K. Cox.

Tomb of Jonathan Mulkey, Sen., in the cemetery at Buffalo Ridge Baptist Church. Taken by S. W. Tindell.

Wilson C. Witt, aged 100 years, 1 month, 1 day, being buried with his Lord
in baptism, July 29, 1917, by Dr. J. M. Anderson.

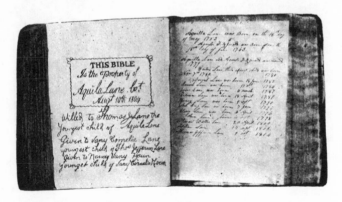

The Bible here photographed has been in the Lane family for
four generations (115 years), descending by "will" from
one generation to another to the youngest member
of the family, and is now in the possession
of Mrs. Nannie V. Haun Jenkins, of
Morristown, Tenn.